The French Revolution
and Historical Materialism

Historical Materialism Book Series

The Historical Materialism Book Series is a major publishing initiative of the radical left. The capitalist crisis of the twenty-first century has been met by a resurgence of interest in critical Marxist theory. At the same time, the publishing institutions committed to Marxism have contracted markedly since the high point of the 1970s. The Historical Materialism Book Series is dedicated to addressing this situation by making available important works of Marxist theory. The aim of the series is to publish important theoretical contributions as the basis for vigorous intellectual debate and exchange on the left.

The peer-reviewed series publishes original monographs, translated texts, and reprints of classics across the bounds of academic disciplinary agendas and across the divisions of the left. The series is particularly concerned to encourage the internationalization of Marxist debate and aims to translate significant studies from beyond the English-speaking world.

For a full list of titles in the Historical Materialism Book Series
available in paperback from Haymarket Books, visit:
https://www.haymarketbooks.org/series_collections/1-historical-materialism

The French Revolution and Historical Materialism

Selected Essays

Henry Heller

Haymarket Books
Chicago, IL

First published in 2017 by Brill Academic Publishers, The Netherlands
© 2017 Koninklijke Brill NV, Leiden, The Netherlands

Published in paperback in 2018 by
Haymarket Books
P.O. Box 180165
Chicago, IL 60618
773-583-7884
www.haymarketbooks.org

ISBN: 978-1-60846-995-6

Trade distribution:
In the US, Consortium Book Sales, www.cbsd.com
In Canada, Publishers Group Canada, www.pgcbooks.ca
In the UK, Turnaround Publisher Services, www.turnaround-uk.com
All other countries, Ingram Publisher Services International, ips_intlsales@
ingramcontent.com

Cover design by Jamie Kerry and Ragina Johnson.

This book was published with the generous support of Lannan Foundation
and the Wallace Action Fund.

Printed in the United States.

10 9 8 7 6 5 4 3 2 1

Library of Congress Cataloging-in-Publication data is available.

Contents

Preface

In 2006 I published *The Bourgeois Revolution in France: 1789–1815*. After many years researching the Old Regime this work marked my first foray into a scholarly field which is the subject of much ongoing controversy. It was meant to challenge the revisionist view of the French Revolution which has dominated academic history since the 1970s. It was intended both as an academic as well as a political intervention. Revisionism rejects the Marxist view that the revolution – the founding moment of modern history – was a bourgeois and capitalist revolution. The aim of revisionism was not only to challenge the Marxist view of the revolution but to put into question its narrative of modern history, whose denouement looks toward a revolutionary transition to socialism. In other words the controversy over the French Revolution is as much about politics as history and is about the future as much as it is about the past. It is my contention that, while there is such a thing as a community of standards and a common methodology in every scholarly discipline, that knowledge is inextricably connected with politics. Nowhere is this more true than in history and especially in a field like the French Revolution.

My book took into account that the revisionists did raise some credible objections to the Marxist view. On the other hand, my analysis suggested that most of these could be answered and more importantly that the revisionists offered no alternative explanation of the revolution. On the contrary, based on current scholarship my work demonstrated that the only plausible interpretation of the revolution remained the Marxist one. The positive reception of this work, especially in France, encouraged me to continue to focus my scholarship on the revolution. Since 2006 I have published a series of articles which challenge various aspects of revisionism. Doing so helped to buttress the case against it but also served to restore the close tie between the history of the Old Regime and the revolution, something that has tended to be lost from sight as a result of academic specialisation. Most notably, contrary to the revisionists, I have tried to demonstrate that the rise of a bourgeois capitalist class has a long history dating back to the sixteenth century. Moreover, I have also shown that the revolution itself played a large role in strengthening the bourgeoisie politically and economically while bringing about the unification of financial and productive capital. Indeed, I have been able to show that the rising of the masses during the revolution, viewed by revisionism as economically regressive, in fact helped to bring about the consolidation of capitalism.

Thanks to Brill Publishers these articles are now presented to readers as a book. Taken together these pieces reinforce and extend my arguments against revisionism and in favour of the Marxist view. Most of the pieces have appeared in the journal *Historical Materialism*. In particular I have to thank Sebastian Budgen, a member of the editorial collective of *Historical Materialism*, for encouraging me to publish these articles as a book. I would also like to thank Pluto Press for permission to publish a piece on Jaurès which introduces a translation of a new abridged version of his *Histoire socialiste de la Revolution française*. Likewise I am grateful to *Science & Society* for allowing me to include a piece, defending the notion of the French Revolution as a bourgeois revolution, which appeared in that journal.

The aim of this book then is to challenge French Revolutionary revisionism and to help restore the Marxist view of the French Revolution. It does so by deepening and extending the arguments I made in *The Bourgeois Revolution in France*. It arose out of a series of articles published in *Historical Materialism* and *Science & Society* in the last few years.

Following an Introduction (Chapter One) which presents an overview of my engagement with the historiography of early Modern Europe and France, the second chapter is meant to briefly familiarise readers with the historiography of the revolution. It does so by reprinting my introduction to a translation of Jean Jaurès's famous *Histoire socialiste de la Révolution française*.[1] Chapter Three tries to set the stage for my discussion of the rise of the bourgeoisie in France under the Old Regime, by means of an extensive review of a monograph by Guy Lemarchand, surveying the history of European feudalism in which France played a central part.[2] Chapter Four, 'La Longue Duree of the French Bourgeoisie', then reasserts the classic Marxist view that the Old Regime saw the slow rise of the bourgeoisie and of capitalism within the interstices of feudalism and the absolute monarchy.[3]

This piece engendered a debate in the pages of *Historical Materialism* which took the form of articles by William Beik and David Parker, who attempted to disprove my claims of the rise of an economic bourgeoisie. Beik's and Parker's articles and my response appear as Chapters Five, Six and Seven of the collection.[4] In the wake of these pieces Stephen Miller attempted to argue that there was no agrarian capitalism in eighteenth-century France and I argued the contrary. This exchange makes up Chapters Eight and Nine.[5]

1   Heller 2015.
2   Heller 2013a.
3   Heller 2009.
4   Beik 2010, Parker 2010, Heller 2010.
5   Miller 2012, Heller 2013b.

The next chapters focus on the revolution itself. Chapter 10 engages with the revisionist historian Sara Maza. Her work claimed that the revolution was not Marxist because the concept of the bourgeoisie as a class and of a bourgeois revolution did not exist in that period.[6] To the contrary it is demonstrated that such concepts did emerge in the course of the revolution and were much debated. Chapter 11 consists of a review article of a book by Jeff Horn, who stresses the role of working-class militancy in shaping the development of the French industrial economy.[7] But I argue that such is the continuing ideological pressure of the revisionist paradigm in Anglophone academe that Horn presents his excellent research while bizarrely eschewing discussion of the bourgeois and capitalist context. In conclusion, Chapter Twelve attempts to confute the revisionist view that the revolution saw no advance of capitalism because the disjuncture between financial and productive capitalism intrinsic to the Old Regime continued through the revolutionary period. On the contrary, through a study of French bankers it is shown that a key feature of the revolution was the effective union of these two forms of capital, facilitating capitalist accumulation.[8]

---

6   Maza 2005.
7   Heller 2012.
8   Heller 2014.

CHAPTER 1

Introduction: French Revolution and Historical Materialism

Marx's interpretation of the French Revolution is central to his understanding of history. For Marx the revolution represented the classic example of the transition from feudalism to capitalism by means of revolution. The revolution of 1789 like no other event demonstrated the truth of the materialist view of history in which changes in a mode of production occur through the revolutionary overthrow of one class by another. Marx saw the revolution as a model for the proletarian revolution in which the working class would sooner or later overthrow the capitalist class and establish socialism. Marx's ideas on the French Revolution were substantiated, elaborated and refined by French historians starting with Jean Jaurès at the turn of the twentieth century and continuing with Albert Mathiez, Georges Lefebvre, Albert Soboul and Michel Vovelle. In France the Marxist view dominated as late as the 1960s but since then has come under attack by revisionist scholars. In the first instance, revisionists concentrated on raising as many objections as possible against the notion that the revolution was capitalist and bourgeois in nature. But inspired by François Furet's insistence that the essence of the revolution was ideological, many revisionists rejected materialist explanations and took a cultural turn. Contrary to the Marxist view that sees culture, politics and ideas as inextricably bound up with social and economic forces, many revisionists split the one off from the other, arguing that the former rather than economic and social forces brought about the revolution.

Whether the Marxist interpretation stands or falls is a scholarly matter but it is also a political question. In the Marxist view the capitalist epoch was born and developed through class struggle and its denouement is seen in terms of a likely revolutionary transformation of the mode of production from capitalism to socialism. The consequences of revisionism were not merely to put into question the Marxist view of the events of 1789, but to raise doubts about its overall interpretation of modern history and its prognostication of the future. This collection of papers is meant to challenge revisionism and to reassert the Marxist viewpoint. Against the revisionist assault on the conception of the revolution as capitalist and bourgeois, the collection brings to bear new historical research while employing the tools of theory to reassert the Marxist case. Most of the pieces included have previously appeared in the pages of the journal *Historical Materialism*. Most address a particular historical question, e.g., absolutism and the bourgeoisie, the financial history of the revolution, revolutionary class consciousness, the nature of the Terror. Brought together as a book these articles offer a substantial critique of revisionism and defence of the Marxist viewpoint.

My interest in challenging revisionism is an outgrowth of a long career devoted to the history of the *Ancien Régime*. The Marxist view has been that in dialectical fashion a capitalist bourgeoisie slowly matured within the aristocratic Old Regime and assumed power with the revolution. Fundamental to the revisionist position is the raising of doubts about the development of a bourgeoisie prior to the revolution. This introduction among other things is designed to show that the existence of this bourgeoisie is confirmed as early as the sixteenth century. Under considerable pressure it continued to develop in the following century and then the development of this class powerfully accelerated in the eighteenth century, advancing to the crisis of 1789. It was the discrepancy between the denials of the revisionists and my own sense of the long pre-revolutionary development of the bourgeoisie which led me to confront revisionism.

It was through the support of *Historical Materialism* that this challenge to revisionism was able to emerge. The birth of this journal was a godsend to me as it opened a sorely needed new venue for Marxist history. Scholarly periodicals that would accept Marxist-inspired historical scholarship are few and far between in the Anglophone world. *Historical Materialism* was born in the late 1990s as a result of an initiative by a group of graduate students in international relations at the London School of Economics who were inspired by the works of Trotsky and Marx. Deliberately non-sectarian, the editorial committee took as its objective the renewal of Marxist political economy from a pluralist and internationalist perspective. Intellectually serious articles on philosophy, economics, culture, contemporary politics and international relations as well as history appeared in its pages and attracted a growing readership. Born in the wake of the collapse of Soviet Communism, the ravages of Thatcherism, the hypocrisies of the Blairite Third Way and the ongoing crisis of British society, it was meant to lay the foundations for a theoretical renewal of Marxism and revolutionary politics in Britain but also globally. Indeed, *Historical Materialism*'s high scholarly standards, its political openness and its annual conferences attracted a growing international audience drawn both by its politics and sophisticated scholarship. Given my deepening commitment to Marxist history and theory and disillusionment with liberal and positivist approaches, *Historical Materialism* offered new vistas to my understanding of Marxism and a new outlet for my scholarship.

Having been won over to Marxism intellectually while in university, I was politically radicalised by the upheavals of the 1960s along with millions of others. Put off by the sectarianism of the Marxist-Leninist parties in Canada and the reformism of social democracy, I affiliated myself with the left-wing nationalist journal *Canadian Dimension*. But it along with the rest of the left was in the doldrums at the turn of the millennium. Moreover, I was not particularly happy with that journal's nationalist orientation. At the same time, I was increasingly dissatisfied with the nature of my scholarship. Although it had definitely taken a Marxist turn it still seemed too far removed from my political and ideological convictions.

The gap between my interest in early modern French history and my political orientation had been a fact of life for me through the Cold War. Although universities and the scholarly disciplines in the United States and Canada paid lip service to academic freedom, the fact remained that universities were ruling class institutions to the administrative and intellectual parameters of which professors were forced to conform. Leading academics in the humanities and social science disciplines were normally politically reliable liberals who for good measure had been thoroughly intimidated by McCarthyism. With a few notable exceptions Marxists during the early Cold War had been largely purged or silenced and later on were for the most part kept on the margins of academe. This was as true in sociology, literature, economics and philosophy as it was in history.

In the discipline of history as practised in the United States the previously influential conflict view of American history championed by Charles Beard was also marginalised by the 1950s. Consensus historiography championed by liberals like Arthur Schlesinger and Richard Hofstadter generally ruled. As for European history, its revolutionary tradition was treated as a pathological condition from which America thankfully was largely immune. Western Civilisation, which bound together the anti-communist states on both sides of the Atlantic and which the United States happened to lead, was transformed into a history course which became the *de rigueur* introduction to the study of history in many universities. The more or less tacit message of the course was that the values of Western Civilization – individualism, human rights, political democracy and economic freedom – had to be defended against threats from the Soviet East and the Third World.

In the United States study of European history, including that of France, had long been an elite and conservative preserve and continued to be so. Nowhere was this more true than in the study of the French Revolution. Reviewing the historiography of American historians of the revolution, Keith Michael Baker and Joseph Zizek noted that few American scholars writing in the 1950s and

1960s found writing history from below and from a Marxist perspective to be acceptable at face value. They admitted that George Lefevbre's Marxist study of the French peasantry deserved respect. But they added that the same could not be said for the communist historian Soboul's pioneering analysis of the Parisian sans-culottes.[1] American critics of Soboul were particularly disturbed by the explicitly Marxist perspective of his work. Regrettably, few historians during the early Cold War were prepared to acknowledge that they too were politically prejudiced. Indeed, it is astonishing how many historians at that time were blind to their own class and social biases. For most professional historians liberal consensus passed itself off as historical objectivity.

Nonetheless the 1960s and 1970s did bring change. *The Crowd in the French Revolution* by George Rude, an Australian academic and former member of the British Communist Historians Group, was widely read.[2] Rude like Soboul studied the Parisian masses but avoided the Marxist class categories employed by Soboul which made American academics so uneasy. But in these tumultuous years historical scholarship in the United States could not escape being affected by Marxism, which pervaded the universities. This was particularly true in American history where the influence of the British Marxist historians and the work of Eugene Genovese, Herbert Guttman and David Montgomery was strongly felt. This Marxist trend in history proper was echoed by a new historical-mindedness in other disciplines, as exemplified by the work of Immanuel Wallerstein in sociology, Eric Wolf, Kathleen Gough and Eleanor Leacock in anthropology and Fredric Jameson in literature.[3] Indeed, the latter pinned his Hegelian Marxist approach to the study of narrative on the dictum 'always historicise'.[4]

But with the fading of the protest culture in the late 1970s the zeitgeist once again changed. As we saw, historians in the United States had been mainly hostile to the French Revolution and especially to its radical phase under the Jacobins. Moreover the social unrest of the 1960s and 1970s was disturbing. Many American historians then welcomed the rise of revisionist and anti-Marxist interpretations of the revolution which began to appear from the 1960s onward. It was Alfred Cobban who began the assault on the Marxist position. Cobban was an English historian with important academic and political connections who was hostile to what he referred to as the social interpretation of

1   Baker and Zizek 1998, p. 363.
2   Rude 1959.
3   Heller 2015, pp. 31–7, 42–4; and forthcoming.
4   Jameson 1981, p. 6.

the revolution. He argued that the politically active bourgeoisie in 1789 were economically hard-pressed professionals and office-holders rather than an economic bourgeoisie. Rather than taking the lead, they were reluctantly pushed into the abolition of seigneurial dues and feudal privileges by an insurgent peasantry. For good measure, concluded Cobban, the revolution left the distribution of wealth, power and the economy in France largely unchanged. If anything it was a revolution against rather than for capitalism.[5] Cobban's interpretation was weakened by his stubbornly myopic empiricism and political elitism, which led to his failure to comprehend the revolution not simply as a political event but a deep-seated and ongoing mass movement the leadership of which took things well beyond the goals of those political leaders who were in place at the start of the revolution. The privileged bourgeoisie of 1789 who sat in the Estates-General and who preoccupied Cobban – participating in the Old Regime certainly, but also revolting against it – were soon displaced by more radical leaders and popular movements and a state from which an already emergent capitalism and a capitalist class was able to develop further. Certainly post-revolutionary France was as much a class society as was the *Ancien Régime*, as Cobban notes. On the other hand, Cobban minimised the immediate achievements of the revolution in improving the lot of the peasantry and strengthening manufacturing and banking. Worse, he ignored the long-term political, social and economic changes that the revolution based on the masses and capitalist property rights brought with it.

But it was the cultural turn that proved decisive in the rise of revisionism. The turn to culture was itself a product of postmodernism or post-structuralism, which became ascendant in the late 1970s. In a work entitled *The Post-Modern Condition* Jean-François Lyotard asserted that postmodernism among other things entailed the rejection of so-called grand narratives, i.e., historical interpretations which are simplistic in their assumption that the past is knowable and that its direction is progressive.[6] There can be no doubt that the ex-Maoist Lyotard's attack was directed against Marxism – the pre-eminent grand narrative. It was Jameson who immediately and most astutely saw through this attack on the Marxist view of history. According to him, postmodernism's anti-historicism was part of the postmodern zeitgeist which was striving to blot out the possibility of understanding the present in historical perspective. Its influence could not be dismissed because it was the cultural expression of an all-encompassing commodity capitalism. But its rejection of history had itself

---

5 Cobban 1968, pp. 53, 67, 172.
6 Lyotard 1984, p. xxiv.

to be historicised, i.e., be understood in the context of late capitalism.[7] Despite such strictures, and under the influence of postmodernism, some historians rejected positivism and foundationalism and turned to the anthropological conception of culture. Culture in the Boasian sense, or as later reflected in the idealist anthropology of Clifford Geertz, implied relativising rather than historicising the past, scepticism toward overarching explanation, respect for complexity and diversity, and distrust of both abstractions and teleology as reductive or false. Some – after the manner of anthropological field workers or, indeed, literary close readers – sought to concentrate on the meaning and interpretation of historical events rather than seeking vainly for their causes. Notable was the questioning of the idea of class, which was seen as an exclusive product of consciousness formed by culture rather than both consciousness and relationship to the means of production.[8] Some even attempted to invoke a reified understanding of culture as itself the cause of events. In these many ways the cultural turn put the Marxist grand narrative into doubt. In doing so it also put the French Revolution – the pivotal event of this historical materialist narrative – into question. Taken to its limit it led to a questioning of the universal importance of the revolution as a Eurocentric illusion.

François Furet did not take things that far. Indeed, initially he claimed no more than that the radical Jacobin Republic interrupted the promising development of moderate constitutional government. But in what proved a decisive step Furet then asserted that this political miscarriage happened not by reason of deep material forces but as a result of the subversive teachings of fanaticised intellectuals.[9] The parallel that Furet suggested with the Bolshevik Revolution was not accidental, as Furet, an ex-communist, was one of the leading anti-communist intellectuals in France at the height of the Cold War.[10] Indeed, the development of revisionism in France must be understood as part of a conservative reaction against Marxist cultural hegemony in that country. Many historians, including those in the United States, disturbed by social and political unrest, enlisted in the ranks of revisionism and under the influence of Furet took the cultural turn. According to them it was the roots and dynamics of pre-revolutionary culture that needed to be understood. Robert Darnton, Lynn White and Keith Baker in the United States – to name a few – produced import-

7   Heller 2015, 4, pp. 6–7; Heller 2016.
8   Heller 2011, p. 194. This refers to my book *The Birth of Capitalism: A Twenty-First Century Perspective*, London: Pluto Press.
9   Furet and Richet 1973, Furet 1978.
10   Christofferson 2001.

ant research by exploring the cultural dimensions of revolutionary politics.[11] To such a degree did revisionism gain ground as a result of the cultural turn that the Marxist interpretation was pronounced utterly discredited in many quarters of Anglophone academe. Wittingly or not, this historiographical reaction against the French Revolution and the Marxist grand narrative formed part of a capitalist ideological counter-offensive from the 1970s onward, gaining momentum with the collapse of Soviet Communism and the ascent of neoliberalism and remaining unchallenged until the 2008 crisis. In the Anglophone world the cultural turn made itself felt through the influence of the Princeton professor of early modern English history Lawrence Stone. In 1979 he published what proved to be a seminal piece entitled 'The Revival of Narrative'.[12] Despite his disclaimers Stone championed a turning away from social and critical approaches to history in favour of return to narrative. In a contradictory way, Stone claimed that a declining interest in ideology and a renewed recognition of the importance of politics was responsible for this narrative turn. It is worth noting that Marx, to the contrary, wrote historical narrative precisely because he thought politics and ideology were both key elements of class struggle. Likewise, he saw narrative as important not as a literary alternative to critical analysis, but rather as a means of bringing together and summing up the findings of critical and analytical investigation. Jameson meanwhile insisted that narrative as a form was finally incomprehensible without accompanying historical materialist analysis. The downgrading of social and economic explanation in Stone's approach opened the door to the cultural turn and the loss from sight of the overall unity of the historical totality in favour of *petite histoire* or biography.

Stone was also indirectly responsible for the most important form of revisionism which appeared in England, and one which had ramifications on the interpretation of the French Revolution. There was to be sure the not very persuasive attempts by conservative historians to undermine the classic Marxist view of the English Revolution which had been developed by Christopher Hill. Hill's many books and articles demonstrated that the English Revolution, like the French Revolution, was a bourgeois and capitalist revolution. Conservative historians attempted to confute Hill by returning to a political interpretation of the overthrow of the Stuart monarchy and the establishment of the Cromwellian republic. Like Cobban they did so by denying the connection between short-term political events and longer term social and economic causes. Instead they dwelt on the fact that some noblemen sided with Parlia-

---

11   Darnton 1984, Hunt 1984, Baker 1990.
12   Stone 1979.

ment and that some of the bourgeoisie supported the King, that Puritans and supporters of Parliament were not the same thing and that the events of 1640 were more about political contingency than anything else. On the contrary, Stone investigated the underlying social and economic evolution of the upper classes in the Tudor and Stuart period.[13] Based on this analysis he interpreted the English Revolution as the result of the temporary economic weakness of the aristocracy, which made it possible for it to be challenged from below. But even before the end of the seventeenth century the aristocrats had more than recouped their political and social position by accelerating their conversion from being feudal to capitalist landlords. There was a revolution from below but it was incomplete in so far as the aristocracy remained the dominant class.

On the basis of Stone's view of the aristocracy, Robert Brenner developed a Marxist revisionism.[14] He accepted Stone's claim of ongoing aristocratic dominance while extending its reach, so that there was never any doubt of its ascendancy over the rest of society and especially a rising middle class during the early modern period. According to Brenner, the English Revolution played at best a secondary role in the transition from feudalism to capitalism, something that Stone did not assert. Brenner claimed that that was because the transition to capitalism had occurred much earlier. In this transition it was the nobility rather than the bourgeoisie who assumed leadership. In making this claim Brenner, a student of Stone's and a professed Marxist, challenged the Marxist interpretation of the revolution by denying its importance to the birth of capitalism, questioning the role of the rural bourgeoisie in its genesis and minimising the importance of the political and legal changes wrought by the overthrow of Stuart absolutism. Whereas Marx had stressed the role of agrarian capitalists in carrying through a sixteenth-century primitive accumulation, Brenner dismissed this as merely the after-effect of changes in social property relations that dated from the fourteenth century. Marx's interpretation was based on the struggle of this rural bourgeoisie to develop capitalism. The latter advanced by gaining ground vis-à-vis the nobility by assuming direct domination over the emerging rural proletariat through growing control of the means of production. This progress was downgraded by Brenner as an after-effect of earlier changes in social property relations which in no way threatened aristocratic control.

Brenner argued that the lineaments of capitalism were already laid down based on the social property relations established between the nobility and

---

13   Stone 1965.
14   Brenner 1976.

would-be tenants during the class struggles of the fourteenth and the fifteenth century. It was the nobility which then took the lead in creating capitalism by imposing economically rational leases on tenant farmers, forcing them to become competitive in the market place. It was these relations, based on changes in the nature and level of rent rather than the new relations of production based on profit, which were determinative in the development of capitalism. Market rationality then dictated all subsequent changes in social relations and *politics* including the revolution of the seventeenth century. Between the end of the fifteenth and the turn of the seventeenth century, class struggle and politics played little role as competitive markets bolstered capitalism. Likewise the role of revolution, fundamental to the Marxist view of the transition from one mode of production to another, was at best an after-effect of inexorable economic forces. Despite these questionable assertions, which were rooted in the false premise that the early modern period economically was based on the operation of a rational market rather than on its formation, the powerful deductive logic of Brenner's argument won over many, and even led to the emergence of a new school of political economy and history, ironically called 'political Marxism'.

The implications of Brenner's view on the understanding of the French Revolution were quite significant. Beginning with Engels, Marxists had assumed that capitalism grew in France in the interstices of the feudal and absolutist regime. But Brenner claimed that based on the social property relations in late medieval France, the economic rationality that drove capitalism forward in England did not exist in France. Arguing from Brenner's premise, his admirer George Comninel argued that the *Ancien Régime* was a land of subsistence farmers with no nascent working class and that capitalism did not really take root in France until the middle of the nineteenth century.[15] The French Revolution may have been bourgeois but it was not capitalist.[16] Despite Brenner's commitment to Marxism and to contemporary revolutionary politics, the interpretation of English and French history by the political Marxist school, in addition to being wrongheaded, had the effect of downgrading in a very non-Marxist way the importance of class struggle and revolution in favour of economism. Political Marxism reinforced the deemphasising of revolutionary politics, which in part reflected the quietism that marked the academic disciplines in the age of post-structuralism and neoliberalism.

---

15   Comninel 1987.
16   Heller 2006, pp. 5, 21, 45–6.

It was in this context that I pursued my research on the *Ancien Régime*, which developed into an account of the long-term rise of the French bourgeoisie. Traditionally the *Ancien Régime* was a field which attracted conservative scholars who regretted the French Revolution and admired the sense of hierarchy and order of the *Ancien Régime*. In the postwar period the very scholarly Roland Mousnier of the Sorbonne, a man of rightwing politics and Catholic faith, was the most important historian upholding this view. Fundamental to Mousnier's position was the denial that economic classes or class struggle in the modern sense had a place in the *Ancien Régime*. Rather politics and institutions centred on the monarchical state was the basis on which society was ordered and controlled, according to rank, status and prestige rather than wealth as in class-based societies.[17] Mousnier's knowledge of the institutions of the *Ancien Régime* was, it must be acknowledged, unparalleled. Moreover, his view that the market economy was constrained within the limits of the political order of the absolute monarchy remains a fundamental historical insight.

It was an insight which was perhaps not sufficiently appreciated by the increasingly influential *Annales* school.[18] This new school of history likewise did not share Mousnier's conservative politics. *Annalistes*, including its founders Lucien Febvre and Fernand Braudel, tended to be mildly socialist in sympathy. On the other hand, the *Annales* shared Mousnier's distaste for the preoccupation of historians with the French Revolution. French historiography until the 1960s was overwhelmingly dominated by the Marxist French Revolutionary school, as seen in the work of Mathiez, Lefebvre and Soboul. This reflected in part the key position the revolution continued to have in French politics. Study of the revolution was linked with the central role that the radical left played in politics and culture in the postwar period. Moreover, spotlighting the revolution underscored the importance of politically decisive events in history – a viewpoint very much in keeping with the Marxist tradition. The *Annales*, which came into its own in the 1960s, represented a turning away or downgrading of political history or what they derisively referred to as *l'histoire evenementelle* and as such was an attempt to break with preoccupation with the revolution. At the same time it reflected a distancing from the revolutionary political culture of the postwar period, in keeping with their more moderate politics. Using the *Ancien Régime* as their template, the *Annales* put the emphasis on continuity rather than change. Making use of anthropology, linguistics and psychology, Febvre pioneered the study of *mentalité*, a concept which under-

---

17   Hayden 1996.
18   Heller 1996, pp. 197–219.

scored the fixity and durability of fundamental popular attitudes and beliefs which reinforced the inertial character of historical change. Braudel and his heir Emmanuel Le Roy Ladurie broke new ground with their total and analytical view of history based on the quantitative analysis of serial data. While stressing the fundamental importance of material conditions, they minimised the importance of class struggle and politics in favour of the long term. So far as the history of the *Ancien Régime* went, change came slowly, based on the difficulty of breaking through the ceiling imposed by the slow development of the forces of production in the face of Malthusian constraints.

The context of early modern European studies in the United States in the early Cold War period was yet more conservative. Until the 1960s the dominant approach was the history of ideas, including an idealist view of the Protestant Reformation. Control of historical teaching and research in the early modern field was in the hands of an establishment marked by a fundamental hostility to Marxism. Economic history was not unknown as, for example, in the work of Earl J. Hamilton,[19] but the Marxist approach to the Reformation, including Engels's account of the German Peasants War, was dismissed as dogmatic and ideological. The flourishing Marxist school of Reformation studies in the German Democratic Republic was made the special object of attack.[20] Even the materialism of the *Annales* was at first regarded with suspicion.

The history of ideas paradigm had been pioneered by Arthur O. Lovejoy at Johns Hopkins. It stressed the continuity of ideas across different historical epochs more or less independently from their historical and social context. While taking ideas seriously was a positive step in an American historiography which tended to neglect their importance, more often than not it tended toward the reification of such ideas.[21] Moreover the assumptions behind such an approach were based on hostility to historical materialism. We can study its effects on the study of the Italian Renaissance – a period dominated by individualism, artistic innovation and realpolitik which proved popular in American universities in the early decades of postwar American wealth and power. Serious scholarship in this field as in others was greatly strengthened by the work of two German Jewish scholars who had fled Nazi persecution, Hans Baron and Paul Kristeller. Baron at the University of Chicago dedicated himself to the study of republican thought, which he thought valuable in defence of liberal values championed by the United States in the face of Nazi dictat-

---

19   Hamilton 1934.
20   Friesen 1974.
21   Skinner 1969, pp. 10–11.

orship and Stalinist tyranny. Kristeller at Columbia downplayed Baron's claim
that there was a connection between Renaissance thought and politics. He
insisted that the Renaissance was essentially about the revival of ancient Latin
and Greek thought and accordingly was an expression of a pure scholarship
and ideas divorced from mundane considerations.[22]

The history of science, an important subject in the age of Galileo and New-
ton, had been the subject of pioneer work by Marxist scholars Boris Hessen
and Henryk Grossman.[23] In reaction an internalist approach based on a thoroughgoing idealism, which insisted on the independence of scientific thought
from social, economic and even technological influence, dominated Western
scholarship.[24] Finally, study of the Reformation was controlled by scholars with
confessional biases. From their perspective the history of religious ideas and
the influence of great men like Luther and Calvin were determinative.[25] As for
the history of the *Ancien Régime*, political history – as exemplified in the work
of Orest Ranum who studied the councillors of Richelieu, and by John Wolf's
biography of Louis XIV – tended to dictate.[26]

By the 1960s new influences began to make themselves felt in American
scholarship. Marvin Becker, Gene Brucker, Donald Weinstein and Lauro Mar-
tines initiated the social history of the Italian Renaissance.[27] Remaining within
an internalist framework, Thomas Kuhn's work (1962) rejected the idea of evolutionary scientific progress in favour of the idea of revolutionary shifts in
scientific paradigms.[28] In the study of the Reformation innovation came not
in German but in French history. Natalie Zemon Davis of the University of
Toronto published a groundbreaking series of studies of French artisans using
the *Annales* approach to the study of *mentalité* as well as the insights of anthropology and sociology.[29] The growing influence of the *Annales* on American
historians of the *Ancien Regime* opened the way finally to a Marxist analysis of
seventeenth-century France by William Beik.[30] Undoubtedly Marxist in its language, it was made respectable in the eyes of the establishment by its emphasis
on the static quality of that epoch in which, according to Beik, a bourgeoisie did

---

22   Muir 1995.
23   Hessen and Grossman 2009.
24   Mayer 2004.
25   Dixon 2001.
26   Ranum 1963, Wolf 1968.
27   Najamy 2005, pp. 272–4.
28   Kuhn 1962.
29   Davis 1975.
30   Beik 1985.

not exist. If this were true it helped to undercut the Marxist view, which since Engels had argued that the revolution was based on the slow incubation of a capitalist bourgeoisie within the *Ancien Régime*.

My own investigations would lead me to confirm the view that not only did such a bourgeoisie exist prior to the revolution but that it originated in the sixteenth century, survived the seventeenth century and advanced strongly in the eighteenth century. Intellectually I was already a Marxist at the time I graduated from the University of Michigan and entered graduate work at Cornell in 1959. In this respect the most important influence was the anthropologist Leslie White, who while not openly proclaiming himself a Marxist nonetheless grounded students in a historical materialist outlook.[31] My Marxism deepened at Cornell, where historical materialist approaches were being pursued by some students in modern French history. On the other hand, such an approach seemed to have little bearing on my thesis on the origins of the French Reformation, which I carried out under the supervision of Eugene Rice. Rice was not closed to the influence of social and economic forces in history, but his interests were in the history of ideas. Moreover, the thesis topic suggested by him, i.e., a study of the French humanist and Biblical scholar Lefèvre d'Etaples and the reformers of Meaux, seemed to hinge on the relationship between politics and theology in a thoroughly conventional way.

But the impact of the civil rights movement and American war against Vietnam drove my hitherto intellectual Marxism in the direction of radical politics. I was particularly exasperated by the attempt on the part of Washington's propaganda to convince the American public into believing that intervention in Vietnam was in defence of freedom. The instrumental and propagandistic use of lies and ideology I found particularly noxious. Yet even here I was able to make a breakthrough based on a growing appreciation of the conspiratorial nature of much of elite politics in the contemporary and early modern world. Analysis of the chronology of the early French Reformation revealed a link between the support of the royal court for evangelical initiatives and hostility to Rome, which had gone unnoticed by previous scholars. My thesis argued that, far from the growth of reform ideas in France simply being the result of the corruption of the Church or the influence of the German Reformation, high Machiavellian politics had played a key role in facilitating the implantation of such influences.[32] Being inspired to pursue these links arose directly out of my growing understanding of the conspiratorial nature of politics in the present.

---

31 Peace 2004.
32 Heller 1969, Heller, Henry 1969.

My conclusions in this regard were largely ignored by historians of the Reformation. This despite the fact that they largely paralleled the early history of the Reformation in England, which likewise was more a matter of high politics than anything else. On the other hand, in the aftermath of completing my thesis, I was finally able to begin to tie the development of the Reformation to social and economic history and in particular to the implantation of radical ideas among the plebeian population.[33] In addition to the work of Davis, Emmanuel Le Roy Ladurie's *Les Paysans de Languedoc* was perhaps the most important work of history I had read while pursuing my doctorate.[34] This massive quantitative study traced the economic and social history of Languedoc from the fourteenth through the eighteenth century. Rooted in a neo-Malthusian perspective, Le Roy Ladurie's study showed that the cycles of demographic and economic growth were based on the stagnant development of the forces of production. His pessimistic conclusion confirmed the *Annales* view of the overall inertia of the Ancien Régime, which was capable only of cyclical growth. However, Le Roy Ladurie did note the dynamism of what he described as the beautiful sixteenth century or the capitalist upsurge that marked the first part of the sixteenth century. Indeed, a former Marxist and member of the Communist Party, Le Roy Ladurie interpreted the development of the French Reformation as a foreshadowing of the French Revolution. Its emergence was rooted in the growth of capitalism and the development of a bourgeoisie made up of merchants, better-off artisans, officials and scholars in the first part of the sixteenth century. In this light the Calvinist revolt could be viewed as an early bourgeois revolution, paralleling the earlier Peasants Revolt in Germany. Ultimately, according to Le Roy Ladurie, early capitalism and the Reformation were still-born in Languedoc as the fulcrum of economic growth shifted from the Mediterranean to the Atlantic (1560–1640).

As I have noted, research had led me to the discovery that far from the Reformation at Meaux being simply a matter of theology and high politics, it had quickly led to popular disturbances. For Le Roy Ladurie, who studied similar events in Languedoc, such disturbances represented premonitions of a crisis in the expansion of the sixteenth-century economy. The crisis exploded in the outbreak of the religious wars and coincided with the open challenge of Calvinism to the hegemony of the monarchy and the established Catholic Church. In this model the Reformation crisis in sixteenth-century France prefigured the revolution.[35]

---

33   Heller 1977.
34   Le Roy Ladurie 1966.
35   Le Roy Ladurie 1966, vol. 1, pp. 353, 357, 381. Heller 1986, pp. 239–40.

Based on this template, I decided to study the development of the French Reformation based on an analysis of its growth in six French towns.[36] Although the history of these towns, located in the four quarters of the Kingdom, significantly differed from one another, investigation revealed a correlation between increasing economic difficulties, growing social polarisation and the rise of Calvinism. I interpreted the rise of Calvinism as a movement which tried to break through the religious and political limits of the established religion and the royal state. Critical junctures between the popular evangelicism of the artisans and that of the more orthodox Calvinist elite of merchants, lawyers and officials created the Protestant movement. Growing economic difficulties marked by a succession of crises facilitated its development, Calvinist ideology ultimately tied the movement together and led to the outbreak of the religious wars in 1562. Insufficiently powerful numerically and economically, the Calvinists were unable to conquer France politically or religiously and were consigned to permanent minority status. Indeed, although the base of the movement remained artisans and merchants, its leadership became aristocratic.

Subsequent to this book on French Protestant origins I published another on the class nature of the religious wars.[37] In this account my premise was that although the Calvinist movement was in origin a class movement from below, its weakness caused it to be subordinated to the nobility. The rival Counter-Reformation party evolved in a like fashion with a popular base and noble leaders. The leadership of both movements waged war against one another, but also carried on a class war from above, particularly against the peasantry. After decades of suffering the peasants and the towns reacted by organising assaults against the nobility which helped to bring the religious wars to an end. Aristocratic alarm at the incipient revolt among the plebeians helped the leaders of both religious parties to rally to the monarchy under Henri IV.

The religious wars were the subject of my next book as well. Le Roy Ladurie had portrayed the outbreak of this conflict as the beginning of the end of the beautiful sixteenth century.[38] Although economic growth continued into the early seventeenth century, the development of capitalism eventually came to an end as the century progressed, as landlord taxes and royal taxes choked off agricultural profit. Indeed, this assumption was the take-off point of Beik's study of Languedoc, which pictured the period as one in which whatever

36   Heller 1986.
37   Heller 1991.
38   Heller 1996.

bourgeoisie there might have been was absorbed into the stratum of royal officials under the control of the absolutist monarchy.

But I began to have my doubts about this model. Le Roy Ladurie along with other historians had pictured the period of the religious wars as one of unrelieved ruin. On the contrary, my research revealed that this undoubtedly chaotic period saw considerable interest in agronomy and agricultural innovation, the development of new technologies and the growth of rural industry. In other words, the *Annales* view that the *mentalité* prevalent in the Old Regime reflected little interest in the development of the productive forces was open to question. The period of the religious wars was, indeed, a period of economic regression. On the other hand, the ongoing violence and wars coupled with debt and other difficulties led to the dispossession of large numbers of subsistence producers and their conversion into wage workers. The increasing availability of wage labour encouraged an interest in developing new technology, increasing agricultural output and developing rural industry. In northern France a process of primitive accumulation comparable to that in sixteenth-century England occurred, which strengthened the middle class and capitalism. Indeed, this was reflected in the growing militancy of townsmen and peasants toward the end of the religious wars. What arrested further progress was not a traditional *mentalité*, but aristocratic reaction reinforced by the fiscal and political power of the Bourbon monarchy.

My next work, which dealt with anti-Italianism during the same period, reached parallel conclusions.[39] It dealt with the development among broad strata of the population of hostility to the Italian merchants, bankers, courtiers and humanist scholars who dominated French economic, political and cultural life under the protection of the Valois monarchy. Nationalism as a mass movement was of course a phenomenon born of the French Revolution and the nineteenth century. Nonetheless, although confined to the middle class and elements of the nobility, nationalism did develop in the sixteenth century in France. In its negative aspect French nationalism was largely directed against Italian dominance. But I argued that the growing strength of this xenophobic movement was largely based on the increasingly literate middle class.

All these books published between 1986 and 2003 pointed to the rise of a capitalist bourgeoisie in sixteenth-century France. This line of argument was made more plausible because it developed out of the *Annales* notion of a beautiful sixteenth century. Infused with Marxism, the publication of these works was also made possible by a growing receptivity to Marxist approaches in the

39   Heller 2003.

study of fields like the Italian Renaissance and the history of science.[40] There was even an opening in the study of the Reformation where the researches of the historians of the German Democratic Republic were assimilated into Western historiography.[41] The waning of the Cold War and the political neutering of Marxism in the West helped make this growing tolerance of Marxist research possible.

The upsurge of the bourgeoisie which I had demonstrated in my successive works was ultimately contained by the Bourbon monarchy, which absorbed its upper layers into its expanding bureaucracy by the multiplication of state offices. The consolidation of the Bourbon monarchy suggested to Beik that no bourgeoisie to speak of existed during the seventeenth century. On the other hand, my own research on the late sixteenth century indicated that a capitalist bourgeoisie actually was growing stronger in the late sixteenth century. Could it simply have disappeared in the seventeenth century? Was there not some continuity after all between this development in sixteenth-century France and the bourgeoisie's strong advance in the eighteenth century? Put another way, the case for the French Revolution as a bourgeois and capitalist revolution could be strengthened if it could be shown that the bourgeoisie had a continuous history during the *Ancien Régime*. Testing such a possibility was in fact inhibited by the way the study of French history was organised in North America. It was compartmentalised into specialties – sixteenth century, seventeenth century, eighteenth century and French Revolution, and modern France – with separate professional meetings, newsletters and periodicals. Thus, for example, Beik's conclusion that no bourgeoisie existed in the seventeenth century was reached without him feeling the need to make any real reference to the implications of such a view on the sixteenth century and especially on the revolution.

While these disciplinary boundaries had a certain legitimacy based on research interest, they did lead to a certain narrowing of perspective – something which was all too common in American academe. In the case of French history, in which it is a truism to say that all roads lead to and from the French Revolution, this state of affairs was particularly crippling. Cloistering of French history into chronologically separate specialities inhibited research into the connections between the *Ancien Régime* and the revolution. In my case this was a real stumbling block, as along with my interest in sixteenth-century France I had always maintained an interest in the historiography of the French Revolution. As a Marxist I had always assumed that the French Revolution

---

40   Freudenthal 2005.
41   Po-Chia Hsia 1988, pp. 5–6.

was the birthplace of modern politics and the model of revolutionary change, including eventual transition from capitalism to socialism. While the great majority of American historians may have been put off by Soboul's work, I considered myself his admirer. The revisionist onslaught had advanced many seemingly convincing arguments against the Marxist approach. On the other hand, my research suggested that events in the sixteenth century – the rise of capitalism and the middle class, the birth of an ideological movement opposed to the established church and the state – foreshadowed the bourgeois and capitalist revolution, or in other words, the coming of the revolution itself.

A breakthrough came with the publication of Jean-Marc Moriceau's study of the capitalist farmers of the Ile de France.[42] He demonstrated that, contrary to the situation in Languedoc which had been stressed by Le Roy Ladurie and Beik, a rural bourgeoisie which had come into being during the French religious wars of the sixteenth century in the Ile-de-France had actually been strengthened in the seventeenth century and flourished in the eighteenth. The families which established themselves as a rural capitalist elite during the religious wars not only persisted but grew stronger on the basis of an increasingly productive capitalist agriculture. Brenner and Comninel claimed that the persistence of small-scale peasant property had blocked the development of rural capitalism in France. Moriceau, on the contrary, showed that large-scale farms were overwhelmingly the rule in the Ile-de-France. In the meantime, I had gone ahead and reasserted the Marxist view of the French Revolution in a book based on recent research.[43] I followed this up with 'The Longue Durée of the French Bourgeoisie', which linked the formation of the French bourgeoisie over three centuries with the *Annales* concept of the long run.[44] If feudal absolutism endured over so many centuries in France, it also incubated over the long term the bourgeois class which would overthrow it. The publication of this article in *Historical Materialism* marked the beginning of my relationship with that journal and the confirmation of my interest in challenging the revisionist approach to the revolution.

Today we stand at a crossroads. Hostility toward Marxism, especially in the form of the idealist current of the cultural turn, still holds sway. But historical materialism, including Jameson's cultural Marxism, is gaining ground, as witness the growth of interest in *Historical Materialism*, the emergence of Haymarket Press books, the circulation of the new Marxist periodical *Jacobin* and

---

42   Moriceau 1994.
43   Heller 2006.
44   Heller 2009.

the growing overall market for Marxist books and periodicals. This advance is spurred by ongoing economic and political crisis. Revisionism still dominates study of the French Revolution, amid signs of a growing resistance to what has become a dogma.[45] Bringing together these published papers helps to advance the arguments against this dogma. They are based on an understanding of Marxist theory which stresses the importance of the development of capitalist agriculture, the role of finance capital in accumulation and the decisive role of the state in the consolidation of capitalism. In the French case capitalism in the countryside helped to undermine feudal social relations and institutions and strengthen a rural bourgeoisie which played a key role in the revolution, enabling it to take control of the countryside. Although its initiatives helped increase production in the countryside and displace more and more small producers, turning them into proletarians, pre-revolutionary agriculture's failure to provide enough food helped set off the urban food riots that accompanied the political revolution.

The existence of finance capital long predates capitalism. But it is the entry of finance capital into production and the institutionalisation of the connection between the two that makes possible ongoing accumulation. The juncture between financial and productive capital was underway prior to the revolution but was greatly accelerated by it. The seizure of the state by the bourgeoisie made possible the dismantling of feudalism and the restructuring of the state and legal system to serve the advance of capitalism. But by confiscating and selling off the extensive lands and buildings of the Church to the bourgeoisie that class was greatly strengthened. Indeed, the last paper in the collection is an extended version of an article which has recently been published in *Historical Materialism*.[46] It amounts to a reversal of the revisionist conception of the state under the Jacobin Terror. The revisionist view of the Terror is largely one of political repression and economic regression based on ideological fanaticism. I argue that the Terror also saw decisive intervention by a powerful revolutionary state which forced the critical connection between financial and productive capital necessary to accumulation, inspired the financial improvisations which saved the revolution and oversaw a massive process of primitive accumulation. The Terror, which for the revisionists was the negation of the economic and the harbinger of modern totalitarianism, I pinpoint as the moment of the birth of capitalism (in France) rooted in the exertion of state power.

---

45   McPhee 1989, McPhee 2002, Lewis 2004, Markoff 1995, Slavin 1995, Jones 1991, Lemarchand 2008.
46   Heller 2014.

As noted, most of the papers collected in this volume were published in order to address a particular historical question. But gathered together they constitute a wide-ranging critique of revisionism. The work begins with a study of Jean Jaurès, who wrote the first scholarly history of the French Revolution based on the Marxist view of the revolution. The text is drawn from an introduction to a translation of an abridgement of Jaurès's *Histoire Socialiste de la Revoloution Francaise*, which has been recently published.[47] Through the lens of Jaures's historical and literary masterwork it seeks to help readers understand the history of the Marxist interpretation of the revolution and its legacy. The French Revolution was a focal point of Marx's thinking in the early 1840s, during which he even contemplated writing the history of the Revolutionary Convention (1792–5). Study of the revolution helped him liberate himself from the influence of Hegelian idealism, formulate his theory of historical materialism and grasp the importance of revolutionary politics. The revolution remained an important reference point for the rest of his life. On the other hand, Marx only adumbrated his view of the revolution's origins and development without offering a full account of it. It was Jaurès who wrote the first fully developed narrative of the revolution based on archival research and a Marxist viewpoint. One of the strengths of Jaurès's work is the skilful way he was able to link the maturation of the bourgeoisie as a class with the growing force and influence of its ideas in a manner which is completely foreign to the perspective of Furet and the cultural turn. Published at the beginning of the twentieth century and re-published only recently, his history remains a valuable instrument of scholarship.[48] The essay links Jaurès's history to the subsequent rich historiography of the revolution, including Marxist and revisionist viewpoints. From first to last this essay shows that the historiography of the French Revolution has been deeply entangled with the politics of France.

The revolution overthrew the feudal mode of production which had existed for a millennium. Despite the fact that modern times date from the sixteenth century, feudalism remained firmly in place in France and most of the rest of France until 1789. In a massive study Guy Lemarchand recently reviewed the history of the feudal mode of production across Europe (1500–1863).[49] France occupies a central place in Lemarchand's wide-ranging account. The second essay, which reviews Lemarchand's work, provides an opportunity for understanding the French *Ancien Régime* in a wide and deeply comparative perspect-

---

47   Jaurès 2015.
48   Jaurès 2014.
49   Lemarchand 2011.

ive.[50] According to Lemarchand, the feudal system reached its perfection in the eighteenth century and nowhere more so than in France. Why then was there a revolution?

Lemarchand, who is a distinguished historian of the *Ancien Régime* and the revolution, finds the answer in the spread of Enlightenment ideas and the degree of class struggle, both of which were exceptionally strong in France. On the other hand, Lemarchand fails to explain the durability of the feudal system faced with the concurrent rise of capitalism in England and Holland and, indeed, within France itself. In this review we show that the concept of uneven development helps to explain the co-existence of feudalism and capitalism in early modern Europe. Likewise Perry Anderson's analysis of absolutism, which fundamentally distinguishes Western from Eastern feudalism, also helps to illuminate this question. According to Anderson, in France the bourgeoisie and a nascent capitalism were imbricated in the absolutist and feudal system. The maturation of the latter only strengthened the former.

The third piece, 'The *Longue Durée* of the French Bourgeoisie', details the development of the bourgeoisie and capitalism in France over the whole period 1500–1789.[51] In doing so it helps to undermine the revisionist contention that there was no bourgeoisie in France prior to the revolution. It reasserts the gradual ascent of a bourgeoisie from the sixteenth through the eighteenth century, a position traditionally espoused by Marxists ranging from Engels to Anderson. Underscoring the progress of capitalism during the religious wars, it notes the persistence of profit through the first decades of the seventeenth century and beyond. It also recalls the growth of commerce and manufacturing, especially in the reign of Louis XIV. Most importantly, following Moriceau, it points to the perdurance of a rural bourgeoisie in the Ile-de-France. Confronting high levels of rent and taxes, it not only survived but increased its productivity in the seventeenth century and emerged stronger than ever in the eighteenth. The publication of this piece occasioned an exchange in the pages of *Historical Materialism* between myself and Beik and David Parker, two Marxist historians committed to the view that because the *Ancien Régime* was feudal there was no bourgeois and capitalist dynamic to it. Their challenges and my responses are included in the text.[52] These arguments demonstrate that what is at issue is not merely the character of the Ancien Régime, but the class character of the French Revolution.[53]

---

50   Heller 2013a.
51   Heller 2009.
52   Beik 2010, Parker 2010.
53   Heller 2010.

There is also the challenge from Stephen Miller, who seeks to undercut Moriceau's work on the bourgeoisie by insisting that *Ancien Régime* France was an unchanging landscape of small producers who were blocked by Neo-Malthusian constraints and a Chaaydovian peasant *mentalité*. In response we insist on the durability of Moriceau's conclusions while also challenging the static and unhistoric conception of petty commodity producers espoused by Miller.[54] Revisionists like Beik and Parker take the view that not only was there no bourgeoisie prior to the revolution but not even during it. This was the contention of Sarah Maza.[55] She claimed that during the revolution the bourgeoisie had no consciousness of itself as a class and that, therefore, the bourgeoisie as a class did not make the revolution. The notion of bourgeois revolution was an invention of the nineteenth century. In a rejoinder published in *Science & Society* and which appears in this collection, I point out that not only does she fail to make the necessary distinction between class for- and class in-itself, but she also does not properly take into account the existing evidence of bourgeois class consciousness which developed during the revolutionary process.[56] At the height of the revolution the bourgeois nature of the revolution was recognised and debated. Its open acknowledgement was delayed, I argue, because it threatened the political unity of the revolution.

The misconceptions foisted upon historians by revisionist hegemony are also evident in the otherwise excellent work by Jeff Horn. In my long review of his book I point to its nearly unprecedented acknowledgement of the significant development of industry and the working class during the revolution.[57] Its account of working-class resistance to industrialisation is particularly noteworthy if perhaps exaggerated. On the other hand, despite acknowledging the importance of the growth of industrial factories and a working class, the significance of the leading role of the bourgeoisie is completely overlooked – and this is not accidental. Acknowledgement of its presence would uncomfortably raise the question of the bourgeois revolution which is still unmentionable in respectable academic circles *en Amerique*.

The last paper in this collection deals with banking and finance during the revolution. A much abridged version has appeared in *Historical Materialism*.[58] But the full text published here, which is around ninety pages, sets out and explains the history of the bankers and state finances during the revolution.

---

54   Miller 2012, Heller 2013b.
55   Maza 2005.
56   Heller 2010.
57   Heller 2012.
58   Heller 2014.

That in itself is noteworthy because the story is quite important and largely unknown (or is otherwise garbled). But more significant is that the piece challenges the revisionist view that capitalism did not exist prior to 1789 because there was no relation between financial and productive capital and that radical democracy represented the negation of capitalism. It shows that the relationship between financial and productive capital began prior to 1789 and that deepening this tie was central to the politics of the revolution. It was precisely the radical democratic regime backed by the sans-culottes which cemented this nexus. In other words there is a direct tie between capitalism and the radical revolution, contrary to the revisionist conception.

Jaurès

Jean Jaurès, the leader of the French socialists, was assassinated on the eve of World War I by Raoul Villain, a nationalist fanatic. As war approached, Jaurès, who was the leader of the Socialist Party, fought valiantly to prevent its outbreak, even calling for general strikes to force peace on the French and German governments. He did so in the face of a rising chorus calling for support of the impending war. Many in his own party, and likewise socialist leaders in Germany, including 'the renegade' Karl Kautsky, succumbed to these bellicose demands. Jaurès resisted because he believed that war would be a disaster for Europe, the French nation and the prospects for socialism. Jaurès took the same anti-war position as had his hero Maximilien Robespierre, the Jacobin leader during the French Revolution. Prior to the outbreak of war between France and the absolutist regimes in Prussia and Austria, Robespierre had insisted that war could only benefit those who opposed the revolution.[1]

Jaurès is remembered as a martyr to internationalism and peace as well as a politician who was able to unite the historically fractious elements of the French left. As the centenary of the outbreak of World War One approaches, Jaurès's political role is being widely celebrated on the left in France. At the same time Jaurès pioneered the Marxist historiography of the French Revolution. His *Histoire socialiste de la Révolution française* was published as a series of journal articles and then in four volumes (1901–4).[2] This massive account of the revolution, which was a highly original work of history as well as a literary masterpiece, is almost forgotten today by the public. Its rhetorical and dramatic character, which is the equal of that of the great nineteenth-century historian Michelet, is felt by some to be too evocative of a bygone age of epoch narrative. Yet Jaurès's monumental work of over three thousand pages was not only a great work of literature, it inaugurated the scientific study of the history of the revolution and is still of use to scholars.

Jaurès's work analysed the revolution from the perspective of Karl Marx's materialist interpretation of history which viewed it as a capitalist and bourgeois revolution. The leading professional academic historian of the revolution, Alphonse Aulard, had established the principle that history had to be based on

---

1   Jaurès 1968, vol. 2, p. 168.
2   Jaurès 1901–4.

a critical investigation of the primary sources. But he was still writing the history of the revolution from the perspective of its politics. Jaurès, too, wrote from a critical investigation of the sources, but he combined this approach with a materialist view of history. The freshness of this perspective deeply impressed contemporaries. Paul Lacombe, a contemporary critic who by no means shared Jaurès's politics, nonetheless conveyed his sense of the originality of Jaurès's approach. Commenting on the opening chapter of the work Lacombe noted that:

> In this work I have come across a ground-breaking inquiry, in large part original, which is without equivalent among other historians of the Revolution: a preliminary but step-by-step review of the economic conditions in which the stratified classes of society, peasants, workers, petit and big bourgeoisie, major and minor financiers, nobility, clergy, court nobility, etc. lived in 1789. After which in logical order there follows a review of the provinces from the perspective of commerce and industry. In short an exposition of the economic activity of France.[3]

Jaurès's subsequent narrative of the revolution then unfolds as a study of the successive conflicts between these social groupings in the years that followed, based on the interplay between revolutionary politics and ongoing social and economic crisis. It was the first assertion of what came to be referred to as the classic or Marxist view of the French Revolution in which the French people *en masse* figured as the main actor. Since Jaurès, the Marxist view has been developed by a long line of twentieth century French historians including Albert Mathiez, Georges Lefebvre, Albert Soboul, Michel Vovelle, Claude Mazauric and Guy Lemarchand. All were sympathetic to the Communist or Socialist Parties and saw their work as an intrinsic part of the political and social movement which it was hoped would lead France toward socialism.[4] In the 1960s and particularly since the failure of the May 1968 revolution, this interpretation came under attack from a counter-movement called French Revolutionary revisionism. Appearing first in England and America, this movement sought to deny the fundamental premise of the classical interpretation that the revolution was bourgeois and capitalist. Without itself being able to articulate an alternative explanation of the revolution, the new school initiated by the English academic Alfred Cobban sought to debunk the idea that capitalism or a

---

3   Lacombe 1908, pp. 164–5.
4   Mazauric 2009.

bourgeois class existed prior to the revolution.[5] In the U.S., Cobban's scepticism was reinforced by George Taylor of the University of North Carolina, who presented a serious case against the economic foundation of the Marxist view.[6] In France revisionist views were supported by François Furet, who first took the view that the radical Jacobin Republic aborted the development of constitutional government in France. Subsequently Furet went further, asserting that this derailment of the revolution had happened not by reason of deep and uncontrollable social forces but as a result of the subversive ideas of fanaticised intellectuals.[7] The parallel with the Bolshevik Revolution was deliberate, as Furet in addition to being a historian was one of the leading anti-communist intellectuals in France at the height of the Cold War.[8]

Indeed, the spread of revisionism can be understood as part of a political and intellectual reaction against the long-standing Marxist cultural hegemony in France and the international threat of revolution which stirred anxiety not only in France but even in England, the United States and the rest of the English-speaking world in the 1960s. As such revisionism was remarkably successful, to such a degree that the Marxist interpretation was pronounced dead in the universities of the Anglophone countries. Inspired by Furet, many historians in the United States took the so-called cultural turn, arguing that the revolution could be explained by the peculiar political culture of France.[9] Insistence on the peculiarities of French culture had the additional advantage of undercutting the universal significance of the revolution. French Revolutionary revisionism must therefore be viewed in the context of the post-structuralist movement, which became hegemonic in the humanities especially from the 1970s in the United States. But this reaction in turn can only be understood as part of the capitalist counter-offensive which gained momentum from the 1970s onward, gaining force with the collapse of Soviet Communism and continuing to be hegemonic.

Despite this apparent revisionist triumph, a strong current of Marxist-inspired historiography persisted in France, most visible in the works of Michel Vovelle, Guy Lemarchand and Claude Mazauric. Vovelle, occupying the prestigious chair of the French Revolution at the Sorbonne, published a continuing series of monographs and articles which encapsulated the new quantitative and cultural tendencies in history inspired by the *Annales* school while con-

---

5   Cobban 1968.
6   Taylor 1962.
7   Furet and Richet 1973, Furet 1978.
8   Christofferson 2001.
9   Christofferson 2013.

tinuing to interpret the revolution within a Marxist framework.[10] Lemarchand cut his teeth on a materialist study of the decline of the feudal mode of production in the pays de Caux in Normandy, which prepared the way for the revolution. He followed this up with a sweeping panorama of French economic history from the 1780s until the 1830s, demonstrating that a decisive transition from feudalism to capitalism occurred during that period, at the centre of which lay the crisis of the French Revolution.[11] Finally there is Mazauric, who spent over thirty years as a historian of the French Revolution at the University of Rouen. Member of the Communist Party and of its central committee (1979–87) and a trade unionist, there has been no more staunch defender of the classic view of the revolution. Mazauric through thick and thin has through his many publications, including works on Rousseau, Babeuf, Jacobinism and Marxist thought and the revolution, combined serious research with an excellent command of Marxist theory and the historiography of the French Revolution.[12]

In the English-speaking world after many years in which cultural preoccupations have dominated there are signs of a revival of interest in the relationship between the revolution and capitalism.[13] Indeed, various scholars including myself have taken a Marxist approach that has begun to challenge revisionist work.[14] The outbreak of the economic crisis since 2008 can only reinforce this trend. But the truth of the matter is that the influence of Jaurès on the scholarship of the French Revolution never went away. As a result of Jaurès's influence in 1903 the National Assembly established a permanent commission to oversee the publication of the economic and social sources of the revolution. The series of works published under its auspices greatly expanded knowledge of the economic and social history of the revolution.[15] Mathiez republished the *Histoire socialiste* in the 1920s[16] and Lefebvre looking back at the historians of the revolution concluded that he considered Jaurès his only master.[17] And Soboul gave Jaurès's text new relevance by providing a new edition undergirded with an up-to-date scholarly apparatus which makes the work even now an indis-

---

10   See Vovelle 1988.

11   Lemarchand 1989, Lemarchand 2008.

12   Mazauric and Louvrier 2008.

13   Livesey 2013.

14   McPhee 1989, McPhee 2002, Lewis 1993, Heller 2006.

15   Peyrard and Vovelle 2002.

16   Jaurès 1922–4.

17   Suratteau 1979.

pensable point of reference.[18] Even Furet expressed his admiration for Jaurès in so far as the latter had conceived of the revolution as not simply a change in the mode of production but a civilizational transformation.[19] In the light of the ongoing interest in Jaurès and renewal of interest in the Marxist perspective it is a stroke of genius that Pluto Press has published an English abridgement of the *Histoire socialiste*, which is both a great historical work and a literary masterwork.[20]

Jaurès was born in 1859 in the Midi in the small city of Castres into a bourgeois family in decline. Young Jean experienced real deprivation as the son of a father who failed as a would-be manufacturer and merchant and was forced to earn his living as a peasant working a fifteen acre farm. On the other hand, Jean had the good fortune to have as his uncle Benjamin Jaurès, an admiral and minister of the navy (1889). Louis, Jean's brother, later became an admiral himself and eventually a republican-socialist deputy. Meanwhile Jean's precocious intellect quickly made itself evident in the collège of Castres, where he received a thorough grounding in the classics. He was rewarded for his diligence and brilliance with admission first to the prestigious Lycée Louis-Le-Grand and then to the École des hautes études, where he came first in the entry exams ahead of the celebrated Henri Bergson. Having majored in philosophy he returned to the Midi where he taught first at a lycée in Albi and then became a lecturer at the University of Toulouse. There he made himself known as a critic of avant-garde literature for a local radical newspaper *La Dépêche*.[21] In 1885 at the age of 25 he was elected to the National Assembly, partly with the help of his uncle. He sat with the Republicans, associating himself with Jules Ferry and other opponents of clerical influence. Having lost his seat in the election of 1889 he returned to teaching at the University of Toulouse, where he received his doctorate in philosophy. His complementary thesis was on the origins of German socialism, which he purported to find in Luther, Kant, Fichte and Hegel. He had already begun to read seriously about socialism, familiarising himself with the first volume of Marx's *Capital*.[22] In 1891 he could affirm that as a left republican he was loyal to both republicanism because it affirmed the rights of man and to socialism because its goal was to submit property to the rights of man.[23]

---

18   Jaurès 1967–73.
19   Prochasson 2011.
20   Jaurès 2015.
21   Rebérieux 1994, pp. 31–8.
22   Rebérieux 1994, p. 52.
23   Rebérieux 1994, p. 48.

His involvement in the bitter strike of the miners of Carmaux the next year moved him definitively into the socialist camp. The strike was occasioned by the dismissal of an employee, Jean-Baptiste Calivignac, by a local mining company because of his election as the socialist mayor of Carmaux. The miners considered this dismissal an attack on the right of the workers to take part in politics and the principle of universal suffrage. As the strike continued the President of the Republic Sadi Carnot, head of a government racked by scandal, nonetheless saw fit to send the army against the strikers to defend the principle of the right to work. In newspaper articles defending the workers Jaurès accused the government of across-the-board siding with industrialists and bankers at the expense of citizens. The government was forced to back down while Jaurès, who proclaimed his conversion to socialism, was rewarded by being elected to parliament as an independent socialist.[24] But then his principled stand in defending Dreyfus the bourgeois and Jew – something that many on the extreme left and peasants and workers rejected – cost him his seat in the election of 1898. Jaurès then became co-editor of *La Petite République*, a republican and Dreyfusard journal, sustaining the moderate socialist Alexandre Millerand in joining the cabinet of Republican Defence of Waldeck-Rousseau.[25] Lenin later would characterise Millerand's action as the first application on a nationwide basis of the disastrous movement to socialist revisionism. But faced with the threat to democracy from the right led by the army and Church during the Dreyfus Affair, Jaurès advocated collaboration with the Radical Party or the liberal and democratic bourgeoisie. He also believed that such an alliance permitted reforms which, if no substitute for revolution, strengthened the working-class movement and a necessary unity with the peasants and petty bourgeoisie. The Republic more and more depended on proletarian democracy, around which the peasants and petty bourgeoisie were being forced to cluster. The development of socialism would follow as proletarian democracy became the main political force in the Republic.[26]

In 1902 Jaurès was re-elected to the National Assembly and helped to pass the anti-clerical laws in the wake of the Dreyfus Affair. In assuming this position of cooperation with the radical bourgeoisie, Jaurès came into conflict with critics on the left – anarchists, Guesdist Marxists and Syndicalists – who argued that the new society could not be prepared within the framework of the old.[27] But

---

24   Rebériuex 1994, pp. 55–6.
25   Stuart 1992, pp. 52–3.
26   Gilles 2011, p. 32.
27   Engelman 1973, p. 198.

from Jaurès's perspective the goal of the Paris Commune, the prime example of
a revolutionary workers government, could only have been the establishment
of such a democratic republic. Moreover he argued that the struggle of the
left since 1871 had been a political struggle toward the same end. By the beginning of the twentieth century, France had become a republican state and the
struggle for socialism had to be defined in these terms. Only by assuming leadership over the democratic republic could the socialists unite the peasants and
petty bourgeoisie under their leadership and move toward socialism.[28] Nonetheless, in order to become leader of the unified socialist movement or *Section
française de l'Internationale ouvrière* (SFIO) [1905] Jaurès had to back away at
least tactically from what seemed to be reformist positions. An engaged and
impassioned politician of the left, Jaurès spent his last years seeking to consolidate the unity of the factionalised left while fighting ultra-nationalism and
social reaction.

The *Histoire socialiste* emerged from this context of struggle for a democratic republic. It was the democratic republic in Jaurès's view which provided
the framework for tying together the peasants, petty bourgeoisie and workers
through the consolidation of the socialist party. It was Jaurès's object to show
that the roots of this ongoing movement toward socialism lay in the French
Revolution. Publishing the *Histoire Socialiste de la Révolution Française* (1901–
7) meant for Jaurès to educate politically the party faithful and proletariat and
help to unify the still divided leaders of the socialist movement in their historic role. Jaurès brought to the task his gifts as an academic and literary critic
as well as his long years of practical involvement in political and social struggle.
During the 1890s he had begun serious research on the project. He read all the
main histories of the nineteenth century – Lamartine, Thiers, Buchez and Roux,
Toqueville, Michelet and Taine – while familiarising himself with the increasingly specialised research of the new century, including the works of Alphonse
Aulard. More importantly he immersed himself in the primary sources found in
the library of the Chamber of Deputies, Bibliothèque Nationale, Carnavelet and
Archives Nationales. Jaurès envisaged his work as part of a broader project on
the history of socialism embracing the nineteenth century, which would draw
in intellectual collaborators from the various currents of the socialist movement including the Guedists, Allemanists and Blanquists. His aim was to use
this collaboration as a way of facilitating the unification of the socialist movement. In this he was only partially successful.[29]

---

28   Labrousse 1967, pp. 10–11.
29   Rebérieux 1967, p. 36.

The inclusion of the word socialist in the title, which took more positivist historians aback, announced the work's purpose. According to Jaurès it was meant in the first place to educate the workers and peasants. Given the price of the volumes it is doubtful that it could do so directly. Rather its view was diffused over many years through the influence of socialist *instituteurs* whose influence on their charges is well known. Furthermore its intent was to show that the French Revolution was based on the people and thereby announced not merely the establishment of political democracy but the eventual establishment of a socialist and democratic republic.[30] This position contrasted with the Guesdists, who asserted that socialism could not be established on the basis of bourgeois institutions but only as a result of a revolution against them. Jaurès's revisionism expressed itself through his apparent rejection of the necessity of a revolutionary break. The republic was founded in revolution and the future of socialism in France depended on the development of a deepening republican democracy. At the same time in his narrative Jaurès made clear that the revolution took place under the auspices of the bourgeoisie: 'the French Revolution indirectly prepared the way for the rule of the proletariat. It created the two indispensable conditions of socialism: democracy and capitalism. But fundamentally it represented the advent of bourgeois rule'.[31] Acknowledging the role of the workers in the revolution, he nonetheless underscored that the working class remained dependent on bourgeois leadership. On the other hand, the people *en masse* already played an indispensable role, opening the way to a future socialism based on economic abundance and a deepening democracy.[32] This view is already manifest in his narrative of the revolution in which there is a clear progression from 1789 until 1794. At the beginning of the revolution the people are clearly subordinated within the Third Estate and see the nobility as the common enemy. But as the revolution unfolds the people more and more come to a consciousness that the bourgeoisie are its enemy as well. Indeed, through thinkers like Sylvain Maréchal and Gracchus Babeuf they come to understand that the workers have an interest which is opposed to those who control property and means of production. But such views can hardly directly influence the course of the revolution. They can however prepare the future, as the great upheavals of the revolution contain the seeds of future democratic and socialist development.

---

30   Labrousse 1967, p. 15.
31   Jaurès 1967–73, vol. 1, p. 63.
32   Antonini 2004, pp. 119, 135.

In terms of research Jaurès fully absorbed the philological lessons of the increasingly influential positivist history that was consolidating itself in the French universities at the beginning of the twentieth century. The *Histoire socialiste* is both an epic and dramatic narrative that is unapologetically partisan in the style of the nineteenth century and a materialist history founded on deep erudition, study of the primary sources and critical analysis. The development of a critical and historical methodology was by no means apolitical. It was based on the aspirations of a new generation of academics to create a scientific historical methodology which could establish the case for the democratic republic in the struggle against political and clerical reaction at the time of the Dreyfus Affair. It created a standard for judging the past that was designed to undercut clerical and chauvinist myths and to intellectually reinforce the struggle for a democratic and secular republic.[33] But in Jaures's hands this technique became an instrument for comprehending the significance of the events of the revolution in terms of their meaning not simply for the present struggle for the Republic but in terms of their potential in building a socialist future.[34]

The *Histoire socialiste* begins with an overview of the Old Regime as it approached its crisis. It continues through the overthrow of the old order, the establishment of the Legislative Assembly and the period of the Convention, coming to a conclusion with the fall of the radical republic at Thermidor. Lacombe noted with admiration the sense of coherence and continuity that Jaurès was able to give his monumental work. He associated this quality with Jaurès's capacity to bring apparently disparate events and currents into order through his oratorical powers.[35] In explaining the revolution Michelet had placed the stress on the misery of the people. According to him, the upheaval was the result of fiscal oppression from above which reached a breaking point. Michelet especially emphasised the role of a regressive system of taxation, which exempted the privileged and ground down the people. Taine echoed Michelet in this respect although he also drew attention to signs of economic growth. Jaurès broke new ground in singling out the rise of the bourgeoisie as the fundamental cause of the revolution. Of course there was misery, Jaurès acknowledged. But what is striking in the eighteenth century is the growing economic strength and confidence of the bourgeoisie.[36] The revolution, he

---

33   Rebérioux 1976, p. 429.
34   Antonini 2004, pp. 120–1.
35   Lacombe 1908, p. 168.
36   Labrousse 1967, p. 23.

was able to document in detail, was a revolution of hope more than misery. Moreover, this advance of the bourgeoisie was registered in both town and countryside and included a stratum of well-to-do peasants. On the growing prosperity of the latter Jaurès pioneered in demonstrating the increasing value of the net product of agriculture in relation to rent. This analysis of the rural economy demonstrated his ability to explain complicated economic matters in a simple and clear style throughout his narrative. Jaurès was able to engage the reader in understanding complicated economic questions as well as political crises. In stressing the ascent of the bourgeoisie, Jaurès perhaps exaggerated the decline of the nobility. Modern research reveals that the fortunes of some lesser nobles declined, but overall the nobility more than held their own based on increasing rents.[37]

While the transformation in the countryside was of great importance the catalyst for the revolution came from the towns. The urban world of the petty bourgeoisie and the working class was closed to Jaurès at the time that he wrote and would have to wait for the result of the researches of Soboul and others. Jaurès's focus was rather on the increasingly wealthy and confident urban bourgeoisie of Paris and the other main cities. He begins with the elite of the world of finance and commerce and is particularly aware of the expansion of overseas commerce and especially of the colonial trade, singling out the progress of port towns like Bordeaux, Marseilles and Nantes. The bourgeoisie of these urban centres was marked not only by their wealth but by their increasing political and cultural maturity. The development of mining, metallurgy, textile manufacturing and construction is taken into account. The launching of a series of impressive real estate projects like the *Palais Royale* is noted.[38] Stressing the growing economic strength of the bourgeoisie, he was unaware of the successive economic crises and grain shortages that marked the century, as well as of the deterioration of the wages of workers; factors which are important to modern interpretations.[39] In Jaurès's account the revolution comes at the end of the eighteenth century because the bourgeoisie reaches intellectual and social as well as economic maturity. At the same time the bourgeoisie needed the support of working people and peasantry whose political consciousness was less formed.[40] While France is the focal point of the narrative, Jaurès finds space at the end of his account of the decisive year 1792 to provide the reader with a vast

37   Labrousse 1967, pp. 17–19.
38   Labrousse 1967, pp. 20–1.
39   Labrousse 1967, pp. 21–2.
40   Labrousse 1967, pp. 23–4.

panorama of the effects of the revolution on Germany, Switzerland and England.[41] Based on his internationalism he escapes the chauvinism with respect
to Germany so typical of his times by providing a sympathetic treatment of
that country.[42] Jaurès's analysis of the crucially important colonial and slavery
question is particularly incisive.[43]

   In Jaurès collective forces dominate the course of the revolution, but to
what degree they determine immediate events is open to question. As Jaurès
represents it, in matters political nothing is decided in advance. The collective
forces only create certain probabilities and more in the long than in the short
term. In the short term the individual plays an important role. Accordingly
human will, moral force and intelligence can affect the outcome of events.[44]
This view emerges from Jaurès's own experience of politics, his study of the
revolution as well as his reading of the ancients. Plutarch's *Lives* particularly
affected his own view of political action. Political figures need to be understood
within the context of their times. Indeed the dominant political figures are such
because they are most characteristically products of their times.[45] Mirabeau,
Necker, Barnave, Vergniaud, Danton and Robespierre, who figure largely in
the narrative of the revolution, were all men of the hour and their decisions
mattered. More often than not Jaurès is able to penetrate to the psychological
core of such figures. During key events such as the overthrow of the monarchy
or during the struggle between the Girondins and Jacobins the actions of
individuals are seen as important to the outcome.[46] Jaurès not only highlights
these individuals in context, he undertakes to judge both them and the morality
of their behaviour. His judgment achieves a certain impartiality despite his own
political commitments. He advances his own view but only in the course of
taking seriously and debating the views of others.[47]

   Despite his attention to political leaders it is class above all which is historically determinative. It is the mediator between the economy and ideology. It
shapes the individual, including his manner of living and his feelings.[48] At the
same time he offers his judgement of particular events, collective attitudes and
political responsibilities. Once again his parliamentary experience serves him

---

41   Rebérioux 1967, p. 434.
42   Guillet 2010, pp. 188–90.
43   Rebérioux 1967, pp. 44–5.
44   Labrousse 1967, p. 25.
45   Jaurès 1967–73, vol. 1, p. 68.
46   Labrousse 1967, pp. 25–6.
47   Lacombe 1908, p. 171.
48   Labrousse 1967, p. 29.

well. The Gironde was revolutionary in terms of its ends but not in its tactics, which became counter-revolutionary. It is the Jacobins, who based themselves on Paris and the unity of France, that embodied the hope of the revolution. He expresses disgust at the September Massacres and while he considered the Terror a regrettable necessity he thought the Law of Priairial which permitted an acceleration of the Terror atrocious and inefficacious. He condemns revolutions by conspiratorial minorities in the tradition of Blanqui or for that matter Babeuf. Among the Jacobins he sides with Robespierre rather than Cambon or Carnot. The latter were administrators while Robespierre was a far-sighted political leader. Historians from Michelet to Aulard had condemned Robespierre as a tyrant and bigot. Jaurès treated him as a hero, a true reflection of popular attitudes and a product of the times.[49] At the same time he condemns him for his bloodthirsty attitude at the time of the September Massacres. Likewise he shows little patience for the demagogy of Marat.

As we have seen, the Marxist interpretation of the revolution initiated by Jaurès has been rejected by the French revolutionary revisionists. But Jaurès's interpretation and its subsequent influence on Marxist historiography has also been attacked from the left. In the 1960s Daniel Guérin published *La Lutte de classes sous la première république, 1793–97*, which argued that the French Revolution already witnessed the mobilisation of a class conscious proletariat, evident in the radical movement that ran from the *Énrages*, Hébertists to Babeuf.[50] Guérin asserted that while Jaurès acknowledged this in a grudging way, he opposed the left in the revolution if it did not ultimately subordinate itself to the bourgeois revolution. According to Jaurès, left extremism endangered the bourgeois revolution necessary to the development of the forces of production under capitalism and the institutionalisation of democracy without which a socialist future was unthinkable. According to Guérin the principle weakness of Jaures's work lay

> In its perpetual oscillation between the Marxist conception of the permanent revolution and the social-democratic conception of the bourgeois revolution. From time to time he does perceive the embryo of the proletarian revolution stirring in the flanks of the bourgeois revolution. But too often he falls in with those who divide history into rigid periods and immobilize it in rigid categories. Having once pinned the label bourgeois on the Grand Revolution he refuses to admit that the prolet-

---

49   Rebérioux 1967, p. 45.
50   Guérin 1968.

ariat entered into fateful struggle with the bourgeoisie in so far as the two
essential conditions for socialism and democracy had not been realized.[51]

In particular Guérin criticised his unconditional endorsement of the *assignat*
as a war measure even though it came at the expense of the mass of the population in the form of inflation while the bourgeoisie were able to escape taxes. He
blamed Jaurès for endorsing the demagogic manipulation of the masses while
endorsing their suppression when they were mobilised by Jacques Roux and
the Hébertists.[52] Protective of his hero Robespierre, Jaurès fails to acknowledge
the common bourgeois outlook of Robespierre and the opportunist Danton.[53]

Guérin's critique of Jaurès and his Marxist followers excited much criticism,
especially from the professional historians who considered themselves heirs
to the legacy of Jaurès. Guérin was denounced for being schematic and not
sufficiently historical. Yet it has to be said that recent scholarship makes clear
that Guérin did not invent his criticisms out of thin air. They were rooted
in fundamental differences in the Marxist movement of the late nineteenth
century, which influenced the perspective of the *Histoire socialiste* and the
subsequent Marxist interpretation of the revolution. As we have seen, Jaurès
evolved toward socialism without breaking from the radical republican and
parliamentary tradition in which he was educated and to which he was deeply
attached. A socialism which entailed breaking from the fundamental institutions of the republic was beyond his ken.[54] The more so in that the political
fights of the *fin de siècle* entailed defending the republic against the immediate threat of military dictatorship and clerical reaction as well as against the
depredations of advancing capital. Even more decisively, Jaurès was convinced
that the assemblage of the coalition of workers, peasants and other petty bourgeois into a unified French socialist party was only possible within the political
framework of the democratic republic. The *Histoire socialiste* was designed to
provide a historical justification for this strategy.

Following publication of the early volumes of Jaures's work, Kautsky – later
Lenin's infamous 'renegade Kautsky' – sharply criticised Jaures's political revisionism from the perspective of orthodox Marxism. Kautsky had long warned
against the pervasive influence of Jacobinism on French socialism.[55] In other
words he warned against subordinating the politics of the working class to that

51   Guérin 1968, vol. 2, p. 412.
52   Guérin 1968, vol. 1, p. 130; vol. 2, p. 78.
53   Guérin 1968, vol. 1, p. 444.
54   Venturi 1966, pp. 6–7.
55   Nygaard 2009.

of the radical bourgeoisie. Encouraged by French revolutionary Marxists led by Guesde, Kautsky authored a short essay which was the first materialist account of the French Revolution which emphasised class struggle and eschewed any romanticism with respect to Robespierre and the Jacobins. Referring to the *Histoire socialiste*, Kautsky then accused Jaurès of throwing the proletariat back to the subordinate position it occupied during the French Revolution.

Writing in *Die Neue Zeit* in January 1903, Kautsky insisted that there were two proletarian politics, one of which was autonomous and the other of which sought to subordinate the working class to the bourgeoisie. According to Kautsky, Jaurès was seeking to replace the class struggle by a return to the forms of political thought of the French Revolution. His aspiration was to base socialism on the Declaration of the Rights of Man rather than those of orthodox Marxism.[56] Kautsky's view of Jaurès was echoed in France by the Guesdists, who applauded Kautsky while clinging to a revolutionary Marxist position which rejected compromise with the bourgeoisie and the illusions of the democratic republic.[57] Likely it was in response to these criticisms that in the introduction to the published first volume Jaurès admitted that the revolution was after all a bourgeois revolution and that the declaration of the rights of man even in the Jacobin version of 1793 above all affirmed the right to property.[58]

The clearest view of this disagreement has been articulated by Neil Davidson, who has insisted that Marx rightly took the view that the roots of permanent revolution appeared during the revolution. The revolution must be understood as having been both a bourgeois revolution and the beginning of permanent revolution. For him the revolution was a great historical event and a precedent for the proletarian revolution. It was an upheaval in which the bourgeoisie undoubtedly assumed power, but also one in which the proletariat did begin to mark out its own autonomous development and, indeed, opposition to the bourgeoisie. On the other hand, Marx perspicaciously added that however uncomfortable the bourgeoisie was made by the actions of the masses during the revolution, the radicalism of the latter ultimately redounded to its benefit. In future the fundamental need of the proletariat was to achieve an understanding of the independence of its interests from the bourgeoisie and to give it political expression. This was Marx's understanding of the idea of permanent revolution.[59]

56   Ducange 2010, pp. 226, 228.
57   Stuart 1992, pp. 59, 222, 233.
58   Rebérioux 1967, pp. 46–7.
59   Davidson 2012, pp. 146–8.

In this light, Kautsky's criticism, echoed by Guérin, amounts to saying that Jaurès favoured the bourgeois revolution at the expense of the permanent revolution. Moreover he did this in order to favour the politics of revisionism. This was no small matter because it spelled out the difference between a revolutionary and reformist politics.[60] Furthermore his historiography shaped the whole of the Marxist historiographic tradition on the revolution. Yet Jaurès's *Histoire socialiste* for all its reformism can still be seen as a work which can inspire revolutionary change, something the world needs more than ever. It is incontestable that, like Marx, Jaurès saw the Grand Revolution of the bourgeoisie as a great example for the working class to follow. Contrary to Guérin, moreover, Jaurès did not see the revolution as one piece, but one which could see radicalisation or revolution within the revolution. Thus, he fully endorsed the Jacobin coup against the Girondins based on the support of the sans-culottes and, of course, championed the armed defence of the revolution. Moreover, he fully approved the subsequent writing of a new and democratic constitution by the Convention. This deepening of democracy was also important to the further development of class consciousness. It can be concluded that the political perspective of the *Histoire socialiste* leaves room for making a revolutionary rather than an evolutionary break from capitalism. This is important in light of the wave of radicalism that has swept over much of Latin America in which, echoing the revolution, armed defence of revolution and the holding of constituent assemblies in Bolivia and Venezuela, for example, are seen as revolutionary steps away from capitalism. Moreover, these unfolding political crises must be seen as part of the ongoing capitalist crisis that marks the new millennium in which further upheavals are in the offing.

---

60   Kurtz 2006, p. 273.

CHAPTER 3

Review of Guy Lemarchand, *Paysans et seigneurs en Europe**

It was in sixteenth-century England (and Holland) that capitalism first appeared. Its origins were dealt with by Marx especially in Part Eight of *Capital* entitled 'So-Called Primitive Accumulation'.[1] This discussion became the foundation of Maurice Dobb's celebrated *Studies in the Development of Capitalism*, which appeared just after World War Two.[2] Dobb's work gave rise to the famous transition debate of the 1950s on the transition from feudalism to capitalism, involving Marxist luminaries such as Dobb, Paul Sweezy, Rodney Hilton and Kohachiro Takahashi.[3] Georges Lefebvre, who held the professorship on the French Revolution at the Sorbonne, was the only French contributor. Lefebvre acknowledged Dobb's emphasis on the role of the petty producers to the transition but, conscious of the long evolution of the *Ancien Régime*, insisted on the importance of merchants and the state to the development of capitalism. Lefebvre underscored that the moment of transition from feudalism to capitalism in France coincided with the revolution and that conflict between petty producers and merchants was an intrinsic element in the revolutionary process.[4]

Lefebvre was part of a line of distinguished French historians who held to the Marxist view that the revolution was capitalist and bourgeois, a view that gradually made itself dominant in France in the aftermath of the Russian Revolution.[5] Lefebvre's interpretation, which came to the fore from the 1930s onwards, was extended by his successor at the Sorbonne, Albert Soboul, whose massive work on the revolutionary urban masses or *sans-culottes* of Paris was published at the end of the 1950s.[6] The Marxist interpretation of the revolu-

---

* Originally published as: Guy Lemarchand, *Paysans et seigneurs en Europe: une histoire comparée, XVIᵉ–XIXᵉ siècle*, Rennes: Presses Universitaires de Rennes, 2011.
1 Marx 1977, pp. 871–930.
2 Dobb 1946.
3 Hilton (ed.) 1976.
4 Lefebvre 1976, pp. 122–7.
5 Mazauric 2009.
6 Soboul 1958.

tion was challenged from the 1970s onward by a revisionist trend whose most important protagonist was François Furet.[7] The revisionist view of the history of the French Revolution was part of a broad reaction against Marxism in scholarship, culture and politics that marked the neoliberal period. Revisionist historiography was especially strong in the English-speaking countries but never established itself as dominant in France despite the influence of Furet. The Marxist interpretation in fact was convincingly reasserted by Soboul's successor in the Sorbonne chair, Michel Vovelle, who successfully incorporated the quantitative and culturalist approaches of the *Annales* school into the Marxist view as can be seen in a masterwork such as *Religion et Révolution: la déchristianisation de l'An II.*[8]

Likewise upholding the Marxist view in the closing years of the twentieth century was Guy Lemarchand of the University of Rouen, who published *La fin du féodalisme dans le pays de Caux*, a profoundly materialist analysis which examined the roots of the crisis of feudalism in Normandy at the end of the *Ancien Régime.*[9] Lemarchand's deep study of the contradictions of feudalism which led to the revolution in the *pays de Caux* was published in 1989, the year of the Bicentennial. In the face of revisionist challenges Lemarchand's patient and exhaustive investigation of the roots of the revolution in upper Normandy coolly demonstrated once again how effective a Marxist approach to the study of the revolution could be. A few years later Lemarchand followed up with an analysis of the overall economic and social history of France during the period 1770 to 1830. Lemarchand convincingly showed that, despite continuities with its rural and traditional past, France as a whole experienced a revolutionary transition to bourgeois rule and the capitalist mode of production.[10]

The transition to capitalism continues to be an ongoing source of interest to scholars.[11] But so, too, does the nature of the feudal mode which was antecedent to the rise of capitalism. Of particular interest is the question of whether feudalism was in fact a mode of production unique to Europe or whether it was common to different formations across Europe and Asia and perhaps might be better understood as part of a more comprehensive mode of production which includes other pre-capitalist formations.[12] The question of the uniqueness of

---

7   Christofferson 2001.
8   Vovelle 1976.
9   Lemarchand 1989.
10   Lemarchand 2008.
11   Heller 2011.
12   Blackledge (ed.) 2011.

European feudalism is directly connected to the transition to capitalism and whether or not capitalism is a distinct product of modern European history – an issue at the centre of contemporary debate on Eurocentrism.[13]

Lemarchand's vast new work does not interest itself in either of these questions. Instead its focus is on the perpetuation of feudalism on the European continent from the sixteenth to the middle of the nineteenth century – the very period which in most historical accounts marks the ascent of capitalism. Embracing the whole European continent from France to Russia, Lemarchand's work offers an immense comparative vista on the development of the feudal system through the modern period. Starting his account with the consolidation of the European states and the onset of economic and demographic stagnation in the 1560s, Lemarchand sketches in succession the reconsolidation of feudalism west of the Elbe and its extension to the East, the development of feudal reaction in both its Western and East European forms during the seventeenth and early eighteenth centuries, the apogee of the system during the eighteenth century and its subsequent demise (1789–1861).

Lemarchand's account of the French Revolution in the *pays de Caux* was distinctive for its emphasis not so much on the rise of a new class or mode of production but on the revolution as a crisis of the feudal mode. It was based on an analysis of the evolution of feudalism's essential structures from the seventeenth century onwards. His new work, which begins in the late sixteenth century, allows us to see that his previous locally-based research unfolded in the light of an ongoing and wider investigation comparing the development of feudalism in states across the whole of the European continent. In this monumental account, with its highly developed scholarship on the *Ancien Régime*, France continues to hold pride of place. But Lemarchand draws on extensive monographic research for the whole of Europe including Russia for this new account. Of course, he recognises that the second serfdom in Central and Eastern Europe fundamentally distinguishes that area from Western Europe. On the other hand, one of the themes of Lemarchand's book is the similarity of the feudal regime across Europe based on the common foundation of the class-rule of the nobility, the institution of the *seigneurie* [lordship] and the absolutist state.

For Lemarchand, feudalism is a mode of production based on the *seigneurie*, the landlord nobility and the peasant producers. But its historical and geographical complexity in the modern period cannot be understood without taking into account its superstructure. This includes not merely the state but

---

13   Heller 2011, pp. 215–39.

also the ideological representations of society and nature produced under the auspices of the ruling class, which he considers integral to the dominant mode of production rather than mere reflections of it. Lemarchand even echoes Althusser, noting that a mode of production is a real abstraction and that the real and concrete manifest themselves in a social formation which may embody different modes of production at the same time. Yet his understanding of feudalism (pp. 12–13) – i.e., the primacy of agriculture of limited productivity, involvement of the largest part of the population in this sector, production for use with limited marketable surpluses, appropriation of one part of the surplus by extra-economic means by a small juridically-defined minority, appropriation of another part to maintain an administrative apparatus considered essential by this minority, social consensus maintained by an ideology based on religion – puts the stress on the relationship between mode of production and its means of production. I would emphasise a forces-of-production approach which gives somewhat more emphasis to class relations, which are partly determined by the forces of production and partly determining of them. In any case, the overall evolution of the system across the centuries and its eventual decline was based on three main contradictions, i.e., the conflict between the forces and relations of production, the increasing influence of the market which undermined the subsistence economy, and conflicts over the appropriation of rent or taxes (p. 14).

Early Modern Feudalism

Lemarchand begins with an overview of the *seigneurie*, the peasants, nobility, the state and the city in the mid-sixteenth century. The *seigneurie* consisted of landed rents and social and legal rights over those peasants who were part of its jurisdiction. Although damaged by the late medieval crisis which in the West had led to the freeing of the peasants, the *seigneurie* survived into the sixteenth century and in many places grew stronger (pp. 98–9). It was present everywhere although there was still much allodial land, especially in central and southern Europe. In the West serfdom continued to decline while it began to make inroads on the *seigneuries* in Eastern Europe for the first time. In southeast England and northern France, especially in the Île-de-France, rich farmers began to accumulate a certain amount of capital. Still, economic life throughout the continent was based mainly on an exploited peasantry of mediocre condition. The village community was at its height in the sixteenth century with its independence being greatest in southern Europe and least evident in Russia, with the spread of the *mir* instituted by the state and firmly under the control of an emerging service nobility. The extent of common lands in Europe was indirectly proportional to the density of population and fertility of the soil in any given region.

In northwest and central Europe part of the nobility had roots that dated back to the thirteenth century or earlier. In contrast this group was virtually extinct in northern Italy and a new nobility with strong ties to the cities emerged there. West Germany, Castile, Poland and Hungary had disproportionally large nobilities. Everywhere the great aristocratic families tied to the increasingly powerful princely courts distinguished themselves from the rest of the nobility below them. A service nobility with legal, administrative and fiscal experience became increasingly important in Spain and France. Most of the nobility had relatively modest resources and struggled to live honourably according to their status. Their situation improved along with the rest of the landed class as a result of rising rents in the sixteenth century. The towns had a juridical status as part of the feudal system and they themselves had a certain juridical role.

Lemarchand concludes this opening discussion by an evaluation of the classic historiographic distinction between *Grundherrschaft* or the *seigneurie* based on free tenant producers in the West and *Gutsherrschaft* based on the large domain worked by corvées of serf labour in the East. Recent research confirms this difference while stressing that it only fully emerged in the seventeenth century while also pointing out that most of the peasants in the West were also increasingly hard-up and that the income derived from the *seigneurie* in that part of Europe continued to be more important than previously believed (pp. 97–100). *Gutsherrschaft* was not quite as stagnant as once thought, developing in the first place as a result of the constant devolution of royal powers in Poland, Russia and Hapsburg territories onto the great nobles whose support was needed owing to the incessant wars in the region. On the Iberian Peninsula and in the south of Italy large estates exploited directly by landlords, farmed out to sub-contractors, or let out to sharecroppers became the pattern (pp. 101–5).

Feudalism and the Absolutist State

The second and largest part of Lemarchand's opus deals with the period between 1550 and 1720, focusing on the feudalisation or refeudalisation of the land. The epoch was marked by wars and economic and demographic regression which were more pronounced in Central and Eastern Europe than in the West. Especially after 1620 and for the next one hundred years the overall economic and demographic conjuncture was negative. Faced with these troubles, the elites responded with social and political reaction, especially through the growing power of the state. The frequent wars between the European powers encouraged what has been called the military revolution in the form of more sophisticated weapons and fortifications and larger armies and navies. The rural population paid the price in the form of the devastation of the countryside and heavy taxation.

Lemarchand agrees that the regression of Eastern Europe and Poland toward serfdom and colonial status was affected by the increasingly unequal exchanges between the capitalist periphery and core as emphasised by Immanuel Wallerstein. But Lemarchand argues that Robert Brenner has the better argument in stressing the internal evolution of these Eastern European regimes as the primary factor for this deteriorating situation. He gives some credence to the argument linking the development of serfdom in the East to low population density. The mobility of the population and the abundance of rich soils in Eastern Europe led lords to tie down the population by imposing serfdom. Limited agricultural output restricted the availability of capital and led to local merchants and manufacturers being overwhelmed by more powerful merchants from the West (pp. 207–8). But the author questions Brenner's insistence that the imposition of serfdom was the result of the weakness of the village communities and their inability to resist the landlords. Moreover, Brenner's further contention that the possibilities of class struggle were reduced is not proven (pp. 122–4, 209). Parallel conditions existed in the states close to the Mediterranean which might have led to the imposition of serfdom. But the higher degree of urbanisation and commercial activity there and the threat of Turkish invasion blocked such an evolution (pp. 210–11).

The nobility's numbers increased during the seventeenth century while their landed revenues held up at least until the second half of the century. The survival and prosperity of this class depended increasingly on the largesse of the state. While the great families and the service nobilities who served the court prospered, the condition of the lesser nobility deteriorated in the course of the century, especially as they were mainly excluded from the magic circle of the princely court. Where they could they entered the service of the great nobles as clients, became the rank-and-file of aristocratic political intrigues, or even the leaders of popular revolts. Overall they troubled the peace with their violence, banditry and duels. Even an increasingly powerful monarchy like France suffered from the effects of noble violence through the first part of the seventeenth century, especially in the Midi. The lesser nobles especially resented the success of the service nobles who in France and Spain more often than not bought their office. Those traditional nobles who could began likewise to buy offices, especially those which brought them close to the prince, or tried to inter-marry with the offspring of the new nobility. Such patterns are evident not merely in France and Spain but even in states like Bavaria, Denmark or the Kingdom of Naples. By the second half of the century there were signs of the weakening of the *seigneuries* as a result of declining revenue, inordinate expenditure or partible inheritance (p. 156).

In the face of upper-class reaction the situation of the peasantry worsened. Increases in rent were coupled with crushing taxation. The weight of these burdens was made heavier by stagnant agricultural prices, growing indebtedness, epidemics and violence. Landlords attacked the communal rights of the peasants and a growing polarisation between better-off and impoverished peasants became evident everywhere. The landless or virtually landless proletariat increased in size while the length of landlord leases shortened. These developments and the growing penetration of market forces promoted the emergence of agrarian individualism and the weakening of the village community. Such trends were by no means confined to capitalist England as is commonly believed. A wealthy peasantry became evident in France, Spain and Italy which combined productive, commercial and usurious activities to different degrees depending on the opportunities available within the constraints of the feudal mode (p. 161). Contrariwise Eastern Europe saw the imposition of a comprehensive system of serfdom comparable to that prevalent in the West during the middle ages.

These trends exacerbated the contradictions of the feudal system. Increases in rents and taxes induced economic stagnation or even regression as surpluses were not re-invested but spent on war and consumption. Increased exploitation of the rural population and blockage of economic growth resulted in the intensification of class conflict between peasants and landlords. In this situation the mentality of the nobility and princes looked to the past. They tended to idealise a stability based on the maintenance of an immobile and static order founded on a hierarchy in which each kept his place. Their aspiration was towards the perfection of feudalism (p. 171).

In short the ruling class aimed at preserving the *seigneurie* as the basis of its continued control over landed property and supremacy over the rest of society. The substitution of the term 'absolutist' for 'absolute' monarchy in recent historical scholarship reflects a recognition that the state of the early modern period was far from an autonomous body. Rather, the nobility largely succeeded in making it serve its class interest and in particular the project of re-feudalising or feudalising society. It is true that in the seventeenth century the practice of the ennoblement of the highest strata of the third estate by the monarchies prevalent in the sixteenth century continued despite vociferous opposition from the nobility. But in response to these outcries over the course of the seventeenth century French, Spanish and even Italian princes limited the number of the bourgeoisie able to ascend to higher status, reinforced the privileges of the nobility, and more and more supported its caste-like pretensions. At the same time a seigneurial reaction on the land saw landlords make new demands or revive old ones.

As part of this trend Lemarchand notes that 'the Catholic or Lutheran clergy, the former re-invigorated by the Counter-Reformation, likewise nourished itself by cultivating traditionalism' (p. 171). However, Lemarchand might have pointed out that this insistence on religious tradition in fact represented something new, i.e., an active policy of confessionalisation whose purpose was to more closely control the population through religious ideology. It was strongly supported by the absolutist state under whose auspices these established religions operated. Indeed, Lemarchand's failure to discuss more fully the ideological aspects of early modern feudalism is disappointing since he considers ideology an integral feature of the feudal mode. Here and there there are references to the contending political beliefs of the established or new nobles and their respective views of the proper relationship between the second estate and the monarchy, but these issues are scarcely developed (pp. 152–3, 155, 185, 188).

In the face of this seigneurial reaction Lemarchand demonstrates that peasant resistance across Europe was widespread. According to the anti-Marxist view championed by the school of Roland Mousnier, despite the frequency and scope of rural revolts in the seventeenth century they were not directed against the society of orders headed by the nobility but directed against taxation by the state.[14] Lemarchand shows on the basis of more recent research that the root of such protests lay in the villages and *seigneuries* and included not only tax revolts, but also subsistence riots and challenges to the incursions of the landlords on communal lands and rights. A veritable *habitus* of revolt, he points out, took hold in the French countryside which was to have lasting consequences (p. 198). Outside of France a similar pattern of resistance developed, although research on such revolts elsewhere is less well-developed. The motivations of peasant rebellions everywhere were quite similar but religion seems to have played little role in the case of France. State authority consistently intervened to put down rural resistance in order to protect its own fiscal power or to back the nobility. On the other hand, the threat of rebellion by the rural population seems to have mitigated to some extent demands for still more rent or taxation.

---

14   Mousnier 1967.

Apogee and Decline of Feudalism

The third and last part of Lemarchand's opus covers the eighteenth and nine-teenth centuries and deals with the apogee and decline of the feudal system. Following an economic recovery which set in between 1720 and 1740 thanks to a reversal in the economic and demographic conjuncture, economic growth increased more or less everywhere in Europe, the *seigneurie* appeared to have recovered its economic strength, and the nobility seemed everywhere unri-valled. In the face of this situation, explaining the collapse of feudalism requires taking into account the subjective factor and especially paying attention to the advent of the new and influential ideology of liberalism and the rising rate of literacy among the lower classes. Above all it is necessary to dig deeper into the structure of European feudalism at the local, national and international level to understand its crisis. The essential problem is to understand why an apparently stable and prosperous order more or less rapidly fell apart.

As everyone knows, the role of the market increased immensely in the eighteenth century and the first signs of the operation of the law of value were evident in international trade from the beginning of the new century. Lemarchand considers the increase in the money supply as a result of the availability of more gold and silver and the printing of money to have been important to the prosperity of the new century, but he fails to explain why this was so in other than monetarist terms. Agricultural prices and rents rose especially after the middle of the eighteenth century while real wages declined. Population increased as did the growth of rural industry in Western Europe, but also now in Eastern Europe as well. Contrary to the view that feudalism was synonymous with economic stagnation, growth was both real and important in the eighteenth century (p. 244). One might add that the economy of *Ancien Régime* France in its last century out-performed that of capitalist England in certain aspects. The expansion of the colonial trade and the export not only of manufactures but also food to the Caribbean and Latin America was particularly notable.

Economic growth certainly led to an increase in the wealth and diversity of the bourgeoisie. Despite this the nobility kept and even consolidated its posi-tion. Its income, much of which still came from the *seigneurie*, exceeded that of its bourgeois rivals by a considerable margin and its control over offices in the state increased. The nobility of the sword and the service nobility strengthened their hand by largely amalgamating. In France the nobility's opening to the financial bourgeoisie and growing involvement in business improved its pos-ition. Despite this apparent supremacy the nobility's actual power eroded, as its numbers declined both absolutely and relatively. The biological extinction

of families, further mortality due to war, the decline of many of the impoverished petty nobility to commoner status, the closing of the ranks of the nobility
to wealthy upstarts from below and the dramatic expansion of the non-noble
population played their part. The political and social danger of such a decline in
numbers was obscured by the seigneurial reaction which intensified (pp. 261–
2).

In France the eighteenth century saw the strengthening of a rural bourgeoisie which was most evident in the Île-de-France but visible elsewhere as
well. Also manifest is a growing popular impatience with what were increasingly regarded as the archaic and unjust constraints of the seigneurial order.
This was all the more the case as the horizons of the rural population widened
as a result of growing education and literacy (p. 250). Respect for the hier-
archical order of society declined on what seemed a day-to-day basis amid
increasing reports of peasant insolence toward authority. The number of anti-
seigneurial revolts rose dramatically as the revolution approached (pp. 266,
270–1). This was in part a response to the renewed seigneurial reaction of the
second half of the eighteenth century. In the past incursions by the nobles
on peasant land and communal rights had been limited by the monarchy's
paternalism. These protective policies were abandoned by the state in favour
of encouraging a liberal agrarian individualism of which the nobility took
increasing advantage. The number of landless or nearly landless peasants grew
(pp. 275–7).

The acuteness of the crisis in France proved unique. The novelty in Central
and Eastern Europe was the appearance of an enlightened absolutism which,
among other progressive steps, attempted to improve agriculture. Lip-service
was given to the idea that serfdom was an evil and certain timid reforms were
attempted. These went furthest in the Habsburg lands but were aborted faced
with the French Revolution and growing noble resistance. The dependence of
the monarchies on their nobilities if anything increased, as did the burdens
on the peasantry. The number of the landless and the growth of rural industry
in Central and Eastern Europe was noteworthy. Parallel to the trend in France,
failure on the part of government to ameliorate the lot of the peasants and the
outbreak of subsistence crises led to large-scale peasant uprisings especially in
Russia, but also in Croatia, Bohemia, Galicia, Transylvania and Saxony (pp. 308–
10).

The abolition of feudalism came from revolution from below in France
and from revolution from above in other places such as Prussia. Lemarchand
attempts to nuance this model of revolution inherited from Lenin by pointing
out that in many cases a third force – the invading French army – brought
about the demise of the system. In fact in many places the liquidation of

feudalism was only partial and redemption payments were more the rule than the exception. Furthermore in the period of reaction which followed the fall of Napoleon efforts were made to reverse the process. The continuing weakness of the bourgeoisie in Central and Eastern Europe reinforced this reaction. The revolutions of 1848 were decisive to the destruction of Central European feudalism. The liberation of the serfs had to wait until 1861 in the Russian Empire. Lemarchand points out, however, that the dissolution of the feudal system, while it destroyed the *seigneurie*, did not bring land reform in the form of serious redistribution of the land from the landlords to the have-nots in France or anywhere else (p. 351).

Feudalism and Uneven Development

Immense achievement though it is, Lemarchand's synthesis fails to locate this perduring feudal mode of production within the historic context of the overall evolution of modern history. It was capitalism that was the transformative element from the sixteenth century onwards, but the relationship between the development of this newer mode of production and the older feudal mode over four centuries is not articulated by the author. Lemarchand earlier noted that feudalism evolved as a result of class conflict as well as the conflict between the forces and relations of production. Furthermore, in the course of the work he especially points to the social differentiation of the peasants, the emergence of a rural bourgeoisie and the growing influence of the bourgeoisie as leading to a crisis in the mode of production. At the end of the work he underscores that the unprecedented ascent of capitalism in the eighteenth century put the system in question (p. 328). But there is no systematic study of the impact of the evolution of capitalism on feudal relations of production over the whole period. There is no discussion of the link between this system and the feudalism of the middle ages or how it differed from it. The case of England is dealt with by viewing it as the great exception. According to Lemarchand, the latter country was marked by the development of capitalism from the sixteenth century onward with the initiative coming from the landlords, who were consequently too divided to defend their interests as a class. This development was capped by a political revolution against absolutism in the seventeenth century (pp. 200–5). Once again, how this innovative English capitalism might have affected the rest of Europe is not explored.

Lemarchand's failure to explain the relationship between the reconsolidation of feudalism in the late sixteenth century, the late medieval crisis and the spectacular revival of Europe in the Renaissance is especially notable. What relationship was there between the feudal revival after 1560 and the earlier spectacular innovations that occurred during the Italian Renaissance, the overseas discoveries, the crisis of the Reformation and the rise of financial and trading centres like Genoa, Augsburg, Lyons and Antwerp? It is the birth of capitalism that these advances have in common, a capitalism rooted in the first place in the creation of value on the farms of the Po Valley, in the mines of Germany and Hungary and on the newly enclosed farms of southeast England based on transformed capitalist relations of production. But this emerging capitalism was also founded on the generalised production of commodities especially in proto-industrial manufacturing – which established itself in the towns and countryside of England as well as in the Netherlands, Italy, France and Germany – in which wage labour played a central role. This new capitalist system was by no means limited to new productive relations but entailed the simultaneous expansion of markets. Much of this new commodity production including the production of gold and silver was aimed at realising itself in the emerging world market, whose inherent tendency was toward indefinite expansion to Africa, America and Asia. Moreover, the financial profits from these ventures were being concentrated in centres like Genoa, Augsburg, Antwerp, Lyons and London not simply as money but as money capital which was available for re-investment. Capitalism had appeared as a totality defined as value capable of indefinite self-expansion through a repeated and widening circuit of production, sale of commodities in the market and realisation as capital in the money-form.

The question is what is the relationship between this capitalism of the late fifteenth and early sixteenth century and Lemarchand's revived feudalism? Part of the answer is to be found in the concept of uneven development. It was Eric Hobsbawm who first applied the conception of uneven development to the historical development of capitalism. He did so as his contribution to the celebrated debate on the transition from feudalism to capitalism back in the 1950s.[15] In this highly original contribution informed by a dialectical view of history – a contribution which has been largely ignored – Hobsbawm put the emphasis on the role of uneven development in the development of capitalism throughout its history.

West European advance came directly at the expense of Eastern Europe and Asia, Africa and Latin America. The process of West European transition throughout its early history entailed turning other areas into dependent economies and colonies. Seizing resources from less advanced areas or later on

---

15   Hobsbawm 1976.

from colonised regions became an intrinsic feature of West European development. In other words, the emergence of capitalism has to be understood in terms of an ongoing world-wide process of appropriation based on uneven development both within and outside Europe. Hobsbawm concludes that 'the net effect of European capitalism was to divide the world ever more sharply into two sectors: the "developed" and the "under-developed" countries, in other words the exploiting and the exploited'.[16] Hobsbawm's conception of the transition is a dialectical one in which unevenness plays a central part. Gain in one place is invariably at the expense of other places, even those that were initially more developed. In this schema the advance of Holland and England toward capitalism entails the refeudalisation of Italy and Germany and the feudalising of Poland, Hungary and Russia as conceived by Lemarchand.

Wallerstein develops this conception further with his notion of the emergence of an early modern capitalist world-system with different labour regimes: coerced labour at the periphery; tenant farming, sharecropping, craft production and usury predominating in the semi-periphery; and wage labour at the core with surpluses flowing toward the capitalist centre.[17] Lemarchand's feudalised European states would belong to the semi-periphery and periphery. Moreover, Wallerstein pinpoints the time of emergence of the European state in a way which coincides with Lemarchand's own dating. The collapse of Habsburg imperial hegemony at the end of the reign of Charles V (1556) was the moment when the independent territorial feudal monarchies began to emerge.[18] Indeed, it is from this point on that the European-wide system of balance of power was born and the Netherlands began its long war of liberation which saw the emergence of the capitalist Dutch Republic. The revolt in the Low Countries testifies to how powerfully sixteenth-century capitalism began to challenge the feudal order and required its re-organisation in the form of the absolutist state.

But Wallerstein's view has problems which make it difficult to link it to Lemarchand's perspective. In Wallerstein's conception, from the sixteenth century there is a single capitalist world-system which questionably makes the Russian noble extracting labour from a serf, a French noble collecting rent from a subsistence peasant in the Auvergne, and an English noble collecting rent from a capitalist farmer in Kent equally capitalist. But French and Russian nobles cannot remotely be considered capitalists from the perspective of

---

16   Hobsbawm 1976, p. 164.
17   Wallerstein 1974, pp. 86–7.
18   Wallerstein 1974, pp. 181, 184–5.

Lemarchand. Likewise untenable is Wallerstein's notion of strong states at the centre and less strong ones toward the periphery, which does not fit the historical evolution of absolutist states as outlined by Lemarchand.

The most serious weakness of Lemarchand's work is its failure to theorise the relationship between the evolution of feudalism and the development of capitalism from the perspective of the development of the absolutist state. As we have seen, Lemarchand acknowledges how important the state was to the survival and perpetuation of feudalism in the modern period. Moreover, in passing he recognises the plausibility of the Althusserian idea that a mode of production can co-exist with other modes of production within a given social formation. It is surprising, therefore, that Lemarchand has ignored the important work of Perry Anderson, published more or less coincidentally with the work of Wallerstein and Brenner with which he is familiar.[19] In Anderson's work the co-existence of modes of production within the same social formation plays a primary theoretical role. Covering more or less the same ground as Lemarchand, Anderson traces the history of the absolutist state as the ultimate defensive rampart of feudalism – a conception identical to that of Lemarchand's. But while Lemarchand stresses the similarity between feudalism in the East and West, Anderson emphasises their differences. The prevalence of serfdom in the East fundamentally marks its feudalism off from that of the West. A related and no less essential distinction is that Anderson sees the Western absolutist state as the cradle of capitalism: a mode defined by the existence of free labour. As Anderson expresses it, 'thus when the Absolutist States were constituted in the West, their structure was fundamentally determined by the feudal regroupment against the peasantry, after the dissolution of serfdom; but it was secondarily *over-determined* by the rise of an urban bourgeoisie which after a series of technical and commercial advances was now developing into pre-industrial manufactures on a considerable scale'.[20] In other words the structure and evolution of these Western absolutisms was shaped not simply by the fact that they protected the interests of the noble class, but that they contained within them and provided a space for the emergence of a capitalist bourgeoisie. Anderson concludes that 'the threat of peasant unrest, unspokenly constitutive of the Absolute State, was thus always conjoined with the pressure of mercantile or manufacturing capital within the Western economies as a whole, in moulding the contours of aristocratic class power in the new age. The peculiar form of the Absolute State in the West derives from this

---

19   Anderson 1974.
20   Anderson 1974, pp. 22–3.

double determination'.[21] Moreover while recognising the exceptional strength of capitalist forces in Tudor and Stuart England Anderson rightly considers it an absolutist state along with those on the other side of the English Channel. Anderson's formulation captures the double character of Western absolutism in stressing its dominant purpose of safeguarding noble class-power but in simultaneously underscoring its provision of a framework for the growth of capitalist elements which were latent inside it. While in Lemarchand the presence of capitalist elements in the absolutist state is additive and cumulative, in Anderson such features are intrinsic to the absolutist states in the West. In a curious reversal, Anderson, born into an English-speaking empirical tradition, brilliantly applies Althusserian theory to European history. On the contrary, the Frenchman Lemarchand appears a prisoner of empiricism. Anderson's work cannot match the overwhelming wealth of Lemarchand's scholarship. On the other hand, its theoretical and dialectical power continues to make it more than a match for the latter.

---

21   Anderson 1974, pp. 23–4.

CHAPTER 4

The *Longue Durée* of the French Bourgeoisie

Marxists in academe sometimes complain about how hard done-by they are by non-Marxist scholars. They gripe that their work is dismissed, marginalised or misinterpreted by mainstream academics. But this can hardly be said to be the case when we look at the current state of historical studies of France in the seventeenth century. At the moment, it seems as if Marxist perspectives are taken very seriously, especially in the English-speaking world. In particular, the works of two Marxist scholars, William Beik and David Parker, have found great resonance among scholars both favourable and unfavourable to Marxism.[1]

Likewise, in the study of early modern England, the work of the avowedly Marxist historian Robert Brenner is held in great esteem. His accounts of the development of capitalism in early modern England and of the English Revolution have attracted much favourable attention.[2] Beside their shared commitment to Marxism, all three scholars have in common a similarly sceptical view of *ancien régime* France. Beik, Brenner and Parker agree that early modern France was unable to break the fetters of feudalism and absolutism. More significantly, they are unable to discover a capitalist bourgeoisie in France in the early modern period. As a result, these Marxist scholars – unwittingly or not – have greatly reinforced the currently popular revisionist view that rejects the notion of the French Revolution as a bourgeois and capitalist revolution. The essay which follows does not reject the view of France as being under the thrall of feudalism during the *ancien régime*. But it does argue that these scholars have over-stated the dominance of feudal relations of production to the point of erasing the bourgeoisie and the dynamic of class struggle. To the contrary, it re-asserts the view that a capitalist bourgeoisie appeared in France in the sixteenth century, persevered in the seventeenth and took the offensive in the eighteenth century leading to the revolution of 1789.[3]

---

1   Beik 1985; Parker 1996. Beik's work is extolled, for example, in reviews by Wood 1986 and Ranum 1986 while Parker's book is highly praised by Rowlands 1999; Lewis 1998.

2   Brenner 1985, 1993. For reviews of the latter work see Morrill 1994; Miskimin 1994; Callinicos 1994.

3   Needless to say, the existence of such a capitalist bourgeoisie has to be grasped within the legal and political modalities of the *ancien régime*. The most sophisticated and historically informed discussion of the place of the bourgeoisie in the *ancien régime* from a Marxist perspective is in Robin 1970, pp. 18–52.

The Rejection of the Classical-Marxist View of Seventeenth-Century France

Beik takes his point of departure from the well-established fact that seventeenth-century France was, at best, a slow-growth economy. In contrast to the sixteenth century, when agricultural profits were high, Beik notes that the seventeenth century was an age of high rents and oppressive taxation. Under such circumstances, nobles and officers benefitted while entrepreneurial activity in town and country was crippled. Money moved out of productive activity toward financial dealings.[4] According to Beik, in Languedoc 'a hidden bourgeoisie of dealers in grain and wine, cloth merchants, silk entrepreneurs, and organizers of rural industries made its presence known from time to time, but these were still political small fry whose importance was limited unless they acquired offices in church or state'.[5] An economically weak bourgeoisie enjoyed a twilight existence, but was largely invisible socially and politically. Under such circumstances, the bourgeoisie, weak as they were, were unable to mount a significant opposition to the rule of privileged nobles and landlords. Meanwhile, co-operating more often than competing with the officials and agents of the absolutising monarchy, the landed ruling class enjoyed a virtual monopoly of power in Languedoc and the rest of France until the death of Louis XIV.

In the first instance, Beik's view of seventeenth-century France represented a challenge to the viewpoint of Roland Mousnier who, in the early decades of the Cold War, argued for the autonomous existence of the Bourbon state. According to Mousnier, the absolute monarchy was dominated neither by the aristocracy nor the bourgeoisie.[6] Rather, the centralising monarchy enjoyed an independent political position located above the competing social orders.

Marxist that he is, Beik argued instead that 'the story of seventeenth-century absolutism was ... the story of a restructured feudal society'.[7] The absolute monarchy was an outgrowth of and embodied the perspective of the ruling noble class. Rather than conflicting, as Mousnier would have it, the centralising monarchy and the still locally powerful nobility, more often than not, mutually reinforced one another.

But, in insisting on the class basis of the seventeenth-century monarchy, Beik took his distance from classical-Marxist interpretations of the period.

---

4 Beik 1985, pp. 40–1.
5 Beik 1985, p. 41.
6 Mousnier 1979, 1984.
7 Beik 1985, p. 31.

He rejected the view espoused by Engels that the absolute monarchy held the balance between the nobility and the bourgeoisie. Engels had maintained that with the virtual disappearance of serfdom there began a period of petty-commodity production and primitive accumulation signalling the appearance of early capitalism. According to Beik, such a view makes sense with respect to England, but not for France, where the society of landlords and dependent peasants persisted for centuries.

It is from this perspective that Beik then criticised the viewpoint of two Soviet scholars, Boris Porshnev and A.D. Lublinskaya.[8] Porshnev had become known to Western historians as a result of his discovery of the recurrent waves of peasant and urban revolts that marked the first part of the seventeenth century in France. In the course of recounting this history, Porshnev echoed the view of Engels: '"French society in the seventeenth century was already profoundly affected by the new distinction among men based upon the opposition between labour and capitalist property which was breaking down the old feudal and corporative barriers".[9] Porshnev regarded the emergent French bourgeoisie as behaving in a contradictory fashion in the seventeenth century. On the one hand, he saw the bourgeoisie acting as an independent and, at moments, revolutionary class. On the other hand, he recognised that the bourgeoisie at this stage of its development was ultimately captive to the feudal aristocratic system. It was subordinated to this system politically through venality of office, socially by acquiring titles of nobility, and economically through tax farming, involvement in state finance and dependence on mercantilist privileges.

In characteristically dialectical fashion, Porshnev saw this class as caught between these two positions, alternating between submission and revolt. Beik, however, refuses to accept this dialectical perspective. Instead, he insists on the total economic and political subordination of the bourgeoisie. While endorsing Porshnev's recognition of the relative weakness of the bourgeoisie, he rejects the Soviet historian's notion of its economic independence or occasional rebelliousness. He dismisses this view by rhetorically demanding 'where is the capitalistic side of his [Porshnev's] bourgeoisie?' According to Beik, Porshnev provides little evidence of its economic independence and strength. As to its political force, Beik notes that Porshnev can point only to its revolutionary behaviour during the Fronde.[10]

---

8   Porshnev 1963; Lublinskaya 1968.
9   Porshnev 1963, cited in Beik 1985, p. 24.
10   Beik 1985, p. 25.

In a similar fashion, Beik gives short shrift to the views of Porshnev's col-
league Lublinskaya. According to Beik, Lublinskaya downplayed Porshnev's
notion of the revolutionary political or social stance of the bourgeoisie. Yet, if
anything, she insisted even more strongly than Porshnev on its independent
economic existence. According to Lublinskaya, the royal officials and financiers were feudalised, but there was also a trading and industrial bourgeoisie
distinct from them. The latter economically active class needed absolutism
to protect and develop its potential for capital accumulation. This indigenous
class of merchants and traders was geographically subdivided, split by religion
and imperfectly developed. But it was slowly rising without having reached
the point where its interests would be incompatible with the feudal régime.
Its influence was great enough to push the state towards developments which
prepared the way for the rise of capitalism.[11]

Beik's view of this is equally dismissive. According to him, the very existence of Lublinskya's trading and industrial bourgeoisie is open to question.
Beik complains that Lublinskaya uses only circumstantial evidence – economic
treatises and a few isolated cases – to argue for the importance of a group which
is exceedingly hard to find in the sources.[12] Like Porshnev, Lublinskaya admits
that the seventeenth-century bourgeoisie was subordinated to the nobility and
absolutist state. But Beik will not admit even this much. For him, the bourgeoisie did not exist. On this point, Beik supports himself with the scholarship
of another Anglo-Saxon historian, David Parker. In his work on La Rochelle,
Parker underlined what he asserted to be the scant evidence for the existence
of an independent bourgeoisie in La Rochelle and, indeed, in France.[13] Parker
reiterates this view in his recent study of seventeenth-century France, *Class and
State in Ancien Regime France*.[14] Parker's new work, it should be said, represents
an important and persuasive new synthesis of seventeenth-century French history. At the same time, his book powerfully reinforces Beik's overall view.

According to Parker, aristocratic control of the state apparatus as well as
continuing seigneurial domination over the land ensured noble domination
over French society to the end of the *ancien régime*. As for the bourgeoisie
and capitalism, they were crippled by the absence of absolute property rights,
by a parasitic and stifling bureaucracy and tax system, as well as by overall
aristocratic control. A rural or urban bourgeoisie can hardly be said to have

---

11   Beik 1995, p. 27.
12   Ibid.
13   Parker 1971, pp. 67–89; Parker 1980, pp. 180–5.
14   Parker 1996.

existed. Especially brilliant is Parker's demonstration of the ongoing ideological dominance of the nobility and its enduring control of the machinery of the state. As for capitalism, Parker compares France and England, asserting that the political and legal basis for capitalism did not exist in the former country.

As a result of his enquiry, Parker reaches conclusions of considerable import. According to him, 'the conception of bourgeois revolution derived from the *Communist Manifesto* is significantly modified. This postulated a growth of capitalism inside the womb of feudalism and the birth of a bourgeois class which then seized power from its feudal masters'.[15] Based on his study, Parker finds that, compared to seventeenth-century England, it is 'difficult to identify a bourgeois class in late eighteenth century France'.[16] Capitalism and the bourgeoisie were weak in the seventeenth century. The weakness of the bourgeoisie continued to the eve of the French Revolution. Parker's inescapable conclusion is that the revolution of 1789 could not have been based on the bourgeoisie. His view thus dovetails with what has come to be called the revisionist view of the French Revolution.

While Beik does not take things so far in this direction, the implications of the work of both historians are far-reaching. It has been a common premise of both liberal and Marxist historians that the history of the *ancien régime* was marked by the slow rise of a bourgeoisie based on capitalism. Beik and Parker reject the notion of a long historical gestation of the French bourgeoisie within the tissues of the French absolutist regime. Directly or indirectly, their view amounts to a discounting of the idea of a nascent bourgeoisie and capitalism within the *ancien régime*. Indeed, with Beik's dismissal of any notion of simple commodity production or primitive accumulation as applicable to France prior to the seventeenth century, such a notion is explicitly rejected.

The Dialectic of Rent and Profit

Regarding France from the perspective of English development, Brenner's views powerfully support those of Beik and Parker.[17] England was the place where a capitalist breakthrough first occurred. This was the outcome of the class struggle between lords and peasants which took place in that country

---

15   Parker 1996, p. 280.
16   Ibid.
17   The concordance between Brenner's and Beik's views is pointed out in Miller 2008, pp. 8–
       10.

at the end of the Middle Ages. According to Brenner, these conflicts saw the
English landlord class gain control of the greater part of the arable land at the
expense of the subsistence peasantry. Such landlord control made it possible
for them to re-organise agriculture on the basis of large farms rented out on
short-term and competitive leases to enterprising farmers. The latter increasingly were able or were compelled to exploit displaced peasants as wage-labour
and, by systematic improvement, initiate a process of capital accumulation
which transformed the English economy.[18]

According to Brenner, this breakthrough toward capitalism occurred
uniquely through a change in the social relations of production in the sixteenth-century English countryside. This emphasis on the rural roots of capitalism is Brenner's key insight in the debate on the origins of capitalism. But,
in the course of arguing this point, he has turned France into the foil or negative example to make the case. According to Brenner, France experienced the
same upsurge of class struggle as England in the late Middle Ages with a quite
different outcome. In the former case, the peasants were able to keep control
of roughly forty-five or fifty percent of the land as against only twenty, twenty-
five or thirty percent in England.[19] As a result of the greater share of property
retained by the peasantry, no restructuring of agriculture along English lines
was possible in France. Whatever tendency there was towards capitalism in
sixteenth-century France was aborted. From Brenner's perspective, the problem of an absent bourgeoisie in France is not merely a reflection of the dearth of
manufacturers and traders. It is also, and above all, about the lack of a *rural* capitalist bourgeoisie. It is the differing allocation of property and the contrasting
relations of production which determined the divergent evolution of the two
countries in the early-modern period. In the eyes of Brenner, France is seen as
the counter-example to England's success in terms of the early development
of capitalism. England is the normative example of capitalist origins. France is
the *Other*.

But, then, as in the case of Beik and Parker, the question arises, what of the
French Revolution? The traditional Marxist view of that revolution was that,
like the English Revolution, the French Revolution was a bourgeois and capitalist revolution. The Brenner thesis could suggest that, given the non-capitalist
evolution of France under the *ancien régime*, such a notion of a bourgeois
and capitalist revolution was, on the face of it, dubious. In a curious way, it
should be pointed out that Brenner's view (based on Marxism) like those of

---

18   Brenner 1985, pp. 48–9; Brenner 1986, pp. 23–53.
19   Brenner 1985, p. 61.

Beik and Parker dove-tailed with the developing scholarly and political trend against the Marxist view of the French Revolution known as French revolutionary revisionism.[20] This historiographical current which became ascendant by the 1980s attacked the idea that the revolution in France could be understood as a bourgeois and capitalist revolution. Among those who denied the capitalist basis of the revolution was George Comninel, also a self-professed Marxist.[21] According to him, the bourgeoisie in France prior to the revolution was not capitalist because it based itself on rent rather than on profit. Moreover, wage-workers were dependent not on their wages but on their own sources of subsistence.[22] This view coincided with Brenner's notion of the ongoing hold of the French peasantry on the land. Indeed, it is probable that, in assuming this viewpoint, Comninel was substantially influenced by Brenner.[23] In the case of the account of capitalist origins by Comninel's teacher Ellen Meiksins Wood, the influence of Brenner is explicit. As Brenner has established – according to Wood – the origins of capitalism are to be found exclusively in the social relations of production of the English countryside. Under French absolutism, feudal rent dominated to the point that there was no capitalist bourgeoisie. The French Revolution was a bourgeois but *not* a capitalist revolution.[24]

The conception of France as a society ruled by a nobility which exercised its power over the peasantry through the absolutist state thus has gained, if not unanimous acceptance, then serious consideration among leading English-speaking Marxist scholars as well as others. Far be it for me to criticise this conception with which I basically agree. As to the bourgeoisie, although they exaggerate its impotence, Beik and Parker are correct to insist on the ongoing absorption of the upper reaches of the bourgeoisie into the political apparatus of the state. At the same time, some profits from industry and commerce were transformed through commercial privileges, venality of office, tax-gathering, the purchase of *rentes* and ennoblement. Indeed, the liquefaction of peasant surpluses on which the regime depended was based on these quasi-commercial processes.

In the light of this perspective, Beik and Parker refuse to accept Porshnev's ideas of class struggle. The latter portrayed the bourgeoisie as suspended between a position of subordination and one of opposition to the bourgeoisie.

---

20   The varieties of revisionism are described in Vovelle 1990, pp. 749–55.
21   Comninel 1987.
22   Comninel 1987, pp. 190–1, 200. Comninel does not explain why workers would work for wages if they could assure their own subsistence.
23   Comninel 1987, pp. 160, 192.
24   Wood 2002, pp. 50–63.

On the contrary, Beik and Parker are at pains to deny the strength and con-
tentiousness of the bourgeoisie. In so doing, they succeed in demonstrating its
weakness and largely refuting Porshnev's conception. But, in rebutting Porshnev, they have gone too far: Beik and Parker have rejected the notion of opposition or conflict between the bourgeois and noble classes. It is this denial of
the conception of class conflict between nobility and bourgeoisie in the seventeenth century that this chapter questions. It contends that their dismissal of
such class conflict deprives seventeenth-century France of a sense of dynamic
development. Moreover, it cuts this century off from any real connection with
developments which occurred later and, in particular, the revolution of 1789.
Finally, in so far as it would deny the continued existence of a bourgeoisie in
seventeenth-century France, their view is not in accord with the historical evidence. The views of Brenner, Wood and Comninel are likewise not sustained by
current research in French history.

Class War from Above

The starting point of Beik's analysis of class relations is his view of the French
agrarian economy. In this respect, his discussion is mainly dependent on the
work of Le Roy Ladurie. Yet, it would seem that he has misconstrued the latter's
overall view. In accord with Le Roy Ladurie, he notes that the sixteenth century
had been a great age of agricultural profits. It was an age, to re-iterate Beik,
that 'favoured the initiative of enterprising middle-to-large-scale farmers'. In
contrast, he underlines that the seventeenth century was an age of increasingly
high rents and oppressive taxation. Citing Le Roy Ladurie, Beik argues that
demographic pressure and land hunger played a part in the increase in rents.[25]
But such increases in rents, we would emphasise, cannot simply be accounted
for by the play of the market. As Le Roy Ladurie also points out, in Languedoc as
in much of the rest of France, increases in rent were connected to increases in
state taxation as proprietors linked rent increases on tenants to tax increases.[26]
Indeed, the decline of profits and rise of rent must not be understood as merely
the inexorable struggle of reified economic concepts. Rather, as Le Roy Ladurie
suggests, the respective level of rent and profit should be seen as economic
metaphors expressing the outcome of a struggle to impose a new political and
social order.

---

25   Beik 1985, p. 40.
26   Le Roy Ladurie 1966, I, p. 468.

If we follow Beik, rent constituted the only form of rural surplus extraction from the beginning to the end of the seventeenth century. Rural capitalism, from his perspective, is nowhere to be seen. If this were so, we would be dealing with a society of seigneurial power and subsistence farming little different from the twelfth century. In fact, the age of merely feudal rent had long since passed. In accord with Le Roy Ladurie, Beik is certainly correct to conclude that rents were step-by-step driven higher. What he fails to appreciate is the implications of Le Roy Ladurie's correlation of rents in relation to profits (and wages) through the sixteenth and seventeenth centuries. Le Roy Ladurie's comparison is rightly premised on the ongoing existence of a class of profit-minded rural capitalists. The rural middle class, he explains to us, 'play an important role in the seventeenth century under Louis XIII and Mazarin'.[27]

No doubt, the great majority of French peasants were subsistence farmers or even farm labourers, but, while small in numbers, the capitalist element noted by Le Roy Ladurie and which had originated in the sixteenth century owned or, more typically, rented a disproportionately large part of the arable land which it exploited with the help of its own operating capital and wage-labour.[28] Capitalist rent collected from profit-minded peasants thus constituted a substantial, if indeterminately large, element of the rural surplus throughout the period.

Beik's misreading of Le Roy Ladurie's dialectical appreciation of the ongoing relationship between rent and profit leads to a fundamental distortion in his appreciation of the seventeenth century. In Beik's view, the triumph of rent can be dated to the beginning of the seventeenth century. Profit apparently disappeared, and the social and political effacement of the bourgeoisie followed. Le Roy Ladurie's account is more evolutionary and dialectical. Where Beik sees a sudden and definitive victory for rent, Le Roy Ladurie offers the perspective of a long-drawn-out struggle. According to the latter, the sixteenth century had seen an offensive of profit against rent that went on through most of the century.[29] The tendency began to reverse itself in 1580 or 1600. In the Île-de-France, Jean Jacquart dates the reversal to as late as 1620.[30]

But, at this point, this new direction is only a reversal of a tendency, a counter-offensive or reaction, not yet a triumph. In other words, half or two-thirds of the next century is marked by a long and continuing offensive of rent against profit. The advance of rent was as prolonged an affair as was the

27   Le Roy Ladurie 1966, I, p. 172.
28   Goubert 1990, p. 1167.
29   Le Roy Ladurie 1966, I, pp. 291–313.
30   Jacquart 1990, pp. 68–9, 196.

preceding offensive of profit. It is only in the reign of Louis XIV that rent and taxes may be said to have overwhelmed profits as a result of this long-drawn-out and sustained offensive.[31]

Beik appears to see class conflict only as overt rebellion from below. With the leading elements of the bourgeoisie having been co-opted into the ruling class, the popular revolts of the period were not class-based uprisings.[32] Parker, somewhat paradoxically, insists that such rebellions did have a class basis, albeit based on the hopeless revolts of the craftsmen and peasants.[33] He takes this position while arguing as strongly as Beik that there was no bourgeoisie. Yet, if there was little or no class-based challenge from below, the offensive of rent against profit makes it evident that there was a strong and ongoing class offensive from above. It took the form above all of the relentless pressure on profits of increasing rents and taxes.

Beik and Parker take the triumph of rent as an established state of affairs that determined all other facets of the seventeenth century. In truth, the seventeenth century was characterised not by a given condition – the static weight of rent – but, rather, by a process in which rents advanced and profits were progressively eroded. The subtlety of Le Roy Ladurie's conception of this relationship is expressed in the following passage:

> The expansion of the sixteenth century was favourable to the profit of enterprise: that of the following [century] prolongs it [profit], but bears rent with it and the surplus value it radiates goes toward the enrichment of the landlord.[34]

A class of rural capitalists remained in existence, albeit increasingly burdened by the imposition of higher rents. In other words, the class struggle continued,

31 Le Roy Ladurie 1966, I, pp. 585–92; Postel-Vinay 1974, p. 17.
32 Beik puts his viewpoint rather cryptically. Citing Porshnev's view of the popular revolts, he notes that 'I am not convinced that they constituted the primary class struggle in seventeenth-century France' (Beik, 1985, p. 190). Beik does not say what the primary class struggle was. A class struggle involves a conflict between at least two classes. Having dismissed the economic and political significance of a bourgeoisie, Beik obviously does not believe that they were part of either the primary class struggle or popular revolts. At the same time, it is not clear from his subsequent work on popular revolts in the seventeenth century (Beik 1997) whether or not he regards the peasants and artisans who did participate in popular revolts as members of a class.
33 Parker 1996, p. 95.
34 Le Roy Ladurie 1966, I, p. 467.

with the initiative coming from above rather than below. Moreover, such an assault did not assume the shape of a violent social confrontation. On the contrary, it took the form of increases in rent to be sure, but also state construction, the increasingly more complex hierarchies of society, a growing sophistication of upper-class manners, and corresponding social and religious disciplining of the lower classes. Despite this offensive, the rural bourgeoisie may be said to have been bowed, but by no means broken, and they emerged from this onslaught with renewed strength in the eighteenth century. It is Le Roy Ladurie himself who takes note of this durability toward the conclusion of his great work: 'On the whole it is indeed the *fermier* class, the group of substantial *labourers* which collapses (in Languedoc) from 1680 (but not forever to be sure)'.[35]

Whither the French Bourgeoisie?

Beik and Parker systematically minimise the existence of the bourgeoisie, questioning its very existence. Engels had postulated a period of petty-commodity production and primitive accumulation as initiating the origins of capitalism. Beik rejects this, maintaining that it makes sense for England but not France. Although there was a decline of serfdom, no period of petty-commodity production, let alone primitive accumulation, occurred. In Beik's view then, there is no evidence of proto-capitalist or capitalist activity in France. Beik makes this claim despite his quite contradictory acknowledgement of Le Roy Ladurie's view that the sixteenth century was a period in which the initiative in the countryside lay with middle- to large-scale profit-seeking farmers.

One wonders what the basis is for his denial of an initial period of petty-commodity production and primitive accumulation. Even Brenner is struck by the parallel between French and English development at this stage. The economic recovery in France from the late-medieval crisis, which began around 1450 and continued in more or less uninterrupted fashion to about 1520, closely approximates to the Marxist conception of a period dominated by simple-commodity production. In this phase, which was common to Languedoc as well as the rest of France, there was a proliferation of markets and market exchange. Merchants were active, but they did not yet fully dominate the marketplace. Taxes and rents were still relatively low. As a result, small-scale rural and urban producers were an important factor in exchange and enjoyed unpre-

---

35   Le Roy Ladurie 1966, I, p. 592.

cedented prosperity.[36] The following period from 1520–60 saw the definitive triumph of merchant capitalism focused on Lyons. The financial power and control associated with the import of silk cloth and spices gave the Italian-Lyonnais merchant-bankers a remarkable degree of influence over regional and local markets throughout France.[37] Meanwhile, in the countryside, the possibility of substantial profits prompted the development of agrarian capitalism. From Normandy and the Île-de-France in the north to Languedoc in the south, the tendency was for the peasantry to become increasingly differentiated between a mass of producers dependent on wages and a kind of rural bourgeoisie. *Pace* Beik, primitive accumulation was an integral and necessary aspect of this process.[38] Certainly, this emergent agrarian capitalism was immature and incomplete. The continued strength of the middle peasantry, the persistence of seigneurial forms of domination and communal rights, the consolidation of the bureaucratic state and a kind of mental inertia or *habitus* in favour of agricultural routine inhibited this emergent rural capitalism.

Despite fetters on its development, capitalism grew in strength in the countryside during the religious wars. The process of peasant expropriation which had begun in the first part of the sixteenth century accelerated. Pillaging, heavy taxation and indebtedness led to a dramatic acceleration of the concentration of land into the hands of wealthy peasants and the urban rich. The partial or complete loss of land experienced by producers, which continued into the seventeenth century, entailed a growing dependence on wage labour.[39]

Summing up this transfer of land from the mass of the peasantry to the rural and urban bourgeoisie on a national level, Jacquart notes that:

> the great wave of appropriation of the soil by the bourgeoisie took place between 1530 and 1600. Afterwards there ensued a continuation and consolidation of a hold which has never since been brought into question despite political, economic and social revolutions.[40]

It was the bourgeoisie who most benefitted from the expropriation of part of the peasants' land, the appropriation of their property and its inclusion in the circuits of commercial exchange. At the end of this process, the peasantry was left with, on average, fifty percent of the soil and, in some places, with

---

36 Bois 1984, pp. 348, 351–3, 361–2; Fourquin 1971, p. 182.
37 Gascon 1971, I, pp. 320–6.
38 Bois 1984, pp. 289–90.
39 Heller 1996, pp. 28–32.
40 Neveux, Jacquart and Le Roy Ladurie 1975, p. 274; Jacquart 1992, pp. 282–3.

as little as one third.[41] According to Jacquart, 'one can affirm that from the seventeenth century three-quarters of the French peasantry were not able to exploit enough land to reach let alone to approach what we today call the vital minimum'.[42] Cooper concludes that 'in open field France there was a trend to larger farms and the pauperization and proletarianization of small peasants as marked as anything claimed for England'.[43] The increased dependence of this expropriated peasantry on wages ensured the availability of abundant supplies of cheap labour for agricultural work. In the wake of these developments, the closing decades of the sixteenth century saw the flowering of an unprecedented interest in agricultural improvement in the form of the introduction of new crops, agricultural implements, irrigation and other methods to increase output. Of 600 works on agricultural improvement published in sixteenth-century Europe, France published 245 as compared to 41 for the Low Countries and a mere 20 for England.[44]

It should be noted that Brenner, along with Beik and Parker, has failed to notice this process of primitive accumulation, social differentiation and growing bourgeois strength in the French countryside in the latter half of the sixteenth century. Brenner placed the emphasis on the class struggle and the distribution of landholding as between landlords and peasants in the late Middle Ages. He was certainly correct to stress the importance of class struggle in France and England at that time. But he overestimated the durability of the victory of the French peasantry at the end of the Middle Ages. By the latter half of the sixteenth century, most of this class in northern France was clearly placed on the defensive by both the nobility and the emerging bourgeoisie. In this context, what proved structurally determinant was the redistribution of property among the commoners themselves, at the expense of the lesser peasants and to the benefit of the bourgeoisie, both urban and rural. Brenner rejects the importance of the process of peasant social differentiation to capitalist origins in the case of English agriculture. Single-mindedly insisting on the importance of class struggle, he rejects the idea that social differentiation among peasants might have been important to the establishment of capitalist social relations.[45]

At the beginning of the seventeenth century, we can conclude, an agrarian capitalism had partially implanted itself on French soil. This was especially the case in the vast grain lands of the Île-de-France and the northern provinces –

41 Neveux, Jacquart and Le Roy Ladurie 1975, p. 275.
42 Jacquart 1990, p. 34.
43 Cooper 1985, p. 171.
44 Heller 1996, pp. 65–84.
45 Brenner's view is criticised in Byres 2006, pp. 17–68.

capitalism in the Midi was in the process of aborting for the time being.[46] Parker discounts the implications for capitalist development of the massive transfer of property that occurred during this period. Given the co-existent progressive and regressive economic tendencies in rural society, the responsibility of the historian is to strike a balance between retarding factors and those elements fostering capitalism. Yet, Parker's approach is to underline all those factors which inhibited the development of capitalism in agriculture, while minimising those aspects which favoured its growth.[47] He insists on the decisive importance of ongoing feudal constraints on the transfer of property and of the absence of an explicit recognition of absolute property rights.[48]

Parker would have it that property rights in the sense of an absolute right to property did not exist in the *ancien régime*. It is the absence of full rights to property, according to Parker, which in part explains the weakness of capitalism in France in comparison to England.[49] Still, it should be pointed out that, in England, no such absolute property rights existed until the Glorious Revolution,[50] yet capitalism had clearly begun to develop there two hundred years earlier. In fact, in sixteenth-century France, feudal rights over the management, sale and acquisition of property were increasingly attenuated. In a practical sense, peasants were more or less able to dispose of property as they pleased. The growing influence of Roman law only accentuated these tendencies.[51] Parker's comparison of England and France would make sense if confined to the period 1500–1640, but to insist on the comparison after 1640 is to compare two societies which were essentially incomparable. As a result of the Puritan Revolution and Interregnum, England largely disencumbered itself of an absolutising monarchy and seigneurial nobility. Capitalism could develop relatively unhindered. On the contrary, these elements were reconsolidating themselves in seventeenth-century France and capitalism could only develop in the interstices of the *ancien régime*. A more apt comparison would perhaps be between France and Tokugawa Japan, where, in both cases, an incipient capitalism developed dialectically within the pores of a strongly seigneurial régime.[52]

---

46 Le Roy Ladurie 1966, I, pp. 326–8.

47 Parker 1996, pp. 58–74.

48 Parker 1996, pp. 232–3.

49 Parker 1996, pp. 56, 153, 232–3.

50 Norht and Weingast 1989, p. 814; Larkin 1930, p. 52.

51 Ourliac and Gazzaniga 1985, pp. 226–8.

52 Anderson 1975, pp. 435–61; Nakane and Oishi 1991.

Primitive Accumulation in Sixteenth-Century France

The development of rural capitalism in sixteenth-century France helped to support the activity of a growing commercial and manufacturing class. Merchants and merchant manufacturers headquartered in such cities as Paris, Lyons, Rouen, Amiens, Tours, Nantes, La Rochelle and Bordeaux prospered in the first part of the sixteenth century.[53] Under their direct or indirect influence, the manufacture of wool, silk, linen and canvas cloth, books, iron and steel and mining ores all forged ahead.[54] To be sure, the religious wars brought serious demographic decline and economic devastation. The eclipse of the financial and commercial centre of the Kingdom, Lyons, dates from the 1570s. The other great pole of the economy – Paris – suffered during the latter stages of the conflict. At the same time, trade and manufacture prospered in coastal towns like Marseilles, La Rochelle, Saint-Malo and, more unevenly, in Rouen and Amiens.[55] Industries such as wool, linen and canvas, and iron and steel manufacture appear to have more than held their own. At the same time, new manufactures like glass and crystal, faience, cotton, ribbon, satin and lace appeared.[56] With the accession of Henri IV, a general demographic and economic recovery began which persisted into the late 1620s.[57]

Major infrastructural programmes, protective tariffs and state financial aid to manufacturers under Henri IV assisted the recovery of commerce and manufacture. Toward the close of the reign of Henri IV, French exports to the Ottoman Empire, especially silk cloth, eclipsed those of the Italians, Dutch or English.[58] The great cloth manufacturing centre of Amiens saw production reach levels which surpassed those of the preceding century.[59]

It was in the period of the religious wars that primitive accumulation and the offensive of profit reached their climax. Despite extensive rural devastation, these processes strengthened the middle class. It is precisely in this period, for example, that the class of rural capitalists numbering no more than a few hundred families consolidated its control over the Île-de-France.[60] Many urban bourgeois meanwhile made killings through the buying and, in some cases,

---

53   Chaunu and Gascon 1977, I, pp. 235–66; Le Roy Ladurie 1994, pp. 39, 47.
54   Heller 1996, pp. 8–19.
55   Heller 1996, pp. 122–3.
56   Heller 2000, pp. 248–51.
57   Heller 1996, pp. 157–8; Le Roy Ladurie 1994, pp. 257–61.
58   Israel 1989, pp. 99–100; Molà 2000, p. 62.
59   Deyon 1963, p. 947.
60   Moriceau 1993, pp. 353–86; Moriceau 1994, pp. 145–341.

resale of rural properties.[61] In 1602, a petition was drawn up asking the government of Henri IV to re-admit foreign merchants to the Kingdom in order to help rejuvenate the economy following the religious wars. These proposals were rejected by Barthélemy de Laffemas's Commission du Commerce. The Commission noted that the wars had only devastated the villages and countryside. The towns not only were not depopulated, but were full of money that had accumulated during the wars. The foreigners were only interested in the towns and were hence of little use to France.[62] We have in this passing comment an important confirmation of the vitality of the middle class at the conclusion of the religious wars and beginning of the seventeenth century. Indeed, the growing strength of the middle class helps to explain its pugnacity. In Languedoc and Dauphiné in the 1570s, the growing assertiveness of the bourgeoisie menaced the nobility and its allies and provoked a seigneurial reaction.[63] The period of the rural leagues and the 1590s saw a broadening scale of similar revolts. Indeed, the strength and organisation of rural leagues, notably in Dauphiné, Normandy, Brittany and Guyenne, appear to have been based on the growing weight of a rural middle class made up of richer peasants and small-town bourgeoisie.[64]

The recent work on the rural league by Jean-Marie Constant makes clear the predominantly urban and bourgeois base of this major political and religious movement.[65] Only a minority of the nobility participated in it and its noble leaders had trouble keeping it under their control. Even more to the point, Constant makes clear that, as important as religion was to the movement and, as anarchic as it later became, it initially did have a coherent political programme. This was embodied especially in the demands of the third estate at the Estates-General of Blois of 1588. These grievances included vehement attacks on the privileged Italian merchants and financiers who were seen as dominating and stifling the initiatives of the indigenous middle class. Beyond these complaints, the third estate went so far as to demand constitutional limitations on the monarchy. Its politically radical demands made the estates of the nobility and clergy ill at ease.[66]

The ongoing sale of offices, the elaboration of a mercantilist programme and the exclusion of the Italians from the ranks of the increasingly powerful

61   Neveux, Jacquart and Le Roy Ladurie 1975, pp. 273–5.
62   Fagniez 1908, p. 10.
63   Le Roy Ladurie 1979, pp. 108, 122, 127–8, 339–70; Heller 1991, pp. 60–3, 86–101.
64   Heller 1991, pp. 111–15, 120–36.
65   Constant 1996, pp. 259–312.
66   Constant 1996, pp. 188–9.

French financiers appears to have temporarily calmed the aggressiveness of the bourgeoisie under Henri IV. Even so, the end of Henri IV's reign brought a renewed surge of bourgeois radicalism. The aspirations of the bourgeoisie were embodied in Louis Turquet de Mayerne's *La monarchie aristodémocrate*.[67] In this work, Mayerne called for the abolition of the traditional aristocracy as a ruling class and the institution of a constitutional monarchy based on an elite whose power was rooted both in trade and ownership of land.[68] The Estates-General of 1614, furthermore, was marked by bitter conflict between the third and second estates.

That same year saw the overthrow of the urban oligarchy of La Rochelle and establishment of a new more democratic commune. In line with his view of the effacement of the bourgeoisie, Parker's description of this revolt rules out any involvement by substantial elements of the bourgeoisie. For him, this rebellion was an affair of shopkeepers and artisans. There was no participation by substantial merchants.[69] The authoritative recent history of La Rochelle by Kevin Robbins places Parker's assessment into question. According to Robbins, 'Parker mentions the 1614 events only in passing and offers no detailed analysis of the social origins and course of the revolt'.[70] Robbins, like Parker, concludes that the petty bourgeoisie constituted the mass base of the movement. But the leadership included elements who were engaged in wholesale and overseas trade, some of whom were as rich as or richer than the members of the ruling oligarchy.[71]

The Endurance of the Bourgeoisie

This revolt in Huguenot La Rochelle, led in good part by merchants, raises the important matter of the role of Protestants in seventeenth-century France, a matter sorely neglected by Beik and Parker. It was the American economic historian Warren C. Scoville who treated the matter extensively in his work on the economic expulsion of the Huguenots from France published some forty years ago.[72] Scoville reached the conclusion that the migration of Huguenots following the Revocation of the Edict of Nantes did not seriously damage the French

---

67   Mayerne 1611.
68   Mousnier 1955, pp. 1–20.
69   Parker 1980, pp. 44–5.
70   Robbins 1997, p. 242.
71   Robbins 1997, pp. 253–6, 260.
72   Scoville 1960.

economy. In so far as the economy suffered, it was mainly because of war and adverse economic trends. Moreover, although some two-hundred thousand Huguenots emigrated, some 600,000 others remained in France.[73] Interesting as Scoville's conclusions are, it is his study of the place of the Huguenots in the French economy which is of special concern to us. His work includes a remarkable survey of the manufacturing and commercial sector of the seventeenth-century French economy. Among other things, Scoville discovers a substantial manufacturing sector which included several hundred factories involving concentrated manufacture.[74] In many towns and cities, it was a Protestant middle class which dominated this activity.[75] There were, of course, Huguenot artisans, office-holders, nobles and even peasants, especially in the Midi. But what is notable about the Huguenots of the seventeenth century was their over-representation in commerce and manufacturing.[76] These entrepreneurs did not confine their activities to the restricted market of the Midi or the Kingdom of France. In Languedoc and Dauphiné before 1685, such businessmen exported salt, grain, pastel and cloth to Geneva and beyond.[77] Through the port of Marseilles, French and Genevan merchants created an important international network for distributing trans-Atlantic products. Indeed, many of those who exiled themselves, particularly to Geneva after 1685, continued to have close business and religious connections with their commercially-orientated brethren in Lyons and throughout Languedoc and Dauphiné. These relationships with the Huguenot diaspora helped to maintain and expand the connection between the French and the European centres of commerce and increasingly of banking. Indeed, the Huguenots who remained in the Kingdom were to play an important role in the expansion of the French economy under Colbert and in the eighteenth century.[78] Geneva constituted a kind of free-trade zone which animated and, ultimately, transformed the French economy of the late-seventeenth and eighteenth centuries.

The Huguenots were by no means the only merchants and manufacturers in seventeenth-century France. But, contrary to Beik and Parker, their existence

---

73 Scoville 1960, pp. 434–47.
74 Scoville 1960, p. 161.
75 Scoville 1960, pp. 133–42.
76 Benedict 2002, pp. 1–2, 27–32, 142–4, 146–8; Ligou 1968, pp. 197–200; Lüthy 1959, I, pp. 68–72; Krumenacker 2002, pp. 16–18, 33, 149.
77 Chaussinand-Nogaret 1970, p. 19; Mottu-Weber 1985, pp. 342–4.
78 These connections in the latter half of the seventeenth and eighteenth centuries are traced in Chaussinand Nogaret 1970, pp. 32–3, 35; Lüthy 1959, I, p. 44; Piuz and Mottu-Weber 1990, pp. 527, 542, 595.

alongside their Catholic counterparts as an urban middle class can hardly be doubted. In any event, Beik and Parker know, or wish to know, little or nothing of the whole earlier phase of advancing bourgeois power at the beginning of the seventeenth century. It is this neglect which helps them to sustain the audacious claim that this class barely existed and more or less disappeared in the following century. It is true enough that, despite a last upsurge of bourgeois radicalism at the conclusion of Henri IV's reign, the offensive of agrarian profit (if not profit itself) appears to have come to an end. A new trend in favour of rent appeared. As we have tried to make clear, this reversal did not occur overnight, was only at its inception during this reign and was part of a long-drawn-out process completed only in the reign of Louis XIV. The offensive of rent was an ongoing movement at least as prolonged as the previous offensive of profit.

Nonetheless, it is true that a reversal of trend did set in during Henri IV's reign, signalled by the propensity of profits to decline and rents to rise on the land. As we have suggested, this trend, which deepened in the following reign, was not merely a response to the play of the market and has itself to be explained. Non-economic factors were at least as important as the inter-action of supply and demand. A new social and political context emerged which encouraged rent and began to undermine profit. Above all, the alliance between crown and nobility, which had broken down during the religious wars, gradually grew more solid. To be sure, the loyalty of the nobility toward the crown was not unquestioned, especially in the early years of the reign of Louis XIII. But, by means of a combination of coercion, bribery and indulgence, such fidelity was re-established in the period of Richelieu's ascendancy.[79]

The context in favour of rent was reinforced by the continuing expansion of venality of office and expansion of the size of the state apparatus. Venality had already reached impressive levels in the reign of Henri III and continued to expand in the reign of his Bourbon successors. The creation and purchase of tens of thousands of offices during this period shifted significant amounts of capital from productive to non-productive economic activity.[80] This movement was strengthened by the perfection of the system of financiers which redirected still more capital into the channels of state credit. The complementary expansion of the army to 50,000 men capped the spectacular expansion in the power of the state. The spiritual recovery of the Catholic Church and the containment

---

79   On the adherence of the nobility to the crown see Parker 1971, pp. 67–78; Kettering 1986, pp. 154–61; Jouanna 1989, pp. 218–22.

80   Le Roy Ladurie estimates the number of officers in 1610 at 25,000 and at 46,000 under Colbert (1994, p. 274).

of the Protestant threat reinforced the social and political order. All of these elements provided a context which made it possible for the state to successfully impose a progressively higher level of taxation. The accretion of state power, in turn, reinforced landlords, facilitating the imposition by them of higher rents. At the same time, the expansion of the number of offices and diversion of capital toward the state entailed a massive co-optation of the upper reaches of the bourgeoisie. Growth of state power, reinforcement of the rule of landlords, co-optation of the upper levels of the bourgeoisie constituted a form of political and social reaction or class war from above. It is this which is the principal characteristic of seventeenth-century French history. Naturally, it provoked a response from below in the form of waves of urban and rural popular protests. But these, in comparison with the popular revolts of the sixteenth century, clearly have a defensive character. Contrasting the fiscal revolts of the seventeenth century with the revolts in Guyenne in the 1590s, Le Roy Ladurie makes an interesting observation. He notes the comprehensiveness of the ideological challenge to the existing order in the case of the rebels of Guyenne, including attacks on the divisiveness of the League as well as on the tithe, rent, royal taxes, usury, excessive commercial profits and low wages. He contrasts the ideological ambition of this programme with the narrowed horizons of the popular insurgents of the seventeenth century.[81] The latter reduced their agenda to one of fiscal protest. Clearly, it is a case of diminished expectations based on a sense of reduced strength. The forces of order were more powerful, while the capacities of the insurgents were weaker.

Porshnev tried to show that such upheavals entailed a somewhat schizophrenic attitude on the part of the bourgeoisie, alternating between fidelity to authority and rebellion. Beik and Parker were at pains to deny the latter. In this argument, the two Anglo-Saxon historians were more right than wrong. As a class, the bourgeoisie was clearly in retreat – its most advanced elements were co-opted to the side of the state. But Beik and Parker have overstated their case. Among the mass of subsistence peasants, artisans and labourers who rebelled as a result of higher taxes, there surely were some substantial peasants or merchants who rebelled as a result of a squeeze on profits.[82] Contrary to the view of Parker, this was almost certainly the case with respect to the Ormée of Bordeaux.[83] In any case, too much has been made of whether or not

81   Le Roy Ladurie 1966, I, p. 495.
82   See the traces of such involvement in Bercé 1990, p. 215; Foisil 1970, pp. 223–4, 226, 250–1; Porshnev 1963, pp. 364–5.
83   Parker 1970, pp. 44–5. See the lists of participants in the Ormée in Birnstiel 1895, III, pp. 218–19; Sarrazin 1996, pp. 177–82.

the bourgeoisie were involved in the seventeenth-century popular revolts. The issue of the existence of class conflict does not stand or fall on this question. The main trend in this respect was one of class warfare from above, of which profit-seeking entrepreneurs among others were the victims, whether they participated in revolts or not.

In the reign of Louis XIV, the fortunes of the enterprising *labourers* and *fermiers* reached their low point. High taxes and rents crushed their profits, forcing many into bankruptcy. But some did survive. Among these were the so-called *fermiers* of the Île-de-France studied by Jean-Marc Moriceau.[84] His path-breaking work follows this class from the time it consolidated itself in the Île-de-France in the late sixteenth century until it assumed power in the course of the French Revolution. In the course of this long trajectory, the latter part of the reign of Louis XIV was clearly the nadir. Some members of this group were weeded out. But its overall survival is what impresses. Family solidarity and the strict rationalisation of operations made it possible for many of them to maintain their profits, while preparing the way for the great prosperity and expansion of their power in the next century.[85] Among notable improvements introduced by such farmers were a successful consolidation of land holdings, a greater degree of specialisation, more intensive manuring and greater traction through improved harnessing of animal draught power.[86] It should be pointed out that these processes of rationalisation and improvement were carried out in response to the relentless compulsion of increasing rents and taxes in a way which is entirely comparable to that experienced by English farmers described by Brenner. Turgot, for example, noted that it was the practice to determine the price of leases of large farms in the region of northern France by competition between capitalist farmers.[87] Recently published works by Guy Lemarchand and Anatoli Ado likewise make clear that the agricultural capitalism of the eighteenth century was rooted in a stratum of rural capitalists which had persevered in the course of the seventeenth century.[88]

In the course of discussing sixteenth-century capitalism, we have noted that flanking the class of rural capitalists a substantial merchant and manufacturing class emerged. Despite adversity, it survived the religious wars and re-emerged

---

84   Moriceau 1994.
85   Moriceau 1994, pp. 611–23.
86   Moriceau, 1994, pp. 631–42; Postel-Vinay 1974, pp. 26, 27, 29 stresses the concentration of land-holding in bourgeois hands and the proletarianisation of the marginal peasants in Soissonais in this period.
87   Cooper 1985, p. 146.
88   Lemarchand 1989, pp. 138–45; Ado 1996, pp. 51, 53.

with renewed vigour in the reign of Henri IV. Its prosperity seemed to have survived longer than that of rural capitalists, being prolonged into the late 1620s. Beik and Parker, as we have seen, have little to say about the fate of this sixteenth- and early-seventeenth-century inheritance. Falling back on the work of Parker on La Rochelle, Beik notes that the latter has been unable to locate a significant commercial and industrial bourgeoisie there or anywhere else in France. In Parker's work the subsumption of manufacturing by commerce, the parochialism, disunity and feudalisation of the bourgeoisie and finally its integration into the state is stressed.[89] As we have seen, in Languedoc, Beik admits to only a hidden bourgeoisie of small-scale merchants and manufacturers of little economic and political account. This enables him to discount Lublinskaya's notion of a trading and manufacturing class independent of the financial elite. Indeed, Parker's discussion of the same group in the seventeenth and eighteenth centuries is cursory and dismissive.[90] We would have to conclude from them that the commercial and manufacturing base that supported it, created by the sixteenth century, either never existed or was more or less annihilated in the following century. In the latter case, little or nothing was carried over in the way of trade and manufacturing. Under such circumstances, the continued existence of an independent merchant class seems out of the question.

A quite different view of the fate of the French merchant class is adopted by Jacques Bottin.[91] Bottin admits the tendency of merchants to assimilate to finance and to move toward office and a higher status. Yet Bottin insists on the continued existence of an independent stratum of merchants in the major towns of the Kingdom. According to Bottin, treatment of this group has suffered from a readiness to view them from the perspective of the regime's mercantilist policy or from the point of view of royal finances. Likewise, they have tended to be seen as a social group in the perpetual process of transition toward banking, office and ennoblement.[92] Yet a lexical analysis of the word 'merchant' as used in the first part of the century supports the view of them as a distinctive social element. Thus, retail merchants or merchants engaged in specialised commerce were referred to with more precise designations: wine merchant, wood merchant, merchant draper, *épicier*. The term 'merchant' used

---

89   Parker 1980, pp. 180–5.

90   Parker 1996, pp. 37–9.

91   Bottin 1990, pp. 962–4.

92   Brunelle notes that 'in reality only a minority of merchants, even in so important and prosperous a city as Rouen, migrated from commerce to the ranks of the *officiers*' (1991, p. 163).

without qualification was reserved for merchants engaged in wholesale non-specialised commerce, usually of an international dimension. Frequently, such large-scale trading was combined with an interest in banking. Such entrepreneurs might involve themselves in loans to the king. But their interest in finance cannot be seen as limited to non-economic kinds of investment. In reality, their involvement in banking was intrinsic to their needs as merchants to transfer funds and settle accounts as well as to facilitate the negotiation of commercial bills of exchange.

As to the overall level of commercial activity, Jean-Pierre Poussou concludes his survey of seventeenth-century French trade by stressing the continuities between the seventeenth and eighteenth centuries. He notes:

> the gap between the eighteenth and seventeenth centuries was less great than has been often asserted, that the latter prepared the way for the former especially in France thanks to the conclusion of a great reign which was much more dynamic and prosperous than is often thought.[93]

Approaching these matters from the point of a comparative and in-depth analysis of Protestant and Catholic populations in Montpellier in the seventeenth century, Philip Benedict notes a surprising increase in wealth in the urban population overall across the century, among whom merchants certainly had their part. His study and others, he concludes, offers further evidence that the larger cities of seventeenth-century France may have been more dynamic centres of economic growth and transformation than was previously thought.[94]

Toward the conclusion of his work, Beik concedes the existence of a considerable textile industry in Languedoc and its success down to 1650. But, faced with this reality, Beik underlines the commercial and manufacturing depression of the next 40 years in Languedoc, conceding that recovery occurred after 1690. He concludes by emphasising 'how little impact this mercantile activity had on the power brokers of Languedoc'.[95] But this conclusion, however true, has no bearing on the question of the continued existence of a merchant class based on trade and manufacturing, the point insisted on by Lublinskaya. Indeed, it would seem that this merchant class had not only survived through the seventeenth century, but was actually growing stronger as the century drew to a close. The internal market being restricted, external markets offered more

---

93   Poussou 1990, p. 365.
94   Benedict 2001, pp. 133–4.
95   Beik 1985, p. 288.

attractive possibilities. It was in foreign commerce and export-oriented manufacture rather than in internal trade or agriculture that substantial profits remained to be had.

Beik and Parker depreciate the importance of the survival and ongoing development of capitalism within the interstices of the seventeenth-century absolutist regime. Indeed, the notion that contradictory economic and political processes could be at work within a given social system appears difficult for them to accept. As to state policy, according to them, seventeenth-century mercantilism was simply a revenue-raising device for a state controlled by aristocratic-minded ministers. From the point of view of economic development, it was a failure.[96] No doubt there were many failures, as Beik insists.[97] We are to understand from Beik's perspective that, like their Prussian counterparts in the eighteenth century, aristocrats *qua* aristocrats could not comprehend the relationship between economic development and state power. Going in the other direction, Parker even goes so far as to suggest that the institution of the Conseil du Commerce in 1700 reflects the weakness rather than the growing strength of the commercial and manufacturing bourgeoisie.[98] But Beik and Parker's notion that state-inspired economic protectionism, canal construction, administrative rationalisation and New World colonialism did not also serve the interests of French merchants in the seventeenth century is simply untenable. In this connection, the recent positive re-evaluation of Colbert's economic initiatives by Le Roy Ladurie serves as an instructive corrective.[99]

Beik does acknowledge that the state's dependence on the rapaciousness of financiers made it possible to form large pools of capital out of which were constituted the fortunes of some of the major French bankers of the eighteenth century.[100] He ignores the significance of these same financiers in Colbert's programme for the development of manufacturing and overseas commercial expansion.[101] A figure such as Dalliez de la Tour, receiver-general of finances of Dauphiné and director of the Company of the Levant, for example, provided a major impetus to the development of the wool cloth, canvas, metal-

---

96   Parker 1996, pp. 28, 29–30, 43.

97   Beik 1985, pp. 288–91.

98   Parker 1996, p. 262. For a contrary, more positive, view of the economic significance of the creation of this body see Schaeper 1983, pp. 179–80.

99   Le Roy Ladurie 1996, pp. 169–77; Stein and Stein is particularly insightful on the close connection between private French commercial interests and the state (2000, pp. 109–116).

100   Beik 1985, pp. 251–2.

101   Chaussinand-Nogaret 1970, pp. 103–4.

lurgical and mining industries in that province. Moreover, the impulse that
he provided to these sectors helped to lay the basis for Dauphiné's industrial
progress in the eighteenth century.[102] Chaussinand-Nogaret concludes that
the financiers of the seventeenth century were far from being simply blood-
suckers. While it is true that a part of national revenue was diverted into
unproductive activities, a significant portion was channelled into productive
purposes.[103] According to this scholar, in the seventeenth century, the financiers of Languedoc correspond only very imperfectly to the notion of financiers as a corps of office-holders divorced from commerce and manufacture.
Overwhelmingly Huguenot, dominant in regional banking, they were fully
integrated into the emergent sector of international banking.[104] While perhaps aware of the unintended connection between oppressive taxation and
finance-capital, Beik appears oblivious to the important progressive economic
consequences of such predatory state finance at the grassroots level of French
society. In discussing primitive accumulation during the sixteenth-century religious wars, we noted an increased availability of wage labour. Throughout the
succeeding period (1598–1715) the transfer of land from the peasantry to the
urban bourgeoisie engendered by a relentless state fiscalism continued. Inevitably, this deliberate state policy prompted a still greater and irreversible development of wage labour. The unrelenting fiscalism of the seventeenth-century
state was thus a major factor behind this steady process of proletarianisation.[105] This increase in the wage-labour-force is all the more remarkable in
the face of the terrible plagues and demographic sluggishness that marked
this period.[106] Indeed, the availability of growing pools of cheap wage labour
became a structural feature of the French economy. The further expansion of
this wage-earning class in the eighteenth century helps to explain the agricultural, commercial and manufacturing dynamism of that period.[107] Consciously
or unconsciously basing themselves on the very Anglo-Saxon notion that state
and market are always in conflict with one another, Beik and Parker view the
French state of the *Ancien Régime* as standing in the way of the development
of capitalism. It is very important that this conception be seen as the half-truth
that it is.

102   Léon 1954, I, pp. 107–8, 118.
103   Chaussinand-Nogaret 1970, p. 22.
104   Chaussinand-Nogaret 1970, p. 312.
105   Lemarchand, 1989, pp. 189–90; Dupâquier and Cabourdin 1988, II, pp. 439–41.
106   Brockliss and Jones 1997, pp. 53–63.
107   See the remarkable chapter by Léon 1970, II, pp. 651–89 on the development of the working
      class in eighteenth-century France.

Conclusion

Based on this review, we can conclude that Beik and Parker's report of the death of the bourgeoisie in the seventeenth century has clearly been exaggerated. Driven onto the defensive, rural capitalism survived a century-long onslaught of increasing rents and taxes. Commercial and manufacturing capitalism similarly endured a prolonged period of depression through the middle years of the century. Yet, it did prosper into the 1620s and emerged stronger than ever towards the close of the period. In their insistence on the hegemony of the nobility, Beik and Parker have both thus overshot and undershot the mark. They have overshot it by denying that a bourgeoisie continued to exist in the face of an assertive ruling nobility. They have undershot it in underestimating the degree of upper-class reaction. The construction of the Bourbon state serving the interests of the nobility was not simply a creation of the predominance of rent. It was, in fact, a long-term social and political reaction to the previous century's offensive of profit. Their insistence not merely on the exclusive rule, but on the exclusive existence, of one class not only belies the historical evidence, it cuts seventeenth-century French history off from what came earlier and what later transpired. Finally, it presents a monolithic and immobile view of the century itself.

In insisting on the survival of the bourgeoisie in the seventeenth century, we in part re-assert the classical Marxist view of the absolute monarchy holding the balance between the nobility and the bourgeoisie. Admittedly, this equilibrium was, in fact, tipped in favour of the nobility. Still, this analysis does restate the traditional liberal and Marxist assumption of a long and continuous development of the French bourgeoisie within the framework of the *Ancien Régime* down to the revolution. However beaten and bruised, the rural and urban bourgeoisie which had emerged in the sixteenth century survived and regained the offensive in the eighteenth century.[108]

---

108   For the further development of the bourgeoisie in the eighteenth century, see Heller 2006, pp. 31, 54–60.

CHAPTER 5

Response to Henry Heller's 'The *Longue Durée* of the French Bourgeoisie'*

William Beik

In 'The *Longue Durée* of the French Bourgeoisie'[1] Henry Heller devotes an entire article to criticising David Parker, Robert Brenner and myself for our approaches to social relations in early modern France. I am pleased to be invited by this journal to respond. I will leave it to Parker and Brenner to speak for themselves. In the interest of full disclosure, I should note that, while I am honoured to find myself in the company of distinguished Marxist scholars such as Parker and Brenner, I cannot myself claim to be a Marxist. Class-analysis and the insights of Marxist historians have been central to my thinking, but I have not studied the principal works of Marx, nor have I consistently adhered to Marxist methodology in my work.

Heller charges that I have undervalued, indeed eliminated altogether, the crucial role of the bourgeoisie in the evolution of class-relations leading up to the triumph of the bourgeoisie in the French Revolution: 'For [Beik] the bourgeoisie did not exist.'[2] He argues that, in distancing myself from 'classical Marxist interpretations',[3] I have joined the ranks of the so-called revisionists who deny the bourgeois origins of the French Revolution. I have also misunderstood Le Roy Ladurie's discussion of feudal rents and land-rents. I have ignored the insights of Soviet historians Boris Porshnev and A.D. Lublinskaya.[4] I have rejected the class struggle between nobility and bourgeoisie, and thereby lost a sense of 'dynamic development'. I have abandoned the concept of a 'nascent bourgeoisie and capitalism within the Ancien Régime' along with 'any notion of simple-commodity production or primitive accumulation'.[5] Moreover, I have missed the importance of markets, merchant-capitalists and

---

* Originally published as: William Beik, 'Response to Henry Heller's "The *Long Durée* of the French Bourgeoisie"', *Historical Materialism*, 18, 2 (2010): 117–22.

1 Heller 2009.
2 Heller 2009, p. 35.
3 Heller 2009, p. 33.
4 Porshnev 1963; Lublinskaya 1968.
5 Heller 2009, p. 36.

international trade, and failed to understand the rise of 'profit-minded rural capitalists' exploiting 'operating capital and wage labour'. I also need to be reminded that 'the age of merely feudal rent had long since passed'.[6]

Henry Heller deserves commendation as one of the few historians who has continued to defend the merits of a Marxist approach, most recently in his provocative history of the French Revolution.[7] But his charges here are way off the mark and surprisingly old-fashioned. His evidence for my neglect of the bourgeoisie is based almost entirely on my 1985 book *Absolutism and Society*, which was about something quite different – the channels of political power and shared influence that linked the royal government and the ruling class of the province of Languedoc.[8] Seen in this context of political influence, the bourgeoisie had hardly any influence. The towns were run by oligarchies of royal officers either enjoying nobility or on the way to acquiring it. Taxes and public expenses were run by the provincial estates, which were, in turn, dominated by twenty-two bishops and a handful of locally-based noble potentates. Of course, Languedoc had markets, merchants, entrepreneurial farmers, even rural manufactories. But those involved were relatively powerless, except in matters of commerce and some local governance. The province was run by noble commanders with delegated powers of command, by an array of top churchmen, and by a circle of elite-families who controlled the principal royal offices and profited from the royal fiscal system. Similar situations prevailed in other provinces.[9] Those who made their fortunes in manufacturing or commerce usually abandoned their businesses after one or more generations and purchased offices for themselves or their sons in order to gain privileged status. These power-brokers were landowners who mostly drew their wealth from the labour of the peasants who paid them rent and dues. This was indeed a 'feudal' situation inherited from the distant past, but it was not static. On the contrary, the tenants continued to resist and obstruct from below, while, within the nobility, a long-term struggle was going on between regional magnates and the centralising royal state over distribution of the agricultural surplus, which came directly from rents and indirectly from taxes. I am in agreement with Porshnev about the fundamental class-orientation of this society, although I have criticised him for overstating the influence of the bourgeoisie.[10] Heller

---

6   Heller 2009, p. 39.
7   Heller 2006.
8   Beik 1985.
9   Collins 1994; Swann 2003.
10 Porshnev 1963.

has no grounds for claiming that I 'deny an initial period of petty-commodity production and primitive accumulation', since this topic was beyond the scope of my project and consequently was not discussed.

Heller concedes that he 'basically agrees' with me that France was 'ruled by a nobility which exercised its hold over the peasantry through the absolutist state'.[11] Where, then, is the problem? It lies in our differing approaches to the agents of change. In a sense, our discussion recapitulates the old Dobb-Sweezy debate of the 1950s.[12] What was behind the dynamic and dramatic transition from feudalism to capitalism? For Sweezy, it was the external push of international trade and the circulation and accumulation of merchant-wealth. For Dobb, it was class conflict emerging within the system from contradictions between social forces and relations of production. Heller, closer to Sweezy, continues to see evidence of capitalism in every economic fact. Wherever he finds merchants, manufacturing, markets, extensive wage labour, agricultural consolidation or technological improvement, he declares that capitalism is on the rise.

To be sure, all these economic and social facts can loosely be designated 'capitalistic' and be attributed to the rising middle class. No one denies that the economy was developing in early modern France. But how was their profit-making different from that of the ancient Greeks or the merchants of any other society? A good Marxist definition should indicate what is distinctive about a given form of class-exploitation and explain its dynamic capacity to transform social relations. We need to know how labour was managed by the dominant class and how the fruits of that labour were distributed. Merely citing merchants or profit-making does not fill the bill.

Heller can certainly cite progressive forces at work here and there, such as the landlord who invests his revenues back into farm improvements and raises production by hiring cheap labour; the merchant-partners who take over and transform the market for a product, say woollens, by employing cheap cottage-labour and taking advantage of economics of scale to produce larger quantities at lower cost; or the banker whose international contacts enable him to transfer money on paper over long distances without moving actual coins, thus lowering transaction costs. All these techniques existed in France, although the French often lagged behind other countries. But the big question is how widespread these new practices were and how much impact they had on social change. We need the whole picture rather than focusing only on certain

11   Heller 2009, p. 38.
12   Harman 2008; Sweezy et al. 1976.

dynamic elements. And it is equally important to ask what obstacles kept the innovators from achieving their potential and what contradictions kept the society from reproducing itself without mutating into something else.

Heller claims that I have missed Le Roy Ladurie's depiction of the 'offensive of rent against profit'. Heller takes 'rent' as signifying traditional payment to the owner for the use of the land, an archaic payment which he at one point assimilates with seigneurial dues, and 'profit' as the net proceeds of a farmer's rural capitalist enterprise. Rent and profit then become stand-ins to measure the struggle of the two sides – the landed nobility and the bourgeoisie. The enterprising farmer gains in the sixteenth century, falls back in the seventeenth century, and triumphs in the eighteenth century. But Le Roy Ladurie is not speaking in Marxist terms. He is talking in market-terms about a conjunctural balance-sheet comprised of land-rent, taxes, wages, and what was left – profit. The changes in rent and profit were determined largely by demographic and political factors, which, in turn, affected supply and demand. Left out of the equation is any consideration of whether the profits were invested in growth which brought fundamental change in yields or in class-relationships. In other words, the process describes the relative prosperity of owner, tenant, and hired employee, but not necessarily the progress of the rural bourgeoisie.

Heller consistently elides the meaning of his terms, seeing a bourgeois under every bush. He finds evidence of a growing bourgeoisie in 'a proliferation of markets', 'merchant-capitalism', 'peasant-expropriation', 'dependence on wage-labour', the 'strengthening of the middle class by the religious wars', 'the grow-ing assertiveness of the bourgeoisie' in Dauphine and Languedoc in the 1570s, the strength of the Catholic leagues in the 1590s, the demands of the Third Estate in 1588, the quarrels of the Third and Second Estates in 1614, the 'demo-cratic commune' of La Rochelle, and the Huguenots' extensive business deal-ings. In the popular revolts of the seventeenth century, he speculates, 'there surely were peasants or merchants who rebelled as a result of a squeeze on profits'. He argues the same for the Ormée-rebellion in Bordeaux in 1651–2.[13] There were indeed merchants involved in the Ormée-movement, along with a cross-section of artisans, legal functionaries and a few nobles, but their griev-ances were about representation, good government and popular control. There was no hint of concern over profits, or even foreign trade. The more character-istic seventeenth-century tax-riots were conducted largely by the *menu peuple* over illicit taxes. The merchants were usually targets, not participants.[14]

---

13   Heller 2009, p. 50.
14   Beik 1997.

With these issues in mind, I see much of Heller's evidence as problematic. First, it is no longer adequate to speak of the bourgeoisie, or indeed any class, as a unified force playing a single purposeful role in history. Second, it is crucial to weigh the forces of resistance and blockage as well as the influence of change. Evidence of an urban investor who was consolidating rural properties does not necessarily show that he was shifting to intensive cultivation of capitalist crops, if the landlord was absentee and the farms were leased out in small plots to local peasants, as we see in Jacquart's study of the Hurepoix.[15]

Evidence of growing masses of landless villagers does not necessarily indicate the emergence of capitalist wage labour. Merchant successes and active markets do not necessarily demonstrate a rise in the rate of production due to improved methods. The rise of new wealth does not automatically transform the system if it is sunk into royal offices and into ownership of traditional farms leased out to traditional peasants. My contention is that much of the potential progress was absorbed into the existing social system, even while new forces were growing and influences from abroad were provoking change. The bourgeois were on the stage but they still had a relatively small role.

Formulae drawn from the *Communist Manifesto* or the writings of Engels do not provide adequate tools for a thorough analysis of the early modern period, which was not, after all, their central concern. A reflective Marxism needs to delve deeply and critically into the forms of exploitation and the uses of capital. Recent scholarship provides ample evidence of the subordinate role played by the bourgeoisie in early modern France. It appears that, contrary to Heller's 'classical-Marxist' focus on the dynamic leadership of the bourgeoisie, this class was not strong enough or conscious enough to seize power. This loosely defined 'middle class' was still made up of groups with contradictory interests. Many were royal officials, professionals of various sorts, craftsmen and artisans with distinctive skills. Many of those who could be defined as bourgeois were still deeply tied to the existing power structure, and, as a group, were not yet strong enough to bring about revolutionary change.

Stating this does not put us in the ranks of the revisionists. There are other ways to think of class conflict in the revolution. The dramatic development of capitalist forces in the later eighteenth century may have altered the situation by 1789. The revolution might be seen as being made not *by* the bourgeoisie but *for* the bourgeoisie. One might postulate that the revolution was caused by the collapse of the old system under the weight of its own contradictions: a new study by Steven Miller on eighteenth-century Languedoc, for instance,

---

15   Jacquart 1974.

finds the collaboration of royal and noble forces still in place.[16] The provincial nobles were still allied with the crown in defence of their privileges, but they were becoming alienated from other aspects of the royal administration and some were leaning towards constitutional resistance. They would both generate demands for change and lead the resistance to change, as the revolution approached.[17]

In the end, Heller and I agree that French society was structured by the class conflict between landlords and peasants and that the bourgeoisie was growing more powerful within it. In his recent book on the revolution, Heller describes these conflicts better. Here, in his haste to defend the concept of a rising bourgeoisie, he holds on to weak equivalencies and overly simplified notions.

---

16   Miller 2008.
17   Miller 2008.

CHAPTER 6

Henry Heller and the *'Longue Durée* of the French Bourgeoisie'*

David Parker

Heller's central argument is that Beik and I have underestimated the weight of an 'independent', that is *capitalist* bourgeoisie in France. He believes that my treatment of the trading and manufacturing class is 'cursory and dismissive'[1] and amounts to no less than a declaration of the 'death of the bourgeoisie in the seventeenth century'.[2] Yet, in the passages to which Heller alludes, I observed that, despite the relatively depressed economic conditions of the seventeenth century, maritime trade continued to expand even if more hesitantly than during the preceding hundred years; notwithstanding significant geographical and institutional obstacles there were, I wrote, identifiable successful 'merchant capitalists' who contributed to a slow integration of local, regional and international-commercial networks.[3]

Heller's view that I have killed off the bourgeoisie is buttressed by the further claim that I have 'failed to notice the process of primitive accumulation, social differentiation and growing bourgeois strength in the French countryside'.[4]

This involved the expropriation and pauperisation of a substantial proportion of the peasantry and the concentration of land into the hands of a bourgeoisie both urban and rural. It is Heller himself who is guilty of not noticing. I dealt at some length with these developments in twenty or so pages devoted precisely to 'The Dispossession of the Peasantry' and 'Agrarian Class Relations'.[5] I even observed, as many others have done, that, despite the remorseless fragmentation of peasant landholdings over the best part of two centuries and the well-documented decline in the number of substantial peasant-holdings, every

---

* Originally published as: David Parker, 'Henry Heller and the *"Long Durée* of the French Bourgeoisie"', *Historical Materialism*, 18, 2 (2010): 123–31.

1   Heller 2009, p. 52.
2   Heller 2009, p. 55.
3   Parker 1996, pp. 31–2, 36–7.
4   Heller 2009, p. 43.
5   Parker 1996, pp. 51 ff.

community still contained a small group of rural notables who occasionally founded farming dynasties which lasted into the twentieth century.

In similar vein, Heller asserts that I concluded that 'there was no participation by substantial merchants' in the extraordinarily successful revolt at La Rochelle of the lesser bourgeois in 1614, a view, he says, disputed by the later work of Kevin Robbins.[6] If I had actually reached such an unqualified conclusion, Robbins would undoubtedly have put me right. In fact, I had been very careful to say that a definitive view of the social composition of leaders of the revolt would require a systematic investigation of the notarial records at La Rochelle.[7]

Robbins subsequently carried out the necessary research and was indeed able to reveal the significant role played by some wealthy merchants in directing and sustaining a movement rooted in the middling groups of the Rochelais community. The coalition of forces which he describes has a striking similarity to those which contributed to the earlier establishment of the Dutch Republic and the imminent revolution in England. Heller might have made more of this, but he was perhaps aware that Robbins's analysis contained a significant rider. 'After 1614', he observed, 'La Rochelle became even more anomalous among French provincial cities, combining a majority of religious schismatics with a substantial influential number of innovative political actors drawn from the middle ranks of urban society'.[8] In other words, developments at La Rochelle during the 14 years in which the lesser bourgeois secured a leading role in the municipal government were not typical of French towns in general; except, it should be stressed, in the sense that the rebellion of the lesser bourgeoisie was itself a reaction to the emergence of a self-perpetuating, increasingly venal, urban patriciate – a process replicated virtually everywhere. No doubt, Heller is right, though he produces no evidence, in suggesting that merchants also played a part in the most celebrated urban revolt of all in mid-century Bordeaux. Antipathy to the office-holding elite was again a significant factor.

In presenting a caricature of my view of French economic and social developments, Heller misses the point. The existence of those whom we may describe as capitalists or bourgeois is not and has never been in dispute. The picture I offered is sufficiently nuanced to accommodate both the discovery of merchants who were not only wealthy but hostile to authority and the existence of the hundred or so *gros fermiers* of the Ile de France identified by

---

6 Heller 2009, p. 47.
7 Parker 1980, p. 44 & note 3.
8 Robbins 1997, p. 329.

Moriceau to whom Heller appeals. Whether they formed part of a bourgeois class is another question. If one assumes, as Heller appears to do, that it is sufficient to define a class by virtue of a common relationship to the means of production, then both merchants and *fermiers* may be said to form two identifiable classes by the mere fact of their existence. But this is clearly inadequate if we wish to be more precise about either the progress of the bourgeoisie or the extent of capitalist development. The key questions are what happened to the bourgeoisie in the seventeenth century, what role did they play in the formation of the absolute state and what merit was there in Engels's view that the monarchy was able to achieve a certain independence because the bourgeoisie now offered a counterpoise to the traditional nobility. On the first of these questions, it transpires that Heller and I are at least in agreement about the way in which capitalist development was arrested in the seventeenth century. He accepts that 'as a class the bourgeoisie was clearly in retreat' and that 'its most advanced elements were co-opted to the side of the state'.[9]

Yet there is more to be said about the way in which the political autonomy and economic vitality of France's urban communities was subverted and constrained by the drive to restore the integrity of the monarchical regime after decades of civil strife. To this end, the crown employed a combination of strategies depending on local circumstances: direct military or political intervention, fiscal pressure and the sale of offices on a vast scale. The latter diverted productive capital to an incalculable extent, offering thousands of willing purchasers the prospect of greater status, influence and security. The bourgeoisie had neither the resolve nor the means to resist what proved to be a very effective combination of carrot and stick. Their uncoordinated and often sectional responses reflected the low level of economic integration and the fragmented character of France's political institutions. Local interests were paramount and, as the capitalist thrust of the sixteenth century stressed by Heller ebbed away, they remained a formidable obstacle to the formation of the bourgeoisie as a class with a clear sense of its own identity. The rebellious Rochelais bourgeois did not constitute part of a cohesive class but a highly localised – indeed isolated – movement within the confines of an exceptionally privileged urban enclave which wanted nothing more than to preserve this position. Of course, in the right circumstances, as in the Low Countries, defence of traditional privileges could acquire a more radical character, but France was not Holland – although the royal apologists found it useful to castigate the Huguenots as would-be republicans.

---

9   Heller 2009, p. 51.

It is nonetheless true that the social and political stresses of the sixteenth century had encouraged a certain development of constitutional ideas and a critique of noble mores and values. Heller cites Louis Turquet de Mayerne's La *Monarchie aristodémocratique*, written in 1591 and published in 1611, as an expression of bourgeois aspirations.[10] Given that Heller takes me to task for underestimating the bourgeois thrust of the sixteenth century, it is surprising that he has nothing to say about my own discussion of Turquet, which acknowledged its significance in unambiguous terms. Turquet's ideas, I said, could 'be seen as a manifestation of the dynamic economic and social impulses of the sixteenth century before they faded away and the implementation of which would have destroyed the *ancien régime*'.[11]

I went on to discuss the 'hegemonic tour de force' by which the nobility recovered the ideological high-ground. If this is what Heller means by 'class-war from above'[12] then there is little between us; but it might be thought that a class-war really requires two sides. Urban oligarchs, though often vexed by the threats to their privileged position, showed less and less inclination, once the Protestant towns had been defeated or isolated, to join either dissident nobles or artisans and peasants in their endemic resistance to the crown. In the end, not being able to produce much more than stray and tenuous references to a rebellious bourgeoisie, Heller virtually concedes as much, declaring that the involvement of the bourgeoisie in popular uprisings is not really an appropriate test of class-conflict.[13]

Given that Heller agrees that the seventeenth century was, on the whole, one of relative economic stagnation with the bourgeoisie in retreat, its upper layers absorbed into the state-machine, and the nobility on the offensive, it is difficult to understand why he persists with the notion that absolute monarchy was in some way the product of a balance between two contending classes. His conclusion is indeed hesitant, defending the classical Marxist view 'only in part' and acknowledging that the equilibrium was tipped in favour of the nobility. This is very wise, given that no one has ever been able to show that an independent, capitalist bourgeoisie possessed anything like the same social and political clout as the nobility. The only Marxist analysis which attempted to do this in any depth was produced by Lublinskaya, who argued that the recovery of monarchical authority in the early seventeenth century and its

---

10   Heller 2009, p. 47.

11   Parker 1996, p. 139.

12   Heller 2009, p. 51.

13   Ibid.

success in overcoming the Huguenots depended on the support of the towns. The bourgeoisie, she suggested, was grateful for the government's programme of economic protectionism. This interpretation founders on objections which I set out at some length.[14] The critical one is that it was the defection of the Huguenot nobility, rather than that of the principal Huguenot towns, which resulted in the royal victory. Despite the social and political conservatism of the urban elites, which may, as at La Rochelle, have been under pressure from the middling sort, the major towns continued to resist after having been abandoned by the great nobles. In any event, such conservatism had little to do with gratitude for the government's mercantilist policies which were rightly perceived to be a threat to urban autonomy. These were certainly not developed at the behest of, or in conjunction with, the merchant-community.[15] Heller, though evidently convinced that Beik treats Lublinskaya in a dismissive fashion, makes no attempt to engage with these questions. What precisely, we are justified in asking, is the evidence to support the view that the trading and industrial bourgeoisie had sufficient influence 'to push the state towards developments which prepared the way for the rise of capitalism'?[16]

Heller introduces Engels's view of the class-equilibrium, which supposedly made possible the rise of absolute monarchy in one brief sentence. The following one moves on to Engels's picture of the dissolution of serfdom, the growth of petty-commodity production and primitive accumulation.[17] Heller does not elucidate the connection between the first and the second, although we might reasonably infer that he sees the latter as a basis for the former. He certainly gives the impression that he sees the dispossession of the peasantry, accompanied by a growing bourgeois strength in the countryside and creating a pool of wage labour, as fundamental. Far from ignoring this development, as Heller claims, I explicitly recognised that the proletarianisation and expropriation of the peasantry was an essential precondition for the development of capitalism.[18] Nonetheless, because of the immense burdens placed on the productive population and the inability of French manufacture to absorb more than a fraction of the potential labour force, the net result was not a rapid development of capitalism but a period of stasis. Le Roy Ladurie's famous study of the Languedocian peasantry, to which Heller mistakenly appeals in order to buttress his view of the progress of rural capitalism, was a major influence in leading me

---

14   Parker 1971.
15   Parker 1980, pp. 71–80; 1966, pp. 29–31.
16   Heller 2009, p. 34.
17   Heller 2009, p. 33.
18   Parker 1996, p. 58.

to this conclusion. Le Roy Ladurie was unambiguous about the consequences which flowed from the polarisation of rural landholding and the concomitant decline of the middle-ranking peasants, stressing that 'capitalism is not built on poverty'.[19]

Nor did the concentration of larger properties in the hands of aspiring urban bourgeois and officeholders of itself introduce capitalism, because these were frequently broken up into smallholdings manageable by their tenants, the use of wage labour was frequently partial and intermittent, whilst capital-investment was low. The *gros fermiers*, to whom Heller refers, undoubtedly displayed entrepreneurial qualities, managing the holdings which they rented with an eye to the profits to be made from selling produce to nearby urban markets. But they were a tiny fraction of a rural population overwhelmingly devoted to subsistence-farming within the constraints imposed by both seigneurial and communal regimes. There was no equivalent in seventeenth-century France to the English yeomanry and resident gentry who were the driving force behind a significant rise in agricultural productivity, which left most French regions lagging far behind. In the following century, there were greater signs of agricultural progress which Heller has assembled to much better effect in his recent study of the French Revolution. Even then, however, he notes that productivity remained low, that most peasants had small amounts of land or none at all and that progress towards capitalist relations was generally 'halting and tentative'.[20]

Absolute monarchy in France emerged at a time when economic conditions make it impossible to explain this by reference to a rising bourgeoisie endowed with the social and political weight to perform the function attributed to it by Engels. Heller, however, is concerned that by denying the central importance of conflict between nobility and bourgeoisie we have deprived seventeenth-century France of 'a sense of dynamic development'.[21] This is a telling comment, indicative of Heller's attachment to a reductionist Marxism which seeks to make the evolution of the French state directly dependent on the balance of class forces. The French state undoubtedly fulfilled a class-function, draining the countryside and towns of their surplus-wealth to the benefit of those with power, influence and status. But this function does not, of itself, explain

---

19   Le Roy Ladurie 1969, p. 163.
20   Heller 2006, pp. 28, 29, 31. Doyle estimates that, in the eighteenth century, the peasant-elite numbered at most 600,000, that is less than three percent of the population. Doyle 1997, p. 197.
21   Heller 2009, p. 38.

the forces which brought absolute monarchy into being. I have set out in various publications, and at some length, the dynamics which pushed France in an absolutist direction, so, here, a rather mechanical list will have to suffice: tension between the decentralising and centralising elements in a feudal body-politic; the pressures of large-scale warfare on an inelastic economy; the drive to religious conformity; economic nationalism and *dirigiste* economic policies; the intense competition for place, influence and a share of the wealth channelled in ever-increasing amounts through the growing state-apparatus. The dialectics of this competition lead both to a concentration of power in the hands of the great royal favourites and then to an appreciation of the need for a ruler who could rise above the fray. The endemic rebellions of the populace further reinforced the willingness of the upper classes to settle their own differences. How convincingly I managed to develop these arguments and how successfully they were incorporated within a Marxist conceptual framework is for others to judge. But it is absurd to suggest that I have ended up with an immobile seventeenth century denuded of dynamics.

By comparison with the seventeenth century, the following one was economically much more dynamic, and, in some areas, notably overseas-trade, the rate of growth was truly remarkable. Heller is therefore on stronger empirical ground in his recent work which seeks to rescue the idea of bourgeois revolution. Economic growth there certainly was and its relationship to the revolution is far from settled, despite the efforts of those who would gut it of its social and economic content. Bourgeois culture and ideas, both political and economic, were increasingly evident, particularly from the 1760s, and affected the thinking of many who were certainly not merchants or manufacturers. Nonetheless the allied question of whether a bourgeois class made the revolution in 1789 remains deeply problematic. Right until the last, the bourgeoisie aspired to join the nobility rather than destroy it, whilst the feudal property-regime was abolished only under duress from an insurgent peasantry. Although the capitalist bourgeoisie grew in numbers and wealth over the course of the eighteenth century, they formed only part of the six percent of the population who could be classified as bourgeois.[22] If the outbreak of revolution had been dependent upon a capitalist bourgeoisie chafing at the limitations of an aristocratic polity, it would not have occurred in 1789. It was the crisis itself and what followed which crystallised latent values and pushed the bourgeoisie into a sense of its own identity. Yet, even when the bourgeois revolution was won, the hegemony of the bourgeoisie remained fragile, its rule subject to fracture and instability

---

22   Doyle 1999, p. 122.

for many decades to come. In contrast, the British ruling class first absorbed demands for political reform and then successfully avoided the revolutions which swept across Europe in 1848.

All this may confirm Heller in his conviction that revisionism has swept the board, disfiguring Marxism in the process. In response, I would simply say that Marxism does not presuppose that class antagonisms are the only contradictions to be addressed, either when explaining the formation of absolute monarchy or when analysing its demise. As Lenin (who knew more than most about making a revolution before the 'objective' conditions had matured) observed, a revolution happens when the old order cannot carry on in the old way. By the 1760s, many Frenchmen, and not just the bourgeoisie, were coming to understand that the monarchy could not carry on in the old way. Central to this realisation was the experience of defeat in their colonial rivalry with Britain, which not only bankrupted the regime but reinforced awareness of the latter's economic superiority. Such awareness stretched back to the mercantilist writers of the early seventeenth century, but now the idea that protectionism offered a solution was discarded in favour of *laissez-faire*. English agriculture and industrial techniques set the benchmark. In a significant sense, it was the comparative backwardness of French capitalism that precipitated the crisis of 1789 rather than the collision of a rising class with the limits of the existing order. This is not a new idea.[23] Here is what Marx and Engels wrote in 1845, although not specifically about the French Revolution:

> ... [A]ll collisions in history have their origin, according to our view, in the contradiction between the productive forces and the form of intercourse. Incidentally to lead to collisions in a country this contradiction need not necessarily have reached its extreme limit in that particular country. The competition with industrially more advanced countries is sufficient to produce a similar contradiction with a less advanced industry.[24]

---

23   Cf. Skopcol 1979; Parker 1996; Teschke 2002.
24   Marx & Engels 1975, pp. 74–5.

CHAPTER 7

Response to William Beik and David Parker

In 'The *Longue Durée* of the French Bourgeoisie' I argued that, despite the ascendancy of the Bourbon monarchy and nobility, a capitalist bourgeoisie continued to exist in seventeenth-century France.[1] As the title of the article suggests, what is in question is the long-term development of a capitalist bourgeoisie through the three centuries of the *ancien régime*. What is at stake is the notion of the revolution of 1789 as a bourgeois and capitalist revolution culminating this long-term development. Such a view represented the standard interpretation of early modern French history among liberal and Marxist historians of the nineteenth and twentieth centuries. According to this interpretation, the revolution cleared the way for capitalism to flourish in the nineteenth century.

In the last generation, this narrative has been challenged by revisionism. Strongest in the English-speaking countries, this tendency has its followers in France as well. Mercurial in its approaches, revisionism's main focus is to attack the idea that the revolution was a bourgeois and capitalist revolution.

It has become my project to argue against such revisionism from a Marxist point of view by reasserting the old view of the rise of a capitalist bourgeoisie through the history of the *ancien régime*. The first part of this plan emerged in the course of researching a book entitled *Labour, Science and Technology in France 1500–1620*.[2] In that work, which was published in 1996, I offered a new interpretation of the religious wars that shook France in the late sixteenth century (1562–98). That period was, for the most part, interpreted as a complex period of fanatical and irrational violence which led to a serious demographic and economic regression. While not completely rejecting this consensus on the religious wars, I highlighted the role of class-conflict in the form of noble reaction, but also of bourgeois and popular resistance. More importantly, I argued that the violence, heavy taxes, usury and economic decline of that period provoked an acceleration of primitive accumulation which led to a substantial decline in landholding by the poorer peasantry and the transfer of much of its property into the hands of rural and urban elites. The consequence was a notable increase in the availability of wage labour and an

---

1 Heller 2009.
2 Heller 1996.

unprecedented spurt of interest in both technological innovation and agricultural improvement.

My findings were reinforced by the pioneering research of Jean-Marc Moriceau who found that it was precisely in this period that an elite of wealthier peasants consolidated itself as a stratum of capitalist tenant-farmers in the Ile-de-France. Already endowed with some land, fixed capital and cash reserves, rich peasants were able to lease the farms controlled by the nobles, urban bourgeoisie and Church while using the wage labour of their hard-pressed neighbours.[3] In other words, far from simply being a period of mere economic regression, the late sixteenth century in France was a period of primitive accumulation quite comparable to what occurred in England in the sixteenth century as classically outlined by Marx in the concluding chapters of the first volume of *Capital*.[4] In those chapters, Marx demonstrated that as a result of such processes the sixteenth century must be regarded as the founding moment of English capitalism. My work, in addition to that of Moriceau, led me to the conclusion that the late sixteenth century must be regarded as a comparable period in France.

The second part of my plan was completed with the recent publication of *The Bourgeois Revolution in France: 1789–1815*.[5] In that work, I analysed the current historiography on the French Revolution and showed that, despite the arguments of the revisionists, an analysis of the evidence overwhelmingly pointed to the fact that the French Revolution was a bourgeois and capitalist revolution. In the revolution, the upheavals in the agrarian sector proved to be crucial. Pushed by mass protest from below, capitalist farmers assumed leadership over the rural revolution which saw the overthrow of feudalism.

The third part of this triadic design is found in the article in question. It seeks to tie together my findings on the late sixteenth century with my analysis of the French Revolution. It argues that, since there was a capitalist bourgeoisie in the sixteenth century, and an even stronger one in the eighteenth century, it is likely that there was continuity in the development of this class in the intervening period. My hypothesis was reinforced by the doctoral thesis of Moriceau, which showed, not only that a rural bourgeoisie took root in the sixteenth century, but that it persisted through the seventeenth century, getting stronger rather than weaker through its engrossing of the land and the rationalisation of its operations.[6] At the same time, I argued that merchant-capital also held its

---

3   Moriceau 1993.
4   Marx 1977, pp. 874–913.
5   Heller 2006.
6   Moriceau 1994.

own during the seventeenth century. As a result of this persistence of the bourgeoisie, it was in a position to resume its progress during the boom of the eighteenth century. In consequence of this analysis, I re-asserted the view that the dominant role played by the bourgeoisie in the revolution was the outcome of a long period of gestation over the three centuries of the *ancien régime*.

In the course of advancing this argument, I challenged some of the principal contentions of the prominent English-speaking historians William Beik and David Parker.[7] Beik and Parker claimed that a capitalist bourgeoisie barely existed or existed not all in seventeenth-century France. In the light of this class's weakness, Beik and Parker inferred further that, although there was a considerable amount of popular unrest in seventeenth-century France, class-war was largely absent. Beik denied that there was a period of petty-commodity production or primitive accumulation prior to the seventeenth century in France, in contrast to England. Parker acknowledged a decline of feudalism in the late middle ages, but insisted that no capitalism emerged in the sixteenth century. According to both Beik and Parker, a mercantile and manufacturing bourgeoisie was scarcely evident in the seventeenth century. In other words, both Beik and Parker denied the existence of a bourgeoisie as a class-in-itself (an economic class) let alone a class-for-itself (an economically-formed and conscious class). Indeed, Parker took this a step further, arguing that it was difficult to identify a capitalist bourgeoisie in eighteenth-century France, thus throwing doubt on the notion that the French Revolution could have been a capitalist revolution.

The point of departure of my objections to the views of Beik and Parker was their neglect and underestimation of the achievements of the sixteenth century. Basing my analysis on the work of Emmanuel Le Roy Ladurie,[8] Moriceau and others, I claimed that the two historians had ignored or dismissed the emergence of a rural and urban capitalism and capitalist bourgeoisie in the sixteenth century, bolstered particularly by the consequences of primitive accumulation. Indeed, I asserted that not only was there evidence of the existence of a bourgeoisie as a class-in-itself, but also one-for-itself, reflected in urban and peasant-protest, demands of the third estate at the Estates-General of 1588 and the anti-feudal writings of figures such as Turquet de Mayerne. This so-called offensive of profit lasted until the late sixteenth or even the early decades of the seventeenth century. On the other hand, the seventeenth century was to be mainly characterised by an offensive of rent.

---

7   Beik 1985; Parker 1996.
8   Le Roy Ladurie 1966.

It is this notion of an offensive of rent, derived from the work of Le Roy Ladurie, upon which Beik and Parker depend as the basis of their interpretation of the seventeenth century. But such an offensive of rent, I argued, has to be understood as coming at the expense of profit, which continued to exist although in retreat. In other words, a capitalist bourgeoisie endured, albeit thrown on the defensive by a class-war carried on from above by the nobility and Bourbon state. Indeed, based on the work of Moriceau, which was admittedly founded on research confined to the Ile-de-France, I pointed out that capitalist farmers successfully adapted to this assault by rationalising and improving their operations, emerging stronger than ever at the beginning of the eighteenth century.[9] At the same time, I brought forward a growing body of research reflecting the continued existence of a mercantile and manufacturing bourgeoisie. In short, whilst agreeing that the sense of a bourgeoisie as a class-for-itself faded in the seventeenth century, I insisted that the bourgeoisie as a class-in-itself continued to exist. It constituted the soil out of which grew the increasingly large and powerful bourgeoisie that developed in the eighteenth century and which eventually assumed leadership over the revolution of 1789.

In his response to my article, Beik claims that his book was not about the bourgeoisie, but rather 'the channels ... that linked the royal government and the ruling class of ... Languedoc'. This is fair enough, as this nexus is fundamental to understanding the political structure of the *ancien régime*. But, in the course of making the argument for a virtual symbiosis between the civil society of the *ancien régime* and the Bourbon state, Beik made a point of dismissing the existence of a capitalist bourgeoisie living off profit. He was perfectly correct to discount the influence of the bourgeoisie politically, but, in doing so, he wrongly erased its continuing economic existence.

As part of his argument he wrote that 'Heller has no grounds for claiming that I "deny an initial period of petty-commodity production and primitive accumulation" since this topic was beyond the scope of my project, and consequently was not discussed'. Yet, in noting the development of Marxist views of the *ancien régime*, Beik approvingly observed that once serfdom, which was intimately associated with feudalism, disappeared, a new mode of production was called for – if not capitalism directly, then a period of 'petty commodity production' or 'primitive accumulation'. This association of the early modern period with the rise of the bourgeoisie and the rise of capitalism made considerable sense for England, where most attention was directed, but not for France, where the society of lords and dependent peasants persisted for cen-

---

9 Moriceau 1994.

turies, the aristocracy consistently renewed itself, and absolutism became a powerful force instead of a hollow shell.[10]

Beik asserts that the difference between us rehearses the old debate between Paul Sweezy and Maurice Dobb, in which the former invoked trade as the external prime mover and Dobb insisted on the importance of class struggle. Beik intimates that he somehow stressed Dobb's relations-of-production approach (class struggle?) while I mistakenly emphasised the importance of trade which Dobb regarded as a regressive force. Actually, Dobb regarded primitive accumulation on the land and the changes in the social relations of production that came with it as fundamental to capitalist beginnings. As noted above, Beik dismissed primitive accumulation in France, while I regard it as the starting point of capitalist origins in France as well as England. It is true that I highlight the evidence for the existence of a trading bourgeoisie as Beik noted. But this is because, once capitalist production begins, exchange is essential to the realisation of surplus-value as capitalist profits. Trade is two-sided, playing a regressive role reinforcing feudal relations of production and blocking innovation, but, once capitalism has entered productive relations, market-exchange is necessary to the realisation of profits and eventually to the emergence of capitalist competition. Of course, Dobb fully understood this.

Beik asserts that my claims of an early-modern French capitalism are superficial and that I need to probe deeply into the relations of production that existed under the *ancien régime* if I want to show that a real agricultural capitalism existed. If he read my analysis of Olivier de Serres's *Le théâtre d'agriculture et mesnage des champs* (1600) in *Labour, Science and Technology* he would realise that I have offered just such an analysis.[11] In Serres, who was reprinted many times and widely read down to the revolution, he would have discovered the reality of a French rural capitalism which has eluded him.

In criticising Beik and Parker, I counterposed their notion of an unopposed seventeenth-century offensive of rent with Le Roy Ladurie's conception of a struggle between rent and profit, stressing that the advance of the one was always relative to the other. As such, profit and a rural capitalist class certainly survived in the seventeenth century, although put on the defensive. In response, Beik claims that the neo-Malthusian Le Roy Ladurie deployed the terms rent, profit and wages in a way that has nothing to do with the vocabulary of Marxism. But the fact is that classical political economy starting from Adam Smith and continuing through Thomas Malthus, David Ricardo and Karl Marx

---

10   Beik 1985, p. 21.
11   Heller 1996, pp. 168–73.

used a common terminology with respect to rent, profit and wages, although they differed with respect to the historical premises and the consequences of their inter-action.

It is true that Le Roy Ladurie in the past expressed intense hostility to Marxism, as was the wont with some former members of the French Communist Party. But the intensity of the Cold War having dissipated, Le Roy Ladurie has called for reconciliation with Marxist colleagues and has expressed admiration for the work of eminent Marxist historians such as Albert Soboul and Guy Lemarchand.[12] Even in the 1970s, the then-Cold Warrior Le Roy Ladurie found it possible to give high marks to the doctoral thesis of the Marxist Guy Bois on late medieval and early modern upper Normandy. In his review of Bois in the pages of *Annales*, he makes clear that he and Bois are speaking about the same thing and from a congruent perspective:

> Under the cloak of a Marxist vocabulary which speaks to us of feudalism and even of centralised feudalism (the name ascribed to the modern royal state) we arrive with Guy Bois finally at the basic facts: they imply a Ricardian-Malthusian (or neo-Malthusian) equilibrium of the eco-system in a more than two centuries *longue durée* and at one and the same time the drift of the said eco-system towards a family-based capitalism. This is what makes this powerful and frequently admirable doctoral thesis truly interesting.[13]

The idea that Le Roy Ladurie employs a terminology which has no relation to Marxism therefore holds no water.

Beik denies that we can see the urban and peasant-unrest of the religious wars and the immediately following decades in class terms. As for the French Revolution, Beik claims that the revolution might be seen as being made not by the bourgeoisie but for the bourgeoisie. This is but part of his larger view that '... it is no longer adequate to speak of the bourgeoisie, or indeed any class, as a unified force playing a single-purposeful role in history'. It is interesting, in this regard, that Beik has had no problem speaking about the nobility as a class. Rather, it is the notion of a class that is an agent of change which appears problematic.

Early in his writings on history and politics, Marx made the distinction between the existence of such a class in terms of its relation to the means of

---

12   Le Roy Ladurie, Lemarchand and Rance 2008.
13   Le Roy Ladurie 1978, p. 124.

production and the degree to which it has consciousness of itself. The former notion of a class-in-itself, in my view, continues to be a fruitful and important one in both historical and economic analysis. From the perspective of history, the notion of a class-for-itself and its relation to that of a class-in-itself appears more problematic. Yet it seems to me that the notion of a class-for-itself can be usefully applied to particular historical conjunctures. The three centuries of the *ancien régime* each have their concrete and particular characteristics which must be carefully taken into account. But the relationship of these phases to their denouement in the French Revolution must also be borne in mind.

In the French Revolution, the dominant discourse became that of *sans-culotterie* and classical republicanism. Nevertheless, it is significant that some revolutionaries did interpret the revolution as a revolution of the bourgeoisie, the middle class and even the capitalist class. Such a discourse did not take hold because it was regarded as too divisive by the revolutionary elites attempting to establish leadership over the common people. The populist idea of the common people united against the aristocrats and of republican virtue appeared more appealing and politically palatable.[14] But it cannot be denied that the notion of a bourgeois revolution was certainly present in the minds of revolutionaries. This was because the revolution of 1789 was, in fact, a revolution in which a bourgeoisie based on a growing capitalism took state power. In other words, there was a convergence between the sense of a class-in-itself and class-for-itself. In this light, it seems appropriate to examine the ferment of the late sixteenth century when, in more tentative and less organised fashion, an emerging capitalist bourgeoisie expressed itself politically, or as a class-for-itself. Le Roy Ladurie, for example, unselfconsciously compared the call of the third estate of Languedoc for confiscation of the temporalities of the Church in 1560 with the passage of the Civil Constitution of the Clergy by the National Assembly in 1791.[15] In seeing the one event as a prefiguration of the other, Le Roy Ladurie, like any good historian, was pointing to the common underlying social dynamic active in both periods.

With respect to the French Revolution, Parker asserted in his book that it was difficult to find a bourgeoisie in eighteenth-century France.[16] But, in light of my work, Parker now grudgingly concedes that a bourgeoisie, however feeble, took power in 1789. Yet he insists that this class was not the product of the long evolution of the *ancien régime* but only of its last years. On the contrary, I assert

---

14   Heller 2010.
15   Le Roy Ladurie 1966, pp. 360–1.
16   Parker 1996, p. 280.

that great events like the French Revolution have proportionally deep causes, in this case the *longue durée* of the bourgeoisie. Parker complains that I ignored his treatment of maritime trade and references to primitive accumulation and social differentiation in the countryside. In fact, his references to maritime trade were cursory. Furthermore, his notion of a *dirigiste* state overriding the views of local entrepreneurs does not square with the emerging consensus on the way that seventeenth-century French mercantilism operated.[17]

As for his discussion of primitive accumulation and social differentiation, I did not ignore them, but complained instead that '... Parker's approach is to underline all those factors which inhibited the development of capitalism in agriculture, while minimising those aspects which favoured its growth'.[18] Parker eventually admits this by noting that, despite the expropriation of the peasantry and their proletarianisation, 'because of the immense burdens placed on the productive population and the inability of French manufacture to absorb more than a fraction of the potential labour-force, the net result was not a rapid development of capitalism but a period of stasis'.

In drawing these conclusions, the authority of Le Roy Ladurie looms large in the eyes of Parker. Indeed, as the absolute master of the history of the *ancien régime*, it could hardly be otherwise. In any case, Parker invokes Le Roy Ladurie as 'a major influence in leading me to this conclusion', i.e., the non-development of capitalism. But we have already cited Le Roy Ladurie to the effect that there was in fact a slow drift to capitalism throughout the course of the *ancien régime*.

Le Roy Ladurie's definitive statement on this question is found in his great summing up of 2002, the *Histoire des paysans français de la peste noire à la Révolution*.[19] Much of this enormous work simply reprints his earlier contribution to the *Histoire de la France rurale and the Histoire économique et sociale de la France*.[20] But about a third embodies new material including an up-to-date bibliography. In a quite dialectical way, Le Roy Ladurie points to the role of the nobility in creating large farms while underscoring the role of the tenants of these farms in the development of agrarian capitalism:

> ... [T]he accumulators of land of the classical age of the sixteenth and seventeenth centuries played the role of sorcerers' apprentices. In creating large domains they saw fit at the same time to create tenants who one

17   Reynard 1999.
18   Heller 2009, p. 44.
19   Le Roy Ladurie 2002.
20   Le Roy Ladurie 1975; Le Roy Ladurie 1977, pp. 483–865.

day, in the eighteenth century, would challenge their descendants. From
the midst of the peasants the amassers of land singled out an élite of farmers who for the times were already modern. In the very long term the latter
traversed the French route toward agricultural capitalism, a route which
itself preceded the 'agricultural revolutions' in the French mode. It is true
that this 'route' was especially characteristic of northern France in which
grain-farming on its fertile and muddy open fields dominated.[21]

Based on recent scholarship, including the work of Moriceau, Le Roy Ladurie
ascribes this evolution towards capitalism to the whole of the north, the most
productive agrarian region of France. In contrast, Parker defends his view of a
non-capitalist France by falling back on Le Roy Ladurie's thesis of 1966, whose
findings were explicitly limited to Languedoc, to the effect that capitalism
failed to consolidate itself in that region. Forced to address the research of
Moriceau on the capitalist tenant-farmers of the Ile-de-France, Parker attempts
to minimise its import for the rest of northern France by noting their relatively
small number, which he compares unfavourably to the in-depth strength of the
capitalist gentry and yeomen of England. That the gentry or even the yeomen
were in the vanguard of English rural capitalism is questionable. But, in any
case, an acknowledged expert on English agriculture, J.P. Cooper, has noted that
the number of large farms in northern France was entirely comparable to the
number in lowland-England.[22]

   In challenging Beik and Parker, my primary purpose has been to re-assert
the old view that, from the sixteenth century onwards, there existed a capitalist
bourgeoisie in France. Moreover, it eventually provided leadership to the mass
of the population during the revolution, assuming control over the state. The
leadership and hegemony of such a bourgeoisie was particularly decisive in
the crucial revolution in the countryside. But my purpose extends beyond this
question to the history of capitalism itself. Far too often, the early history of
capitalism has been seen to be an exclusively English affair. This is a mistakenly
parochial approach. Capitalist relations of production began at more or less
the same time in England and France. In the one case, such relations were able
to advance as a result of the success of the Puritan Revolution. In the latter
case, feudal and absolutist reaction under the Bourbons was able to hold back,
if not extinguish, capitalism in the seventeenth century, delaying its advance
until the next century. It is important to note that capitalism, which always

---

21   Le Roy Ladurie 2002, p. 391.
22   Cooper 1985, pp. 143, 152.

was a single system, in fact began in Italy in the late middle ages and extended into Germany, the Netherlands, France and England in the sixteenth century. Robert Brenner has recently demonstrated the particularity of the Dutch route to capitalism.[23]

The responsibility of European historians is to appreciate that there were different paths to the development of capitalism in the various states of Western Europe. The strengths and weaknesses of its development in each case has to be taken into account if we are to do justice to capitalism's development and to the concrete history of separate states.

---

23   Brenner 2001.

CHAPTER 8

French Absolutism and Agricultural Capitalism: A Comment on Henry Heller's Essays*

Stephen Miller

Friedrich Engels argued, in *The Origins of the Family, Private Property and the State*, that absolute monarchies took shape in a period of equilibrium in the class struggle between the old feudal nobility and the class of townspeople. The warring classes balanced one another so nearly that although the state appeared to mediate between them, it momentarily attained autonomy from both. This argument long informed Marxist thought on the development of the bourgeoisie, capitalism, and absolutism. Yet it did not result from a systematic painstaking analysis, because Engels and Marx devoted nearly all of their attention to their own capitalist society.[1]

Perry Anderson, the first Marxist to carry out a thorough investigation of absolute monarchies, argued, in a revision of Engels, that these states amounted to 'A redeployed and recharged apparatus of feudal domination ...'[2] Anderson further argued that the discrete autonomous authorities characteristic of feudalism made it possible for towns, capitalism and the bourgeoisie to emerge in the interstices.[3]

Conversely, Robert Brenner made the case that capitalism came into being in agriculture as an unintended consequence of feudal class struggle. In the fourteenth century, English serfs fought and won freedom from lordly domination. The lords, however, retained the right to enhance the feudal fees for the use of land. Over the following centuries, the lords began to raise the fees to as much as the farmers would pay. They adjusted the fees to economic conditions and, in this way, involuntarily propelled themselves, their tenant farmers, and the agricultural workforce into a system of commercial rents and capitalist competition. Across the Channel, the peasants of France and most of Western

---

* Originally published as: Stephen Miller, 'French Absolutism and Agricultural Capitalism: A Comment on Henry Heller's Essays', *Historical Materialism*, 20, 4 (2012): 141–61.

1 Engels 1972, p. 1.
2 Anderson 1974, p. 18.
3 Anderson 1974, p. 422.

Europe not only won freedom but also the right to pay fixed monetary dues to the lords for the use of the land during the thirteenth century. Inflation eroded these dues over the course of the fifteenth and sixteenth centuries and put pressure on lordly incomes. The nobles responded, in a long convulsive process, by building up their feudal capacity, under the aegis of absolute monarchs, to appropriate the peasants' surpluses.[4]

William Beik and David Parker refined this line of Marxist analysis in carefully researched works on the ways in which the French aristocracy renewed itself through the absolutist state. Rather than harbour a triangular struggle, as Engels had indicated, between the bourgeoisie, nobility and crown, the monarchy retained feudal trappings for the benefit of the ruling class and for the oppression of the peasant masses that had emerged from the direct lordly exploitation of the medieval period. The bourgeoisie did not develop as a class opposed to the monarchy. In England, by contrast, gentry landlords gained income through agricultural capitalism and did not rely on the absolutist form of governments.[5]

In the article 'The Long Durée of the French Bourgeoisie', Henry Heller agrees with Brenner that capitalism originated in agriculture. But against this whole line of Marxist analysis, Heller highlights a comment of Emmanuel Le Roy Ladurie about the limits of the offensive of *rente* against profit in seventeenth-century agriculture. Heller argues that *rente* (by which he seems to mean the levies of the state and seigneurs) had not entirely eradicated profit (which, for Heller, indicates capitalism).[6] He writes, in his 'Response to William Beik and David Parker',

> [A] rural bourgeoisie ... persisted through the seventeenth century, getting stronger rather than weaker ... As a result of this persistence of the bourgeoisie, it was in a position to resume its progress during the boom of the eighteenth century ... [T]he dominant role played by the bourgeoisie in the revolution was the outcome of a long period of gestation over the three centuries of the *ancien régime*.[7]

Heller actually devotes most of 'The Long Durée of the French Bourgeoisie' to the economic and political significance of urban capitalists rather than to agriculture. But since he writes more concretely about agrarian relations in his

---

4   Brenner 1985, pp. 242–6, 286, 288–9, 293, 295–6, 301.
5   Beik 1985, pp. 21, 25–6, 31; Parker 1996, p. 280.
6   Heller 2009.
7   Heller 2009, p. 134.

'Response to William Beik and David Parker', and since he founds his entire argument, in both essays, on the resiliency of agricultural capitalism in early modern France, I direct these comments solely at this aspect of Heller's work.[8]

I premise my argument on the logic of *Capital*. In the chapter 'The Transformation of Surplus-Value into Capital', Marx argues that accumulation consists of the use of surplus product to create more surplus product and surplus-value. The never-ending drive for more production is a social mechanism of which the capitalist is but a cog. Individual capitalists must necessarily procure new means of production with each new round of accumulation. Competition subordinates each capitalist to the law of capitalist production, compelling each one constantly to extend capital so as to preserve it, and by this extension to beget progressive accumulation. Marx further argues, in 'The General Law of Capitalist Accumulation', that in this cycle of reproduction, competition forces capitalists to produce relative surplus, that is, not profit by extracting more value from the variable component of capital, or labour power, but by adding to the constant component of capital, or means of production, to cut costs. As accumulation proceeds, the variable component of capital increases but in a diminishing proportion in relation to the constant. From this premise, I argue, capitalism did not determine the evolution of French agriculture.

Peasant Agriculture in France

The research on early modern England demonstrates a steady rise in relative surplus, as labour became more productive through the accumulation of constant capital in agriculture. Tenant farmers increased yields, improved implements for sowing, weeding and harvesting, concentrates corn-growing on the lands most suited to it, enhanced farm sizes to economise on the workforce, and, where appropriate, turned to pasture farming, which economises on labour far more than does cereal-growing. In the centuries following the later middle ages, the amount of working capital in arable farming, measured in the number of draft animals relative to sown acres, increased dramatically. At the end of the eighteenth century, French farmers had about 2.1 man-hours of horse labour-power for each one of their own, whereas English farmers had 3.5. The total agricultural labour force slightly declined from about 1.1–1.2 to 1.1 million between 1300 and 1800, while output per head grew approximately three times

---

8   Heller 2009 and 2010.

over. It is estimated that labour productivity rose 4.4 times in cereal agriculture in South Eastern England between 1300 and 1850.[9]

The key to this rise in productivity was the transformation of peasant communities into individual free labourers, variable components of capital, whose costs were calculable and always had to diminish on account of the tenant farmers' competition against one another. Marx called this transformation primitive accumulation, or the dispossession of the rural population. It was absolutely crucial to his argument, because members of peasant villages, in possession of the means to reproduce themselves, do not have to find work and so do not form proletarian labour power abstracted from the community of human existence and made into a variable component of capital. Marx devoted the entire eighth part of *Capital* to this very issue.

Heller argues that, in France, the violence, usury and economic decline of the sixteenth-century religious wars caused 'an acceleration of primitive accumulation which led to a substantial decline in landholding by the poorer peasantry and the transfer of much of its property into the hands of rural and urban elites'.[10] This analysis of the Wars of Religion makes the fundamental class-relationships of capitalism an unintended consequence of the political conflicts of absolutism. It has much to recommend for Marxists, because otherwise, if capitalism were the deliberate design of sixteenth-century people, it would then seem to form part of the human DNA in the manner of Adam Smith's '... necessary ... consequence of ... a propensity in human nature ... to truck, barter, and exchange ...'[11] How otherwise could sixteenth-century people have had the idea to bring capitalist relations of production into being? And if capitalism were 'human nature', how could people ever hope to supersede it?

Disappointingly, Heller then hitches his line of reasoning to the work of Jean-Marc Moriceau, a historian of the Paris Basin, and makes the argument that the bourgeoisie got stronger in the seventeenth century '... through its engrossing of the land and the rationalisation of its operations'.[12] Moriceau is an unabashed adherent of Smith. In the opening pages of his doctoral thesis, which Heller approvingly cites, Moriceau writes:

---

9   Allen 1994, pp. 96, 121; Allen 1992, pp. 214, 224–5; Brenner 2007, p. 106; Brenner 2001, p. 321; Campbell and Overton 1993, p. 83; Clark 1999, pp. 208–9, 238–9; Thirsk 1978, pp. 161–4; Wrigley 2006, pp. 454–6.

10   Heller 2010, p. 133.

11   Smith 1999, Book I, Chapter II.

12   Heller 2010, p. 134.

The Parisian attraction favoured a type of agriculture precociously engaged in capitalism. In an all-encompassing fashion, it incited the shaking
off of the old framework of the feudal organisation. More importantly, it
diffused an aura of modernity in the nearby countryside.[13]

In other words, the urban market presented baubles, à la Adam Smith, and
the spellbound feudal lords ceased to concentrate on building up their power
by gaining the loyalty of knights, and the peasants ceased to concentrate on
subsistence agriculture. The class relations of capitalism require no further
explanation than the compelling opportunity of the towns.[14]

I argue, by contrast, that these relations did not come into being in early
modern France. If one looks at the period from the middle ages through the
nineteenth century, one notices that the peasantry made available landless
labourers and paupers, but not proletarian labour power. By the 1200s, although
the peasants had won de facto rights over the greater part of the land, they
never fully controlled their livelihood, because they faced a lordly class deeply
ingrained in the political and social fabric of the country. The lords came to
accept the legality of the peasants' plots over the following two centuries, at the
same time as they made periodic surveys of seigneurial inventories to define
their perquisites. Duties that had fallen into abeyance were discovered in the
unnoticed implications of customs, others were invented and added to the
tangle of levies, and a heavy seigneurial burden accumulated on the peasants.
These also had to pay tax collectors and vendors of essential goods, and often
had to sell their produce when prices were lowest in order to make ends meet.
After a long period of economic and population growth, from the end of the
1400s until the 1670s and 1680s, peasants faced mounting difficulties, as the
subdivision of their plots among offspring left them with parcels inadequate for
their subsistence. They faced debts and foreclosures, and the nobles ended up
with estates as large as 300 hectares in the Paris Basin amid an overall context
of stagnation which lasted into the eighteenth century.[15]

These estates did not represent the outcome of primitive accumulation so
much as solutions by default, when peasant communities abandoned the land
in a time of crisis. What is more, when prices rose again in the second half of
the eighteenth century – when, according to Heller, capitalist farmers emerged

13   Moriceau 1994b, p. 72.
14   For Smith's description of the dissolution of feudalism, see Smith 1999, Book III.
15   Bloch 1966, pp. 128–34, 140–3, 217, 233; Fourquin 1970, pp. 175–9; Fossier 1968, pp. 555–6;
      Bois 1976, pp. 203–4, 217, 355; Meuvret 1987, pp. 75–6, 86, 88–9; Beaur 1984, pp. 270, 336,
      339; Jacquart 1975, pp. 362–5, 373–5; Brenner 1985, pp. 312–13.

stronger than ever – the estates shed peasant farms. Every carefully researched measurement of property from about 1730 or 1740 through the 1800s shows that the nobles lost ground, and the bourgeoisie found itself on the defensive, as peasants racked up debts to acquire land. The extent of peasant property varied from one region to another and overall amounted to around 40 percent of the total at the end of the eighteenth century.[16]

The peasants succeeded in extending their share of the soil by exploiting their household labour. They had more family members than could be put to work on their plots, and rather than cast off this labour, and make the land yield income relative to the time spent working it, they used the members in labour-intensive lines in which their superabundant capacity for work gave them a competitive advantage.[17]

In the Lyonnais, where the population grew in the eighteenth century into one of the densest concentrations in the realm, peasants possessed more and more of the land, maybe even a majority of it, in farms of fewer than five, often fewer than two, hectares. Many of these resulted from the peasants' indefatigable work converting woods and stony soils into vineyards with the aim of complementing their holdings in rye and wheat for bread, hemp for cloth, and oats for animals. Vineyards did not require outlays of household income on cattle, animal fertiliser, ploughs or carts, and brought in two-and-a-half to five times more income per hectare than did grains. In contrast to grain cultivation and its dead seasons, viticulture filled the calendar year with hewing, layering to multiply the base of the vines, three ploughings with hoes, putting in stakes for vine shoots, preparing vessels and basins, harvesting, fermenting, pressing the wine, and many other tasks, which permitted households to put their stores of labour to use generating additional income for their subsistence.

The Lyonnais countryside buzzed with tiny vineyards spread through the larger arable fields of the landed classes.[18] The peasants of Poitou, in the West, had from as little as 2 percent of the land around Poitiers to as much as 25 percent in areas of the Vendee. Yet they had around 40 percent of the land

---

16 Heller 2010, p. 135; Meuvret 1987, pp. 88–9; Beaur 2000, pp. 32, 38–9; Tulippe 1934, pp. 110, 161–3, 241, 318–19; Jarnoux 1996, p. 268; Lefebvre 1924, pp. 47–50, 57; Berenson 1984, pp. 9–10, 18, 20, 22–3; Price 1975, p. 271; Brennan 2006, pp. 183, 186, 189–90, 193, 197–8; Grantham 1975, pp. 292–306, 324–5; Labrousse 1966, pp. 48–51.

17 My line of reasoning is inspired by a comparative article on England and China by Brenner and Isett 2002.

18 Berger 1985, pp. 183–4; Tomas 1967, pp. 409–10; Gutton 1971, p. 172; Jomand 1966, pp. 126–7; Durand 1979, pp. 230, 291–2, 447, 507–8; Brenot 1980, p. 235; Dupaquier 1995, p. 76; Bianchi 1999, p. 53.

in hemp and 30–85 percent of the land in vines. Hemp required much labour soaking the stems, grinding the dried ones a month later, cleaning and combing the material, spinning it, and then putting the hanks on winders for the making of cloth. Artisans usually worked a quarter of the year in rural cloth workshops, the rest on their parcels of land. They planted turnips after the hemp to bring nutrients to the topsoil and prepare it for rye. This crop, which predominated on the peasants' fields, did not fetch as high a price as did wheat but did better on land lacking fertiliser and helped assure their subsistence.[19]

Cereals covered at least 70, and usually 80–90 per cent of Poitevin fields, especially those of the landed classes. They also took up the main part of the peasants' work. Even so, fodder crops, for commercial cattle, began to appear on the farms of peasants and sharecroppers in the wooded countryside with small irregular-shaped fields and many hedges and copses. The smallholders developed crop rotations of buckwheat to clean, loosen and break down the soil, and then broom, gorse bush, vetches, and sainfoin, along with barley and oats, after the harvest of wheat. The gorse bush on the heaths fixed lime and phosphorous acid (in the same way that legumes do) in these acidic soils naturally deficient in such nutrients. Peasants left the broom and gorse on uncultivated paths to be saturated in rain and animal droppings, and trampled by cattle and people. They obtained excellent fertiliser in this way and had fodder to rear about one draft animal per two hectares, a proportion superior to that obtained on the commercial cereal domains and open fields of northern France.[20]

This animal husbandry required the peasants of Poitou to till plots for several years, abandon them, and then clear the unplanted land. The peasants used resistant hoes to divide the broom and gorse, and to plough several times with the aim of breaking up the roots and taking out the weeds. The husbandry required huge amounts of labour of both sexes and all ages. It appeared as time wasted to observers but actually added up to a means of putting excess labour to use and maintaining a dense population.[21]

The peasants of the Berry, in central France, reared oxen. Horses did farmwork more rapidly but cost more to buy and maintain. Since the peasants did not face pressure to maximise the market value of their labour-time, they saw

19   Peret 1998, pp. 43–4, 94, 98; Guillemet, Pellegrin and Peret 1981, pp. 11, 14–15; Merle 1958, pp. 40–1, 64; Autexier 1947, p. 83; Benoist 2005, p. 120; Benoist 1985, pp. 163–4; Bossis 1980, p. 143; Bossis 1972, pp. 132–3, 135–6; Elie 2003, p. 238; Pichon 2004, pp. 149, 152, 154; Pellegrin 1987, pp. 380–1; Martin 1988, p. 64.
20   Benoist 2005, pp. 184–5, 294–5; Benoist 1985, pp. 163–5, 167; Antoine 1999, pp. 121, 124–6, 128–9, 131; Bossis 1980, p. 143; Tilly 1964, p. 33; Gerard 1990, pp. 42–4.
21   Antoine 1999, p. 129.

the horses as a needless expense. They reserved the best land for subsistence crops rather than fodder, and their oxen did not produce optimal amounts of fertiliser. Yet the peasants still had more manure for their fields than the landed classes of the Berry had for their commercial cereal domains which had extensive sheep grazing, fallow and few farm animals. The peasants intensively applied household labour farming peas, broad beans, and turnips, which renewed the soil and raised yields. Fallow receded from their plots long before it did from the large domains. The peasants laid out gardens and vineyards, and farmed hemp for domestic clothing and sales of the surplus garments. They used spades and hoes, which went deeper into the soil, and turned, ventilated, and weeded it better than did ploughs. Spades and hoes required far more labour, but the peasants only had to take wood from the forests to make them and did not incur costs to maintain and replace them. The peasants saved instead for new parcels to assure their families' livelihood.[22]

In the Paris Basin, the population grew 31 percent in the eighteenth century, making the region the second most densely inhabited of the realm. The Paris Basin is known for large farms of 10 to 40, 120, and even 300 hectares in certain areas. Yet peasant farms, mostly smaller than two hectares, existed in nearly every parish and covered anywhere from 5 to 45 percent of the farmland. These small holdings grew at the expense of the large farms of the bourgeoisie and nobility in the eighteenth and nineteenth centuries, as the peasants took on debts to buy as much land as possible in the hopes of attaining self-sufficiency and security in old age.[23]

The expansion of peasant agriculture in the decades following 1740 stemmed from the rural population's ability to put unpaid family members to use in labour-intensive lines such as market gardening in the parishes bordering Paris to the northeast. Peasants gardened with spades and sickles, even though these did not accomplish much work relative to the labour expended, because replacing these implements with more efficient ones would not have increased output but would have increased the outlays of family income. Peasants of the Paris Basin also created vineyards, which, like the gardens, generated more income per hectare than did wheat fields. They had far fewer prairies and woods than did the urban landowners, yet had nearly all of the regional vineyards.[24]

---

22   Gay 1967, pp. 159–60, 162–3, 169, 184–5, 308.
23   Loutchisky 1933, pp. 121, 123, 134; Jacquart 1974, pp. 104–5, 107, 117; Brunet 1960, p. 284; Vovelle 1980, pp. 85, 217, 202; Ganiage 1988, p. 54; Dupaquier 1995, p. 76; Dupaquier 1956, pp. 145–6, 214, 255; Tulippe 1934, p. 110; Beaur 1984, p. 128; Beaur 1991, pp. 285, 287.
24   Peru 2003, pp. 68–9, 71; Dion 1959, pp. 32, 466–7; Labrousse 1990, pp. 554, 558; Baulant 1979, p. 96.

In short, if any economic vitality existed in rural France it came from the peasantry, not the bourgeoisie. In fact, it was because the peasants possessed so much of the land, and acquired even more of it as prices rose in the decades following 1740, that the upper classes accumulated political power. Politically constituted private property – seigneurial rights, venal offices, tax farms, noble titles, and bonds sold by office holders, municipal magistracies, and provincial estates – redistributed income from the peasantry to the nobility and bourgeoisie. It is well documented that the bourgeoisie rented the right to collect seigneurial dues from nobles and bishops, and purchased lordly rights, venal offices, titles and state bonds, down to the end of the *ancien régime*. Politically constituted private property amounted to the sole means of appropriating the surpluses from the mass of resources possessed by the peasantry.[25]

The Exploitation of Peasant Labour

The most widespread and fundamental form of appropriation was the extra work taken from the entire families of the smallholders. To understand this point, one must keep in mind that the peasant economy gave up poor and dispossessed, but not variable proletarian components of capital. From the 1730s and 1740s onward, increases in output did not take the form of capital accumulation so much as additional outlays of household labour by a growing numbers of peasants eager to eke out income and acquire land. The peasants actually gained less income per time working. In the Paris Basin, their discretionary income for consumer goods shrank, as their growing numbers competed for scarce resources in land, food, and jobs. The majority of peasants did not have the surpluses to speculate on grain markets, and had to buy their subsistence at a time of rising prices. While no one actually starved, the population's malnutrition is well documented.[26]

---

25   Robert Brenner developed the concept of 'politically constituted private property'; see Brenner 2003, pp. 652–3, P. Jones 2003, pp. 28, 73–5; Doyle 1996, pp. 233, 237; Lüthy 1998, pp. 9–10, 15, 17–18, 23; Porshnev 1963, pp. 112–13, 122, 563–6, 572; Althusser 1972, pp. 99–104; Anderson 1974, pp. 18–20, 47–8, 54–5, 97, 125–6, 138–9; Goubert and Roche 1984, pp. 66, 243, 356; Dessert 1984, pp. 43, 46, 59–60, 63, 316, 331, 341, 355, 367; Beik 1985, pp. 21, 245–78; Comninel 1987, pp. 195–6, 198, 200–3; Collins 1988, pp. 111, 122, 136, 144, 146, 155, 164, 214; Descimon and Jouhaud 1996, pp. 78, 155, 173, 189–90; Parker 1996, pp. 100–1, 263–5; Miller 2008, pp. 42–4, 46, 59, 71, 74–81, 93–4, 96.
26   Aymard 1988, p. 235; Bouton 1993, pp. 57–9; Ganiage 1988, p. 41.

In the Lyonnais, only a third of the vintners owned the minimum of two hectares needed to support a family in wine production. The rest had to get resources in other ways, commonly by labouring on the arable fields of the landed classes. The growing population, and its reliance on labour markets for income and on grain markets for food, drove up the price of rye, the staple crop of the region, higher than the agricultural wages. Growth came to a halt as a result of the saturation of vineyards in the region of Lyon. Wine prices rose over the course of the eighteenth century, as consumption regained the levels it had reached prior to the crisis of the end of the seventeenth century. But output eventually surpassed demand, as the urban population sacrificed wine purchases to necessities in years of high prices. Harvests expanded excessively, drove down wine prices from 1776 to 1785, and plunged the peasants into precariousness.[27]

After 1770, rising land rents and rural poverty diminished the market for non-essential goods and provoked a severe downturn in artisanal activity affecting all the households of the Poitou-Charentes that earned ancillary income from hemp. While the price of grain and other products rose, that of wine and flax fell on account of all of the vineyards and hemp fields carved out of the hillsides and poor lands, where cereals did not grow. The vintners of northern Poitou saw the value of their plots decline in the 1780s. The sale of livestock grew exponentially in the fairs of Fontenay and other towns of lower Poitou from 1758 to 1776 but then faced a brutal recession. The lack of fodder made animal fattening impractical, forced sales amid falling prices, yet still led merchants to turn away from markets. The after-death inventories of Poitou, measured against the regional food grains, show a 20 percent decline of fortunes over the course of the eighteenth century and a particularly sharp decline among day labourers and ploughmen without much property. The number of poor and beggars grew in lower Poitou, and the population of the Fontenaysien actually declined in the years preceding the revolution.[28]

The peasants, in a word, faced mounting difficulties wringing subsistence from their plots. Only a minority had the land and livestock to avoid reliance on wages, on leasing small plots to combine with their own insufficient holdings, or even on leasing whole units of production to provide for their families' subsistence. The nobility and bourgeoisie had no thought of expropriating the peasants and turning them into proletarians. The routine practice of pinning

27   Durand 1979, pp. 41–2, 291–2, 507–8; Gutton 1971, pp. 70–1.
28   Peret 1988, pp. 16, 20; Peret 1998, pp. 47, 157; Martin 1988, p. 177; Bossis 1972, p. 136; Dehergne 1963, p. 23: Gerard 1990, p. 55.

down ever more of the peasants' labour to the soil – by dint of overlapping forms of tenancy and remunerated work – generated much wealth for the landed classes. This form of appropriation did not involve the calculation of labour costs, the competitive pressure to reduce them, or the accumulation of surpluses.

The rental agreements of the Lyonnais, Poitou, and Berry, drawn up for the benefit of merchants, office holders and nobles, had traditional, quasi-feudal, arrangements for the payment of seigneurial dues, and for labour services carting agricultural goods to market or to the landowner's table in the towns. They contained many indications that the tenants were bound to the soil in debts they could never redeem. Leases spelled out traditional methods and crop rotations, and restricted the lands for seeding through binding rotations of grains and fallows so as to prevent soil exhaustion. The landowners and their stewards did not worry much about meagre harvests, because these increased the value of their supplies of wheat. Besides, customary rotations suited the purpose of ensuring that the crops amenable to seigneurial dues would be available at harvest time. As the eighteenth century wore on, the leases obliged the tenants to cede more and more, over half in some cases, of their harvests and gave the proprietors little reason to accumulate livestock, stables, fields of fodder crops, and other forms of constant capital. The economy showed no evidence of capitalist cycles of accumulation, in which, according to Marx, '... a part of the annual surplus labour must have been applied to the production of additional means of production and subsistence ...'[29]

This extractive, non-capitalist sort of feudal landlordism also prevailed in the Paris Basin. Heller makes much of Moriceau's research, but what does it actually indicate? Moriceau claims that wheat yields grew 10 to 25 percent in various parts of the Paris Basin, and attained relatively high levels at the end of the eighteenth century, through improved rotations with fodder crops and the application of animal fertiliser. He claims, above all, that tenants accumulated two or three leases of large farms, and added horse-power to carting and

---

29   Marx 1990, p. 727; Couturier 1909, pp. 22, 288, 295–7; Guillemet, Pellegrin and Peret 1981,
      pp. 12, 14; Benoist 2005, p. 144; Louis (ed.) 1877–80, pp. 26, 70, 226–7; Remondiere 1894,
      pp. 74–6; Masse 1956, pp. 24, 28; Elie 2003, p. 236; Autexier 1947, pp. 85, 104, 145, 147–8, 169,
      195; Peret 1976, pp. 101, 132–3, 194, 225; Peret 1988, p. 16; Dehergne 1963, p. 45; Cathelineau
      1912, p. vii; Legal 1995, pp. 331–2, 348–9; Brossard and Delapoix de Freminville 1904–7, p. 51;
      Fournial and Gutton 1974–5, p. 10; Tomas 1968, p. 395; Tomas 1965, p. 116; Berger 1985, p. 178;
      Garnier 1982, pp. 363, 381; Vignon 1978, pp. 451–2; Dontenwill 1963, pp. 123, 127; Zeller 1990,
      p. 70; Gay 1967, p. 276; Gay 1955, pp. 36, 38–9; Surrault 1990, p. 197; Menault 1991, p. 118;
      Meuvret 1987, pp. 103–4.

ploughing, all with the intention of economising on farm buildings and hired labourers and thus of increasing profit.[30]

If one unpacks this research, one notices, first of all, that the tenants' large farms reached their maximum extent of about 200 hectares in 1675–99 but then diminished to 160–70 in 1775–99. This sequence resulted from the vagaries of the peasant-subsistence economy rather than cost-cutting responses to capitalist competition. Landlords were stuck with properties in the crisis of the seventeenth century – as the peasants could no longer make ends meet amid falling prices – but then sold property to peasants willing to take on debts, deploy additional family labour, and wring more from the land as prices rose in the eighteenth century.[31]

Second, looking at Moriceau's figures, one sees that 35 percent of the large holdings of the tenant farmers remained fallow down to the end of the *ancien régime*. Such a vast area plainly shows the lack of capital accumulation. It shows that farmers did not put into practice the interconnected undertakings that made up the hallmark of early modern agricultural revolutions. Specifically, the tenants did not replace fallow with nitrogen-restoring fodder crops, build stables, rear livestock, amass manure fertiliser, and expand the arable surface for the purpose of accruing surpluses and cutting relative costs.[32]

Third, the yields documented by Moriceau resulted from the growth of the market and population, not capitalist development. Feudal lords of the thirteenth century, at a time of population increase and the growth of the urban market, did not accumulate means of production, but rather non-capitalist modes of accumulation. They extracted additional labour, output and revenue from the peasantry. The lords secured profit by enhancing their domination of the rural population and thereby actually contributed to the depletion of the agricultural capital.[33]

One observes the same tendency in the eighteenth century. Arthur Young, the most respected agricultural writer of the time, remarked,

> The greatest fabrics ... are the cottons and woollens of Normandy, the woollens of Picardy and Champagne, the linens of Bretagne, and the silks and hardware of the Lyonnois. Now, if manufactures be the true encour-

30   Moriceau 1994a, pp. 33–4, 50–1, 53, 58; Moriceau 1994b, pp. 460–1, 631, 635, 640–3, 659–60, 779–80; Moriceau and Postei-Vinay 1992, pp. 172–3, 184–5. 191–5, 197–8, 204–6, 209–12, 318, 322.
31   Moriceau 1994b, p. 631; Jacquart 1975, pp. 362–5, 373–5.
32   Moriceau 1994b, p. 640.
33   Brenner 2007, pp. 50–1.

agement of agriculture, the vicinity of those great fabrics ought to be the best cultivated districts in the kingdom. I have visited all of those manufactures, and remarked the attendant culture, which is unexceptionably so execrable, that one would be much more inclined to think there was something pestiferous to agriculture in the neighbourhood of a manufacture, than to look up to it as a mean of encouragement.[34]

The proliferation of smallholders and their critical need for income led farm managers to squeeze extra labour out of the peasantry for intensive hoeing and tilling in the pursuit of extra output for the Paris market. This extractive landlordism explains the yields recorded by Moriceau. Jean-Michel Chevet has gone over Moriceau's evidence and shown that it does not demonstrate the consolidation of landholdings. He has shown, significantly, that Moriceau's evidence does not indicate the addition of horse power and improved ploughing. Moreover, the tenant farmers used more labourers, not fewer, in the herding of sheep and the harvesting of oats and hay. Chevet has shown, in short, that the tenant farmers controlled the labour of peasant families and communities and thus did not have to calculate and curtail their costs through investment in constant capital. For this reason, the profitable crop-growing detailed by Moriceau coincided with the abysmal state of agriculture noticed by Young.[35] Fourth, Gerard Beaur has also gone over Moriceau's findings and pointed out that Moriceau's typical tenant farmer did not amass surpluses. In contrast to this distinguishing feature of capitalists, as described by Marx in the chapter of *Capital* titled 'Money, or the Circulation of Commodities', the tenant farmer depleted his profits in an apparently fierce quest for land. The tenant undertook risk, used up revenues, even went into debt, and sterilised investment so as to secure landholdings for the maximum number of offspring. He adhered to a traditional economic logic of assuring social respectability for his sons.[36]

Lastly and most importantly, the body of research on the Paris Basin, beyond Moriceau's, a long list of empirical studies, points to traditional seigneurial relations, not to an emergent capitalist agriculture. In the eighteenth century, as the rural population and grain prices increased, landlords were in a powerful position to force extra work from peasant families. They added many stipula-

---

34   Young 1969, pp. 432–3.
35   Chevet 1994, pp. 118–19, 123–7, 136, 138–9; Beaur 1996, p. 374. For Young's negative assessment of farming in the Paris Basin, see Young 1969, pp. 14, 267, 299, 307, 441–2.
36   Beaur 1996, pp. 381–3, 385.

tions of a feudal character to leases with the aim of extracting produce, work and money. Peasants often had to provide the landlord with seigneurial dues, fruit from gardens, and chickens or other animals on Christmas Day. Leases had stipulations for rents in kind and in money, and often resembled debts forcing the lessee to submit to all sorts of burdens, such as obligatory carting services, hardly distinguishable from medieval servitudes and the feudal corvees.[37]

The tenant farmers of the Paris Basin resembled seigneurial stewards more than they did rural capitalists. They threw their weight around in the lord's name, managed his farms, hired local labourers, engaged artisans, collected dues, and stored grain for charity, wages and other sorts of influence. They often held the peasantry in debt and benefited from the lord's tax privileges. Landowners and their stewards relied on traditional leasing practices to appropriate extra work and produce from the peasantry and thus to profit from rising grain prices. They did not build up stocks of nitrogen-restoring fodder, facilities for animal rearing, and other means of production necessary to cut costs. The Paris Basin showed no evidence of a ceaseless drive toward more means of production, more commodities, and capital accumulation on an ever-greater scale.[38]

Class Conflict

The fact that the rural economy did not evolve according to a capitalist logic does not mean that we should eschew a dialectical approach to its study. One of the best recent works on the period shows the pervasiveness of class conflict. About 8,500 popular revolts shaped the period from 1660 to 1789. Nearly 40 percent of them targeted the royal tax farms, not to mention hundreds of further revolts against direct taxes.[39] Royal taxation, we have seen, was crucial to the class relations in redistributing revenue from peasant communities to aristocrats of the royal court, as well as to noble and bourgeois investors in state bonds and offices. It sustained the royal judiciary and army, which, in turn,

---

37   Jacquart 1974, pp. 272–4, 757–8; Jacquart 1975 pp. 359, 362–3; Lejosne 1989, pp. 61–2; Parker 1996, pp. 63–4; Venard 1957, pp. 72–3, 83; Mireaux 1958, pp. 112–13; Loutchisky 1933, pp. 141–2; Fromont 1907, pp. 522, 526–7, 578–9.

38   Bouton 1993, pp. 44–5; Beaur 1996, pp. 381–3, 385; Mireaux 1958, pp. 117–18, 120–1; Aymard 1988, pp. 222, 225; Fromont 1907, pp. 517, 519; Jacquart 1974, p. 317; Grantham 1978, pp. 332–3; Ado 1996, pp. 57–8. George Comninel provides a good description of this non-capitalist commercial agriculture of the Paris Basin; see Comninel 1987, pp. 183–93.

39   Nicolas 2002, pp. 29, 56, 12.

upheld the entire complex of seigneurial domination. The revolts obviously limited the monarchy's options as it sought to cope with financial difficulties and keep the regime afloat in the 1780s.

Bread riots, though not as common as fiscal revolts, grew in number over the course of the eighteenth century, especially in the Paris Basin. They occurred more often in the towns than in the countryside. The riots not only speak to the failure of agriculture to raise output sufficiently to bring down relative food prices. They also speak to the trends of population growth, the subdivision of landholdings, the inability of households to make ends meet on tiny farms, their movement into labour-intensive lines of cash crops, and their growing reliance on tenancy, sharecropping and day labour. Although the peasants increased output, they still grew more dependent on grain markets for their subsistence. They undoubtedly found it unjust that landlords took saleable crops from increasingly oppressive terms of tenancy, wage labour and seigneurial rights.[40]

Most importantly, the popular revolts show that the passing of time did not change the character of violent episodes. The cohesion of the common people remained everywhere the norm. Village solidarities persisted. The peasants had not seen their work abstracted from the community of human experience into a variable component of capital.[41]

Conclusion

In Heller's view, the line of argument of Beik and Parker, by neglecting the development of the bourgeoisie in early modern France, abets the revisionist challenge to the idea that the revolution of 1789 was bourgeois and capitalist. I would argue, however, that currently the main focus in early modern and revolutionary studies is not, as Heller argues, '... to attack the idea that the revolution was a bourgeois and capitalist revolution'.[42] On the contrary, the latest Penguin history of eighteenth-century France, a work of over 600 pages, fully supports the idea of bourgeois revolution. Like Heller's 'The Long Durée of the French Bourgeoisie', it focuses on the dynamism of *ancien régime* society.[43]

Liberal and Marxist historians, Heller states, long had argued that 1789 was a bourgeois and capitalist revolution. Today it is the liberals who revive this

40   Nicolas 2002, pp. 227, 252–3.
41   Nicolas 2002, pp. 76–7; Comninel 1987, p. 193.
42   Heller 2010, p. 132.
43   Jones 2003.

thesis. In fact, the only common theme discernible in the recent historiography is not a rejection of bourgeois and capitalist revolution so much as an aversion to class analysis or conflict. The latest Penguin history leaves aside the seigneurial regime and gives no indication that the political actions of the 90 percent of the population residing in the countryside contributed in any way to the evolution of the country.[44]

As for the rural economy, the current consensus – represented by Philip Hoffman, whose work concurs in every respect with Moriceau's – is that a transition to capitalism requires no explanation whatsoever. Agriculture became productive when stimulated by the economic demand of the towns. Rural social history and conflict between peasants and lords have no place in the studies of Moriceau and Hoffman.[45]

Market dynamism and bourgeois revolution permit liberal historians to present the essential relations of capitalism without any explanation, as the inherent response to prospects for gain. The social structures, which beget inequality and poverty, need not concern historians, who can assume them to have developed naturally as unfortunate results of progress. This is the current consensus which Marxists ought to challenge.[46]

---

44   Heller 2009, pp. 33, 36; Heller 2010, p. 132; Jones 2003.
45   Mouriceau 1994b, pp. 54, 72; Hoffman 1996, pp. 144–6.
46   Heller 2009, pp. 33, 36; Heller 2010, p. 132; Comninel 1987, pp. 192–3.

CHAPTER 9

Stephen Miller on Capitalism in the Old Regime: A Response

The relationship between the *ancien régime* and the French Revolution lies at the core of the dispute between Stephen Miller and myself. At the conclusion of his critique Miller announces the startling news that liberal historians like himself accept the view that the French Revolution was bourgeois and capitalist. On the other hand, lest I pop the champagne too soon, Miller hastily offers a caveat. Liberal historians accept that the revolution was bourgeois and capitalist but do not accept that class and class-conflict were primary factors behind the revolution.[1] However if class and class-struggle had little or nothing to do with the revolution it would seem incumbent on him to suggest some other explanation for the transition from feudalism and aristocratic rule to capitalism and bourgeois dominance that even he agrees marked the revolution. Adding to the puzzle, a page earlier Miller acknowledges that class conflict was chronic in the period from 1660 until 1780, embodying an ongoing struggle between peasants and plebeians and seigneurial and state power.[2]

This might have provided the basis for an explanation. But Miller refuses to explore the connection between such struggles in the *ancien régime* and the revolution or even to logically reconcile his own contradictory assertions regarding class conflict. The objective of his piece is rather to try to insist on the non-capitalist nature of the whole French countryside so as to forestall the idea that a bourgeoisie might have assumed leadership over the peasant revolution.[3]

Marx argued otherwise, asserting that the bourgeoisie who led the revolution arose dialectically within feudal society. Although study of Marx is today experiencing a revival, the view still lingers that his understanding of history is dépassé, that 'new', 'archivally'-based scholarship has long since superseded his work. Marx in fact extensively studied the scholarly works and published documents of the French Revolution, and, more importantly, brought to bear on them unequalled theoretical insight.[4] On the question of the capitalist and bourgeois nature of the revolution his most valuable observations are to be

---

1 Miller 2012, p. 155.
2 Miller 2012, p. 154.
3 Miller 2012, p. 145.
4 Lowy 1989.

found in Volume One of the *Theories of Surplus Value*, the so-called fourth volume of *Capital* referred to by him as the historical, historico-critical or historical-literary part of *Capital*.[5] In this work Marx attributes the discovery of surplus value in the sphere of production to the Physiocrats, whose

> system is presented as the new capitalist society prevailing within the framework of feudal society. This therefore corresponds to bourgeois society in the epoch when the latter breaks its way out of the feudal order. Consequently, the starting-point is in France, in a predominantly agricultural country, and not in England, a predominantly industrial, commercial and seafaring country.[6]

In England where capitalism was already highly developed, the attention of economic thinkers like Adam Smith was focused on circulation. In France, on the contrary, the sudden rise to prominence of capitalist relations of production in agriculture prompted the Physiocrats to recognise that the source of surplus-value lay in the exploitation of agricultural workers. Some of the Physiocrats, reflecting the interests of the bourgeoisie, went so far as to urge that taxes be imposed on rent and not on profit-generating activity since, they argued, rent was the only real form in which the surplus was embodied. According to Marx, this position anticipated the legislation of the French Revolution.[7]

In Marx's view, then, the decisive arena in which capitalism developed and the capitalist bourgeoisie emerged was the countryside, and he saw this occurring in France prior to the revolution, just as he describes the earlier breakthrough of capitalism in sixteenth-century rural England in the eighth part of the first volume of *Capital*. In putting forward this perspective, Marx was especially influenced by Turgot who, alongside Quesnay, was the most influential of the Physiocrats. Turgot was aware of the evolution of France toward capitalism and attempted to theorise it within the terms of a society which was still politically and socially feudal. Never quite abandoning his Physiocratic assumptions, which stressed the importance of agriculture, Turgot nonetheless arrived at the view that value or wealth derived from the surplus labour of workers which produced capitalist profit both in agriculture and manufacturing. In his principal work, the *Reflexions sur La formation et la distribution des richesses* (1766), Turgot repeatedly underlines his fealty to the basic principles

---

5   Marx 1963, p. 13.

6   Marx 1961, p. 50.

7   Marx 1963, p. 52.

of Physiocratic doctrine. Nonetheless, in a backwards and forwards fashion, he moves toward recognition of the value-creating potential of both industry and agriculture, of the essential role of capital to the activity of both farmers and manufacturers, and to the common condition of both agricultural and industrial workers in competition to sell their labour to employers in return for a wage.[8] The primary focus in Turgot's work becomes not land as a material entity which produces wealth but capital as a value which attempts to expand and realise itself whether in farming or manufacture.[9] While Turgot harked back to the original Physiocratic definition of wealth as the net product from agriculture at various points in the *Reflections*, he increasingly acknowledged the role of the category of profit in capitalist activity.[10] Turgot also underscored that the more productive and advanced form of farming based on capitalism had become prevalent throughout the north of France.[11] Turgot's economic principles, we conclude – like those of other French theorists of the time – was a reflection and theorisation of the new capitalist relations which had begun to emerge and which he hoped would develop further.

Both Turgot and Marx believed that in the eighteenth century a capitalist bourgeoisie had emerged among the farmers of northern France. The source of their wealth was the exploitation of the labour of rural wage workers. Jean-Marc Moriceau's thesis on the farmers of the île-de-France offers an important historical reinforcement of this viewpoint.[12] According to Moriceau, it was in the latter part of the sixteenth century that an elite of wealthier peasants first consolidated itself as a stratum of capitalist tenant-farmers in the île-de-France. Already endowed with some land, tools and cash reserves, they leased farms held by the nobility and Church while using the wage labour of their hard-pressed neighbours.[13] During the heyday of the Bourbon absolutist state in the seventeenth century, family solidarity and the strict rationalisation of operations made it possible for many of these farmers to sustain profits in the face of increased taxes and rents while preparing the way for the great prosperity and expansion of their power in the next century. Among notable improvements introduced by such farmers were a successful consolidation of land holdings, a greater degree of specialisation, more intensive manuring, and

---

8   Morilhat 1988, pp. 158–9, 164, 168–9, 171.
9   Morilhat 1988, pp. 156, 173–4.
10   Morilhat 1988, pp. 167–8.
11   Turgot 1898, p. 24.
12   Moriceau 1994a.
13   Moriceau 1994a, pp. 145–351.

greater traction through improved harnessing of animal draught power.[14] By the beginning of the eighteenth century this elite had engrossed the greater part of the land in the île-de-France and had reduced the majority of producers to wage workers.

These rich peasants lobbied in favour of a free market in grain as introduced by Turgot during his brief tenure as minister of finance in the 1770s. They organised production using their own tools and equipment and employed a workforce paid in wages. Based on their operations, they derived a profit and as a result paid their landlords what amounted to a capitalist rent.[15] Indeed, the farmers of such enterprises had to pay not only these rents, but usually also seigneurial dues, taxes, and tithes. But since their farms were on fertile lands that were close to good roads and towns, they were able to take advantage of high prices and to enjoy profitable returns. They often enhanced their revenues by farming ecclesiastical tithes and seigneurial obligations. As such, the incomes of such farmers were made up of both capitalist profits and feudal rents, something that Miller finds perplexing. Through their business and social connections and their lifestyle, these farmers constituted part of the bourgeoisie alongside those of the middle class who lived in the surrounding bourgs and towns.[16] Peasant differentiation, including the existence of a rural capitalist bourgeoisie that dominated the rest of the rural population, is something else that Miller has difficulty coming to terms with.

Looking for a moment at northern France as a whole, this elite of wealthy farmers constituted a smaller fraction of a more numerous and broader group of prosperous peasant ploughmen or labourers. On a lesser scale than the wealthy farmers, they, too, hired wage labour and loaned grain, ploughs, wagons, and money to their less well-off neighbours. As such, they, too, were part of an emergent class of rural capitalists. More generally we can say that the French countryside, especially in the north, saw a halting and tentative progress toward capitalist relations in agriculture and the development of an agrarian bourgeoisie.[17] Moriceau notes that in the île-de-France and over much of the rest of the north of France genuine agricultural improvement took place. Especially in regions close to cities that were affected by new agronomic ideas and by the growing availability of manure, productivity significantly increased in the second half of the eighteenth century.[18]

---

14   Moriceau 1994a, pp. 611–23, 631–42.
15   Ado 1996, p. 51.
16   Moriceau 1994a, pp. 703–69; Moriceau 1989, pp. 46–7.
17   Ado 1996, p. 53.
18   Moriceau 1994b.

Undermining Moriceau's perspective is the principal objective of Miller's critique, bent as he is on showing that capitalism did not exist in France prior to the revolution. Miller claims that the large estates of the nobility were not the result of primitive accumulation but rather of defaults due to the widespread abandonment of the land in the crisis of the late seventeenth century.[19]

Apparently Miller does not realise that defaults which were the result of economic crisis as well as other factors like heavy rents and taxes and violence are at the crux of the long-term historical process of primitive accumulation. Miller does seem to be aware that this process of primitive accumulation was not confined to the late seventeenth century but went on from the sixteenth through the eighteenth century.[20] But it is a process the consequences of which he refuses to engage with or outright denies in the name of the idea of the peasant's persistent and enduring connection to the land. Despite his attempts to cover up the results of expropriation by pointing to the partial comeback of small property in the eighteenth century,[21] the overall result of the secular process of primitive accumulation was an unprecedented concentration of property in the hands of rich farmers and the transformation of most of the producers into full or part-time wage earners.

Miller's pointing-out of the persistence of small holdings in the île-de-France is part of his attempt to assimilate agriculture in the north to that of the Midi. His account of the latter is rooted in Chayanovian conceptions of a sempiternal economy of subsistence and *Annaliste* notions of neo-Malthusian cycles that have nothing to do with capitalist development but rather are redolent of the conservative populist ideology of the agrarian myth.[22] In fact he would do better to understand the evolution of the situation in the Paris basin and elsewhere in France by developing Kautsky's insight into the historic and persistent role of small farmers in supplying wage labour to larger agricultural enterprises – the secret of the long-term survival of this stratum and one of the keys opening the door to an understanding of the evolution of feudalism and capitalism in France and Continental Europe and indeed in the rest of the world.[23] As a matter of fact, Kautsky's views have become part of a sophisticated attempt to redefine the complicated and ever-changing relationship between the exploitation of wage and non-wage labour in the history of capitalism.[24]

---

19   Miller 2012, p. 146.
20   Miller 2012, pp. 145–6.
21   Miller 2012, p. 148.
22   Brass 2000.
23   Kautsky 1988, pp. xiii–xvi.
24   Brass 2011.

STEPHEN MILLER ON CAPITALISM IN THE OLD REGIME: A RESPONSE   125

All the more so as Miller is at pains to insist that 'if one looks at the period from the middle ages to the nineteenth century, one notices that the peasantry made available landless labourers and paupers, but not proletarian labour-power'.[25] Evidently this included the majority of the French rural population, since Miller is forced to admit that in the eighteenth century 'only a minority had the land and livestock to avoid reliance on wages ...'[26]

For Miller, the essence of the accumulation of capital is the generation of increasing amounts of surplus value as a result of the creation of more and more relative surplus value attendant on the progressive substitution of fixed capital for variable capital – a process driven by market competition. Such a transformation is evident in England but not in France, according to Miller.[27]

Actually, accumulation in the first instance involves an increase in the amount of both fixed and variable capital employed by capitalists and in this light the farmers of the Paris basin were undoubtedly capitalists. The substitution of relative surplus for absolute surplus value, which is never complete, is a by-product of this process and in this respect there is no doubt that England was ahead of France especially in the eighteenth century. On the other hand, that there was also agricultural progress in the île-de-France, as noted above, is unquestionable. In a selective and tendentious way Miller brings forward the research of Jean-Michel Chevet on the île-de-France to try to suggest that Moriceau is wrong on all counts.[28] Interesting as Chevet's research is, it does not cast into doubt the radical polarisation between landholding and the land-less and the concomitant process of accumulation as outlined by Moriceau. It merely questions the latter's understanding of how one measures gains in pro-ductivity. Even so, Chevet reaches the important conclusion that the eighteenth century saw a fifty percent gain in the productivity of agricultural workers.[29]

Miller offers a backhanded compliment by noting that my account of prim-itive accumulation at least has the merit of arguing that the inception of sixteenth-century capitalism was the unintentional result of religious viol-ence and seigneurial reaction rather than Moriceau's view that it was the con-sequence of the intentional logic of growing market demand.[30] In fact I argued that both factors helped to initiate capitalist accumulation. In any case, Miller condemns me for hitching my wagon to Moriceau whom he dismisses as being

---

25   Miller 2012, p. 145.
26   Miller 2012, p. 150. The pervasiveness of wage labour is stressed in Heller 2006, pp. 46–7.
27   Miller 2012, pp. 143–4.
28   Chevet 1994.
29   Chevet 1994, p. 140.
30   Miller 2012, p. 144.

unapologetically Smithian in his account of the inception and development of capitalism.[31] In fact Miller misrepresents Moriceau's approach, in which the ongoing influence of his training in the Annales school is evident, embracing in its striving for total history human geography, technological innovation, demography, family history, class and class-struggle as well as the history of primitive accumulation and capitalist accumulation proper and finally the role of the market to explain the long-term development of capitalism in the Paris basin. It is doubly ironic that in his conclusion Miller insists that today historians are concerned with the dynamism of the Old Regime rather than the revolution.[32] For while his own view is marked by a sense of historical immobility, the discounted Moriceau, as editor of the vanguard *Histoire et societes rurales*, has placed himself in the lead in creating a new kind of rural history which is interested in the long-term evolution of the French countryside – a history which includes its capitalist phase but predates it and is a history not of stasis but of movement.[33]

---

31   Miller 2012, p. 145.
32   Miller 2012, p. 155.
33   Moriceau 2002.

CHAPTER 10

Marx, the French Revolution, and the Spectre of the Bourgeoisie

Revisionism has been the dominant trend in the study of the French Revolution since the 1970s. This is especially the case in the English-speaking countries, but its influence is felt as well in France as a result of the authority of François Furet. As is well known, the object of revisionism has been to challenge the long-established Marxist view of the revolution. The Marxist school of historians, which included Albert Mathiez, Georges Lefebvre and Albert Soboul, flourished in the first part of the twentieth century. It looked upon the revolution as a bourgeois revolution whose power was based on the development of capitalism in the eighteenth century. In a multitude of ways revisionists have attempted to deny the significance of the bourgeoisie and capitalism in the revolution. They have questioned the link between the two terms. They have cast doubt on the strength of both capitalism and the bourgeoisie. Some have even sought to deny the meaning of the terms. Finally they have questioned the significance of the revolution to French history, which, it is claimed, is a history of continuity rather than change.

Among prominent historians who continue to defend the Marxist view has been Michel Vovelle. In his recent work *Les mots de la Revolution*, Vovelle puts forward the following assessment of the still evolving character of the bourgeoisie at the time of the revolution:

> It is a bourgeoisie of a mixed sort. It associates the 'self-defined' rentier bourgeoisie with the representatives of the commercial bourgeoisie which is beginning to become industrial and is connected to the world of services.

This balanced view of the evolving and changing nature of the bourgeoisie allows Vovelle to conclude: 'With due caution and with a consciousness of the evolution of language it does not misrepresent things to maintain the classic designation of the revolutionary historiography of the French Revolution of a bourgeois revolution based on popular support'.[1]

---

1 Vovelle 2004, p. 16.

Revisionism has multiple and contradictory threads, as I have noted. Some adherents have argued that capitalism was weak or even that it did not exist. Others allow that it was strong but derailed or retarded rather than advanced by the revolution. Still others argue that capitalism had nothing to do with the revolution. As for the leading role of the bourgeoisie, it has been asserted by revisionists that this class was non-capitalist, or even that the nobility rather than the bourgeoisie were capitalism's *avant-garde*. The implication of the latter point is that the overthrow of this class was in retrospect a retrograde step.[2] Such revisionist arguments have in common their focus on trying to refute the social and economic aspects of the Marxist interpretation of the revolution.

The present chapter focuses on cultural revisionism, an approach pioneered by Furet. Turning his back on attempts to explain the revolution's causes by trying to tie together a multiplicity of factors including the social and economic, Furet and other cultural revisionists lay emphasis on the development of a radical political culture which had its own internal momentum and logic. A cataclysmic event like the revolution could not have been the result of the mere oscillations or cycles of French social and economic history as detailed *ad infinitum* by the Annales school. To the contrary, the revolution was the consequence of a fundamental cultural and ideological shift. In consequence, historical understanding comes through the hermeneutical analysis of the new revolutionary discourses, political cultures, and identities which in themselves are seen as the causal agents of this transformation.

Perhaps the foremost advocate in France of this view is Mona Ozouf, who with Furet is the editor of a revisionist historical encyclopedia entitled *Dictionnaire critique de la Revolution française* (1988). Ozouf has been described as a sentinel who guards the gates against the intrusion of any kind of social explanation that could contaminate the closed realm of discourse analysis. For Ozouf all attempts to link discourse to social and economic forces are arbitrarily dismissed as discredited, inherently constraining, and reductionist.[3] As the Marxist school perhaps did not pay sufficient attention to the creation of a new revolutionary and republican culture, this current of revisionism in reaction has gained credibility among some historians who take seriously the importance of culture. This line of interpretation gains intellectual credibility from the fact that all parties agree that the revolution represented a change of epic proportions. The depth of cultural transformation inherent in this profound event, it is then argued, cannot be reduced to economic and social factors. Not only can this momentous event not be reduced to the socioeconomic, argue these

---

2   Heller 2006, pp. 9–23.
3   Kaplan 1995, pp. 54, 61–2.

revisionists, but the socioeconomic is essentially irrelevant to it. Without the existence of a revolutionary political culture, revolution cannot occur regardless of the socioeconomic context. Hence a spate of historical work on the political culture of the revolution, which de-emphasises or deliberately ignores the material basis of the upheaval.

Never mind that Marxists have always insisted that analysing political consciousness or the so-called subjective factor in politics is indispensable to understanding the occurrence of revolutionary change. Without the development of a revolutionary politics and consciousness, there is no revolution. But, however indispensable, political consciousness is not a sufficient condition for a revolution, according to Marxists. In a balanced way, they have generally stressed that the strength of political consciousness – revolutionary or otherwise – must be related to the social and economic context. Ideology and culture by themselves could never induce a revolution. Nor could merely material factors bring about a revolution, which by definition entails a political and ideological transformation. It is a combination of material and non-material factors that lie behind a revolution. Accordingly, Marxists insist that the social and economic context was far from irrelevant to the French Revolution.

Cultural Revisionism

Thus, from the Marxist point of view the French Revolution was quintessentially the result of the developing strength of the bourgeoisie as a class in itself and for itself. Put simply, the bourgeoisie developed both as a class economically and socially and in terms of its consciousness of itself. Given the maturation of this class during the eighteenth century, it was able to seize political power by revolutionary means in the crisis of 1789. To the contrary a preoccupation with discourse in the case of some cultural revisionists has led to a virtual flight from historical and material reality toward a pure idealism. A case in point is an American historian of the revolution with more than a little creditability, Sarah Maza, who denies the economic and social development of the bourgeoisie as a class as a factor in the French Revolution. Fixing on the development of bourgeois consciousness of itself as a class and, indeed, fetishising the term 'bourgeoisie', she insists that the French Revolution was not a bourgeois revolution.

In her recent book, *The Myth of the French Bourgeoisie*, Maza makes her central thesis the memorable notion 'that the French bourgeoisie did not exist'.[4]

---

4   Maza 2003, p. 5.

Justifying this position, Maza asserts her belief 'that language is not passive but performative: identities are constructed by the cultural elements they
absorb and then articulate as individual and collective stories'.[5] Designating
this approach cultural constructionism, Maza insists 'that the thesis of bourgeois nonexistence derives from my belief that classes only exist if they are
aware of their own existence'.[6] According to her account, there is no sign of
a sense of the bourgeoisie as a class in French discourse until after 1820, and
then mainly in a negative sense. As such, the existence of a bourgeois class was
largely mythical. It follows that there was no bourgeois revolution in France. In
taking this position, Maza evidently seeks to put a last nail in the coffin of the
Marxist interpretation of the revolution.

Marx and Classical Republicanism

In my view it certainly is important whether or not there existed a notion
of the bourgeoisie as a class at the time of the revolution. The existence of
such a concept is in part related to the actual strength of that class in French
society. But the existence of the concept ought to be properly considered in
conjunction with the question as to whether or not such a class had a social
and economic basis in French society rooted in profit-making commercial and
industrial activity. In other words, the existence of such a class for itself goes
hand-in-hand with its existence as a class in itself.[7] If there was such a class
in France that carried through the revolution, we should expect that it would
make its weight felt politically and socially and that contemporaries furthermore would be aware of and refer to its existence. On the other hand, it would
be quite wrong to allow our discussion to fixate merely on whether or not the
term 'bourgeoisie' was or was not employed by contemporaries. We should not
view the use or non-use of the term 'bourgeoisie' as determining our understanding of the historical reality. On the contrary, Maza herself seems obsessed
with the currency or not of a term which she fetishises or endows with a life
of its own. Other terms such as 'middle class', 'capitalists' or even 'merchants
and bankers' should properly be considered as evidence for the existence of a
bourgeoisie in the Marxist sense. Moreover, we should realise that along with
all other aspects of French society language itself was undergoing rapid change

5   Ibid., pp. 6–7.
6   Ibid. p. 6.
7   Heller 2006.

during this tumultuous period. The appearance or disappearance of the notion of a bourgeois class had a great deal to do with the evolution of the politics of the revolution.[8] Moreover, it should constantly be borne in mind that the term 'class' is always as much a political as an economic and social one. In this perspective, to speak of a bourgeois class is to speak of it in opposition to other classes and in terms of an evolving historical and political context.[9]

In undertaking this critique of Maza's denial of the French Revolution as a bourgeois revolution it is only fitting to begin with the views of Karl Marx, the foremost proponent of the idea of bourgeois revolution. As is well known, Marx inherited his notion of bourgeois revolution from earlier historians like Augustin Thierry, Francois-Auguste Mignet and François Guizot.[10] He most fully asserted his conception of the French Revolution as a bourgeois revolution in the celebrated and poetic opening passages of *The Eighteenth Brumaire of Louis Napoleon*. We find there a view of the revolution which at first sight is surprisingly congruent with that of Maza:

> Men make their own history, but they do not make it just as they please; they do not make it under circumstances chosen by themselves, but under circumstances directly encountered, given and transmitted from the past. The tradition of all the dead generations weighs like a nightmare on the brain of the living. And just when they seem engaged in revolutionising themselves and things, in creating something that has never yet existed, precisely in such periods of revolutionary crisis they anxiously conjure up the spirits of the past to their service and borrow from them names, battle-cries and costumes in order to present the new scene of world history in this time-honoured disguise and this borrowed language. Thus Luther donned the mask of the Apostle Paul, the revolution of 1789 to 1814 draped itself alternately as the Roman Republic and the Roman Empire, and the revolution of 1848 knew nothing better to do than to parody, now 1789, now the revolutionary tradition of 1793 to 1795 ...

> Consideration of this world-historical necromancy reveals at once a salient difference. Camille Desmoulins, Danton, Robespierre, Saint-Just, Napoleon, the heroes as well as the parties and the masses of the old French Revolution, performed the task of their time in Roman costume

---

8   Lafargue, 1894; Guilhamou, 1989; Guilhamou, 1989a.

9   Camfield 2004.

10   Nygaard, 2007, p. 154.

and with Roman phrases, the task of unchaining and setting up modern *bourgeois* society. The first [of these heroes] knocked the feudal basis to pieces and mowed off the feudal heads which had grown on it. The last [of these, Napoleon] created inside France the conditions under which free competition could first be developed, parcelled landed property, exploited and unchained the industrial productive forces of the nation, and beyond the French borders everywhere swept the feudal institutions away, so far as was necessary to furnish bourgeois society in France with a suitable up-to-date environment on the European Continent. The new social formation once established, the antediluvian Colossi disappeared and with them resurrected Romanity – the Brutuses, Gracchi, Publicolas, the tribunes, the senators, and Caesar himself. Bourgeois society in its sober reality had begotten its true interpreters and mouthpieces in the Says, Cousins, Royer-Collards, Benjamin Constants and Guizots; its real commanders sat behind the counter, and the hogheaded Louis XVIII was its political chief. Wholly absorbed in the production of wealth and in peaceful competitive struggle, it no longer comprehended that ghosts from the days of Rome had watched over its cradle. But unheroic as bourgeois society is, it nevertheless took heroism, sacrifice, terror, civil war and battles of peoples to bring it into being. And in the classically austere traditions of the Roman Republic its gladiators found the ideals and the art forms, the self-deceptions that they needed in order to conceal from themselves the bourgeois limitations of the content of their struggles and to maintain their passion on the high plane of great historical tragedy.[11]

The importance of classical republicanism as the dominant ideology of the revolution has long been a commonplace of revolutionary historiography. But preoccupied by culture and ideology as it is, the recent historiography of the revolution is giving it renewed attention.[12] Unlike Marx, Maza fails to deal with the hegemony of classical republican ideology during the revolution. But in complete accord with Maza, it is noteworthy that Marx recognises that the revolutionaries of 1789 appear to have had no sense of themselves as champions of a bourgeois revolution. Based on his own extensive reading of the texts of the revolution, he observed that the revolutionary bourgeoisie had no consciousness of itself as a class in itself. Instead, right down through the Napo-

---

11   Marx 1978, pp. 103–4.
12   Monnier 1994, 2003, 2005, 2006.

leonic period they wrapped themselves in the heroic mantle of classical republicanism.[13] It is only in the aftermath that the heirs of the revolution began to
understand it as a bourgeois revolution. Maza and Marx apparently are in full
agreement and Maza's attack on Marx appears to be tilting at windmills.

Of course the real difference between Marx and Maza is not over the appearance of things but over what, if anything, lies below. According to Marx, the
protagonists of the revolution had an ideological or illusory sense of their
actions, based on the weight of tradition upon them. Marx characterises this
tradition of classical republicanism inherited from past generations negatively,
as a nightmare lying on the brains of the living. In any case, it is this classic
republican ideology inherited from the past that Marx sees as dominating consciousness during the revolution. It is this deeply political kind of thought that
helped obscure the social and economic realities of the revolution.[14] This is
a particularly celebrated illustration of Marx's notion of false consciousness.
Underneath this illusory surface lies Marx's bourgeois revolution, which only
rises to the surface to be consciously articulated in the aftermath of the revolution. Maza, on the contrary, is content with studying the surface of things.
Indeed, for her nothing exists apart from appearance. Nothing lies below or can
be abstracted from the way things appear. What is represented, namely culture,
engenders everything else.[15] On the face of things, then, she finds no ideology
of bourgeois revolution. In the absence of any apparent evidence of bourgeois
self-consciousness, she concludes that there was no bourgeoisie and no bourgeois revolution.

Marx's emphasis on the weight of tradition and the importance of false consciousness continues to make a certain amount of sense in the interpretation
of the French Revolution. In his view revolutionaries at first did not rationally
understand the consequences of their own actions. It is only when the smoke
cleared in the wake of the revolution that a realistic understanding of the significance of the event emerged. It has recently been suggested that Marx's notion
of bourgeois revolution must be understood in terms of his conception of the
central role of the state as the forcing house of bourgeois revolutionary transformation.[16] This insight helps to account for the prominence in the revolution
of this socially alienated political language of classical republicanism.

---

13   Boudon and Bourdion 2006.
14   Furet 1988, p. 25.
15   Maza 2003, pp. 3–4, 67, 163–4.
16   Nygaard, 2007, pp. 162–4.

Revolution and the Bourgeoisie

On the other hand, I will argue in opposition both to Maza and Marx that a sense of the bourgeoisie as a class and of a bourgeois revolution did develop in the immediate wake of the taking of the Bastille in 1789. In the early politically and socially tense years of the revolution, I will show, some revolutionaries did in fact understand the revolution in these political-economic terms. A Marxist understanding of the bourgeoisie as a class did not emerge. Nor should we expect it to. But the class conflicts and successive crises of the revolution led revolutionary leaders to begin to refer to the better-off among the supporters of the revolution as the bourgeois class. Moreover, the foundations of this class was understood to be its economic power. Further, I will argue that the decline of this kind of class-based discourse and its replacement by that of classical republicanism was not the result simply of the influence of the classical republican tradition, as Marx would have it. The weight or power of a certain tradition on consciousness is itself a historic circumstance that needs to be explained. Rather, the triumph of the ideology of classical republicanism came about in response to the specific and urgent political and social circumstances generated by the revolution. In particular, *the emergence of a language of class and of class conflict threatened bourgeois leadership over the revolution.*

The question is then whether at the time of the revolution a sense of the bourgeoisie as a class and of a bourgeois revolution existed. Contrary to the assertions of the revisionists, current research demonstrates the existence of economic foundations for the emergence of the eighteenth-century bourgeoisie as a class-in-itself.[17] In northern France, an increasingly well-off rural bourgeoisie consolidated itself prior to the revolution. Commerce, especially overseas trade, grew prodigiously during the eighteenth century. There was an enormous expansion of rural industries but also the beginning of a concentration of manufacture into mechanised factories. The bourgeoisie was the overwhelmingly dominant element in this economic advance, and the beneficiaries of it in the form of enhanced profit.[18] Moreover, this economic advance continued during the revolution when money was made through the seizure of land, war-profiteering and eventually a renewed expansion of trade and manufacturing.[19] In the revolutionary crisis that broke out in 1789, merchants and manufacturers strongly backed the National Assembly, which reflected their

---

17   Heller 2006, pp. 14–16.
18   Heller 2006, p. 53.
19   Heller 2006, pp. 27–37, 54–6, 133.

interests.[20] Bourgeois control of the state and cultural life after 1789 made that class stronger and more confidently aware of itself.[21]

Having however briefly established the existence in the revolution of the bourgeoisie as a class-in-itself, we must turn to the question of the degree of its existence as a class-for-itself. In order to do so, we must first assure ourselves as to whether or not people at the time had a sense of class, in the sense of society divided into economically differentiated social groups. Dallas Clouatre has shown that the notion of economic and social classes became widely prevalent from the middle of the eighteenth century onward. By the time of the revolution there was indeed a widespread sense that French society was divided into such classes. Contrariwise, the older notion of orders and estates which was rooted in the legal and political distinctions of the *ancien régime* was increasingly less used. The influence of the Physiocrats was particularly important in bringing about this change of perspective.[22] Indeed, the increasing use of economic categories was the result of the rise of a political-economic discourse in late eighteenth-century French society, which was related to the notion of the reform and renewal of the *ancien régime*.[23]

The notion of economic classes had thus developed prior to the revolution. On the other hand, although the word 'bourgeoisie' already had a long history, the concept of the bourgeoisie as constituting a class was not evident before the revolutionary crisis. The word 'bourgeoisie' prior to the revolution had varied connotations. It could refer to a member of the third estate, to a member of the ruling elite of a town or to one of its inhabitants or citizens. It could mean a person who lived off rent, someone engaged in contemptible economic activities, or someone who was a boss (who hired and employed the labour of others). Among these definitions the last would be closest to the Marxist conception. But the term 'bourgeois' had yet to be used to describe a social and economic class.[24] *It was the convulsions of the revolutionary process that would produce the sense of the bourgeoisie as a class.*

In the political debate prior to the meeting of the Estates-General the term 'bourgeoisie' was absent. It was rather the political-legal term third estate that occupied the foreground of discussion. By far the most popular expression of the claims of the so-called third estate was the Abbe Sieyès's *Qu'est-ce que le*

---

20   Heller 2006, pp. 71–9.

21   Heller 2006, 110–11, 127–9; Jessenne 2007, pp. 11–12.

22   Clouatre 1984, pp. 232–4; Shovlin 2006, p. 106; Piguet 1996, pp. 65, 87–8, 95.

23   Shovlin 2006, pp. 11–12, 50.

24   Piguet 1996, pp. 93–4.

Tiers-etat?.[25] This text is justly considered the foundational text of the elites who assumed leadership of the revolutionary process in the spring of 1789. In his manifesto Sieyès sought to present not the bourgeoisie but the commoners or mass of the non-privileged population making up the great majority of the French populace as the third estate. He put forward the notion of the commoners as the real nation united in their political demands against the privileged orders of the nobility and clergy. Sieyès's conception of the third estate was in part a strategic choice in response to the exigencies of the political situation. The nobility and clergy defended their privileges on the basis of their political and legal rights under the *ancien régime*. Sieyès, in reaction, advanced the demands of the commoners in the name of the third estate, which already had a definite legal and political existence within the context of the same regime. Made up of agriculturalists, those engaged in manufactures, those in trade and those devoted to providing services, these elements of the third estate stood together as constituents of the nation in opposition to the privileged orders. In Sieyès's conception, there is no distinction according to rank between members of these four groups of commoners. The class devoted to service, for example, includes domestic servants as well as lawyers and physicians.[26]

Faced with the obduracy of the nobility and clergy, it was evidently in Sieyès's interest to represent the third estate as united and socially equal. Indeed, Sieyès insisted that such unity should continue to be the case in a new political order based on representative rather than democratic government. In this representative order the so-called 'available class' made up of the leisured and educated among the commoners could effectively represent the rest.[27] It is evident that Sieyès's conception assumed that future leadership of the third estate would be permanently vested in educated members of the middle class. Not all agreed with him. An engineer with democratic proclivities, Louis Pierre Dufourny de Villiers, published *Les Cahiers de Quatrieme Ordre*, which appeared in April 1789, asking:

> Why is it that the immense class of day labourers, wage labourers, and un-employed, that class which has so many grievances to bring forward, why is it rejected from the midst of the nation? ... We belong to the third estate but not one of its representatives is from our class and it appears that everything has been done in favour of the rich.[28]

---

25   Sieyès 1970.
26   Sewell 1994, pp. 57, 58; Forsyth 1987, p. 85.
27   Sewell 1994, pp. 60, 68–9, 149–52; Forsyth 1987, p. 85; Sonenscher 2007, pp. 67–94.
28   Roux 1951, p. 259.

From the inception of the revolution, Dufourny de Villiers among others questioned the notion of a unified third estate by invoking the language of class to advance the claims of day labourers, labourers and the unemployed. If perhaps Dufourny de Villiers's sense of a working class is not quite the same as our own, it nonetheless represents a step in that direction. Moreover, we should note that the use of a language of class in this context was by its nature disruptive and was meant to be so.

Still, the use of the term 'bourgeoisie' in reference to a class was absent prior to the revolution of July 1789. But it appeared almost immediately after the upheaval. In the wake of the revolutionary violence of the summer, the restoration of order by the mobilisation of moderate and politically reliable supporters of the revolution became an urgent matter. A debate ensued in which a variety of opinions about the recruitment of a National Guard was offered. In a text dating from August 1789, an anonymous author openly avowed that he looked at the question of the recruitment of the National Guard from the perspective of the bourgeoisie. The document's author insisted that the Guard should be recruited exclusively from the bourgeoisie, none of whom should be exempt from serving. Those who would serve for wages (the lower orders) should be excluded. At the same time, the author insisted that the regime that has been established is that of equality.

> But it is an equality which agrees with that class which we form in the state, I mean, the Bourgeoisie: to whom it essentially and exclusively belongs. The same spirit, the same interest ties us together. Our families, our enterprises and our fortunes depend on our surveillance.[29]

According to this anonymous author, the new state is based on an equality from the perspective of the bourgeoisie who form a class within the state, indeed, to whom the state now belongs and who have a stake in preserving property and wealth. One could hardly wish for a more direct articulation of the notion of bourgeois revolution in the sense of a class assuming political control over the state and in particular its means of violence. This immediately throws into doubt Maza's notion that the sense of the bourgeoisie as a class or of a bourgeois revolution was unknown at the time of the revolution.

It should be said, however, that the forthright articulation of a notion like the one above was a rarity at that moment. In the early years of the revolution the idea of the bourgeoisie as a class was not common and the term's meaning was still up in the air. In 1791, for example, Adrien Duquesnoy used the term

---

29   Genty 1993, pp. 67–8.

'bourgeoisie' as an inclusive one to distinguish all the middling sort from both the great in society and the riff-raff and brigands. According to him, the people are made up of the bourgeoisie, of that mass of employed and virtuous men who are corrupted neither by opulence or misery. They are truly the nation, the people.[30] But in a revealing aside Duquesnoy admits that his use of the term bourgeoisie to refer to the middling sort is something of a novelty: 'I make use of the word bourgeois because at present there doesn't exist any other word which expresses my thought'.[31] Clearly the term 'bourgeoisie', like many others, was in flux and was in the process of being redefined or even invented in response to the social upheavals of the revolution. Duquesnoy understands the word as referring to all those who either by their labour or their legitimate possession of property produce means of existence. He excludes only those who do not work, 'those who are part of the court or that mass of brigands who are paid by them. The latter steal for a living, whether they are in rags or wear cloth of gold'.[32]

Duquesnoy's use of the term 'bourgeoisie' doesn't conform to any pre-revolutionary usage. In it there are still echoes of the term as referring to a member of the third estate or to the citizens of a town. But it is clear that he is using the term in a sense that passes beyond these pre-revolutionary usages. His inclusion of even those who work, including those who work for wages, clearly contradicts pre-revolutionary usage. In the latter case it was used to refer to a boss who employed labour, excluding those who might labour for wages. It suggests that Duquesnoy was interested in maintaining a sense of solidarity between employers and employees, especially as between the former and skilled workers.

The Economic Power of the Bourgeoisie

The complex evolution of the term 'bourgeoisie' is illustrated by its appearance in the writings of Joseph Antoine Barnave. Barnave, a lawyer with roots in the merchant class of Dauphiné, played a major role as a member of the National Assembly in the early years of the revolution. In a letter dating from October 1789, Barnave described the mobilisation of the Parisians that culminated in the march on Versailles. He distinguished the attitude of the bourgeoisie, who were

---

30   Gruner 1976, p. 415.
31   Ibid.
32   Ibid.

incensed at the King's obstruction of the work of the National Assembly, from that of the people, who he says were also agitated by the high price of bread.[33] In this case Barnave uses the term bourgeoisie to distinguish the upper class inhabitants of Paris from the lower class, whom he calls the people. Barnave is making a distinction which can be viewed as a familiar one under the *ancien régime*.

But in the following few years Barnave was able to extrapolate this usage to a more abstract level in which the term 'bourgeoisie', or its somewhat more abstract synonym 'middle class', undoubtedly refers to a class that has both an economic and a political existence. By 1793 Barnave had not only fallen from political grace but in fact sat in prison under the Terror. There he worked on a manuscript which was posthumously published as the *Introduction a la Revolution Française*.[34] Barnave had compromised himself by continuing to champion the cause of constitutional monarchy in the face of growing demands for the establishment of a political democracy and a republic.[35] Indeed, he was alarmed by the growing threat of popular government. Faced with increasing pressure for a democratic franchise in the wake of the King's flight to Varennes in June 1791, Barnave rejected the idea that participating in elections was a civic right. In a speech to the Legislative Assembly, he insisted that the right to vote should be reserved to the middle class (*classe mitoyenne*) which was educated, was more interested in public affairs and had independent economic means. According to Barnave, in the wake of the revolution only this class should have the right of suffrage.[36] A month earlier, Barnave had been at pains to forestall the end of the monarchy and the establishment of a republic. The king's attempted flight had opened the floodgates of demands for the establishment of a republic.[37] He denounced those who pointed to the American republic as a model which France should emulate. America is sparsely populated, has a large territory mainly devoted to agriculture and is not threatened by foreign rivals. As such, Barnave insisted, it is totally unlike France, which needs to remain a monarchy.[38]

In 1792 France moved toward the creation of the republic of which Barnave disapproved. Therefore, while acknowledging the economic causes of the rev-

---

33   Barnave 1906, p. 24.
34   Barnave 1971.
35   Bates 2001, p. 445.
36   Monnier 1989, p. 82; Chagny 1990, p. 142; Gueniffey 1990, p. 163.
37   Monnier 2003, pp. 93, 99–100.
38   Barnave 1971a, p. 11.

olution, he was bent on demonstrating that the middle class could not directly rule France by establishing a republic. Referring now to the bourgeoisie rather than to the middle class, Barnave acknowledged the possibility of rule by a new aristocracy, albeit a bourgeois and commercial aristocracy, arising from the triumph of industrial property: 'In small states the power of the people will allow it to become master of the government. A new aristocracy, a kind of bourgeois and merchant aristocracy, can arise from this new form of wealth'.[39] Elsewhere he explains that by aristocracy he means government by the rich.[40] But he insists that such a republican elite could only rule over small states like those in Italy. Political and military necessity, he argued, demanded that a great state like France continue to be ruled by a monarch, albeit a constitutional one:

> the progress of capital [*propiete mobiliere*] which is the element of demo-cracy and the cement of the unity of states in Europe has successively transformed all political regimes ... Where it has progressed the most ... it explodes assuming its place in government while establishing limited monarchy.[41]

Writing at the moment that the republic was taking shape in France, Barnave realistically discussed its prospects, while predicting its fracture into at best a federation of smaller republics.[42] Nonetheless, for our purposes, it is important to understand that his reference to a new aristocracy of a 'bourgeois' and industrial kind is not merely a dismissive reference to an insignificant Italian state but what was being increasingly discussed and advocated in France. Barnave's deployment of the term bourgeoisie still has the connotation of an urban ruling class in the fashion of the *ancien régime*. But used as an adjective in conjunction with the term industrial to describe a ruling political elite of the rich it takes on a meaning that transcends the usage of the *ancien régime*.

Barnave, as I have noted, had meanwhile used the term 'middle class' and insisted that this class alone should have political rights in France. Indeed, a contemporary to Barnave had already asserted that the revolution had been made by this class. In 1789 Philippe Antoine Grouvelle spoke of the middle class, 'a class insufficiently recognized', as 'the focal point of morality and public rationality out of which stems common sense, justice and liberty. The present

---

39   Barnave 1971, pp. 9–10.
40   Barnave 1842, p. 51.
41   Ibid., p. 14.
42   Barnave 1971, pp. 9–10.

revolution is its work and it is it which gives to it its moderate character'.[43] Grouvelle's middle class should certainly be taken as a synonym for the bourgeoisie.[44]

The Workers and the Bourgeoisie

Meanwhile, workers began to use the term 'bourgeoisie' in ways that passed beyond the simple idea of a boss or employer of labour, and began to approximate the notion of exploiter of labour and political master. George Rude was one of the scholars of the last generation who took note of the development of working-class agitation independent of the rest of the Parisian population. Accounting for this upsurge in the fall of 1789, Rude pointed out that workers in the luxury trades and domestic servants suffered particularly after the revolution as a result of a decline in employment brought on by the political crisis. But in the immediate wake of the revolution, it is a significant reflection of their growing political consciousness that the demands of these domestic employees were political rather than economic. Already in the late summer a large number assembled, asking among other things for rights as citizens, the right to attend district assemblies and the right to enrol in the National Guard. It is true that the National Guard was likely open to the most skilled and well-paid of the 100,000 workers in Paris. But it is fair to say that joining the National Guard was beyond the means of most workers. Workers were in fact under-represented and their membership was discouraged by the dominant bourgeoisie.[45] In any case, the authorities persuaded these domestics to disperse quietly and they did not carry out their original threat to assemble *en masse*, 40,000 strong. But the feelings that had been aroused could not so easily be suppressed.

A few days later an unemployed cook, Eugene Gervais, was arrested in the Palais Royal for inciting domestic servants and workers against the National Guard. He allegedly declared that

> the *garde bourgeoise* and all those who wore the uniform were all j.f. [Jean Foutres, buggers] and that ten thousand servants could take all the j.f. with their blue suits and white facings and make them dance: that all the *bourgeois* ... were j.f. with no exceptions ... that there were sixty thousand

43   Monnier 2005, pp. 130–1.
44   Staum 1996, p. 196.
45   Clifford 1990, pp. 849–78; Devenne 1991, pp. 50–65; Genty 1993, pp. 61–88.

servants in Paris who could get together with the workers in different trades, and then you'd see all those j.f. go hide away at home with their f[ucking] uniforms.[46]

It is possible to interpret the reference to the bourgeoisie in the text as referring simply to bosses, in other words, in terms of a traditional usage of the old regime. Maza, who quotes this text taken from Rude at length, does precisely that.[47] But this attempt at containment flies in the face of much new scholarship, which reflects growing unrest and self-awareness among workers at the time of the revolution. Part of the reason for the unhappiness of workers lay in a reduction in their salaries. David Weir tends to minimise this. He notes only a slight decline in wages in the period 1726–87. Instead, he stresses a sense of grievance arising from wage-workers' awareness of the substantial increase in the level of profits and rents in this period as against a slight decline in workers' wages.[48] On the contrary, Steven Kaplan claims that the decline in wages was substantial, between 20 percent and 30 percent in the period between 1725–41 and 1785–89.[49] Technological innovation was also a cause for worker dissatisfaction. There had already been scattered protests against the introduction of machinery during the eighteenth century. The riot at the Reveillon wall paper factory which initiated the violence of the revolution in the French capital in April 1789 was sparked not only by the threat of lower wages, but by the threat of a new technologically innovative capitalist industry to the traditional crafts workers in the city.[50] Indeed, by the time of the revolution the growing introduction of machinery was provoking widespread protest. Between 1788 and 1791 in Normandy, Champagne, Lille, Paris, Troyes, Roanne, and Saint-Etienne there were riots by workers that involved the breaking of machines.[51] At Rouen, Darnetal and Sotteville attacks on machinery constituted one element in the popular revolutionary uprising of the summer of 1789. It was those employed in the traditional sectors of the cloth industry rather than those who worked in the new mechanised factories who took the lead in such Luddite attacks.[52]

The region to the north and east of Paris meanwhile was hard hit by so-called *bacchanales* or rural strikes on the capitalist farms. Such strikes in the Parisian

46   Rude 1959, p. 65.
47   Maza 2003, p. 89.
48   Weir 1991, pp. 920–1.
49   Kaplan 1979, 192.
50   Rosenband 1997, pp. 481–510.
51   Ballot 1923, pp. 19–22; Chassagne 1991, pp. 220; Horn 2006, pp. 90–125.
52   Mazauric 1985, pp. 511–16.

countryside had increased in frequency and intensity in the years leading up to the revolution. Word of the revolution aroused further militancy in Paris that continued over the next two years.[53] The most militant among workers in the years after the taking of the Bastille proved to be the companion printers, who formed the *Club typographique et philanthropique*, this organisation combined political radicalism with highly effective demands for improvements in wages and working conditions.[54] In the Faubourg Saint Marcel, long-simmering salary disputes came to a head in the wake of the revolution. Workers at the Gobelins tapestry manufacture and the Paris stone quarries were able to make significant gains in their wages as a result.[55] The construction site of the Church of Sainte Genevieve became a major focus of worker unrest. There the workforce combined demands for higher wages with agitation for political democracy and calls for the democratisation of the workplace.[56]

Kaplan has recently argued that the widespread working-class unrest, both urban and rural, in fact represented the birth of modern working-class politics in the midst of the revolution.[57] Such a politics entailed a sense of self-identification as a worker, as for instance Gervais's consciousness of the common interest of workers in all the trades of the city. It also included a sense of the enemy, which Gervais clearly identified as the bourgeoisie who were seen as not merely economic bosses as Maza would have it, but as in control of the National Guard. Dufourny de Villiers's notion of wage workers as constituting a class or fourth estate not represented in the third estate is also indicative of a sense of a working class in gestation, in opposition to the rich and propertied. In 1791 Jean-Paul Marat produced a still more mature sense of the working class. He denounced the Le Chapelier Law as an attempt to prevent the 'innumerable class of wage earners and workers' to 'meet to discuss their interests in an orderly fashion'.[58] According to Marat, their rights as workers and citizens were being denied. The sense of the bourgeois class as collectively repressive of the popular element in the revolution is clearly reflected in the assertion by Marat in the same year that 'we won't allow ourselves to be lulled to sleep by the bourgeoisie as we have been until now'.[59]

---

53   Bernet 1999, pp. 153–86; Moriceau 1985, pp. 421–33.
54   Minard 1989, pp. 25–33.
55   Burstin 2005, pp. 175–9.
56   Ibid, pp. 306–9.
57   Kaplan 2005, pp. 449–50, 546, 550, 564.
58   Marat 1963, p. 40.
59   Roux 1951, p. 261.

Growing hostility to the bourgeoisie is reflected in an anonymous article in the radical and popular *Revolutions de Paris*, published in the spring of 1791.[60] The bourgeoisie is described in this piece as a class of citizens in Paris and the other towns of France that had little or no role in the revolution. The bourgeoisie did not take part in the events going on around them and based their behaviour on calculations of personal security and interest. According to the anonymous author,

> they are preoccupied by minutiae and a view of the whole almost always eludes them. For them only the present moment exists. Their view of things is too short-term to allow them to see into the depths of the future.[61]

> Most are honest enough, but such probity often cannot resist the hope of gain, however modest. Grand passions, elevated feelings and all that involves energy, strength and pride of self are foreign to them. They are egoists by education and habit.

> The bourgeoisie are not democrats. They are monarchists by instinct. Sheep likewise bleat for the authority of a master. Nothing can detach them from their shepherd who nonetheless fleeces them to the point of skinning them alive.[62]

The grand bourgeoisie imitate the nobility, although they lack its sense of loyalty and energy. Having denounced the bourgeoisie in general and the upper bourgeoisie in particular, the author of the text relents a bit and adopts a more positive view of the middle and lesser bourgeoisie. The so-called *bonne bourgeoisie*, which includes some lawyers, magistrates, intellectuals and merchants, behaves more honourably. But it is the *petite bourgeoisie*, the author concludes, who have openly sided with the revolution and who have ranged themselves on the side of the people.[63]

---

60   *Revolutions de Paris* 1791, pp. 453–57.
61   Ibid, p. 453.
62   *Revolutions de Paris* 1791, p. 454.
63   *Revolutions de Paris* 1791, pp. 456–7.

The Debate on the Bourgeoisie

But the climax of the discussion of the place of the bourgeoisie in the revolution came about as a result of a letter by the democratically inclined mayor of Paris, Jerome Petion. The letter was published in *Le Patriote Français* on 10 February 1791, and attracted national attention.[64] At this point Petion had broken with his erstwhile friends the extreme Jacobins, including Robespierre, and would emerge as an influential figure among the Girondins. On the other hand, he insisted on the need for the bourgeoisie to reunite with the people.[65]

According to Petion, it is the privileged, i.e., the nobility, who continue to represent a danger to the revolution. When the privileged argue that the monarchy has been overthrown, that the king no longer has any authority, aren't they really saying that the privileges which exist do not exist, and that they wish to fight to reestablish them?

> The bourgeoisie, that large and well-off class, is splitting itself off from the people. It is placing itself above it. It thinks of itself as the equal of the nobility. The nobility meanwhile disdains it and only waits for a favorable opportunity to humiliate it.[66]

For Petion a clear line continues to separate the bourgeoisie from the privileged. The bourgeoisie would be blind not to perceive a truism based on this evidence: it would have to be mad not to make common cause with the people. Based on its misperception it thinks that the nobility no longer exists and can no longer exist. As a result, it has no sense of distrust of them and does not perceive their intentions. According to Petion,

> The people are the sole object of its suspicions. The bourgeoisie have been told so many times that a state of war exists between those who have property and those who don't that this idea has taken possession of them ... On the other hand, the people have become exasperated against the bourgeoisie. They are indignant at its ingratitude. They recall the services the people have provided to them. They remember that they were all brothers during the heady days of liberty. The privileged

---

64   Guihaumou 1998, p. 209.
65   Burney 1995, pp. 33–44; Burney 1996, pp. 100–7; Tackett 2003, pp. 40, 82–3.
66   Chenier 1872, p. 366.

are secretly fomenting this war which is leading imperceptibly to our ruin. The bourgeoisie and the people together made the revolution. Their reunification alone can preserve it.[67]

In the eyes of Petion,

> All kinds of factions and parties have developed which confuse and dis-tract citizens. Those hostile to the revolution seek to divide them. But there are really only two parties and they are the same as they have been since the Revolution. One wants the constitution and has created it. The other side does not want it and is opposed to it. Do not be deceived. Things haven't changed. It is time that the third estate opened its eyes and rallied together or it will be crushed. All good citizens should give up their petty personal grievances, silence their particular feelings and sacrifice all to the common good. We should have only one cry, 'alliance of the bour-geoisie and the people'; or if one likes, 'union of the third estate against the privileged'.[68]

The third estate for Petion is composed of both the bourgeoisie and the people. In accord with the view taken by Vovelle, which is not at all an anachronism, the revolution is seen as the product of the union of the bourgeoisie and the people. The role of the people in the revolution is as essential as that of the bourgeoisie. Indeed, the latter cannot do without the former, and vice versa.

Petion's letter elicited a diversity of reactions. Duquesnoy accused him of wanting to set one class against another, i.e., proletarians who have no property and whose numbers are limited, against property owners, a class which every-where in France is the most populous and which wishes to eliminate anarchy. Petion risks blaming the proprietors, accusing them of *incivisme*. Those who are known as the bourgeoisie are already becoming known as enemies of the people. The citizens are already showing themselves to be against a part of themselves. In every town they are arbitrarily dividing between bourgeoisie and people, to use the terminology of Petion. As a result a war, a new division, will be born, one that will be particularly tragic.[69]

If Duquesnoy criticised Petion for fostering class conflict, the Girondin leader Jacques-Pierre Brissot defended him, while trying to reassure prop-

---

67   Ibid.
68   Ibid.
69   Guilhaumou 1998, p. 209.

erty owners. Toward the end of February he wrote in the pages of *Le Patriote Français* that Petion in no way sought to create a new class, i.e., that of the bourgeoisie. On the contrary, he preached union and fraternity. The principal aim of Petion's letter was to restore the consciousness of citizens to what it was at the time of the revolution, giving it the same high purpose and energy.[70]

Andre Chenier's critique of Petion went way beyond that of Duquesnoy. Duquesnoy accused him of encouraging class conflict between the bourgeoisie and the people. Chenier, on the other hand, threw down the gauntlet, championing the bourgeoisie while altogether dismissing the popular element in the revolution which Petion had defended.[71] As a moderate revolutionary adhering to the so-called *Feuillants*, Chenier like Barnave was by 1792 increasingly disturbed by the radicalisation of the revolution. Like many other moderates he was more and more worried by the growing power of the Jacobins and the Parisian masses. Replying to Petion, he offered the following definition of the bourgeoisie: 'he should consider that this class which he designates by the word bourgeoisie, being that which is placed at an equal distance between the vices of opulence and those of misery, between the prodigalities of luxury and extreme need, is made up essentially of the true people in all places and times where words make some sense'.

Notable is the fact that Chenier, like Duquesnoy, has the sense that the use of the term bourgeoisie to refer to the middle class is something of a novelty. For all that, Chenier asserts that the bourgeoisie is the middle class between the nobility and masses, the one marked by the vice of extravagance and the other by poverty. This middle ground is seen as the location of virtue, as Chenier makes evident by insisting that they are in effect 'the people' in any meaningful sense of the term. Chenier accords them the title the 'true people'. Chenier is of course harking back to a conception of a well-ordered polity dominated by the middle class first articulated by Aristotle. According to Chenier, 'this class is the most serious, most intelligent, most active and the one most filled with what honest industry can create of what is good and laudable'. Chenier's conception of this class then would include the economic bourgeoisie, but also the professional and rentier element. He concludes that 'when this whole class is discontented it is necessary to point to some secret vice in the laws or the government'.

For Chenier the laws are not at fault. He is full of praise for the Constitution of 1791. According to Chenier, its statutes have re-established equality

---

70   Ibid., p. 210.
71   Chenier, 1958, 277–8.

among men. At the same time, the Constitution opens the way for the most ambitious and unfettered enterprises. No doubt these laws have their imperfections. All human endeavours do. Yet these laws were destined to establish concord and happiness for all on the basis of the common interest. It follows that these laws cannot be the basis of the discontent of this class. The problem lies with the government. Either the government is not governing according to the law or does not have the power to do so. Chenier then proceeds to a list of complaints that alienate the bourgeoisie: the courts have no authority, the administrators command no power or respect, and the public finances, level of debt and taxation cause alarm. As a result, individuals are anxious about their private affairs. In consequence fear and a lack of confidence are putting a stop to or forcing overly hasty commercial transactions, the most legitimate of speculations have become dangerous, prices have increased and money devalued. In short, the bourgeoisie have lost confidence in the government.

A year earlier Chenier had published *Reflexions sur l'esprit de Parti*, directed against the Patriot Party. There he made clear his sense of the difference between this class of the bourgeoisie and the rest of the populace. According to Chenier, the majority of the nation, the sage and industrious class of merchants, retailers and farmers, require that peace be based on good laws. They wish it so. It was for them that the revolution was made. They are truly the French people.[72] In other words, the revolution was a bourgeois revolution founded on an economically based middle class. As for the rest of the population, Chenier notes in passing, 'the largest class of citizens', 'the last class of the people', 'they know nothing, have nothing and take no interest in anything'.[73]

It seems clear that in the initial years of the revolution a language of class developed in France which included the conception of the bourgeoisie as a class and even the notion that the revolution was made by this class or by this class together with the people. The evidence of a discourse of a bourgeoisie in itself, of a bourgeoisie conscious of its role, tends to confirm the existence of the reality of the revolutionary bourgeoisie as a class both for and in itself. I conclude that Maza's denial of this reality is simply untenable.

---

72   Ibid., p. 228.
73   Quean 1989, p. 87.

The Triumph of Republican Discourse

Yet this terminology of class did not become the dominant discourse of the time. This was likely because it was too divisive. Indeed, it emerged as part of the growing conflicts within the revolution. By 1792 economic divisions between the peasants, artisans, workers and bourgeoisie were becoming acute.[74] Duquesnoy's complaint that Petion was trying to set one class against another is particularly pertinent in this respect. So, too, was Brissot's assurance that Petion was not trying to set the bourgeoisie up as a separate class. What was needed from the perspective of those who aspired to dominate the revolutionary process was a discourse of reconciliation and unity among its supporters. Kaplan has suggested that the language of *sansculotterie* and indeed the language of citizenship became one of the means of achieving this.[75] Indeed, Michael Sonenscher has recently argued that it was in the wake of the Petion-Chenier dispute that the republican notion of *sans-culotte* was born.[76] A language that could tie together those who supported the revolution became all the more necessary following the royal flight to Varennes. The discrediting of the monarchy opened up a huge political and ideological space in the heart of the revolution.[77] The language of classical republicanism proved to be the answer to both the political and social fractures besetting the revolution. This kind of discourse had begun to be used as early as 1789, if not earlier. It became the preferred discourse as the Jacobins assumed political control. The primary goal of the Jacobins once in power was to crush counter-revolution at home and abroad and to consolidate the revolution. But in order to do so they needed to suppress developing class divisions and to promote unity within the ranks of the revolution by taking populist and egalitarian measures as well as by resorting to outright repression. Resort to the language of republicanism was an obvious alternative in the face of the stubborn refusal of the monarchy and its closest allies to accept the revolution. It was also a language that, having suppressed the political differences between active and passive citizens, could insist on the equality of all citizens. The enemies of the revolution could still be denounced as nobles, privileged, even rich, or as anarchists and terrorists. But among those considered loyal to the Republic the stress was put on the people, citizenship, heroism, patriotism and sacrifice, a language of virtue

---

74   Vovelle 1984, pp. 215–17.
75   Kaplan 2001, pp. 548, 557.
76   Sonenscher 2008, 355–9.
77   Monnier 2005, p. 83.

rather than of class. At the same time the Jacobin state did all it could to minimise class differences among citizens.[78]

Marx saw this use of the language and forms of classical republicanism as a way of justifying and giving a pedigree to what in the end turned out to be a not so heroic bourgeois revolution which based itself on production and the market. Marx explains this resort to the language of classical antiquity as the result of the weight of tradition upon the revolutionaries, which he describes as a kind of self-delusion or even a nightmare. The essence of the nightmare was the attempt to force the communitarian ideals of ancient republican politics onto a society that was moving toward market individualism. The ideals of the ancient city-state masked the emergent individualistic and egotistical reality of civil society based on the relations of the market. This is a brilliant insight, which still holds much truth. So much so that it has been lately revived as the basis for a new interpretation of the Terror by Patrice Higonnet.[79] But, as I have attempted to show, in the initial years of the revolution some at least were prepared to use the language of class and to understand the epochal events they were enmeshed in as a revolution presided over by the bourgeoisie. Indeed, in my view Marx's interpretation is too idealist. He sees the ideology of classical republicanism as effectively postponing the issue of class conflict. In fact it was used to repress it. The triumph of republican ideology was a response to the political and social crisis of the regime in the transition from monarchy to republic. A political-economic discourse of class and of bourgeois revolution had itself become divisive and dangerous to the survival of the regime, and so it was eclipsed.

But suppose that a sense of the bourgeoisie as a class and even of bourgeois revolution emerged in the period of the national legislative assembly (1789–92). Barnave's adumbration of an economic interpretation of the French Revolution and Chenier's assertive defence of the bourgeoisie and the bourgeois revolution are perhaps its outstanding manifestations. They and other acknowledgements of the role of the bourgeoisie are admittedly important confirmations of a sense of class-based revolution. But these utterances were after all responses to the exigencies of the moment. They are far from a full-fledged theory of bourgeois revolution. Indeed, as part of her thesis discounting the notion of bourgeois revolution, Maza claims that such theories only make their appearance retrospectively in the 1820s. Come to think of it, as Marx suggested, should one expect otherwise? Yet, surprisingly, in the writings during the revolution of

---

78   Gros 1987; Daline 1960, p. 397; Tonneson 1960, p. 418.
79   Higonnet 2006, pp. 121–64.

Pierre Louis Roederer it is possible to discern the emergence of an increasingly clear consciousness of the historic role of the bourgeoisie.

A Theory of Bourgeois Revolution

Roederer played a major political role in the period of the national legislative assembly (1789–91). As a political democrat he was among the leaders of the most radical elements of the Girondin Party. Under the Jacobin dictatorship he was discredited politically and abandoned his democratic ideas. Instead, he became preoccupied with liberal economic theory and with developing a sociology of order that could help to stabilise a new postrevolutionary regime. Indeed, he played a significant part in the *coup d'etat* of 18th Brumaire (1799) and became an influential figure in the subsequent Napoleonic regime. Living through the entire revolutionary period and playing a major role through most of it, no one had a better appreciation of its meaning than Roederer.

Prior to the revolution Roederer had already championed the rights of non-landowning capitalists. During the height of the Terror, when private property appeared threatened, he defended private property rights in a series of lectures before the newly created *Lycee des Arts*.[80] At the beginning of the Consulat he reappeared before the *Lycee* to deliver a second set of lectures on what ought to be the rightful role of capitalists in the new order established under Napoleon.[81] In the new conservative environment the doctrines of physiocracy were being used to try to reserve political power exclusively in the hands of landlords. On this occasion Roederer defended the critically important productive role of both industrial and agricultural capitalists and their consequent right to enjoy political rights.[82] It is significant that throughout this text Roederer does not refer to political rights per se but rather to *droit de la cité*, which translated properly means bourgeois right. In making this argument it is noteworthy that Roederer also claimed that the National Guard in 1789 and in 1800 was made up overwhelmingly of capitalists.[83] It is capitalists who were the guardians of the new revolutionary order. Indeed, he went so far as to note that under the Terror – a regime controlled by proletarians according to him – capitalists tended to stay in France, while it was landlords who were prone to flight.[84]

---

80   Scurr 2000, pp. 105–26.
81   Roederer 1840.
82   Allix 1913, pp. 297–348; Whatmore 2000, p. 100.
83   Roederer 1840, p. 61.
84   Ibid., pp. 63–4.

Roederer summed up his view of the revolution in a work published in 1831 entitled *L'esprit de le Revolution de 1789*.[85] In the preface Roederer notes that he had actually composed the work toward the end of 1815, but renounced the idea of publishing it under the weight of the censorship of the restored Bourbon monarchy.[86] According to him, to understand the coming of the revolution one must comprehend that movable capital gradually arose alongside land as a form of wealth. Over time, the value of such capital overtook that of the land as it expanded throughout industry and labouring activity. In the same way it soon flowed back from the towns into the countryside, where it gave an immense impetus to agricultural production. Capital became the unit in which the value of all kinds of goods, including land, was measured.[87]

> At that point, the bourgeoisie, the leading possessors of capital – just as the seigneurs had been the leading possessors of land – held in their power the greater part of the national wealth. The unique owners of all kinds of industry, they became landowners as well ... Seigneurs became the vassals, indeed, the subjects of wealthy plebeians.[88]

Roederer clearly saw the importance of the bourgeoisie in both the urban and rural sectors. The revolution was self-evidently a capitalist revolution, both in town and country. Moreover, he specifically names the bourgeoisie for the first time not as simply capitalists but as the bourgeoisie.

Roederer had a clear understanding of the decisive role of the economic bourgeoisie. But reflecting his mature sense of class, it is noteworthy that he gave equal stress to the historical development of the cultural capacity of the same class. According to him, both the development of the mentality and the increase in the capital or moveable wealth of the bourgeoisie over time gave it more power: 'The development of its intellectual power and the increase of its capital enhanced the importance of a part of the third estate'.[89] Only they were capable of providing the needs of society; to make known and to savour the higher pleasures. Only they could tighten the connections of society by means of communications of the mind and through the moral force of a public opinion which included all persons and actions. It is only from the estate of commoners that all public and private services came to be provided.

---

85   Roederer 1831.
86   Ibid., p. ii.
87   Ibid., pp. 15–16.
88   Ibid.
89   Ibid., p. 20.

It is from this estate that those who practice literature and art came: 'Brilliant savants and great writers contributed to the rise of the third estate not only through their ongoing effusions of enlightenment and feeling but through the eminence they achieved in society'.[90] With the development of science and philosophy in the eighteenth century a new nobility of the human race developed alongside the old nobles. They further contributed to the rise of the third estate and the emergence of public opinion.[91] 'The revolution was the indestructible product of the growth of civilization which itself was the result of the growth of riches and enlightenment'.[92] Roederer thus views the relationship of the emergence of the economic and non-economic bourgeoisie as unproblematically intertwined with one another. The growing prominence and power of both are understood as part of a single process. By 1815 Roederer was able to see that the significance of the revolution was that it had seen the triumph of this bourgeoisie.[93]

---

90   Ibid., p. 24.
91   Ibid., p. 26.
92   Ibid., p. 14.
93   Guizot 1860, III, pp. 152–3.

CHAPTER 11

Review of Jeff Horn, *The Path Not Taken: French Industrialization in the Age of Revolution, 1750–1830*

Jeff Horn's new work on French industrialisation during the age of revolution unfortunately reflects the anti-Marxist bias we have come to expect from most English-speaking scholars of the French Revolution. In the early pages of his book, Horn complains of a class-based Marxist reductionism which fails to capture the more positive aspects of the *ancien régime*'s policing of labour.[1] This means that Marxists lay too much stress on the repression of workers prior to the revolution. He then applauds the collapse of the Marxist paradigm and the recent emergence among American scholars of more cultural approaches to the development of class and the factory-system.[2] Noting these comments, a reader might legitimately conclude that Horn adheres or pays necessary lip-service to the consensus among most English-speaking academic historians known as French-revolutionary revisionism. The *sine qua non* of this view is a rejection of the Marxist idea of the French Revolution as a bourgeois and capitalist revolution. The sense of an anti-Marxist bias is strengthened by the fact that, in his narrative of the take-off of French industrialisation, Horn seldom if ever uses the term capitalist or bourgeoisie. The farthest he ventures in this direction is to refer delicately to the activity of entrepreneurs. In lieu of the capitalist or bourgeois class as the agent of French industrialisation, Horn instead emphasises the primary role of the state.

Given this approach, Horn's work would appear to offer little which would compel the interest of those who cling to the view of the French Revolution as bourgeois and capitalist. Yet there are aspects in his approach which can interest those who continue to espouse a Marxist approach to history. Having eschewed any discussion of the revolutionary bourgeoisie, Horn surprises by placing the violent struggle of workers at the focal point of his discussion of French industrialisation during the revolution. It is their violent resistance to technical innovation in the form of machine-breaking which forced the new revolutionary state into assuming a central role in fostering and controlling the industrial process. In contradiction to the views of most revisionist historians,

---

1   Horn 2006, p. 18.
2   Ibid., p. 20.

furthermore, Horn rejects the notion that the period of Jacobin rule was a political and economic disaster. On the contrary, he insists that it was the economic policies of the Jacobins which helped save the revolution and opened an alternative path to industrialisation.

Horn's stress on the significance of the industrialisation process during the revolution represents a breakthrough from the perspective of an area of scholarship dominated, at least in the Anglo-Saxon world, by revisionism. French scholars such as Serge Chassagne and Denis Woronofff, untainted by revisionism, have taken the lead in demonstrating the importance of industrialisation during the eighteenth century and the revolution.[3] A limited number of English-speaking historians have likewise bravely interested themselves in the history of French industry during this period.[4] But from the perspective of an Anglo-American historiography which in the last decades has been preoccupied with culture or, at best, with the culture of the market, Horn's insistence on the importance of industrialisation and questions of class during the revolution is something of a departure. Horn's work is thus of interest to Marxist scholarship because it concedes in a back-handed fashion the progress of capitalism in France in the wake of the revolution. Furthermore, while largely ignoring the bourgeoisie, no doubt to avoid so-called class-based Marxist reductionism, Horn in paradoxical fashion underlines the key role of the working class and class-struggle to the industrialisation process in France. In a contradictory way, and despite himself, Horn ends up speaking the language of Marxism instead of culture.[5]

Horn's primary objective is to counter the Anglo-centric view of modern economic history as exemplified in David Landes's highly influential *Unbound Prometheus*.[6] From the latter's perspective there was only one path to industrialisation, based on the pure laissez-faire economy of the English type. In this view, France was a second-best economy held back by cultural or irrational constraints, especially an emphasis on the family-firm which failed to value profit-maximisation and relentless expansion of output. Horn to the contrary points out that France experienced high growth-rates between 1815 and 1850, that French per-capita income was only 20 percent below that of England in 1914, and that the French economy adapted well to the so-called second industrial revolution of the late nineteenth century. France successfully pur-

3 Chassagne 1991; Woronofff 1994.
4 Among others, Lewis 1993; Johnson 1993; Hafter 2007.
5 It is of course not necessary to choose between the two.
6 Landes 1969.

sued industrialisation along its own path, he concludes. It must not be judged according to the English pattern which was the path not chosen.[7]

Horn argues in the first place that, prior to the revolution, policy-makers in France attempted to follow what they understood as the English model of industrialisation. But contrary to a preconception which was common in the eighteenth century and has been ever since, economic experts in the French government regarded the English state not as laissez-faire but as every bit as mercantilist or interventionist as the state in France. Moreover, while they acknowledged some English commercial and industrial advantages, they thought it possible for France to compete successfully in many other economic sectors. In a fashion that can only be welcomed, Horn insists on the importance of politics to the process of industrial development in both France and England.

Horn then claims that French attempts to emulate English policies were interrupted by the radicalism of the French Revolution. The possibility of radical revolution in the period 1789–94 on the part of the labouring classes ensured that neither the French state nor entrepreneurs could easily pursue profit-maximisation or introduce technological innovations in response to labour militancy. On the contrary, in England the state brutally and systematically repressed working-class resistance to industrialisation, allowing industrial entrepreneurs to pursue the accumulation of profits without real hindrance.

Unable to pursue the 'liberal' path to industrialisation of the English, Horn argues that the French state embarked on a different path forged first by the Jacobins in the midst of war, national mobilisation and the reign of terror. In a context of economic distress and the threat of counter-revolution, the state was put at the heart of the economic process. The statist command-economy of the Year 11 (1793–4) represented both a return to the *dirigiste* policies of the *ancien régime* and under new and revolutionary circumstances a powerful alternative model of economic development. The Jacobin regime was swept aside by the Thermidorean reaction, but a more moderate version of the interventionist state was perfected by Napoleon's Minister of the Interior Jean-Baptiste Chaptal (1800–4). Chaptal kept the threat from below at bay while encouraging the growth of industry through state-support of science, technology and entrepreneurship, cautious subsidisation of industry, and cartelisation of the heights of the economy. In the aftermath of the collapse of the Continental System and the Napoleonic regime, Chaptal's interventionist economic policies were

---

7   Horn 2006, pp. 3–5.

adopted by the Bourbon Restoration and subsequent French governments in the nineteenth century with considerable success.

Horn's treatment of government economic policy under the *ancien régime* in Chapters 2 and 3 reflects much of the current historiographic consensus. In response to English competition it is agreed the regime combined ongoing state intervention with increasing moves in the direction of laissez-faire. But viewing these efforts from the perspective of the government elites, Horn minimises the responsibility of economic liberalism in bringing on the popular upheavals of the revolution. The first great experiment in liberalism came with the appointment of Turgot as Controller-General. The physiocrat minister attempted to introduce free trade in grain (1774) and dissolve the guilds (1776). Horn deals with the attempt to dissolve the guilds without really relating it to the consequences of the freeing of the grain-trade. On the contrary, as Turgot realised, the fate of the first initiative, freeing the market for subsistence, and the second, opening the labour market, were closely connected to one another.[8] The freeing of prices precipitated a massive rebellion (the 'guerre des farines' of 1775) which anticipated the social upheavals of the revolution. Liberalism was temporarily discredited, the dissolution of the guilds became a dead letter and the state was required to re-regulate the labour market on a national basis.

Horn treats the signing of the commercial or free-trade treaty of 1786 with England again without relating it to the previous liberal experiment under Turgot. In fact, the treaty was nothing but a second attempt to liberalise, but this time through the back door – introducing free trade from without. There is an uncanny mirror-image of these episodes in the recent French experience with neoliberalism running from Mitterand to Sarkozy – *plus ça change, plus c'est la même chose*. Horn concludes that the treaty was good policy unfortunately interrupted by the revolution. In fact, while it did not cause the revolution, there is little doubt that it deepened the economic recession which brought massive popular revolution. In the light of these events only a liberal ideologue could consider this treaty good policy. People in the streets seem to have a recurrent problem with the impeccable logic of economic liberalism.

If Horn does not deal adequately with popular violence in the closing years of the *ancien régime*, he more than makes up for it in the next chapter, which becomes the keystone of the work. Entitled 'The Other "Great Fear": Labor Relations, Industrialization, and Revolution', it lays out the results of Horn's detailed research on machine-breaking during the early phase of the French Revolution. As part of the massive peasant and urban upheavals of 1789, textile-workers as

---

8   Kaplan 2001, p. 120.

well as other wage-earners carried out damaging attacks on factories, mines and machinery in the textile-regions of Normandy, but also in Champagne and in the coal and iron-region around Saint-Etienne (Lyonnais). While machine-breaking largely died down in subsequent years, the persistent fear of such incidents played a major role in retarding further investment in mechanisation and the intrusion of large-scale capital into industry.[9]

Horn's assertions seem to be contradicted by French experience under Napoleon. As Horn himself notes in Chapter 6, the output of machine-spun cotton at least quadrupled between 1806 and 1810. Wool, silk, mixed textile-materials and hardware-production all also notably expanded production. There was a major retooling of French industry during this period, often with the latest technology. Mechanisation of the cotton-industry was the most spectacular success in this upward surge. In 1789 there were six large-scale mechanised cotton-mills in France. By 1814 there were 272. At the highest point of the Napoleonic Empire, industrial production was at least 50 percent higher than under the *ancien régime*.[10]

It is admirable that Horn takes note of this industrial progress, as it reflects the post-revolutionary boom of capitalist industry which is swept under the carpet in contemporary revisionist history. But a hundred pages earlier, Horn had stressed the retardation of the mechanisation and capitalisation of industry owing to labour-militancy. Yet other than noting in passing that the surge was made possible by the quiescence of labour owing to military conscription, Horn does not seriously account for this Napoleonic industrial boom in terms of his thesis. At the very least, Horn would seem to have overstated his initial claims of the influence of labour-resistance on the path of French industrialisation. Indeed, there are those who question at least part of the retardation-thesis. Recent firm-based research has shown that French industry was much more expansive and technologically advanced in the nineteenth century than once thought. In certain sectors, French industries were entirely competitive with England and Germany.[11]

At best, we can continue to entertain Horn's thesis as a claim of the overall retardation of French mechanisation and concentration of industry relative to England. Yet, even on these terms, his monocausal explanation based on the persistent threat of machine-breaking seems to be an exaggeration. In passing he notes the frequency of strikes in the first decade of the revolution.[12] We

9   Horn 2006, p. 120.
10   Ibid., p. 223.
11   Smith 2005, p. 4.
12   Horn 2006, p. 120.

know that there was at times a close relation between such militancy and the threat from technological innovation as suggested by the causes underlying the riots at the Reveillon wallpaper-factory in the spring of 1789.[13] Yet, compared to his treatment of machine-breaking, he does not probe into how strikes and other kinds of labour militancy may have had a bearing on the progress of industrialisation. Indeed, although he mentions it, Horn does not do justice to the wide extent of working-class unrest in this period – an unrest that goes beyond machine-breaking. Strikes and indiscipline on the part of workers in the period 1787–9 were especially notable in Paris and its region leading up to the revolution. Following the taking of the Bastille, strikes multiplied and new forms of worker-militancy and sociability appeared.[14] In reaction, the National Assembly enacted the Le Chapelier Law of 1791, prohibiting combinations.[15]

The Jacobins made real efforts to placate workers, especially by passage of the maximum on prices. But the containment of ongoing working-class unrest became a focal point of the agenda of the Jacobin regime, especially after the imposition of the maximum on wages. Contrary to Horn's view of labour unrest inhibiting technological innovation, the Jacobins fostered such innovation in the national armories as a way of overcoming worker unrest.[16]

The subsequent Conspiracy of Equals led by Babeuf (1796) has been dismissed by most historians as insignificant, its membership not even based on workers. The recent researches of Jean Marc Schiappa have revealed that it advanced a communist ideology and had a considerable working-class following in many places in France. The Babouviste political conspirators were fully conscious of the misuse of technology to exploit workers.[17] Horn's emphasis on machine-breaking as inhibiting mechanisation is no doubt a point well taken. But it should be seen as part of a larger picture of working-class resistance that tended to inhibit the capitalisation of industry and forced the intervention of the state.

How necessary a wider view of worker resistance is to Horn's argument is illustrated by his unconvincing comparison of machine-breaking in France and England. His account shows that Luddite violence in the latter country was far more extensive and prolonged than it was in France. Horn quite rightly points out how important the brutal repression by the so-called liberal English

---

13   Rosenband 1997.
14   Sibalis 1986.
15   Burstin 1993; Kaplan 2001, pp. 548–50.
16   Alder 1997, p. 277.
17   Schiappa 2003.

state was to breaking this resistance and clearing the way for industrialisation there. Strangely, Horn asserts that the danger in France was greater, but fails to demonstrate the ongoing threat in the absence of major outbreaks of machine-breaking after 1789. It is only in the context of evidence of working-class militancy, strikes, and revolutionary conspiracy in the 1790s that Horn's argument can hold water.

Emphasising the resistance of the working class to industrialisation, Horn does not even begin to take into account the difficulty large-scale industry had in recruiting a workforce as a result of the revolution. The fact is that while the revolution in the French countryside may have been led by a capitalist element, its radicalism reinforced the grip of the lesser peasantry and even the previously landless on the land. While in England the process of enclosure was being pursued to the bitter end and issued in the emergence of the industrial working class, the revolution made the peasantry cling ever more fiercely to the land. Peasants who went to the mines and factories on a temporary basis stubbornly resisted permanent proletarianisation.[18] Primitive accumulation continued in France but at a much slower pace than in England, inhibiting the formation of the large and permanent pools of unskilled and low-wage labour that industrialists and mine-owners required.

The accumulating evidence of working-class agitation in the form of machine-breaking, strikes and conspiracy is in a way a vindication of Daniel Guérin's *La lutte de classes sous la Première République, bourgeois et 'bras nus'* (*1793–1797*) of 1946.[19] In that work, Guérin stressed the working-class character of the popular movement in Paris and underlined Jacobin repression of its demands. Guérin's view arose in part from his commitment to the idea of permanent revolution and his opposition, along with fellow Trotskyites, to the post-liberation *Parti communiste français*'s policy of cooperation with that part of the bourgeoisie untainted by Vichy. Guérin at that time came under attack from the French historical establishment and especially from Albert Soboul.

The latter was a member of the Communist Party who was in the process of becoming the historian of the sans-culottes or the popular movement of the revolution.[20] Soboul and others castigated Guérin for his provocative and anachronistic assertions which, it was claimed, lacked a scholarly foundation. No doubt there is some truth to this critique.[21] At the same time, there was a certain prescience to Guérin's view as reflected in recent research.

---

18   Woronofff 1994, p. 290.
19   Guérin 1946.
20   Soboul 1973.
21   Berger n.d.

Soboul did not deny that there was a proletarian element to the popular movement. But, in fact, leadership over it rested with well-to-do craftsmen, small-scale merchants and manufacturers who lived and worked with their workers and were able to dominate and subordinate them in the so-called sans-culottes movement.

The ideology espoused by them and which they imposed on their workers and the rest of the plebeian population in Paris was focused around questions of subsistence, productive work and democratic politics. From Soboul's perspective Guérin's stress on the proletarian character of the Parisian masses seemed overstated. Soboul's view has itself been questioned by Richard Mowery Andrews, who carefully delineated the incipient class-differences between what we can call the petty-bourgeois leadership and the plebeian element in the popular movement.[22]

Soboul's position nonetheless continues to make a certain amount of sense. Faced with constant threats to the revolution from counter-revolution abroad and internal subversion, as well as ongoing problems of subsistence, it seems plausible to see the sans-culottes as a popular movement no doubt riven by tensions but with a common ideology and programme. How fruitful this approach has been was demonstrated in the recent work of Haim Burstin, who has produced an unprecedentedly sweeping and minutely-detailed political history of the movement.[23]

We mention Soboul and Burstin in the context of this review because their historical studies of what can be described as an emergent lower middle-class with a capacity for revolutionary action points to a fundamental weakness in Horn's approach. It was not only workers who found themselves opposed to technological innovation and the capitalisation of industry. During the revolution and through the first part of the nineteenth century, well-to-do craftsmen, small-scale family-manufacturers and lesser merchants fought an important rear-guard action against large-scale industry and big business in a struggle that was both economic and political. In dismissing Landes's critique of the influence of the family-firm, Horn too hastily dismisses the inter-class rivalry between big and little capital in explaining French resistance to the English path to industrialisation.

Horn likewise makes little or nothing of the international division of labour in explaining the French path to industrialisation. French industry was certainly less capital-intensive and mechanised than most of industry in England.

---

22   Andrews 1985; Kaplan 2001, pp. 572–3.
23   Burstin 2005.

But it could be argued that English success along the path of mass-production and achieving economies of scale tended to force France back on its traditional strength in more labour-intensive and higher-quality production for the export-market. France inserted itself differently but successfully into the international marketplace, stressing the manufacture of higher-end and better-quality products. Its industrialisation was comparable to England's, but based more on craftsmen and small manufacturers than on large-scale industry.[24]

Praiseworthy as Horn's research is on machine-breaking, we conclude that it is insufficient to explain the French path to industrialisation. The latter was clearly the product of a multiplicity of factors that Horn does not sufficiently take into account. On the other hand, Horn deserves credit for rehabilitating the economic reputation of the Jacobins. Horn's fifth chapter, entitled 'La patrie en danger: Industrial Policy in the Year II', recalls the history of the Jacobin dictatorship (1793–4). But instead of harping on the excesses of the Terror as do the revisionists, Horn emphasises the success of the interventionist state of the Jacobins, which marshalled the material and moral forces of the nation in order to overcome economic and political crisis. According to Horn, 'the raw, almost unbridled economic necessities that gave rise to the Reign of Terror allowed the revolutionaries to tame rampant inflation, feed the nation, and equip an army that dominated Europe for more than a generation'.[25] Based on extensive archival research, Horn offers us a detailed review of this period of sweeping economic mobilisation, including an account of the maximums on prices and wages, state-directed or controlled war-production, the creation of a scientific and technological brains-trust, unprecedented initiatives in technological education and technical innovation, the politics of labour-control, and the role of representatives on mission in implementing the industrial and economic policies of the central government. Coupled with political repression and mass-mobilisation, these policies enabled the Jacobins to defeat counter-revolution and save the revolution. Chaptal never went so far in controlling the economy as did the Jacobins. Nonetheless, as Horn details in Chapter 6, he, too, championed state-intervention whose success he had personally witnessed during the Year II. According to Chaptal, the state must promote commerce and industry while mediating the varied private interests in behalf of the public good.

Horn's positive treatment of the industrial policies and record of the Jacobins and of Chaptal in the Napoleonic period is welcome. But focused as he

---

24   O'Brien and Caglar 1978.
25   Horn 2006, p. 128.

is on the state, he fails to fully contextualise these policies. He thereby fails to completely grasp the limits and choices of French industrial development in the revolutionary period. The latter cannot finally be grasped without taking into account the still-dominant agrarian sector of the economy and the role of revolutionary class-struggle. We have already noticed this failure in Horn's treatment of economic liberalism in the dying years of the *ancien régime*. It persists in his one-sided account of the industrialisation-process under the revolution. It is the theoretically informed work of the Russian Marxist histor-ian Anatoli Ado that we have to turn back to in order to find such an adequate analysis.[26]

According to Ado, the fundamental obstacle to the development of indus-trial capitalism was the overwhelming dominance of rent and the constriction of profit under the *ancien régime*. The popular violence of the revolution in country as well as city which reached its peak under Jacobin rule destroyed feudalism and seigneurialism and allowed even poor peasants some access to the land. Ado sees the agrarian radicalism of the Year II as opening the way to the emergence of a dynamic market dominated by petty producers. According to him, this could have constituted the starting-point for an accel-erated process of capitalist accumulation based on the emergence of a power-ful class of agrarian and industrial capitalists and the eventual proletarianisa-tion of the mass of producers. Following its successful revolution, the United States became the most outstanding example of this developmental path. More recently, Mao's China appears to have taken a similar direction.[27]

In Horn's view, revolutionary violence inhibited capital accumulation and forced the intervention of the state. To the contrary, Ado regards class-struggle as opening a wider path toward the development of capitalist forces of pro-duction. Some supporters of the Jacobins and members of the Directory paid lip-service to fostering the strength of petty producers, but failed to support a sufficiently radical or thoroughgoing land reform. The result was that, while feudalism and seigneurialism were abolished, rent continued to have an excess-ive influence inhibiting the accumulation of profits in both the agricultural and industrial sectors following the revolution. The implication of this view is that, however laudable the initiatives of Chaptal, they were fundamentally constric-ted by the regime of landed notables that consolidated itself under Napoleon on the basis of the persistence of rent. The sweep and power of Ado's view demonstrates the force of the Marxist mode of analysis. Welcome as Horn's re-

26   Ado 1996.
27   Byres 1996.

engagement with the economic and social history of the revolution is, there is no mention of Ado in his work. Horn's inability or unwillingness to take Marxism seriously fundamentally constrains his viewpoint.

CHAPTER 12

Bankers, Finance Capital and the French Revolutionary Terror, 1791–4

The production of commodities bearing surplus value is at the heart of the accumulation of capital. But the financing of production and the realisation of profit in the market depends on the availability of credit in the form of liquid capital. Fully functioning capitalism requires the integration of the productive and commercial economy with a credit system which serves to facilitate its expansion. In the absence of a system of credit a full-blown capitalist economy cannot exist. The absence of such a system of capitalist finance prior to the revolution was the principal point of an important article by George V. Taylor on the Paris stock exchange prior to the revolution which appeared in the *American Historical Review* in 1962.[1] It alongside several other articles on the forms of property and types of enterprise under the Old Regime made it possible for Taylor to argue that the Marxist idea that the French Revolution was a capitalist revolution was wrong.[2]

Taylor was a historian for many years at the University of North Carolina, and he approached the history of the French Revolution from an unabashedly Christian perspective. In the context of Cold War America his version of Christianity brought him into open opposition to Marxism.[3] His work proved important to the consolidation of the anti-Marxist or revisionist school of the French Revolution, which began to emerge in defiance of the revolutionary mood of the 1960s. Taylor appeared to provide serious economic arguments backing up the political and cultural critique of the Marxist interpretation of the revolution made by historians like Alfred Cobban and François Furet. Taylor's work, it is not too much to say, constituted the economic basis of the revisionist school of French revolutionary history that flourished from the 1970s onward. The revisionist school challenged the Marxist method and its view of the trajectory of European and world history based on the idea of revolutionary change. Taylor in particular challenged the Marxist conception of the revolution as a creative response by the French bourgeoisie and people in which the long term progress

---

1   Taylor 1962.
2   Taylor 1963; Taylor 1964; Taylor 1967.
3   Taylor 1956.

of capitalism was threatened by fiscal, political and economic crisis. According to Taylor, the revolution did not eliminate the obstacles to the further advance of capitalism since capitalism did not really exist.

This chapter disputes Taylor's view, claiming that a proper appreciation of the evolution of the relationship between financial and productive capital between 1760–1830 demonstrates that the revolution was both capitalist and bourgeois. Taylor asserts that because investment banks did not exist prior to the revolution and the small amounts of capital that were available for investment were raised locally, capitalism barely existed. We take the position that Taylor's view is fundamentally anachronistic. According to Taylor, the absence of what later came to be called *La Haute Banque* or investment banking prior to the revolution largely precluded the formation of productive capital. On the contrary, we argue that the development of investment banking in the first half of the nineteenth century was the outcome of a long history which included the period of the revolution, in the course of which the link between financial capital and a growing mass of productive capital slowly was forged. Investment banking in the nineteenth century was an outcome of this process, not a pre-condition of it.

As we have noted, Taylor argues that credit for enterprise was only available locally. That capital for productive investment was available at the local level is no argument against capital in sufficient amounts being at hand to foster accumulation. As is well known, most of the initial capital behind the early Industrial Revolution in England came from the pooling of local capital through country banks.[4] Prior to the revolution a similar pattern is discernible in France. Even more important is the fact that Taylor completely ignores the role that commercial credit provided by Parisian banks played in the financing of the burgeoning overseas trade during the eighteenth century. Furthermore, as a result of this trade there developed an increasing market for manufactures, which provided an important stimulus to the development of French manufacturing. In the initial development of such industries it is well known that the most important requirement was not fixed capital but affordable commercial credit.[5] The Parisian banks played an important role in providing this capital.

Taylor furthermore ignores the degree to which bankers themselves both before and during the revolution began to invest their capital in productive sectors of the economy. We argue that the money capital of the bankers which

---

4   Pressnel 1956.
5   Blackburn 1997, pp. 541–2.

was closely tied to commercial capital began to be invested in land, mines and manufacturing prior to 1789 and that this trend gained momentum during the revolution, in part owing to radical and popular political pressure which narrowed opportunities for speculative investment. Popular political pressure which restricted speculation helped to force finance capital toward productive investment. Especially notable was the purchase during the Terror of national properties by bankers in the form of capitalist farms and ecclesiastical buildings which were turned into factories. This rapprochement between finance and productive capital continued under the Directory and was reflected in the composition and mandate of the Bank of France, at least as conceived by Napoleon.[6] Under the revolution and especially under Napoleon industry grew rapidly and came increasingly under the control of the bankers.[7]

The Progress of Capitalism

Like other historians, Taylor characterised the speculative bubble that developed in the 1780s in Paris as an aspect of the impending political and economic crisis of the Old Regime. But for him the bubble emerged not from the gap between finance capital running ahead of productive capital, which is typical of a capitalist crisis, but because of the growth of finance capital in the virtual absence of productive capital. In a companion piece published a few years later Taylor backed up and explained this argument by insisting that the greater part of wealth in eighteenth-century France came from what he described as 'proprietary sources', i.e., rents on land, bonds and annuities which he described as non-capitalist.[8] According to Taylor's categorisation, land cannot be considered productive capital and the absence of significant productive capital signified that capitalism did not exist prior to the revolution. Hence he concluded that describing the revolutionary crisis in terms of a bourgeois and capitalist revolution was mistaken.

Rent of course was the major source of wealth prior to the revolution. Moreover, a significant portion of rent was admittedly non-capitalist or feudal (although Taylor did not like the term). Taylor seemed not to know or chose to ignore that the definition of capitalist wealth is surplus made up of profit, interest and rent derived from the surplus value generated by producers who

---

6   Jacoud 1996, pp. 31, 52, 67, 71, 283–6.
7   Bergeron 1978, p. 319.
8   Taylor 1967, p. 471.

work for wages. Such profits are by no means limited to the manufacturing sector but are also produced from land if the land is treated as a capitalist means of production. Indeed, in the Marxist view the development of capitalist relations on the land is decisive to the development of capitalism. In the case of France much of the agricultural land in the île-de-France and elsewhere in northern France prior to 1789 had already become capitalist, i.e., worked by capitalist farmers or tenants employing wage labour.[9] *Pace* Taylor, rents paid to landlords were rents of a capitalist nature.

Capitalist production relations had also developed in the agriculture of the Midi although not so generally.[10] Capitalist coal mining, iron mining and iron and steel manufacture and fabrication likewise experienced significant expansion. Particularly noteworthy was the expansion of cotton manufacturing, especially Indian cotton manufacture, the latter imitating and replacing the hitherto popular imported Indian cottons.[11] Although the construction of large fully integrated factories in this sector was only in its early stages prior to the revolution and only took off with the revolution, nonetheless the rising number of so-called cotton proto-factories reflected the increasing importance of growing investment of significant amounts of capital, the expansion and concentration of wage labour, growing division of labour and a continuous stream of new production techniques in this sector.[12]

As the revolution approached the spread of capitalist relations of production seems to have destabilised French society both in the towns and countryside. By then many French producers worked either part- or full-time for wages in agriculture, but also increasingly in manufacturing and mining for employers who sought profits from the commodities so produced. Part of the surplus generated under such circumstances might be paid to owners or creditors not in the form of profit but in the form of rent or interest. If so such rents or annuities themselves must likewise be considered capitalist. The rest of the surplus produced in this way would be retained as profit which would remain in the hands of capitalist farmers, merchant-manufacturers, factory or mine owners. Given the expansion of grain production and the accompanying growth of industry both based on the increased use of wage labour, we can say that the role of profit and capitalist wealth generated from agriculture and industry significantly expanded as the eighteenth century unfolded. As a result of this evolution there is little doubt that after 1750 the French economy began

9   Lefebvre 1954a, p. 61.
10   Heller 2006, pp. 29–30.
11   Lemarchand 2008, pp. 97–101.
12   Chassagne 1991, pp. 92, 169, 181–4.

to transcend the limits of merely reproducing the feudal economy.[13] Prior to the revolution these new economic relations of course remained constrained within feudal structures and much of agriculture, especially south of the Loire, continued to be carried on at the level of subsistence production.

The Attack on Speculation

Taylor's research on the Paris stock exchange was based on the earlier investigations of Jean Bouchary.[14] Bouchary's works, which were mainly published around World War II, while eschewing theoretical analysis, were empirically rich. What emerged from his scholarship was a stress on the speculative rather than the productive character of the activities of the Parisian bankers and stock brokers, many of whom had close ties to the court and government. Taylor, who added to Bouchary's research, noted that the bankers dealt with foreign exchange, state loans and the shares of joint-stock companies like the newly formed Paris Fire Insurance, Water, Life Insurance, and Lighting Companies. These were essentially speculative ventures which in large part were designed to attract the money of investors. Stocks in these companies rose and fell on the stock exchange based on the puts and calls of stock jobbers and bankers trying to manipulate prices and to take advantage of runs on the market. Like Bouchary, Taylor saw the speculative bubble of the 1780s largely as a recapitulation of John Law's Mississippi Company Bubble of the early eighteenth century.[15]

Taylor took this position because he claimed that most economic assets in pre-revolutionary France were non-capitalist, the financial sector existed apart from productive activity and commercial capitalism barely existed. According to Taylor, the merchant capitalism of the pre-revolutionary period mainly consisted of family firms and modest partnerships rooted in small-scale putting-out enterprises. Among conservatively-minded merchants who controlled such enterprises, speculators were fundamentally distrusted and most merchants raised their own capital as needed. Taylor did concede that the speculators of the pre-revolutionary period were in advance of their age, resembling in inspiration and technique the finance capitalists of the post-1830 period with its railways, canal and large-scale manufacturing requiring large-scale invest-

---

13   Perrot 1975, p. 31.
14   Bouchary, 1937; Bouchary 1939–43; Bouchary 1942; Bouchary 1940–2; Bouchary 1946.
15   Taylor 1962, pp. 967–7.

ments based on loan capital. But he also argued that there was a fundamental difference between the speculators of the Old Regime and the finance capitalists of the Orléanist monarchy. The latter were laying the foundations of industrial capitalism in France, while the former had nothing to do with it. On the contrary, the financiers of the pre-revolutionary decade were involved with the debts of the French state, the privileges that could be obtained by serving the court and speculating with the floods of capital accumulating in Paris in the decades leading to the revolution. The joint stock companies which were created had more to do with stock jobbing and price-fixing than productive or commercial activity: 'the boom of the 1780s ... was built on the aristocratic and monarchic institutions of the old order rather than the unborn industrial and financial system of the nineteenth century. It exemplified not the so-called Industrial Revolution but the court capitalism of early modern Europe'.[16]

Taylor's conclusions with regard to capitalism were three-fold: first, that the opportunity to place capital in substantial productive investments did not exist because up to 1789 large-scale capitalist enterprises in France were scarcely to be found. Second finance was confined to speculative investments or loans to the government and aristocracy. Investment banks did not exist and capital for enterprise was raised locally by merchants. Third, industrial capitalism dates from the third decade of the nineteenth century and has no relationship with the French Revolution. Capitalism in France prior to 1789 was weak and consequently the revolution cannot be considered a capitalist revolution.

The evidence of the tumultuous first years of the revolution at first glance reinforces this view. Bankers were widely seen as speculators who operated at the expense of the productive elements of the population. The words 'speculator' and 'banker' were virtually synonymous in the eyes of the lesser merchants, craftsmen and workers of Paris and other towns who constituted the rank-and-file of the revolution. A constant refrain against the bankers was that they were essentially parasites living off the productive activities of peasants, workers and craftsmen, failing to add anything to the real economy. Bankers along with rich merchants furthermore were accused of collaborating with the nobility and the court, being in league with foreign enemies, conspiring with counter-revolutionaries to the left and right, illegally transferring gold and silver outside France and speculating against the new national currency.

The enragé Jacques Roux's *Discours sur le jugement de Louis le dernier* (1792), for instance, demanded not only that the king be punished for treason follow-

16   Ibid.

ing his flight to Varennes, but that economic traitors too be summarily dealt with. Addressing the sans-culottes, he asserted that 'you ought not be starved, ruined, rendered frantic and attacked by poisonous reptiles, parasitic speculators and vampires, who through the deadly combination of monopoly seize hold of the food trade and consume properties, manufactures and liberty itself and through usury make one arrive at the gates of counter-revolution'.[17] According to Roux, implacable war must be made on monopolists and speculators and all others who were discrediting the *assignats* and who were carrying the price of goods of the first necessity up to unreasonable levels.[18] For Roux the truly productive element in the economy were the small producers who were being victimised by wholesale merchants and bankers.

Jacques Hébert, the leader of the extreme Jacobin faction known as *enragés*, similarly denounced the bankers as 'jean foutres':

> privileged beings who would like the right to seize hold of everything. Oh fuck we know how to abolish the privileges of the speculators, we know how to reduce you to the level of the rest of the people from which you come, messieurs *jean foutres*. Seeing your carriages clog the rue Vivienne one would take you for important people. But I only see a crowd of beggars ... Only repeated thrashings ... will drive you people off.[19]

Hébert further claimed that if one got rid of the so-called merchant and farmer 'aristocracy' and gave land to the urban sans-culottes, productivity would increase and grain shortages and high food prices would disappear.[20]

The productive part of the population worked with their hands and produced real goods which were of use to people. On the contrary, the bankers and speculators, not to speak of the nobility and clergy. lived off other people's labour and were essentially parasitic.[21] Such views of course echo those of the petty producers and had little to do with capitalist accumulation. But in the context of the revolution in which the sans-culottes achieved extraordinary political influence they deeply influenced Jacobin politicians and those who had money to invest and were running scared.

In less extreme form these attitudes were shared by many Jacobins, including Robespierre and Saint Just. In their view the normal and natural economy

---

17   Roux 1792, p. 7.
18   Roux 1792, p. 8.
19   Hébert 1791, no. 14.
20   Hébert 1792, no. 341 cited in Walter 1968, p. 394.
21   Sewell 1980, pp. 110–11.

was one in which the rights of property and unimpeded exchange in the market ought to be the rule. But unfortunately bankers and wholesale merchants were using their financial power to fix the market, taking advantage of wartime conditions and their privileged economic position in order to manipulate and disrupt normal exchange through speculation, monopoly and hoarding.[22] The revolutionary regime's initial reply to growing fiscal and economic disorder was to try to create a new national paper currency and then to impose controls on prices – measures strongly favoured by the sans-culottes. Bankers, not to speak of merchants and rich farmers, tried to resist and undermine these policies which threatened their interests. The Jacobins responded with the Terror, which was directed not only against the political but also against the economic enemies of the revolution. Jacobin and sans-culotte hostility to speculation should be seen as an aspect of their commitment to what they considered the productive elements of the economy whose needs they were determined to protect.

Already in August 1792 the actor turned revolutionary Fabre d'Eglantine denounced bankers as part of an English plot to speculate against the *assignat* – the new paper currency – in order to undermine it. The next year representatives on mission invited patriots to seize bankers' assets and hand the bankers over to the guillotine. In June 1793 the Paris Bourse, on which many bankers traded, was suspended.[23] Two months later the government ordered the closing of France's first national bank, the *Caisse d'Escompte*, compromised on account of being mixed-up in speculation and no longer of service to the finances of the state. At the beginning of September 1793, as the Terror took hold, a decree ordered all operations by banks and exchange agents halted and their business premises and assets sequestered. Although this decree was never fully enforced, many bankers were imprisoned, their assets were seized and over twenty met their death. Under the Terror the primary functions of the bankers under the Old Regime – financing loans to the government and facilitating foreign trade – disappeared. Indeed, with the ordered dissolution of all private companies, which included such entities as the East India Company and the Paris Life Insurance, Water and Lighting companies, the apparently limited role that bankers had in economic life seemed to have vanished.

Under the Terror bankers were imprisoned and killed. Among bankers who became victims the brothers Gabriel and Louis Tassin were among the most important. The Tassins, adherents of the Feuillants, members of the municipal

---

22   Hincker 1993, pp. 211–24.
23   Crouzet 1993, p. 246.

government of Paris and officers of the national guard, were condemned by the Revolutionary Tribunal for having tried to defend the royal family in the Tuilleries from the attack of the sans-culottes (10 August 1792). Perhaps the most powerful banker who suffered death was the Girondin Etienne Clavière, who made a fortune in the stock market prior to the revolution, and as revolutionary Minister of Finance then tried to defend the *assignat* from speculators. Following the fall of the Girondins he was imprisoned and then committed suicide rather than face the guillotine. On the news of his death, his wife Marthe-Louise Garnier immediately poisoned herself. Among the most interesting of the guillotine's victims were two Jewish bankers, the brothers Emmanuel Junius and Simon Junius Frey. French Jews, especially those living in the provinces of Alsace and Lorraine, were initially bewildered or suspicious of the emancipation that the revolution offered. The Frey were not French but Moravians, bankers to the Habsburgs, who moved from adherence to orthodox Judaism to the heresy of Frankism and then to Free Masonry. Responding to the new freedom offered by the revolution with unreserved enthusiasm, the brothers ended up in Paris, befriending the Hébertists, the extreme faction of the Jacobins. The Frey are fascinating because in important respects they anticipate the emancipatory experience of much of nineteenth- and twentieth-century Jewry on the way to modernity. However, their ties to the Hébertists, suspected involvement in speculation and a growing xenophobic reaction encouraged by Robespierre doomed them. All told over twenty-two bankers and stock brokers were executed under the Terror.[24] Perhaps as many as forty or fifty others suffered imprisonment. Some bankers avoided confinement or the guillotine by suspending their operations, fleeing into exile, expatriating their capital or safeguarding it by purchasing so-called national properties.[25] In the eyes of the Jacobins and their supporters the sans-culottes bankers stood for speculation, hoarding and parasitic rather than productive economic activity. The Jacobin and sans-culottes view of bankers as essentially opposed to productive activity would appear to confirm Taylor's view that the finance of the pre-revolutionary period was essentially non-capitalist.

---

24   Rabourdin 1988. Wholesale merchants suspected of cornering the market in one way or another likewise suffered. 97 were executed under the Terror. See Greer, 1935, p. 154. Plessis 1989, pp. 107–8. See Greer, 1966, p. 133.

25   Plessis 1989, pp. 107–8.

Overseas Trade

But as we have already seen, Taylor's view that capitalism did not exist is untenable. In fact capitalism's rapid progress in a still largely rural feudal society was largely responsible for the destabilisation of the towns and countryside at the onset of the revolution. Scepticism is likewise warranted when it comes to Taylor's view of commercial life. His treatment of this economic sector is to say the least incomplete, incorrectly insisting that commerce was a relatively small-scale affair. His understanding of commerce under the Old Regime is based on study of small and medium-sized commercial enterprises in Lyons, which were largely financed by merchants raising their own capital from other local merchants and investors. His view of such merchants is one of deep economic and social conservatism.[26]

But if we consider what commerce's and especially overseas trade's role in the French economy actually was, we get an entirely different picture, and one that reflects spectacular dynamism. At the beginning of the reign of Louis XV, the value of France's external trade had been less than half of Great Britain's. Between the years 1716–20 and 1784–8, French external commerce multiplied by a factor of 3 compared to a British expansion of 2.4. By 1788 French foreign trade was superior to that of its British rival dominating the sale of manufactures to Spain, Italy and the Levant. France's colonial trade was growing at an annual average rate of 2.8 percent and it was leading in the re-export of colonial products to the northern European countries. Especially striking was the expansion of trade through the port of Bordeaux as well as other Atlantic and Mediterranean ports. The slave trade and the sugar plantations of the West Indies were the most profitable part of trade. Overall the increase in wealth in the hands of the merchants involved in overseas trade in the eighteenth century was dramatic and their importance to the French economy can hardly be overstated.

Taylor leaves the impression that the activities of pre-revolutionary financiers were essentially speculative, having to do only with stock market manipulation, loans to government and the handling of foreign exchange. But in addition to speculating in rents, stocks and other financial instruments including government bonds, bankers played a key role in financing this overseas expansion through providing letters of credit and loans. Indeed, it is difficult to see how overseas trade on such a scale could have developed without access to a well-developed system of credit as provided by the Parisian bankers. It was the finan-

---

26   Taylor 1963, p. 60: Taylor 1967, pp. 482–4.

cing of trade rather than loans to courtiers or speculation on the stock market which was the chief source of their profits. And as we have stressed it was the expanding colonial and overseas trade which these bankers helped finance which was the major source of the dynamism in the French economy of the eighteenth century.[27] In Lille the rise of the all-important cotton manufacture was admittedly initially the result of the pooling of local financial resources.[28] But this does not confirm Taylor's notion of economic parochialism. It rather reflects the local basis of the process of industrialisation in its early stages, which we have noted is observable on both sides of the Channel. Moreover, from the beginning the commercial credit extended by the banks of Lille as well as Paris was indispensable to the development of the long-distance operations of these manufacturers.[29] Indeed, the further growth of Indian cotton manufacturing in Lille was financed in part by the profits of the colonial trade and the slave plantations.[30] We see a like pattern in the emergence of manufacturing in Dauphiné. The growth of canvas, paper and metallurgical manufacturing and its eventual development into large-scale industry was directly tied to the expansion of the West Indian market. The important Dauphinois Perier bank appears to have been an outgrowth of such operations.[31] The commercialisation of the products of the iron and steel manufacturers in Burgundy appears likewise to have been dependent on local banks tied in with the Parisian credit market.[32] Taylor's failure to consider the weight of overseas commerce is serious as it relates to the major role of banking prior to the revolution. Most of the growth of the export sector was based on commercial credit and the greater part of this credit was supplied by the Parisian bankers.

The Crisis of Public and Private Finance

Taylor's turning a blind eye to the role of Parisian commercial credit in financing overseas trade must lead us to fundamentally question his analysis of capitalism and the role of finance prior to the revolution. All the more so as we know that banking and credit was one of the central political and economic issues in the period of speculative fever leading up to the revolution. The cre-

---

27   Antonetti 1963, pp. 249–50, Potofsky 2011, pp. 92–4, Forestier 2011, pp. 55–6.

28   Hirsch 1991, pp. 114–15, 330–1.

29   Hirsch 1979; Claeys 2011, p. 1927.

30   Hirsch 1991, pp. 114–16.

31   Léon 1963, pp. 25–7, 33.

32   Woronoff 1984, p. 511.

ation of the *Caisse d'Escompte* in the 1770s was not only intended to address the immediate problem of financing government debt.[33] It also was meant to respond to the growing demand for more accessible commercial credit on a national scale, as the relationship between confidence in the public debt and the availability of commercial credit was close. A system of public finance which would allow the state to finance its need to fight wars and at the same time maintain and expand the economy became a central issue as the revolution approached.[34]

In the course of the 1780s it became evident that the credit made available through the *Caisse* was restricted to the government, court and elite of big merchants and bankers and failed to meet national commercial needs. In a similar manner the last ditch attempt by Calonne to save the finances of the French state by inflating economic demand and thereby generating more fiscal resources aborted because the expansion of credit during his ministry extended to only a narrow circle and failed to increase the purchasing power of the mass of the population. The failure of Calonne's experiment in demand-creation was in turn rooted in the more fundamental problems of social and economic inequality. Meanwhile the flagrant political manipulation of the finances of the *Caisse d'Escompte* as well as the French-controlled Bank of Saint Charles in the same decade helped to undermine the legitimacy of the regime. Indeed, the scandals surrounding the political manipulation of the market, the stock exchange and the banks prepared the way for the constitutional crisis of 1789.[35] There developed an increasing awareness that excessively high government debt was driving up interest rates and discouraging the investment of capital in new enterprises, complicating the economic crisis that struck in the late 1780s and becoming part of the developing political crisis.[36] The solution to the problem of government debt and the creation of a proper national bank which would in principle be at arms-length from the government became part and parcel of the question of the establishment of a constitutional or responsible government.[37] At the local level the restoration of the credit of the state was understood to be tied directly to resolving the problem of commercial credit.[38]

---

33   Lüthy 1959–61, vol. 2, p. 701.

34   Laffon de Ladébat 1807, pp. 3–4, Legay, Félix and White 2009, pp. 183–201.

35   Lüthy 1959–61, vol. 2, p. 703.

36   Root 1994, p, 180; Butel 1974, pp. 206–7; Lüthy 1959–61, vol. 2, pp. 77–81.

37   Root 1994, pp. 170–210; Luckett and Lachaier 1996, pp. 291–2; Bosher 1970, pp. 257–75; Whatmore 2012, pp. 21, 213–16, 219; Sonenscher 1997, pp. 268–325.

38   Hirsch 1991, p. 194.

The development of a more appropriate system of banking and finance was not only key to the future operations of the government but also to hopes for the renewed growth of the French economy. A wide-ranging debate around the creation of a national bank developed which drew in not only Necker and Clavière but also the banker François Louis Jean-Joseph de Laborde de Mereville, Dupont de Nemours, Olympe de Gouges, Marat and Condorcet, among many others, reflecting the centrality of the issue of public and private finance to the revolution.[39] Condorcet's views were particularly insightful, calling for reducing the power of the Parisian financiers by decentralising control of banking into the hands of provincial assemblies which could better serve the credit needs of local enterprises. Condorcet furthermore made the sophisticated observation that not only could the existence of a national bank or public debt have an effect on all aspects of an economy but that these effects could be calculated.[40] That the question of a national bank was at the centre of political discussion in the revolutionary crisis must lead us to question Taylor's view that the crisis of finance had little to do with capitalism and was simply an expression of the recurrent financial problems of the Old Regime. Among the forces that impelled the revolution was not only the issue of the immediate crisis of government revenues, but the need to create a more efficient system of public and private finance in response to a French economy which had reached a turning point. In 1789 the government's inability to pay its debt helped to burst asunder the existing political system while the future of banking and credit remained one of the central questions facing the new revolutionary regime. The fact that after the temporary suppression of private banking during the period of the Terror the government of the Directory went on to experiment with free banking and then under Napoleon moved to create the Bank of France (1803) – which brought together most of the leading French capitalists, including bankers and industrialists, to create a bank of banks – reflects the centrality of the question of finance to the revolutionary process.[41] A clear evolution toward the creation of a new financial system more effectively tied to the new capitalist political and economic order emerged during the revolution. This overall evolution leads us to delve more deeply into the role of banking and state finance at the height of the revolutionary crisis.

39   Stasavage 2003, p. 148.
40   Condorcet 1793–4, vol. 1, p. 570.
41   Jacoud 1996, pp. 255–66.

The Bankers

There were about seventy private bankers in Paris at the time of the revolution. Some were French, but most foreign – Dutch, English, but principally Swiss, especially Genevan. Most of the Genevans came from Protestant families which had abandoned France following the revocation of the Edict of Nantes. But descendants of these exiles filtered back into the Kingdom and set themselves up as bankers in Paris in the course of the eighteenth century in response to expanding economic opportunities and growing religious tolerance. The Parisian town houses of these bankers served as both residences and places of business and were located mainly between the Place Vendôme and the rue Beaubourg. As noted above by Hébert, the centre of activity for most of the bankers was the rue Vivienne in the quarter named for the monastery known as the Filles de Saint-Thomas.[42] Under Napoleon the site of this monastery became the location of the Parisian Bourse – a building built by the revolutionary architect Alexandre Théodore Brogniart. Set on fire during the events of May 1968, it is today, in the age of the internet, a shopping centre.

The new townhouses of the bankers built in this quarter reflected the Parisian construction boom in the years leading up to the revolution, which was mainly based on profits from the Atlantic trade. The substantial investment in Parisian real estate signalled the prosperity enjoyed by overseas merchants and bankers. At the same time the real estate boom perhaps also reflected the still limited opportunities for profitable investment within the productive sectors of the French economy.[43] In a typical operation on the eve of the revolution, the Parisian Insurance Company, a company initially floated to cash in on the stock market boom of the 1780s, agreed to pay off the debts of the Duke de Choiseul. In return the company acquired a set of houses owned by the duke in and around the new Théâtre des Italiens, located in this same quarter where real estate was booming.[44]

Speaking of the rue Vivienne, Sebastien Mercier noted: 'There is more money on this street than in all the rest of the city. It is the pocketbook of the capital. The big banks and notably the *Caisse d'Escompte* are to be found there. The bankers, money changers and stock brokers and all others who trade in money are located there. As the whole of their science consists of buying low

---

42   Bourdin 1937, pp. 16–17.
43   Potofsky 2009, p. 11.
44   Lüthy 1959–61, vol. 2, p. 713.

from some in order to sell high to others, everything favours their avarice ... All things which constitute speculation and that by nature is hostile to the sanctity of agriculture is to be found in proximity to this street'.[45] Mercier shared the common view that bankers had no interest in the productive side of the economy and that their trade in money was hostile to it.

As early as September 1789 Marat, responding to attacks on the inflammatory stories in his new journal *L'Ami du people* that were emanating from the district of the Filles de Saint Thomas, noted that: 'I would have believed such a thing impossible if I had not known that the district is that of the stock exchange agents, bankers, financiers and speculators, that is, men who build their fortune on the ruin of others, who drink the blood of people and whose rapacity which is a real plague of humanity is one of the principal causes of public misery'.[46] In the aftermath of the revolution the rue Vivienne and the monastery of the Filles-Saint Thomas were included in the new municipal section known as *La Bibliotheque* (later *Lepeletier*), embracing most of the financial district. About a quarter of the active citizens of this section were made up of bankers, money changers, treasurers and financial clerks. Based on this electorate in 1791, the section elected Etienne Clavière and the banker Jean-Louis Monneron as delegates to the Legislative Assembly.

A Protestant sensibility diluted somewhat by Enlightenment rationalism persisted in the Parisian banking families and was reinforced by a strong endogamy.[47] Some formed part of the Calvinist or Lutheran congregations in Paris while most focused their faith on family devotions discreetly confined to the home.[48] Although the Protestantism of the bankers was no longer held against them by most Parisians, the bankers remained aware of their embattled heritage. During the revolution counter-revolutionaries reminded them of this. In the debate in the Constituent Assembly leading to the expropriation of ecclesiastical property Cardinal Jean Maury alluded to the religion of the bankers by denouncing the 'Genevan' or 'foreign' bankers who wanted to usurp the lands of the Gallican Church to guarantee the national debt.[49] Later on a royalist paper the *Annales monarchiques* more directly accused the Protestant bankers of being the money behind the revolutionary agitation which was being whipped up in the wake of the flight to Varennes:

---

45   Mercier 1994, vol. 1, pp. 730–1.
46   Marat, *L'ami du peuple*, no. 20, 30 September 1789.
47   Biancarli 1995, pp. 137–9.
48   Lods 1992, p. 273.
49   Maury 1827, vol. 4, pp. 171–4.

The Protestants, the patriots in the sense of the revolution, are at work realizing enormous gains. Monsieur B.de M. (François Louis Jean-Joseph de Laborde de Méréville) at Bordeaux has seized hold of all the coin and numeraire there. All of the former rebels of Holland, a large number of the Protestants of England and all of the beggars of the Constituent Assembly who have enriched themselves at the expense of our misery, have united to create a fund of 150 million livres and with this tainted money are getting ready to once more rouse the people who at this moment are afflicted by misery and by that means to draw them into a new course of crimes more vast and atrocious than all of the precedent ones.[50]

The importance of the overseas trade to the Parisian bankers is reflected in their reaction to demands for the abolition of slavery, which began to be voiced from 1789. The growing chorus against slavery led the Caribbean planters and the merchants of Bordeaux to demand that the National Assembly and the city of Paris support the slave trade and the continuation of slavery in France's West Indian colonies.[51] In February 1790 a resident of the Section Filles Saint-Thomas, Louis Lizin de Mily, who was born into a prominent family in Martinique, published a warning that abolition would set off a race war in France's West Indian islands.[52] The appearance of this work immediately won the plaudits of the Club Massiac or Parisian pro-slavery lobby.[53] A resolution was then passed in the assembly general of the Section Filles Saint-Thomas by an overwhelming majority noting that calls for the abolition of slavery were at the very least premature. The end of black slavery would mean the loss of these islands as colonies and the forfeit annually of 300 million livres in cash and 250 million in sugar and other commodities. It would mean the loss of a further 150 million livres in exports. Such losses would lead to the collapse of the maritime towns and the merchant fleet. It concluded that Paris, like the rest of France, had a stake in the prosperity of these colonies. The resolution called on the other districts of Paris to likewise endorse the maintenance of the slave trade and slavery and noted that Rouen has already done so. Very few other districts of Paris heeded this appeal. On the other hand, the resolution backed by the Parisian bankers and financial community reflects a sophisticated understanding of the importance of the West Indian slave economy to their interests.[54]

---

50   Bouchary 1939–43, vol. 2, p. 22.
51   Liébart 2006.
52   Lizin de Mily 1790.
53   Challamel 1895, 1974, p. 74; Debien 1953, pp. 185, 193, 322, 323.
54   Lacroix 1894–1955, vol. 4, pp. 374–5; Antonetti 1963, p. 209.

Lüthy distinguishes between the private bankers and the financiers of the Old Regime. The latter were directly tied to government finances, holding state office and adhering to the Catholic faith.[55] The former had to do mainly with international trade, operated at a remove from the state, and were mainly Protestants. Jean Bouvier, on the other hand, insists that the differences between the groups ought not to be exaggerated. There was an overlap between the two, according to him, private bankers who made or organised loans to the court and government and financiers who became involved in discounting letters of exchange.[56] The Caisse d'Escompte had as its administrators both financiers and Protestant bankers. The above mentioned François Laborde de Mereville, who was the son of the marquis Jean-Joseph de Mereville, the celebrated court banker, was himself a merchant banker and a deputy for the third estate in the Estates-General of 1789. Father and son were deeply involved in the overseas Caribbean trade and sugar plantations centred on the port of Bordeaux.[57] Perhaps the clearest instance of this overlap were the Lecouteulx of Rouen and Paris, an old bourgeois Catholic family which combined an interest in the debts of the court with overseas trade and even the financing of mines and manufactures.[58] The Lecoutuealx experienced massive losses on their Western Indian investments as a result of the Haitian revolution.[59] Many of the private bankers, on the other hand, were not even subjects of the French king. Clavière, a citizen of Geneva, for example, at first could not directly participate in French politics and only obtained naturalisation after the revolution. Like Clavière many had migrated to Paris as a result of the growing financial needs of the monarchy, the development of overseas commerce and the increasingly tolerant attitude of the government toward the Protestant religion.

The Revolution of 1789

When the revolution arrived most bankers supported it. The fact that these powerful men – the financial mainstays of the Old Regime – did so was of incalculable importance to the initial success of the revolution. Their support for the party of constitutional government and civil and human rights as against the party of absolute monarchy and privilege was of immense import

---

55   Lüthy 1959–61, vol. 2, p. 774.
56   Bouvier 1964, pp. 118–19.
57   Potofksy 2011, pp. 93, 106; Claeys 2011, vol. 2, pp. 1204–24; Fourbert 1990.
58   Zylberberg 2001, pp. 163, 167.
59   AN F7 4774.

in redefining their own social and economic functions. But at first sight their support for the revolution is surprising, since many were deeply involved in buying or selling royal debt and were by instinct conservative. Nonetheless some had undeniably been affected by the liberal ideas of the Enlightenment. The sympathetic attitude of others like Clavière may have been shaped by the anti-oligarchic revolution which had shaken their native city of Geneva (1782). Many had supported the Genevan revolution which had then been suppressed by the intervention of the French monarchy. In their eyes the revolution in France seven years later vindicated their previous failure.[60] More decisive in determining the attitude of most bankers was the dire nature of the crisis. They were alarmed by the court's dismissal of one of their own, the Genevan banker Jacques Necker, as minister of finance. They feared that the ouster of Necker foreshadowed the monarchy's repudiation of the national debt and imminent and catastrophic financial loss from which they could not extricate themselves – an important point.[61] As a result, abandoning their usual caution, they were led to support the taking of the Bastille and the establishment of the Paris Commune. The banker Etienne Delessert, for example, who had befriended Rousseau and had employed him as a tutor, encouraged his son, clerks and servants to participate in the ransacking of the Invalides for arms prior to the assault on the Bastille. The basement of Delessert's townhouse in the rue Coq-Héron near Palais-Royal was turned into an arsenal during the siege. Delessert then provided money to support the unit of the national guard established in his district. The bankers Aimé Gabriel Fulchiron, Jean-François Perregaux, Gabriel and Louis Tassin, Jean Cottin and Théodore Jauge became national guard officers. Joseph Lefebvre, a banker who lived in the rue Beaubourg, meanwhile was appointed commissioner of enrollments for his district. Among the rumours circulating in the wake of the taking of the Bastille was that the rue Vivienne, in other words, the bankers, had secretly bought the loyalty of the king's own guard – the so-called *gardes francaises*.[62] According to Marat, a few months later, on the arrival of the king at the Hôtel de Ville following the March on Versailles, the bankers, money changers and speculators assembled and fiercely acclaimed Necker. He was considered their idol, someone ever ready, as Marat puts it, to sacrifice the happiness of the nation to themselves.[63]

---

60   Whatmore 2012, pp. 5–12.
61   Caron 1907, pp. 666–7.
62   Bourdin 1937, p. 17.
63   Marat, *L'ami du peuple*, no. 28, 8 October, 1789.

As a result of the revolution's abolition of legal privilege the power of the bankers, who based their influence essentially on money, dramatically increased. The sudden rise in the status of the bankers following the revolution is reflected in a report of the Ambassador of Saxony. At the conclusion of his account of the March on Versailles, which according to the ambassador was a day filled with outrages, he notes that one of Lafayette's *aides-de-camp*, the banker Jauge, dressed in military uniform, saw fit to enter the *cabinet du roi* uninvited in a way that no duke or peer would have dared to do prior to the revolution. Addressing himself to the Foreign Minister Count Montmorin de Saint Herem, Jauge noted that the Count's carriage had not been allowed into the courtyard of Versailles and explained that he had ordered the gates be kept closed. 'Under the circumstances', he explained, 'it is necessary to learn how to suffer'. The ambassador concluded: 'My head is still unable to comprehend this change of circumstances'.[64] Indeed, in abolishing the privileges of the nobility and the influence of the court financiers and by reducing step-by-step the government's involvement in the economy, the revolution greatly increased the influence and power of the private bankers, giving them every incentive to continue their support.

The bankers tried to use their newfound influence to shape the politics of the revolutionary regime. Their primary concerns during the peaceful two year interlude which followed Louis XVI's return to Paris was guaranteeing the national debt through the confiscation of the lands of the Church and the drawing up of a liberal constitution. They pursued these objectives by means of their participation in moderate political clubs like the Société de 1789, the Feuillants and the Club de Valois. In the meetings of these clubs could be found such leading figures in Parisian banking circles as Perregaux, Walter Boyd and John William Ker, Jean Cottin, Laurent-Vincent and Jean-Barthélemy Lecouteulx, Guillaume Mallet, Louis Greffuhle, Jean Marc Montz, Jean Boscary, Etienne Delessert, Jean Girardon and Théodore Jauge.[65]

It was reassuring to the bankers that while the monarchy lasted, two Genevans, the bankers Necker and Clavière, were ministers of finance. In an effort to continue to retain the bankers' confidence following the overthrow of the monarchy, Clavière was named finance minister once more under the short-lived Girondin republic. Summing up the cause and consequences of the revolution, Edmund Burke argued that as a result of the enormous national debt, 'a great monied interest had insensibly grown up, and with it a great

64   Mathiez, Albert 1913, 1989, p. 75.
65   Challamel 1895, 1974; Bouchary, 1939–43, vol. 2, p. 14.

power'.[66] According to him, the revolution marked the triumph of this moneyed interest over the traditional landed interest. Seizing the lands of the Church then made possible a vast expansion of public credit through the creation of the *assignats*: 'by this means the spirit of money-jobbing and speculation goes into the mass of land itself, and incorporates with it. By this kind of operation, that species of property becomes (as it were) volatized'.[67] Burke concluded that a new Paris-based financial oligarchy had come to power: 'it is through the power of Paris, now become the center and focus of jobbing, that the leaders of this faction direct, or rather command the whole legislative and the whole executive government'.[68] Burke's conception of the revolution fails to capture the popular and class nature of the revolution, and does not properly grasp the contradictory effects of the institution of the *assignats* on the operation of the private banks. But *pace* Taylor and other revisionists, the view of Burke, the leading counter-revolutionary theorist of the time, is impressive in its grasp of the new political power of finance capital and the concomitant transformation of landed property into capital which followed the revolution. Likewise Burke understands the link between the immediate crisis and the longer term conflict between rival economic orders, the one based on traditional control over land and the other on finance capital.

In addition to writing a new constitution and securing the state debt, financial reform including the creation of a national currency and bank were important goals of this initial liberal stage of the revolution. As a remedy to bankruptcy and in order to restore economic confidence, Necker proposed that the Caisse d'Escompte be transformed into a national bank whose notes would be backed by the free gift of wealthy citizens and especially the property of the king and clergy.[69] Clavière planned a central bank based on mono-metallism and the abolition of the long-standing distinction between real money and money of account. Clavière was the primary agent behind the *assignats* in their first form, i.e., convertible bonds used as a means of guaranteeing the national debt. At the same time he envisioned a national bank as a bank of deposit for individuals or for other regional banks which would create money, issue government-backed bonds and serve as a clearing house at the national level for loans and debts. It is noteworthy that Clavière's scheme included further provisions which would have smoothed the way toward the fuller development of private investment

66   Burke 2001, p. 274.
67   Burke 2001, p. 360. See Pocock 1985, pp. 193–212.
68   Burke 2001, p. 365.
69   Necker 1789, pp. 160, 168; Crouzet 1993, p. 206; Dorigny 1985, pp. 99–100; Antonetti 2007, pp. 74, 91.

banking. Claviere's scheme indicates an awareness of the need to link finance capital with investment in productive activity. The plans of Necker and Clavière make clear that the establishment of a national bank was not simply a question of restoring the finances of the government but part of an overall plan for overcoming the political and economic crisis which had intensified as a result of the revolution and which could only be ended by the restoration of confidence, especially among those with money.

Among those with money whose confidence needed to be restored the bankers were foremost. Their initial support for the new regime was strengthened by a renewal of economic expansion after the crisis of 1789.[70] Many bankers and merchants at first assumed that after the upheavals of 1789 the political and economic problems facing France would be resolved. In their view the revolution had created the possibility of an unobstructed path toward the development of a productive, commercial and financial capitalism whose different sectors would operate in concert. Indeed, far from the revolution fostering an atmosphere of commercial and financial caution, the years which immediately followed the storming of the Bastille were marked by renewed economic growth, expansion of foreign trade and a flurry of speculation.[71] True, over the course of the next three years the propertied classes step-by-step began to dump the newly established national currency in exchange for gold and silver. Yet the gradual erosion of the exchange rate at first served to quicken economic life. Seeking safety, investors and savers exchanged the new French paper currency for commodities and thereby boosted demand. Likewise the depreciation of the currency actually favoured exports, which prospered during 1791 and 1792.

The expansive liberalism of Adam Smith made itself fashionable and even became briefly hegemonic, eclipsing the hitherto dominant Physiocratic school.[72] In the name of laissez-faire regulations over the buying and sale of property, monopolies and barriers to commerce of all sorts including regulations on prices and wages were relaxed. The Law of Allarde (2 March 1791) took a decisive step toward a much vaunted economic freedom as corporations, guilds, and royal manufactures were abolished. The Goudard Decree of the following September lifted all regulations on manufacturing.[73] Many journeymen and apprentices, evidently inspired by the notion of economic freedom, took

---

70   Perrot 1975, p. 32.
71   Poussou 1993, p. 102.
72   Whatmore 2002, pp. 65–89.
73   Hirsch 1989, pp. 1286–7, Fitzsimmons 2010, pp. 51–6.

the opportunity to leave their masters to try to set up in business for themselves.[74] The loosening of the economic reins also made possible the multiplication of new small private banks and other financial institutions amid general
acclaim.[75] Important in fostering the creation of these latter bodies was the
demand for credit and the opportunity some of these new institutions offered
small producers, shopkeepers and skilled workers to buy annuities.

Private Money

The creation of new banks was above all meant to find an immediate remedy
to the increasing shortage of small change to pay workers and to buy and sell
goods in local retail markets.[76] The paucity of small metallic coins initially was
the result of the import of large amounts of grain to deal with the subsistence
crisis and also the consequence of the commercial deficit due to the economic
and political upheavals attendant on the revolution.[77] But over the longer term
it reflected the fact that despite enormous popular support for the revolution
the possessing classes – including well-to-do peasants and merchants – began
to hedge their bets by hoarding or expatriating bullion or metallic coinage,
especially following signs of accelerating inflation that became evident in
1791. A shortage of coin backed by gold or other precious metal is no mere
technical matter. Without sufficient coin not only is foreign trade inhibited
but the capacity of productive capital to employ and pay workers and realise
profits in a money form is fundamentally constrained. In any case, in France
the growing shortage of numeraire began to stir popular unrest, especially
among workers, who increasingly found themselves not being paid or not being
paid in full. As the crisis deepened the regime tried to counter the lack of
liquidity by gradually transforming the *assignat*, which had begun life as a kind
of convertible bond meant to guarantee the national debt, into a new paper
currency issued in smaller and smaller denominations. But even aside the
fact that the *assignat* lacked the backing of sufficient liquid and exchangeable
metallic coin owing to increased hoarding and expatriation, the distribution of
the *assignats* lagged behind demand and markets became increasingly flooded
with new local currencies, private as well as public, backed by little or nothing
in the way of reserves.

---

74   Heller 2006, p. 88.
75   Bouchary 1939–45, vol. 3, pp. 9–10.
76   Bouchary 1940–2, vol. 2, pp. 9–11, 15.
77   Bouchary 1937, p. 61.

Meanwhile the French economy took a turn for the worse in the aftermath of the revolution in Haiti. Cut off from the continuing flow of sugar, coffee and cotton from the West Indies from the late summer of 1791, it was impossible for France to offset the ongoing entry of English manufactures and to pay for the inflow of Spanish coin while stemming a growing flight of precious metals. The expatriation of gold and silver accelerated in the face of declining political confidence and growing inflation. Among those most immediately affected were the bankers Laborde, closely tied to the West Indian trade, as well as the Parisian banker Jauge, linked to the important wholesale firm owned by his father, the Bordeaux merchant Simon Jauge.[78] In the crisis that followed several Parisian banks went under. In the meantime the detention of Louis XVI following the disastrous flight to Varennes led to the outbreak of war between revolutionary France and its neighbours in April 1792.[79] The growing scarcity of liquid capital and the outbreak of war made the maintenance of the export trade increasingly difficult. The financing of overseas trade had been the life blood of the bankers and the source of the exchange necessary to keep the *assignat* stable. The revolution began as a crisis of credit. It entered a new stage when it became a crisis of money, circulation and exchange.

In the face of the shortage of coinage in 1791 the government allowed hundreds of so-called *caisses patriotiques* to open across France, which issued their own currencies known as *billets de confiance*.[80] The existence of a multiplicity of different monies was nothing new in France. It should be remembered that under the Old Regime there had never been a national currency. Save only for money of account calculated in livres and sols, trade had long been carried on using different kinds of numeraire both foreign and domestic. The French therefore to begin with were comfortable with the idea of different local monies.

These largely public local banks it should be noted were approved by the Legislative Assembly, which was in principle strongly attached to the idea of political decentralisation and local economic initiatives. Most of these new banks were organised under the aegis of municipal or departmental authorities and were required to maintain a reserve in *assignats* to back the local issue. These currencies appear at first to have functioned well, helping to sustain local markets. They were of course established and dominated by the local bourgeoisie but enjoyed support at first from the small producers and workers

---

78   Butel 1974, pp. 200, 216, 308, 315.
79   Antonetti 1963, pp. 197, 209; Crouzet 1993, p. 199.
80   White 1990, pp. 251–76.

as well.[81] Indeed, they were very much in accord with the laissez-faire spirit of
the early phase of the revolution, which sought to minimise state interference
in the economy with the belief that unleashing the market, especially at the
local or regional level, would foster growth.

In Paris revolutionary sections like the Section Bibliothèque created their
own *caisses patriotiques*.[82] But the situation in the capital and in other major
centres like Lyons, Lille and Bordeaux and in manufacturing centres appears
to have been different from less important centres in that private interests
played a larger role in the circulation of billets de confiance. In Paris alone
some sixty-three distinct *billets de confiance* were issued, including those created by private bodies like manufactures, bakeries and even theatres. Profits
came from charging fees to exchange *assignats* at a discount for *billets*. Likewise
money was made by speculating with the accumulated funds in the absence
of safeguards ensuring adequate reserves.[83] The problem of a lack of eventual accountability is suggested by the fact that the Girondin leader Brissot,
while he was president of the Section Bibliothèque, casually appropriated 580
livres from his section's account in the *caisse patriotique* and did not pay it
back.[84]

Several of the new banks in Paris were able to achieve a wide reach, allowing
their notes and currencies to circulate at a national level. The Banque Monneron was the most ambitious of these schemes. Founded by the brothers Monneron, who were important merchant bankers involved in the Caribbean trade,
the new bank exchanged *assignats* for stamped copper coins known as mon-
nerons which circulated throughout the country.[85] Also operating on a national
scale was the so-called Maison de Secours whose notes circulated in the millions throughout northern France.[86] Notable, too, was the Caisse Lafarge, which
accumulated 50 million livres in savings and had nearly 120,000 subscribers at
its height in 1793.[87] Also important was Antoine Lacornée's Caisse de Commerce, which put itself forward as an alternative to the big banks designed
to serve the needs of small-scale producers in Paris. Threatened with clos-
ure, Lacornée was able to fend off critics by mobilising the support of some
merchants and sans-culottes, who claimed that the institution represented an

81   Bloch 1910, pp. 143, 45, Houssay 1907, pp. 33–40, Becchia 2000, pp. 387–8.
82   Bourdin 1937, p. 53; Burstin 2005, pp. 302–4.
83   Mathiez 1927, p. 53.
84   Brissot de Warville 1877, p. 448.
85   Bruguière 1986, p. 87.
86   Bouchary 1940–2, vol. 2, pp. 73–156.
87   Thullier 1999, pp. 3–4.

alternative to the hated speculators. It was able to attract the savings of thousands of investors.[88]

The fact that the men who controlled the state in 1791 would allow the creation of a multiplicity of private currencies to circulate throughout France attests to the limitations of the unfettered liberalism which characterised the immediate post-revolutionary period. In adhering to the principle of laissez-faire to the point of allowing money itself to become a matter of private enterprise, they demonstrated that they did not understand the necessity of the state regulating the means of exchange and the market for credit in developing a capitalist economy. Paradoxically it was the Jacobins who understood this better.

We know that influential Parisian bankers became involved in these private operations. Guillaume Sabatier, a director of the East India Company, later imprisoned under the Terror, was a principal backer of the Caisse Lafarge.[89]

Another important private bank, the Caisse patriotique de Paris, with an initial capitalisation of more than three million livres, had as its principal shareholder Delessert.[90] Another investor in this *caisse* was Jean-Pierre Germain, a close associate of Delessert, director of the Paris Insurance Company, partner with Delessert in the acquisition of national properties and future regent of the Bank of France.[91] Jacob Bidermann, who headed the important Senn-Bidermann Bank, was implicated in the affairs of the Monneron Bank. Monneron coins, the numeraire issued by the bank, were machine-manufactured in England at high cost and because of their significant metallic content were hoarded by the French public while the *assignats* they exchanged for them depreciated. As a result the Monneron Bank was in crisis by January 1792 and had to be re-financed by Bidermann's Bank as well as those of Bontemps, Mallet, Tourton and Ravel, and Rivier and Jean Louis Baux. In the absence of any controls the Monneron Bank then clandestinely speculated against the *assignat* on a massive scale, with the help of an intermediary, the Lyonnaise banker Johannot Léozat. This proved a miscalculation, forcing the bank to declare bankruptcy at the end of March 1792.[92] The failure of the Monneron Bank provoked widespread consternation.[93]

---

88   Seligman 1904, pp. 49–50.
89   Claeys 2011, vol. 2, pp. 2168–9.
90   Bouchary 1940–2, vol. 2, p. 59.
91   Szramkiewicz 1974, pp. 129, 134.
92   Antonetti 2007, p. 81.
93   Antonetti 2007, pp. 80–1.

Meanwhile rumours of the failure of the Maison de Secours created its own panic. *Le Moniteur* reported that news of the bankruptcy spread rapidly throughout France, with merchants in many towns refusing to accept its notes, provoking popular commotions.[94] In Paris there were threats of riots against speculators and bankers in the wake of the failed operations.[95] Bidermann does not appear to have been directly involved in the Bank's failure. However, as the executor of the bankruptcy he helped its director François Guillaume escape from prison and flee abroad. His associates were not so lucky. They were killed in the September Massacres, which led to a scandal and Bidermann's temporary detention.[96] Meanwhile Lacornée's Caisse de Commerce not only proved itself insolvent, it became involved in royalist intrigues to try to keep itself afloat. It was shut down once the Jacobins took power and one of its directors, Pierre-Paul Kolly, a bankrupt ex-farmer-general and royalist sympathiser, ended on the guillotine as a counter-revolutionary.[97]

Already in the port city of Nantes in September 1791, workers took things into their own hands. Starting in the naval yards, workers throughout the city rebelled against being paid in *billets de confiance* and demanded the suppression of the local *caisse patriotique*, which they had come to see as a creature of the local employers. According to their complaints, payment in paper as against hard currency had fuelled inflation, effectively enabling employers to cut their wages. So far as they were concerned the billets were a confidence trick being played at their expense. Nostalgia for the more stable currencies of the Old Regime was voiced. Moreover, in the minds of the workers bourgeois members of the national guard sent to repress them were directly involved in keeping this oppressive and fraudulent set-up in place.[98] Similar events occurred at Lille, where wholesale merchants and local bankers established a private bank which issued a currency to pay workers. When the workers rebelled against being paid with this private money, demanding payment in *assignats*, the municipality was forced to take the private bank under its protection.[99]

The excesses of the *caisses patriotiques* provoked a like reaction in Paris.[100] According to Camille Desmoulins, writing in Marat's *L'ami du peuple* on 8 June 1791:

94   *Réimpression de l'ancien Moniteur ... 1789–99* (1843), pp. 66, 132.
95   Jaurès 1968–73, vol. 2, pp. 385–6.
96   Mathiez 1929, pp. 577–89.
97   Bouchary 1940–2, vol. 1, pp. 165–7; Seligman 1904, *passim*; Claeys 2011, vol. 2, pp. 1177–80.
98   Guicheteau 2008, pp. 214–19.
99   Hirsch 1991, p. 211.
100   Bouchary 1940–2, vol. 2, pp. 16–20.

A company made up of vampires (the Caisse Patriotique de Paris) at the head of which are the said (Etienne) Delessert, the so-called Count d'Estaing (Admiral Jean Baptiste Charles Henri Hector), and several deputies of the National Assembly has been formed to suck the blood of the people to the last drop. These greedy speculators contend that there is not enough numeraire and have perhaps themselves contributed to its scarcity by hoarding. You know that a formal decree has ordered that 100 million *assignats* worth 5 livres apiece be put in circulation. This measure if well-directed could benefit the arts, agriculture and commerce. Those backing the caisse have done all that they could to block this measure. Being unable to do so they have established a caisse that they call patriotic but which in fact is a disastrous enterprise. It exchanges assignats worth 50, 100, 200 and 300 livres against notes signed by who knows who ... The operation of these speculators is to discount the assignats against letters of exchange or against prospective gains on the stock market with the purpose of benefiting from the rise and fall of values while monopolizing national properties, perhaps in order to pay for the 20 millions livres worth of national properties that Delessert has already monopolized.[101]

Delessert, who socialised with the Girondin leaders Brissot and Clavière, was arrested under the Terror and barely escaped with his life.[102] Among the charges against him was that in the face of his misdeeds in the management of the Caisse patriotique the public treasury had had to step in and assume the losses. He was also suspected of colluding with foreign agents and the Girondins of Lyons while undermining the *assignats* through speculation: 'it is to be feared that this man whose fortune exceeds the limits of hope can become very dangerous in a moment of crisis ... there is reason to believe that he could serve the interests of foreign powers with money and credit'. In his defence Delessert reminded the Revolutionary Tribunal of his role in the taking of the Bastille, his purchase of national properties and the fact that his son Benjamin was serving as an officer in the revolutionary army, all reflecting patriotism.[103]

The link made between revolutionary patriotism and productive investment was a noteworthy response to the criticism emanating from the Jacobin radicals and sans-culottes. The bourgeoisie, both rural and urban, already held about thirty percent of the land prior to the revolution. But the sudden acquisition

---

101   Bouchary 1940–2, vol. 2, pp. 61–2.
102   Brissot de Warville 1877, p. 343.
103   AN F7 4667, de Coninck 2000, p. 26.

of ten percent more assured them of political and social hegemony. It also amounted to a massive investment of money capital in productive activity. As we have seen, Burke noted the political and economic significance of the sudden and large-scale entry of financial capital into the land, freeing it of feudal entailment and 'volatilising' or transforming it into capital. Bankers obtained a significant proportion of this capital.

Overall the purchase of such national properties on the part of bankers was most evident in the nearby île-de-France. Most of the properties acquired by them took the form of large capitalist farms formerly held by ecclesiastical corporations, which were beyond the financial reach of affluent farmers and labourers. As a group the bankers of Paris – Delessert, Giradot de Marigny, Sabatier, Guillaume and Jacques Mallet, Louis Julien, Jean Dupont, Thomas-Simon Bérard – acquired the largest amount of such properties.[104] Delessert was accused of using his ill-gotten gains from speculation to buy twenty million livres worth of national properties. This was undoubtedly an exaggeration for at his death in 1816 he held only six farms whose worth was estimated at 1.5 million francs.[105] Bérard bought almost 1.5 million livres worth of such properties, which represented the repatriation and re-investment in the French economy of a substantial amount of colonial wealth.[106] Purchase of these properties was represented as an act of patriotism showing on which side of the revolution one stood.[107] But of course acquisition of a national property was more than an act of patriotism or even a hedge against uncertain economic times. Acquisition of these highly productive farms also made good business sense, as the confiscation of national properties put more on the market, significantly lowering their price while the rents on them remained at about the same level.[108] Purchase of such capitalist farms reflected a significant step toward tying productive and finance capital together. It is noteworthy that the movement of capital in this direction was not merely an economic matter but was encouraged by the increasing political restrictions placed on speculation.

104   Moriceau 1989, pp. 218–19, Moriceau 1990, pp. 442, 444–7, 463, 465.
105   Bergeron 1978, p. 71.
106   Claeys 2011, vol. 1, p. 197.
107   Bernard Bodinier and Eric Teyssier 2000, p. 310. See also the testimony of the banker Girardot de Marigny before the Parisian Revolutionary Tribunal, following his arrest in AN F7 4226.
108   Perrot 1975, pp. 32–3.

Assignats

A month after Desmoulins's denunciation of the *caisses* in the press the first signs of opposition to the *billets de confiance* appeared in the local revolutionary organisations of Paris. On 12 July the Section Mauconseil passed a resolution calling for the establishment of a single Parisian currency in place of the *billets de confiance*. The executive of the section then took up the matter. According to its deliberations the absence of a proper money in small denominations had led to disorder and a breakdown in relations between buyers and sellers in the market. The problems were being exacerbated by the manipulations of the merchants of money who were attempting to profit from the existing confusion, especially by controlling the availability of *billets de confiance*. Numeraire is only a representative sign of money and paper only a representation of numeraire. The existence of many different *billets de confiance* in the city's sections is compounding the problem. The solution is the creation of a single paper money in small denominations issued in the name of the united revolutionary sections of Paris.[109] Based on the subsequent discussion of the issue that took place in the Section des Postes it becomes clear that the idea began to take hold that the new currency for Paris should be the basis of a single new currency for France as a whole.[110] In other words, in response to the economic crisis that had been exacerbated by the *billets de confiance*, the productive citizens of revolutionary Paris began to press for the rapid transformation of the assignat into a national currency.

The reaction against the *billets de confiance* was intensified by the outbreak of the Parisian sugar riots. Jean-Marie Boscary, a member of the Legislative Assembly who directed the wholesale merchant house of Choll Boscary and Company, found himself the focal point of popular anger during the riots which rocked the popular quarters of the Faubourg Saint Marcel and Saint-Antoine in January 1792. Boscary's father Jean was a banker, a director of the Paris Life Insurance Company and of the *Caisse d'Escompte*, while his brother Jean-Bapiste-Joseph Boscary Villeplaine was a broker on the stock exchange. His firm Chol Boscary and Company was involved in the West Indian trade as well as in the export and re-export trade all over Europe. In addition Boscary and his partner and relative Chol operated a hat manufacture in Paris which employed 150 workers. Following the taking of the Bastille Jean-Marie became politically active, getting himself appointed secretary of the assembly of representatives

---

109   Lacroix 1894–1955, vol. 7, pp. 433–4.
110   Braesch 1911, pp. 54–5.

of the Paris Commune and elected to the Legislative Assembly. A supporter
of the constitutional monarchy, he was a member of the Club de la Sainte
Chappelle.[111]

As we know, the question of the price of grain driven up by speculation and
hoarding was central to the mentality of the popular classes in Paris during the
revolution.[112] But in fact sugar had also become a regular part of the diet of
Parisian artisans and workers and the sudden increase in its price provoked
deep anger. Along with other wholesalers Boscary Chol and Company suddenly raised the price of sugar to an unprecedented level, claiming shortages in
the wake of the Haitian Revolution.[113] The result was that their warehouses as
well as several other wholesale merchants were pillaged by the sans-culottes
over several nights in late January.[114] Boscary complained to the Legislative
Assembly '... my fortune and those of my friends are in danger. I call upon the
law – the safeguard of property – not only on my account but for the sake of
all the merchants of Paris'.[115] Writing in the journal *L'Assemblee nationale* on
23 January, Charles-Frederic Perlet, by no means a radical, noted 'that it is principally the merchants of money and the companies of so-called patriotic billets
who have hoarded sugar and other commodities through the enormous profits
they have made on their capital as a result of speculating on paper money'.[116]
Widely execrated, Boscary was singled out as a hoarder in the Jacobin Club
by Le Clerc de Saint-Aubin, another merchant and friend of Danton.[117] As a
result of this humiliation Boscary was forced to resign his seat in the Legislative Assembly. The radical press meanwhile raged against the secret hoards
of sugar and other goods allegedly being kept by merchants in warehouses in
Paris and in the main ports. A reporter for one of these papers, the *Revolutions
de Paris*, sarcastically noted that it was incorrect that, as rumoured, there was
a vast stash of sugar hidden in the cellars of the Abbaye of Saint-Germain-
des-Près. Rather the banker François-Sylvain Laurent de Mézières, rue Saint-
Benoît, had an immense store of wine, spirits, wax and coffee which he kept
there.[118] Indeed the banker Laurent de Mézières's agent Louis Desisnard ended
up on the guillotine.[119]

111 Bouchary 1942, pp. 9–11, 13.
112 Kaplan 1982, pp. 1–79; Burstin 2005, pp. 169, 800–11.
113 Jaurès 1968–73, vol. 2, pp. 328, 332–9.
114 Burstin 2005, pp. 332–4.
115 Quoted in Jaurès 1968–73, vol. 2, pp. 342–3.
116 Bouchary1940–2, vol. 2, p. 20.
117 Bouchary 1942, p. 14.
118 Jaurès 1968–73, vol. 2, p. 352.
119 AN W 431.

As a result of the rioting the first hesitant voices were raised in the Legislative Assembly questioning the use of *billets de confiance* and calling for the rapid dissemination of *assignats* in smaller denominations as a way of undercutting the activities of speculators.[120] Then on 26 Jan 1792 a deputation from the militantly revolutionary Faubourg St. Antoine presented a petition in the name of more than 10,000 citizens demanding measures to suppress speculation. It called for the issuing of a decree ordering stricter control of the *caisses patriotiques* which were issuing *billets de confiance* and measures to assure the use and availability of *assignats* in their place.[121] Addressing Boscary's charge that his property had been damaged, the petition warned: 'let the disturbers of the public peace tremble! The patience of the people is at an end. We denounce hoarding of whatever kind. Everything including commodities of the first necessity is under the control of these greedy assassins of the people. These brigands speak of property. Isn't this property itself a crime of lèse-nation?'[122] In response to this petition, which had wide backing, the Assembly voted to put the *caisses patriotiques* under closer scrutiny. The Assembly was in fact responding to what was becoming a grassroots movement toward the creation of a single money which was spreading through parallel resolutions being passed in more and more of the revolutionary sections of Paris. The increasing fear that the revolutionary commune of Paris might act independently from the Convention, posing the threat of dual power, appears to have influenced the attitude of the politicians in the Assembly.

The growing clamour against the *billets de confiance* intensified with the entry in opposition of Clavière and Brissot, who were the leaders of the increasingly ascendant Girondin party.[123] They were not in principle hostile to the bankers, with whom they were closely associated, but rather concerned about the chaos reflected in the multiplication of local *caisses patriotiques*. Their opposition to the *billets* also reflected their understanding of the shift in the popular mood which had become utterly exasperated by financial speculation and which the Girondin leaders now repudiated in principle.[124] By February 1792, Cambon, to the left of the Girondins but still committed to laissez-faire, voiced reservations at the continued existence of the *billets de confiances*. Created amid general enthusiasm, he now claimed that the *billets de confi-*

---

120   Lacroix 1894–8, vol. 8, pp. 94–5.
121   Bouchary 1940–2, vol. 2, p. 20.
122   Lacroix 1894–8, vol. 8, p. 95.
123   Antonetti 2007, p. 76.
124   Bouchary 1939–43, p. 63.

ance issued by the *caisses patriotiques* were undercutting the *assignats*, causing a shortage of numeraire, the decline of the French currency on foreign exchanges, and the hoarding of goods including necessities. It was even possible that they were being used by counter-revolutionaries to buy up *assignats* in order to send them abroad, with the aim of causing shortages of currency. In any case, they lent themselves to counterfeiting operations and their circulation should be terminated.[125]

Following Cambon's critique a lengthy petition from the Section des Lombards underscored that the multiplication of *billets de confiance* had facilitated the operations of speculators buying up and hoarding goods and by this means gouging the people.[126] At the end of March 1792 the question of the *billets de confiance* was debated at length in the Legislative Assembly. On 29 March the Jacobin Jean-Francois Crestin delivered a wide-ranging and stinging indictment of the *caisses patriotiques* in which the behind-the-scenes intrigues of the Parisian bankers were especially underscored. Like Cambon, Crestin acknowledged that the *billets de confiance* at first had had the enthusiastic support of the people. However, he insisted that by now they had become a malediction. They have become the pivot of hoarding and speculation and as such were pumping the substance out of the people. It is well known that speculation is one of the most dangerous enemies of France and of the new Constitution. As a result of the ongoing speculation of the banks and financial companies, the standing of the new national money has been depreciated in the eyes of public opinion. In particular speculation has led to an excessive decline in the value of French currency in foreign exchange markets. 'By virtue of speculation metallic currency has virtually disappeared, the hoarding of commodities of the first and second degree of necessity has been facilitated and the price of goods made exorbitant. This is why the anxieties of the people have been intensified, feeding the troubles which are the consequence of these anxieties while nourishing the hopes of the enemies of liberty'.[127]

It is well know that the *billets de confiance* make possible such speculation. It is not the exchange agents of the Place des Victoires nor the stockbrokers of the Bourse who are the fundamental source of this blood-sucking. They are merely its secondary agents. It is the bankers who are the particular adepts in this kind of activity. Only by getting rid of the primary cause of speculation

---

125   Cambon 1792, p. 5; Lacroix 1894–8, vol. 8, pp. 100–1.
126   Lacroix 1894–8, vol. 8, pp. 105–7.
127   Crestin 1792, p. 4.

can public credit be restored. The art of speculation consists in provoking a rise or fall in exchanges by dint of personal interest and at the expense of the public good. It is the bankers who are particularly skilled in this kind of activity. When bankers get together and under cover of professed patriotism and devotion to country put forward plans for public institutions, such offers should be looked at askance. It is inconceivable that the initial proposals for the establishment of *caisses patriotiques* did not conceal a carefully calculated project of speculative gain in the interest of the bankers and at the expense of the people.[128]

At the moment that the *caisses* were established there was a shortage of metallic currency because of the flight of the emigres and the vagaries of the revolution. The Caisse d'Escompte contributed to the difficulties by continuing the practices of the *ancien régime* under the guise of utility and with the sanction of the Minister of Finance (Clavière). The bankers offered to make *billets de confiance* available based on the reserves or backing of *assignats* which at the time were only available in large denominations. The people desperately seized on the idea and the Constituent Assembly evidently accepted it uncritically. Since the establishment of the *caisses* all the above problems have only been compounded.[129] The caisses have multiplied, even divided into branches, *billets de confidence* of all types have been established throughout the country and the activities of the *caisses* have gone so far as to include the issuing of coins. All told some 400 million livres worth of *billets de confiance* are in circulation with the state having no idea of the resources that back up such notes. In the space of ten months all means of exchange including *assignats* and metallic currency have been largely replaced in the form of the circulating notes of the Caisse d'Escompte, Caisse Patriotique de Paris, Maison de Secours, bankers' letters of exchange and the *billets de confiance* issued by the towns of France. The reserves of the Caisse Patriotique de Paris, it should be pointed out, consist not of *assignats* or metallic currency, but in notes on national properties, the East India Company and other enterprises which lend themselves to further speculation.[130]

The *caisses patriotiques* exchange their notes and bills for *assignats* or exchange *assignats* of higher denomination for those of lower, both discounted at a certain rate of interest. The *caisses* use those of higher denomination to discount letters of exchange or to make loans on the collateral of the notes

128   Crestin 1792, pp. 5–6; Baker 1979, p. 279.
129   Crestin 1792, p. 6.
130   Crestin 1792, p. 7.

of private companies or deposits of bullion. In other words, the *caisses patri-otiques* were carrying on the business of fully-fledged banks and were closely associated with them. The Caisse d'Escompte has been involved in this busi-ness but it at least has significant reserves. The lack of reserves in the Caisse Patriotique de Paris and the Maison de Secours should be particularly noted.[131] In the meantime the expansion of credit made available through these insti-tutions has allowed merchants to hoard enormous quantities of necessities, driving up prices and striking fear in the population.[132] The fall in the value of the assignat on foreign exchange has in similar fashion increased the prices of imported goods. It is said that this is the result of the lack of confidence in the *assignat* on the part of foreigners. But the truth is 'that it is not the for-eigner who has lacked confidence in our paper. It is the capitalist, it is the Parisian banker, they are the ones who have speculated to the point of ima-gining a lack of confidence, a lack of confidence fostered and disseminated by themselves and fed by means of the caisses of which I speak'.[133] This has been done so that the banks and the caisses can speculate more assuredly in numeraire and foreign exchange. The negative political convictions of the counter-revolutionaries have been used to facilitate and cover up these opera-tions. Crestin concludes that the way to end such speculation is to cancel the semi-official status of the *billets de confiance* and instead to defend the new paper money.

On 30 March, the day following Crestin's speech, the Assembly forbade the circulation of further quantities of *billets de confiance* by private entities while ordering a verification of the accounts of the public *caisses* which should be undertaken by the municipalities. But a report by André-Daniel Laffon de Ladebat in early June noted that despite these decrees the situation was getting worse.[134] On 10 August 1792, the day on which the Tuilleries was attacked by the sans-culottes, Nicolas Haussman, deputy for the Seine-et-Oise, denounced the Caisse Lafarge, concluding that: 'it is time to close down all these gambling ventures, lotteries, *caisses* and *tontines* where speculators' exorbitant profits are guaranteed and where those who join have a chance of a return only if there are large numbers of early deaths or there a sufficient number of fools among those who participate. If the poor and workers are able to save something they should invest what they save in their art or craft which is a

---

131   Crestin 1792, pp. 8–9.
132   Crestin 1792, pp. 10–11.
133   Crestin 1792, p. 12.
134   *Archives parlementaires* 1879, vol. 44, p. 695.

solid, pure and fruitful source of wealth. It is from a love of work that prosperity accompanied by good morals issues'.[135] Once again the productive labour of the small producers was invoked in contrast with the unproductive commerce of those involved in money and finance. It is in investment of capital in the latter which is the source of wealth and a virtuous life.

The *caisses patriotiques* were finally ordered shut down in November 1792 by the Jacobin government, which by then had assumed power. It decreed that losses incurred by local *caisses* were to be made good by a special tax on the rich imposed locally.[136] In the mind of the radical politicians and the mass of the public the experience of the *caisses* had been a bitter lesson of the consequences of unregulated speculation. Moreover, it seems clear that in the popular mind, bankers large and small were responsible for this episode. The public attitude toward bankers had been negative prior to the revolution. The animus that developed on the part of the public as a result of the experience of the *caisses patriotiques* helps to explain popular support for the attack on the bankers and the suppression of most kinds of speculative activity under the government of the Terror. Moreover, it serves to explain why the Jacobin government attempted to create a highly regulated and centralised system of public finance in which private banking could find little place.

Crestin had put his finger on the role of the bankers in the operation of the *caisses patriotiques* and the speculative excesses their activities made possible. But he also identified the bankers as the principal opponents to the consolidation of the *assignat* as the national currency. Yet using interest-bearing bonds guaranteed by land instead of gold and silver as the backing for a national paper currency had its own problems, especially with respect to maintaining liquidity and carrying on foreign trade. On the other hand, the establishment of the *assignat* as a national money represented an audacious scheme on the part of the leaders of the revolution in response to popular demands. The establishment of the *assignat* was associated with restoring not only the market but also the productive economy. It was likewise aimed at overcoming the fiscal and economic parochialism that had characterised the French economy under the Old Regime, which whatever tendencies it had toward political centralisation had never come close to creating a national currency.[137] Furthermore, the *assignat* backed up by the reserves of the confiscated national properties represented a serious threat to the previously unregulated speculative exchange and

---

135   *Archives parlementaires* 1879, vol. 47, p. 629.
136   Herrmann-Mascard 1990, p. 22.
137   Blanc 1994, pp. 81–111.

loan operations of many bankers and, particularly, to the latter's long-standing ability to profit from the financial instability of the French state. The institution of the *assignat* which was opposed by the bankers is a perfect illustration of the principle that private interests may profit from capitalism but cannot create its framework. Only the power of the state can do so. Indeed, it is impossible to understand the nature of capitalism without understanding the indispensable tie between the modern state and the creation of a level economic playing field for the accumulation of capital. Such a playing field requires that the state be able to regulate private finance. It was especially for this reason that the private bankers resisted the *assignat* as a national currency.

The idea for the *assignats* had initially developed in reaction to the problem of looming state bankruptcy as we have noted. As the financial crisis which brought on the revolution reached its climax, there were more and more outcries against the direct involvement of bankers in the financing of government through private loans controlled by them. As early as 1789 the National Assembly began to consider measures to remove all private enterprise from direct involvement in the system of public credit. It was asserted that the government should be able to borrow on the basis of its own credit. Fingers were pointed at the private and court bankers who advanced the government money while profiting from administering the accumulated debt. The Caisse d'Escompte which was run by a committee of such bankers was viewed as being at the centre of such machinations. As we have seen Necker had proposed that a reconstituted Caisse d'Escompte be used to issue a new set of securities backed by the state. But the National Assembly more and more lost confidence in the Caisse. Based on the national properties taken from the Church, *assignats* began to be issued by the government as early as 1790 in place of notes from the Caisse. Mirabeau strongly endorsed this move, noting the resistance of the bankers whom he claimed were accustomed to receiving ten percent interest on their loans. The issuing of the *assignats* would open up a new source of credit. The resulting competition would lead to lower interest rates. The objections of the banks are a signal of hope to the manufactures whose enterprises, according to Mirabeau, would be restored as a result of access to cheaper credit.[138] Based on such conceptions aimed at restoring the economy based on cheapening the cost of borrowing, the National Assembly worked out a scheme for paying off the national debt held by financiers, bankers and other creditors based on public rather than private credit.[139] There seemed less and less

---

138   Levasseur 1903, 1969, Vol. 1, p. 148.
139   Bosher 1970, pp. 262–5.

place left for an institution like the Caisse d'Escompte, especially following its role in the speculative excesses involving the *billets de confiance*. The Jacobins were to order its dissolution in 1793. In its place the Jacobins would eventually come up with the idea of a public mortgage bank which would reduce interest rates forcing capitalists to make available credit to agriculture and commerce at competitive interests rates.[140]

Meanwhile raising revenue through taxation was foreclosed by the continued reluctance of the population, especially the well-off, to pay taxes – a fact of astonishing import when one considers it. Despite the absence of a fiscal foundation the revolutionary government abandoned step-by-step the policy of trying to finance its growing expenditures by borrowing from the bankers, whose past involvement in financing debt made them suspect. Between 1789 and 1793 the new regime instead issued currency backed in the first place by the confiscated national properties and then more and more resorted to using the *assignat* as fiat money in the face of an absence of sufficient numeraire and the growing need to finance war expenditure. The contrast between the policies of Clavière and Cambon in this regard illuminates the evolution toward fiat currency. As a result of the debacle of the *billets de confiance*, Clavière and the Girondin leadership wholly committed themselves to the establishment of a unified national currency. In the course of his tenure as minister of finance (1791–2) Clavière increasingly resorted to defending the *assignat* by speculating in its favour while fostering its consolidation as a unique and credible paper money. At the same time as minister of finance he called for the cessation of the circulation of any other form of money in a circular to the departments (20 October 1792):

> The circulation of all *billets de confiance* issued by *caisses patriotiques* must cease. The emission of assignats in small denominations, the large-scale fabrication of copper sous ... has rendered the *billets de confiance* useless. And the abuses and disorder to which they have given rise must end as soon as possible. Act with the greatest dispatch so that nothing appears in circulation any longer which is not national.[141]

But faced with the increasing and concerted attempts by foreign governments to undermine the *assignat*, he came to agree with Brissot that a war policy against the Habsburgs, which would among other things *impose* the assignat on

---

140   *Archives parlementaires* 1879, vol. 90, p. 220.
141   Leroux 1922, p. 231.

conquered territories, was a necessary means of bolstering the currency. Only those who think that economic assets alone determine the value of a currency in international markets will find this policy incredible. Resort to war and imperialism in the past and the present can provide governments with both real and intangible assets including confidence in the value of their money.[142] The immediate aim in this case was the imposition of the *assignat* on the territory of France's enemies and, as Daniel Guérin has suggested, the disruption of the English entrepôt in Belgium. But more deeply it may be seen as the beginnings of a reorientation of the French economy away from the colonial trade in the wake of the Haitian Revolution and toward expansion on the Continent. In any case, the ultimate result, namely, the French conquest of Belgium (1794) was suddenly and dramatically to unleash the potential of capitalism there. In the wake of the French occupation the abolition of internal barriers to trade, the opening of the French market and transformation of ecclesiastical property into national properties overnight opened this highly developed country to capitalism.[143] As occupier, France benefited enormously from this transformation.

On the other hand, Claviere clung to the idea that the *assignat* had to be backed by the possibility of land redemption through purchase of national properties and on that basis called for the sale of government bonds to finance the rising costs of war and other government expenditure.[144] Meanwhile behind the scenes the regime was being strengthened by the rising power of new elements of a bourgeoisie that was buying up the confiscated national properties confiscated from the Church and émigrés while tying themselves to the future of the revolutionary government.[145] Cambon, who assumed power in 1793, took matters a step further. Faced with insufficient revenue, internal political crisis and mounting war expenditure, Cambon concluded that the solution was to print money: 'we must resort to our *assignats* and to our *assignats* without stopping'.[146] Clavière's policy reflected an astute grasp of the relationship that should be struck between politics, war and a sound currency.[147] On the contrary, Cambon recognised that in time of war and revolution the salvation of the state and the consolidation of the new order was the highest priority. The credit of the state and the guarantee of the new national paper currency would

---

142   Patniak 2009, p. xvii.
143   Bodinier Bernard and Eric Teyssier 2000, pp. 280–97; Godechot 1958, p. 7.
144   Antonetti 2007, pp. 75–6, 81.
145   Guérin 1968, vol. 1, pp. 341–3.
146   Antonetti 2007, p. 88.
147   Whatmore 2012, p. 246.

be founded on victory against the counter-revolution at home and abroad.[148] In a report to the National Convention, Cambon retrospectively justified his policy with considerable eloquence:

> Since the creation of this money that covers the whole of France it has rendered great service to the revolution, allowing the value of the national properties to enter into circulation, providing the means of nourishing, equipping and maintaining an army of 1,100,000 men, creating fleets, scouring the land to extract saltpeter, manufacture arms and providing work for all our citizens ... From the introduction of the *assignats* until the beginning of 1793 national wealth has increased ... when minds will be reassured or feel themselves at peace national industry will take another leap upwards.[149]

What stands out in this statement is the emphasis Cambon puts on using the new money to mobilise the productive forces of the nation, including its labour, in order to overcome crisis and defend the revolution.

At the same time as galvanising the economy and the finances of the state on behalf of the revolution, Cambon consolidated the national debt, which he explained would help to block speculators from playing on the depreciation of the *assignat* and rising price of commodities while trying to profit by imposing exorbitant interest charges.[150] Cambon's *Grand Livre de la dette publique*, like the indiscriminate printing of the *assignat*, appears to have been an improvisation in the face of crisis. Among its immediate objectives it was designed to achieve a partial repudiation of state debt while meanwhile raising some revenue by a transaction tax on trading in the new issue and by imposing a forced loan.[151] But unlike the *assignat*, which fell by the wayside, the establishment of the *Grand Livre* proved decisive in the systematisation of the public debt, which became the float against which all future private debt could be measured – an essential step in the direction of the emergence of a capitalist credit market.[152] Meanwhile, in the shorter term the printing of money and the rampant inflation which followed amounted to a tax on those forced to buy their subsistence and a further opportunity for profit for those who sold means of subsistence.

---

148   Antonetti 2007, p. 154.
149   Cambon 1795, p. 2.
150   Cambon 1793, pp. 8–9.
151   Hermann-Mascard, *L'emprunt forcé*, pp. 48–51.
152   Redlich 1948, p. 141.

When confronted by mounting resistance from the popular classes, whose support was indispensable to the revolution in the short run, Cambon tried to sustain the *assignat* and manage the course of inflation and its political and economic consequences by resorting to the fixing of prices.[153]

It was only by coercion that the revolutionary government was able to enforce these policies. As is well known, the most severe and widespread punishments fell upon those who violated the maximum or hoarded grain.[154] But harsh measures were also taken against those sabotaging the value of the *assignat* by trading in money. On 25 February 1793 Cambon introduced a plan calling for a blanket prohibition on the sale of gold and silver. The *assignat* should become the only money in circulation and the army paid only in the new paper money. At first the Girondists succeeded in blocking the plan. But in April the Assembly passed measures to pay its bills only in *assignats*. Then with the ouster of the Girondins the way was open to impose the *assignat* by draconian measures. On 1 August it became a crime to refuse to accept *assignats* or to accept them at a discount and in September it was decreed that such a crime could be punished by death. In November it was declared that all specie which was being kept hidden should be confiscated to the benefit of the Republic. As a result there was a rush to exchange specie for *assignats*. The value of the *assignat* strengthened and even foreign observers remarked on the efficacy of these extreme measures. Similar steps were taken with respect to foreign exchange. By the end of November it was reported that the buying of foreign currency had abruptly ceased as those who tried to do so were held suspect. It was decreed that all sums held by French citizens abroad were to be repatriated and requisitioned and to be reimbursed at par.[155]

Based on these successes, some radical Jacobins advanced the idea of suppressing the circulation of gold and silver altogether. In October Chaumette proposed the substitution of labour for gold as the measure of value: 'in the system based on the people one carries out tasks with labour and nothing is done with gold'.[156] According to the *Journal de la Montagne*, in order to make factories and manufactures operate, 'working hands rather than gold are required'.[157] At the end of November the Cordelier Society demanded that no new coinage be struck until peace was concluded and this was seconded by a deputation of the Paris Commune which presented its petition to the Convention. In order

---

153   Antonetti 2007, p. 134; Crouzet 1993, pp. 144, 46, 154–5, 160–8.
154   Guérin 1968, vol. 1, pp. 175–89.
155   Guérin, 1968, vol. 1, pp. 164–9.
156   Quoted in Guérin 1968, vol. 1, p. 169.
157   Ibid.

to curb inflation Cambon himself proposed to limit the circulation of gold and silver. On 1 December Cambon presented a proposal which recommended that gold and silver no longer be exchanged for *assignats* but only be accepted to pay taxes and forced loans, to pay for the purchase of national properties and to meet the obligations of the state. To many sitting in the Convention such a prohibition seemed to go too far. Forbidding the use of gold and silver in exchange seemed tantamount to the confiscation of property, and Cambon's proposal was shelved.[158]

For a state controlled by the middle class to try to force acceptance of its currency in the absence of the agreement of bankers seems quixotic in the long term. This is especially true if we are speaking about the eventual establishment of a functioning capitalism, as indeed we are. On the other hand, the imposition of a national currency by the French state made a certain amount of sense in the midst of a state of emergency faced by a revolutionary regime struggling for its existence. The political and social base of the Jacobins were small producers and an emerging class of manufacturing and landed capitalists, most of whom had no love for bankers. Moreover controlling the price of subsistence while allowing inflation to wipe out the debts of producers served to reinforce this support. In the long run the attempt to create a national currency represented an important step toward creating a national market and eventually an effective system of money and credit. Running the printing press enabled the regime in the short run to free itself from dependence on the bankers, to partially repudiate the debt and successfully to finance the wars and mobilise the economy. At the same time fixing prices allowed the Jacobins to keep the support of the urban artisans and workers as well as rural wage earners.

But the price was the discrediting of this first attempt to create a paper currency. As we have seen, inflation was undoubtedly a problem as early as 1791 and intensified when war broke out. But the accelerating inflation that developed from then on was undoubtedly caused by this excessive printing of money. The effects of this increase in the money supply were compounded by shortages of supply and increasing demand stemming from crop failures, labour shortages, the hoarding of commodities, mounting war expenditure, increased overall consumer demand and supply bottlenecks. By the time of the Jacobin takeover (July 1793) the *assignat* had lost 80 percent of its value on international exchanges and Parisian banks had ceased operation.[159] While inflation

---

158   Ibid, p. 170.
159   Antonetti 1963, pp. 210, 220, 234, 235.

alienated workers, rentiers and other creditors, borrowers like wealthy peasants and tradesmen benefitted by paying off loans in depreciating currency.[160]
The state's response in the form of growing control over exchange, including
foreign trade and prices and insistence on fostering the *assignat* as a paper
currency, were incompatible with the speculative profits of the bankers, who
turned decisively against the revolutionary government.

Bankers and Counter-Revolution

The discrediting of the monarchy as a result of the flight to Varennes was an
important milestone. Contrary to the growing radicalisation of public opinion, the bankers responded with growing impatience with popular unrest and
increasing estrangement from the revolution.[161] This alienation is reflected in
the private correspondence of the banker Jean-Louis Grenus, who although
long resident in Paris was eventually forced to flee to his native Geneva as
an alternative to prison under the Terror. In a letter to a foreign correspondent dated 19 July 1792, at the moment when the Prussian army was massing
around Coblentz, Grenus remarked: 'our exchanges reflect no great movement
although our situation is getting worse and people expect the entry of foreign
troops from one day to the next: but many see that as a boon and think that
business will improve'.[162] In the wake of an outburst of popular turbulence in
the wake of the Declaration of Brunswick (25 July 1792), Grenus opined that 'it
is to be feared that it is only foreign armies that can put us in accord'.[163] Shortly
after the fall of the monarchy (10 August 1792) he advised a correspondent not to
refer to politics because at present discretion is necessary.[164] In the throes of the
September massacres he identified himself to the head of the section Grange-
Batelerie as a foreigner who had lived in France since the beginning of the
revolution. He dispatched 2000 livres to be distributed to citizens serving the
republic with the wish that all of France's enemies be defeated.[165] On rumours
of further popular unrest in the Vendée he commented to a correspondent
(19 March 1793): 'it is impossible to continue business with this regime. I am
doing nothing but liquidating my positions and I am counting on being clear

---

160   Hoffman 2000, pp. 186–7.
161   Mathiez 1929, p. 398; Zylberberg 1993, pp. 422–3.
162   Bouchary 1940–2, vol. 2, p. 170.
163   Ibid.
164   Bouchary 1940–2, vol. 2, p. 170.
165   Bouchary, 1940–2, vol. 2, p. 173.

by May'.[166] An important letter on 15 April informs us 'that at the point where the exchanges are at today I fear to offer credit, for government expenditures are growing as a result of the depreciation of the *assignats* and as the emission of them is increasing each month the deterioration of this currency can lead us to the point that the system will collapse of itself ... The assignats made the revolution, I fear that they can make the counter-revolution'.[167]

While Grenus expressed growing misgivings, the attack on the Tuilleries (10 August 1792) saw several bankers openly break with the revolution. Indeed, it was this event which saw the collapse of the faction of constitutional monarchists or Feuillants made up of liberal nobles and rich bourgeois, including many bankers. The banker Etienne François Gallet de Santerre appears to have been part of this group accused of being close to Lafayette as well as having contact with foreign enemies. Eventually consigned to the prison in the Convent of the Carmelites des Carmes, he was accused of becoming involved in a prison conspiracy during the last stages of the Terror and was guillotined.[168]

More politically prominent were Gabriel and Louis Tassin, commanding the Battalion des Saintes-Filles de St. Thomas formed out of citizens of the Section Bibliotheque (Le Peletier). As officers of the Battalion their primary responsibility was the defence of the residence of the royal family. Having openly sided with the counter-revolution during the attack on the Tuilleries, the Tassin brothers were subsequently arraigned and sent to the guillotine by the Revolutionary Tribunal on 3 May 1794.[169] The Tassin were Parisian bankers connected to a wealthy and established Orleannais family whose fortune was based on refining sugar from the islands of the Caribbean.[170] Gabriel Tassin was promoted to the council of administration of the Caisse d'Escompte in 1786.[171] Following the revolution the brothers were alternate delegates to the Third Estate of the National Assembly and officers of the Batallion des Filles de St. Thomas, while continuing their role as partners in one of the wealthiest Parisian banks.[172] Gabriel was a member of the Society of 1789 and then the Club of the Sainte-Chapelle, which was absorbed into the Feuillants. As attacks increased on the monarchy Gabriel proved to be a passionate defender of royalty and vehemently anti-Jacobin.[173]

166   Bouchary 1940–2, vol. 2, p. 186.
167   Bouchary 1940–2, vol. 2, p. 188.
168   AN W 429.
169   AN W 357.
170   Lüthy 1959–61, vol. 2, pp. 313–4.
171   Lüthy 1959–61, vol. 2, p. 699.
172   Antonetti 1963, p. 23.
173   Cointet 1965, p. 457.

The Tassins lived in the Section Bibliothèque, which we have seen was inhabited by a substantial number of employees of the financial institutions located in the quartier including the Bourse, Caisse d'Escompte, Hôtels des Domaines et Trésor, Régie générale, Hôtel des Loteries and Compagnie des Indes. These bodies were dominated by an elite of money managers made up of bankers, money changers, farmers-general and receivers-general of finance.[174] By 1792 the restaurants, cafes, gambling houses and book stores of the adjacent Palais-Royal had become the focal point of counter-revolutionary talk and plotting.[175] The headquarters of the increasingly suspect pro-slavery Club Massiac lay in the nearby Place des Victoires. Marat noted that the Section was politically dominated by speculators, bankers and lawyers who were open enemies of the revolution. It was from this section that counter-revolutionary proposals emanated which supported the plans of the government, the Paris mayor Jean Sylvain Bailly and the commander of the National Guard Lafayette and other counter-revolutionary army officers.[176]

Prior to the attack on the Tuilleries, Brissot, who lived in the Section, complained 'that the section was divided between the part that was patriot and the other which was the infected part made up of financiers, exchange agents and speculators who since the beginning of the revolution have done more damage to the establishment of liberty than all the armies of Prussian and Austria'.[177] Having organised the defence of the Tuilleries against the attack of the sans-culottes as commander of the Battalion des Saintes Filles, Louis Tassin and Gabriel were imprisoned along with other members of the Battalion. At his trial Louis was accused of mounting patrols along with other bankers, stock brokers and bank employees in order to harass and intimidate citizens prior to the attack on the Tuilleries.[178] He tried to buy support for his counter-revolutionary activities by offering hospitality to likely supporters and recruited as many counter-revolutionaries as he could into the Battalion. He was violently hostile in opposition to the Jacobins.[179]

Jean-Philippe Weinmaring, a bank clerk and captain of the Batallion de Saintes Filles, who also participated in the defence of the Tuilleries, went to the guillotine along with the Tassin brothers.[180] Weinmaring, who for a time

174   Cointet 1965, p. 453.
175   Schmidt 1867, vol. 1, p. 41; Gendron 1993, p. 41.
176   Marat, *L'ami du peuple*, no. 369, 2 December, 1791, Lacroix Sigismond 1894–8, Vol. 3, p. 704.
177   Coudart 1990, p. 201.
178   Lacroix 1894–8, vol. 2, pp. 140–1.
179   AN W357.
180   Ternaux 1866–81, vol. 2, pp. 472–3.

served as secretary to the Parisian Committee of Subsistence, which was made up largely of bankers, was accused of recruiting criminals into the Battalion in concert with the Tassin. Etienne Delessert's son Jacques-Etienne, likewise a member of the Battalion, had to flee to New York following the attack on the Tuilleries, where he attempted to set up a bank, dying shortly thereafter.[181] Another member of the Batallion and victim of the guillotine was Antoine Gregoire Geneste. He was chief clerk of the bankers Boyd and Ker, who doubled as spies for the English government in Paris. The two Englishman were able to avoid arrest by fleeing across the Channel. But the agents they left behind to act for them suffered in their place. Boyd and Kerr pretended to liquidate their business while arranging to have Geneste serve as their front man. He was guillotined during the Terror for his part in the defence of the Tuilleries as part of the Batallion as well as illegally transferring funds outside of France in concert with Kerr.[182] Another agent of the Boyd and Kerr Bank was Thomas Simon Bérard. No mere clerk, he was a major overseas merchant partnered with the merchant-banker Pourtalès and became the director of the Company of the Indies prior to its liquidation. Bérard was a founding member of the Club Massiac and likely helped draw up the pro-slavery petition that emanated from the Section Bibliothèque.[183] As we have seen, he acquired massive amounts of national properties in the île-de-France.[184] As an officer of the Battalion he was condemned to death by the Revolutionary Tribunal.[185]

Among those who escaped the guillotine for his part in the events of 10 August was Boscary de Villepain, second in command of the Batallion and brother of Jean-Marie Boscary, the disgraced wholesale merchant. While his father was a banker and brother a merchant, Boscary de Villepain became a major figure on the stock exchange. Following the revolution he joined the Society of 1789. During the events of 10 August he is reported to have advised the King to escape Paris under an armed escort. Increasingly under threat, the two brothers and the father fled Paris and took refuge on their estate in the nearby Brie. The revolutionary committee of Melun accused them of preparing to emigrate, of being supporters of Lafayette and of being part of a club of bankers who were engaged in nothing but speculation. An informant told the committee that their cook said of them 'they make semblance of being patriots which perhaps they once were but they are not friends of the

---

181   de Coninck 2000, pp. 30–1.
182   AN W182, AN W348; Claeys 2011, vol. 2, p. 1205, n. 7501.
183   Claeys 2001, vol. I, p. 198.
184   Moriceau 1990, pp. 445, 409–528.
185   AN W357.

revolution although they have gained the major part of their fortune from it. They are quite adroit and calculating'.[186] The father and Jean-Marie were brought back to Paris and imprisoned while Boscary de Villepain crossed the border into Switzerland.[187] All three were rehabilitated under the Directory.

While the Tassin and other officers of the Batallion openly sided with the monarchy on the barricades, in secret the bankers Jean Barthélemy and Laurent Lecouteulx, heads of one of the most important banks in Paris, engaged in more serious conspiracies behind the scenes. While centring their commercial activities in their home town of Rouen, they became deeply involved in the finances of the court and through this connection developed close ties to banking interests in Spain and its colonial empire.[188] As a result, on 29 November 1793 the Committee of General Security accused the two directors of Lecouteulx & Company of corresponding with and passing money to the enemies of France. They were sent to the Concergerie in February and were not to be liberated until after 9 Thermidor.[189] Shortly thereafter Laurent succumbed to the effects of his imprisonment.[190] Their lawyer Pierre-Nicolas Berryer claimed that they had been spared the guillotine by the fact that they had offered the notorious head of the Revolutionary Tribunal Antoine Quentin Fouquier-Tinville a job at the beginning of the revolution.[191]

The Lecouteulx connection with Spain was well known to revolutionary radicals. The brothers were named in a pamphlet, the *Complot d'une banquerote generale de la France, de l'Espagne, et par contre-coup de la Hollande et d'Angleterre ou les horreurs de l'ancien et nouveau regime*, published in 1791 by the provocateur and later police agent Louis Heron. The tract detailed a pre-revolutionary conspiracy organised by Calonne to control the whole of Europe's finances through the Bank of Saint Charles. The scheme in fact was part of the wave of speculation that marked the early 1780s, which were designed to inflate the shares of the Bank of Saint Charles as well as the Caisse d'Escompte.[192] Heron had served as an intermediary in this scheme, being sent to Havana in order to arrange the transfer of bullion from Spain to France in return for a widely subscribed French loan organised by a syndicate of bankers including the Lecouteulx. Prior to becoming an agent in the service of Robes-

---

186   Bouchary 1942, p. 27.
187   Bouchary 1942, pp. 27–8, 37.
188   Claeys 2011, vol. 2, pp. 1333–9.
189   Zylberberg 2001, p. 316; Flamein 2010, p. 11.
190   Claeys 2011, vol. 2, p. 1337.
191   Berryer 1839, vol. 1, pp. 138–9.
192   Lüthy 1959–61, vol. 2, p. 702.

pierre, Heron came under the protection of Marat, who published his pamph-let.[193] The tract argued that the machinations of the bankers such as that organised around the Bank of Saint Charles had not ceased with the revolution but were intensifying.[194] In the hearing before the Revolutionary Tribunal the Lecouteulx were denounced for using the funds of the Bank of Saint Charles to buy shares in the Caisse d'Escompte. Abraham Ducange, a Jacobin sympathiser who had lived in Madrid, testified that the Lecoutuealx had been able to buy these shares for 2.7 million livres and sold them at more than twice their value. Ducange demanded that the nation confiscate at least 4–5 million livres from the Lecouteulx as such transactions '[were] all that one can expect to get from men of this class for whom hearing the very word republic is a martyrdom'.[195] Indeed, suspicion of the financial dealings of the Lecouteulx is further reflec-ted in the report by those who evaluated their income in response to the forced loan imposed by the Jacobins (1793). The commissioners charge that the broth-ers had under-reported their real incomes in their tax declaration by at least a factor of five.[196] On the other hand, Fouquier and the Committee of Gen-eral Security remained unaware that the Lecouteulx, who sympathised with the Feuillants, were involved in a major plot to save the King by attempting to bribe the members of the Convention with money from the Spanish court.[197] At the same time they put themselves forward as earnest republicans, publishing a pamphlet arguing that immediate execution of the King would be politically inexpedient for the republic.[198]

The wives of the Lecouteulx published a defence of their husbands, who were languishing in prison. In their pamphlet they flatly denied that their spouses were bankers at all. In order to appeal to the prejudices of the Jac-obins they played up their commercial or industrial interests. According to this apologetic, Lecouteulx & Co. was really a firm of merchants and industrial-ists. The Parisian branch of the company carried on several activities useful to the industry of the nation. The branch at Rouen was involved in importing raw materials for manufacturing and for finding markets for the manufactured products of the burgeoning industries of Normandy. The branches at Cadix and Le Havre were engaged in competition with English rivals to extend the market for French manufactures. Furthermore they had established a manufacture of

193   Heron 1791, p. 2; Zylberberg 1993, p. 318.
194   Heron 1791, pp. 29–30.
195   AN F 7 4774.
196   Hermann-Mascard 1990, p. 216, n. 219.
197   Zylberberg 2001, p. 317; Zylberberg 1993, p. 424.
198   Lecouteulx 1792.

fish oil in a suburb of Rouen, a tobacco factory at Morlaix and a foundry for laminating copper at Romilly-sur-Andelle.[199]

Meanwhile in December 1793 another banker, Louis Pourrat, who was a business partner of the Lecouteulx and was related to them by marriage, was abruptly arrested and, after languishing in prison, guillotined. Pourrat had played an important part in speculating in government debt prior to the revolution and had become notorious for getting into a fist-fight with Clavière on the floor of the Paris stock exchange.[200] His connections to the Lecouteulx, his daughter Fanny marrying Laurent Lecouteulx, seems to have played a critical role in his condemnation.[201] Fanny had been the muse of the Feuillant poet Andre Chenier, who also was guillotined. Known to be in sympathy with the Feuillants and Girondins, Pourrat was denounced and arrested while sitting on the benches of the Jacobin Club. After languishing in prison for seven months, he was executed in July, shortly before 9 Thermidor.[202] According to the memoirs of Berryer, Pourrat 'perished precisely because of the extreme caution that he took to preserve his life. Although he was a banker he arranged to be admitted to the Society of the Jacobins in order to avoid being put on the Index. Nonetheless he was arrested in the midst of a Jacobin meeting, thrown into prison and sent to his death. It was as if the Jacobins wished to avenge themselves for the fact that he had attempted to cover himself by donning the mantle of patriotism'.[203]

The Dutch bankers Antoine Auguste, Jean Baptiste and Jean-Baptiste Vandenyver were also denounced by Heron as being involved in the Spanish loan advanced by the Bank of Saint Charles in the previous decade.[204] Like many other bankers the Vandenyver initially sympathised with the revolution. They were closely related to Anarchasis Cloots, the scion of an ennobled German banking family who moved to Paris and became a Jacobin. Cloots became celebrated as the foremost champion of a cosmopolitanism whose objective was to universalise the ideals of the revolution. He was later guillotined as a Hébertist sympathiser. The Vandenyver Bank was one of the most well-established and important banks in Paris.[205] But in 1789 the Vandenyver quietly

---

199   AN F 7 4774; Zylberberg 2001, p. 163; Bergeon 1978, p. 302.
200   Lüthy 1959–61, vol. 2, p. 696.
201   AN F 7 4774, AN W 437.
202   Lüthy 1959–61, vol. 2, p. 727.
203   Berryer 1839, vol. 1, 139.
204   Heron 1791, pp. 3, 18.
205   Lüthy 1959–61, vol. 2, p. 322; Claeys 2011, vol. 2, pp. 1259–64. On the growth of Dutch investment in French debt, see Riley 1973, pp. 732–60.

renewed their ties to the court and once the revolution radicalised they began
to supply Madame Du Barry and other nobles with money. Their trial and condemnation before the Revolutionary Tribunal was designed to be an object
lesson to those bankers guilty of aiding aristocrats. They were executed by the
guillotine on 17 frimaire an. 11.[206] An example was also made of the banker
Jacques Henry Wiedenfeld, originally from Aix-la-Chapelle, who in defiance of
the prohibition against the export of bullion was discovered to be sending gold
outside the country secreted in pots of pomade. Brought before the Revolutionary Tribunal, he was condemned and executed 26 pluviose an 11.[207]

With the fall of the monarchy many bankers who sympathised with the
Feuillants now pinned their hopes on the Girondins as the more moderate
element among the republicans. It was reassuring to them that Clavière, one
of the Girondin leaders, had served as Minister of Finance in the last few
months of the constitutional monarchy. In order to build confidence in the
new republican state he was once again given charge of the finances. But he
was arrested along with other Girondins a year later. The announcement of
his upcoming hearing before the Revolutionary Tribunal on 8 December led
him to suicide, followed by the suicide of his wife. A month later Jean Andre, a
banker and merchant from Nîmes, was guillotined for Girondin sympathies.
Faced with an increasing challenge from the sans-culottes to his business
interests and elite political position in Nîmes, Andre compromised himself by
showing sympathy for the federalist revolt. When the Jacobins seized power in
Nîmes in January 1794, Andre was arrested and transferred to Paris for trial and
execution.[208]

Two other bankers, Théodore Jauge and his associate and brother-in-law
Jean Paul Marie Cottin, were accused of involvement in the attempted assassin-
ation of the scourge of the Girondins, Collot de Herbois. Cottin had pioneered
in the development of French cotton manufacturing. Through his marriage to
Marie Risteau, Jean Cottin became connected by marriage to the Bordeaux
overseas merchant community.[209] His tie to Jauge represented a further reinforcement of his links to textile manufacture and Bordeaux overseas commercial interests. Before coming to Paris Jauge had been a banker in Bordeaux who
alongside his father had a major interest in the French colonial trade while
holding estates in the Bordelais. As we have seen, Jauge became an aide-de-
camp to Lafayette in the wake of the taking of the Bastille. His bank provided

206 AN T 508, AN 1671, AN W 300.
207 AN W324.
208 Lehideaux-Vernimmen 1992, pp. 128–37.
209 Claeys 2011, vol. 1, p. 553.

large credits to the revolutionary government.[210] Initially associated with the Feuillants, the flight to Varennes led Jauge to shift his support to the Girondins more out of prudence than conviction.[211] In 1792 Jauge, along with his wife, visited England in order to buy grain for the revolutionary government. The fact that his wife remained in England instead of returning to France aroused suspicion. At the end of January 1793 he was arrested, interrogated and released as part of a large-scale round-up of bankers. They were accused of monarchist sympathies, associating with counter-revolutionaries, speculating against the *assignat* and in some cases of being implicated in the Massacre of the Champs de Mars.[212] In September Jauge was re-arrested. Cottin meanwhile was found dead in his bed by those who came to arrest him.[213] Jauge went to the guillotine on 17 June 1794 as part of a mass execution of suspected conspirators.[214]

Fundamental to the Girondin viewpoint as analysed in recent scholarship was a belief in private property as not merely a social but also a natural right. Indeed, as the right to property came to be questioned more and more, the Girondins put the emphasis on property as a natural right antecedent to society. Property was the fruit of labour but also without it society itself was threatened with destruction.[215] The views of Clavière may again be taken as representative. Like many other Girondins, Clavière was a fervent advocate of the separation of the market from government, believing that government interference hampered economic growth, corrupted morals and fettered individual liberty. In taking this view Clavière had the practice of the Old Regime before his eyes. The economic sphere flourished if it was regarded as a private matter, while government intrusion was inherently corrupting.[216] The national bank which he advocated would be authorised by the government but was designed to provide the sound currency and public credit necessary to the functioning of the private market. Investment would be left the responsibility of bankers, merchants and manufacturers.

210   Bouchary 1939–43, vol. 3, pp. 113, 116, 117.
211   Bianciarli 1995, pp. 142, 179, 199.
212   Bouchary 1939–43, vol. 3, pp. 121–2; Claeys 2011, vol. 1, p. 553.
213   Lüthy 1959–61, vol. 2, p. 310; Bianciarli 1995, p. 213.
214   AN W389.
215   Dorigny 1983, pp. 16–20.
216   Whatmore and Livesey 2000, pp. 1–26.

War Capitalism

The Jacobin policies which led them toward more and more control over the market were driven partly by their egalitarian ideology and partly by necessity in a context of war, economic crisis and counter-revolution. A willingness to use the state in order to mobilise the economic and military defence of the revolution differentiated them from those committed to a policy of laissez-faire. The Girondins falsely accused the Jacobins of threatening private property. On the contrary, their notion of equality led them to believe that everyone should own property. They distrusted large landed property but were not hostile to substantial industrial enterprise. But the Jacobins were divided. The Jacobin regime included not simply ideologues suspicious of laissez-faire like Robespierre and Saint Just, but also politicians like the Montpellerians Joseph Cambon and Francois-Victor Aigoin and the associate of Bidermann Jean Johannot, who despite their banking and manufacturing interests and belief in the freedom of the market were prepared to regulate the economy to defend the new revolutionary state. They were backed by an influential stratum of financial administrators in the state bureaucracy carried over from the Old Regime, who on the contrary believed in principle in state regulation of the economy.[217] Moreover many Jacobin clubs during the radical phase of the revolution contained a small but important minority of the grand bourgeoisie, including manufacturers who saw the necessity of a strong national government.

The most interesting example of a backer of the Jacobins from among the bankers was Claude 'Milord' Perier. Born into a prosperous merchant dynasty in the Dauphiné, Perier moved from trade and the manufacture of canvas into banking. Expanding his activities into importing sugar via Marseilles, he also began manufacturing Indian cottons on his estate at Vizelle. The link between overseas trade and manufacturing in Dauphiné alluded to earlier seems clear, as does the development of local investment capital through Perier's bank. On the eve of the revolution Perier was the richest man in Grenoble. Remarkably, he held aloof from the local nobility despite having acquired a title and estates. He then became the principal backer of the revolt of the representative assemblies that emerged in Dauphiné and elsewhere in France from 1788 and then an enthusiastic supporter of the revolution. On the other hand, his ongoing banking activities led to attacks on him by radicals.[218] In August 1790 the Jacobin *Journal patriotique* attacked 'this banker rolling in

217   Brugière 1986, pp. 73–107.
218   Barral 1964, pp. 23–32.

money who nonetheless is extracting a premium on the exchange of *assignats* on which the salvation of the Kingdom depends'.[219] He was also denounced for speculating by buying and hoarding commodities.[220]

Unlike most others involved in banking Perier took the side of the Convention in the face of the Girondin revolt. But even this was not enough to secure him from further attacks. He found himself being denounced as a Crassus by the radical Jacobins advocating the institution of the Terror in Grenoble. He was warned that he would have to demonstrate loyalty by generous acts towards the revolution, which he duly came up with in the form of substantial amounts of cash.[221] The war and the Law of the Maximum led to major losses on his commercial ventures. In 1793 he prudently dissolved his bank and saw the bankruptcy of his Indian cotton manufacturing business. But in a calculated move he then opened an arms factory, 'the Société des Sans-culottes Republicains', employing 140 workers in a national property which had been the Convent of the Minimes in Grenoble. This venture, too, failed. Perier undoubtedly suffered financial reverses but he also later clearly exaggerated the losses he experienced during the period up to 9 Thermidor.[222] In any event, his subsequent activities make it clear that his reserves must have been enormous. At the head of a consortium which included the Lecouteulx and the bankers Guillaume Sabatier and Pierre Desprez, in 1794 he took control of Anzin, the largest and most technologically advanced coal mine in France, which was acquired as a national property. Most of the capital involved in this transaction derived from the now liquidated Company of the Indies, another instance of the re-investment of colonial profit directly into the French economy.[223] Moving to Paris and resuming his banking activities under Napoleon, Perier came to write the rules of the Bank of France.[224]

Another success of this tumultuous period was that of the Burgundian banker Jean Baptiste Bureau. Head of a regional transport company, Bureau invested in a multiplicity of iron and steel works in the Burgundian region. During the decades leading to the revolution he established ties to the Mallet and Lecouteulx banks while taking up residence in Paris. In 1793, like Perier, he prudently abandoned banking. On the other hand, during the same crisis he

219   Barral 1964, p. 33.
220   Barral 1964, p. 36.
221   Barral 1964, pp. 32–3.
222   Barral 1964, p. 37.
223   Prunaux 2006; Claeys 2011, vol. 2, pp. 2168–9.
224   Szramkiewicz 1974, p. 301.

used his accumulated capital to lay the financial and commercial foundations for the Messageries Nationales, the first national transportation company. At the same time he formed a syndicate which took control of one of the choicest of national properties, Le Creusot, a technologically advanced iron and steel works and coal mine.[225] While exceptionally successful, the careers of Claude Perier and Jean Baptiste Bureau under the Jacobins demonstrate that Jacobin rule, despite its economic interventionism and populism, was not incompatible with the development of capitalism in the long term.

The construction of the Jacobin state was not simply based on countering the threat of counter-revolution from within and without. It was in fact a regime of war capitalism, which suspended the normal rules of the market in order to create the framework and foundations of a capitalist state. The creation by the Jacobins of a nation in arms, the weapons, munitions and uniforms of which were supplied by private and public manufacturers, went with the establishment of a strongly protectionist regime aimed at reinforcing the national economy. Prohibition of English manufactures, the encouragement of French industries and control over the export of grain and raw materials sealed the close alliance between manufacturing – the core of the emergent national economy – and the popular classes.[226] Indeed, the Jacobins were explicitly committed to protecting the nascent capitalist industries which had already emerged prior to the revolution, especially cotton manufacturing. Low-cost food was essential to keeping wages in check, ensuring the survival of the industrial sector. It goes without saying that price controls on food also favoured self-employed artisans and artisan manufacturers.[227] While place was found for capitalists who were interested in production rather than speculation, Robespierre and his faction believed in a republic dominated by small-scale property.[228] He and his adherents stood for political democracy and a market based on small-scale property owners. As such they were hostile to big merchant and banking capitalists, whom they regarded as parasitic and monopolistic. But there is a difference between intended and unintended consequences. As a matter of fact a capitalist economy based on the production of petty producers, as in the early history of the United States, is likely to produce a particularly strong agricultural and industrial base for the full development of capitalism. Capitalist development along this path has been explored by

225   Woronoff 1993, pp. 63–76.
226   Démier 1990, p. 286.
227   On the relationship between food costs and industrialisation in this period, see Patniak 2011, pp. 17–27.
228   Gross 1997.

Lenin, Terrence Byres and Anatoli Ado.[229] It was this path that the Jacobins also favoured. The politics of the Jacobin state therefore cannot be seen as entirely anti-capitalist in the short run and certainly not in the long term. In fact in the face of the ongoing largely negative impact of rent and interest on the expansion of the French economy from the Directory onwards, Jacobin economic policies opened up a crucial space for rural and urban small-scale producers and for emergent manufacturing industry, without which French capitalism might have been even more retarded than it was – especially as compared to England. What was at issue in the aftermath of the revolution was not the emergence of capitalism but whether that capitalism would be more or less dynamic. In other words, the short-term interests of bankers or big merchants should not be seen as necessarily coincident with the long-run development of a capitalism with a significant productive and industrial potential.

Speculation and Terror

While they governed, the Jacobins tied the hands of capitalist bankers and wholesale merchants who controlled not the production but the circulation of commodities. In response to the subsistence crises, war and counter-revolutionary revolts that troubled France during the Terror, the Jacobin leaders firmly insisted that the right to property should not include things vital to subsistence. Subsistence being vital, it could not be considered private property. What is sacred to life is as precious as life itself. As such food could not be thought of as private property but must be regarded as common property. The right to subsistence precedes all other rights and all other rights are subordinate to it. Property itself exists for the purpose of subsistence to which it must be subordinated.[230] In the form of the Maximum on prices the Jacobins placed fundamental constraints on the trade in grain – overwhelmingly the most important food product and most important market commodity. During the national political and economic emergency of the Terror speculative activity, i.e., the playing of the market by capitalist farmers, millers, grain merchants, big merchants and last but not least bankers was considered criminal.[231] Such restrictions on the operation of merchant and finance capitalism was enforced

229   Lenin 1964, vol. 3, pp. 32–3; Lenin 1972, vol. 13, pp. 238, 423; Byres 1996; Ado 1996; Heller 2006, pp. 101–3; Heller 2011, pp. 141–2.
230   Gauthier 1992, p. 73.
231   Aulard 1889–97, vol. 1, p. 285.

in order to protect the interests and secure the political support of workers, craftsmen and other small producers and in order to sustain the nascent industrial sector. In lieu of the market, the state fixed prices, including the price of labour, and suspended the operation of credit markets.

Being attacked for speculation and hoarding by a populace made up largely of craftsmen and workers was a serious impediment to the activities of the bankers. But their difficulties were compounded by growing government interference in foreign exchange transactions. In defiance of threats of punishment, bankers attempted to evade government prohibitions by continuing to speculate against the *assignat* and illegally exporting bullion.[232] Bankers were suspected of assisting the royal family and court aristocrats in transferring money abroad or by being in collusion with the English, Prussian and Austrian governments in counterfeiting and undermining the value of the *assignat*. With the fall of the monarchy, popular hostility to those who traded in money became more intense. In February 1793 a petition against the sale of money was presented to the National Convention, claiming it was responsible for the depreciation of the *assignat* and growing inflation. At the beginning of March a similar petition from all the revolutionary sections of Paris was presented. By a decree of 11 April 1793 the *assignat* was made the only legal currency and exchange in the market; using any other numeraire was made illegal. Cambon in a speech to the National Convention attacked the very idea of money as a commodity which could be speculated upon.[233]

But the surreptitious trade in money did not end.[234] In the Convention on 27 June, the Jacobin Georg Friedrich Dentzel denounced the speculators still operating in the rue Vivienne. On 29 August the Section Unité complained of speculators exchanging money in the gardens of the Palais-Royal. Agents of the Jacobin regime meanwhile kept constant surveillance on bankers, speculators, money changers, suspect aristocrats and jeunesse dorée, especially in the Section Bibliothèque where such types still congregated.[235] On 21 February 1793 the Conseil général of Paris adopted a motion of the Cordelier Club calling for restrictions on the circulation of numeraire until the signing of a peace. In particular the Cordeliers called for all merchants and others dealing in money to hand their gold and silver over to the mint in order to block any exchange of bullion for *assignats*. Beyond attacking the trade in money, the sans-culottes

---

232   Antonetti 1963, pp. 134, 138, 159; Crouzet 1993, pp. 181, 185, 201; Tuetey 1890–1914, vol. 2, pp. 141, 148.
233   Soboul 1958, p. 475; Crouzet 1993, pp. 243–4.
234   Bouchary 1937, p. 73.
235   Coudart 1990, p. 204.

denounced the institutions which supported commercial and financial capital. At the beginning of May 1793, the Sections Faubourg-du-Nord and Contrat Social demanded the Bourse be closed. With the Girondins purged and under pressure from the sans-culottes, the Assembly decreed its closing on 27 June.[236] The sans-culottes displayed a like hostility to other financial enterprises. At the end of July a citizen of the Section Sans-Culottes expressed astonishment to see 'on the one hand a Caisse d' Epargne, on the other the Tontin of the Elderly, in one direction the Tontin of Life Insurance and at that gate the Patriotic Lottery of the rue du Bac'. These businesses, he concluded, are simply means to hoard money. 'These rich men, masters and entrepreneurs of *caisses* are those which one must fear the most'. They harm 'commerce and contribute to the difficulties of the Republic. The Convention should seize the *caisses* of these rogues'.[237] On 24 August the assembly ordered all financial companies shut down. The following April all companies of whatever sort were ordered closed.[238]

Foreign Conspiracy

The hostility of the Jacobins toward bankers was not merely an economic matter. It developed as part of a deepening suspicion of foreigners and fear of counter-revolutionary conspiracy inspired by France's enemies. At the beginning of the revolution in 1789 the dominant mood in Paris and elsewhere had been one of generous cosmopolitanism. The common opinion was that the revolution was not merely a French affair but an event of universal significance. Many citizens in other countries enthusiastically agreed. A host of foreigners were attracted to the new revolutionary France and took up residence in Paris. They were welcomed especially by moderate revolutionaries inside and outside government who were proud of their country.[239]

By the fall of 1793 the mood had shifted radically. The Girondins who had championed liberalism and cosmopolitanism were discredited while the Jacobins now in power became increasingly nationalistic and xenophobic. The growing suspicion of foreigners fed on the threat of invasion and faction fights within the ranks of the government. Measures against the bankers, many of whom necessarily had close ties outside of France, must be seen as part of a

---

236   Soboul 1958, p. 476; Crouzet 1993, p. 246.
237   Soboul 1958, p. 477.
238   Ibid.
239   Mathiez 1918, pp. 15–17.

growing distrust toward foreigners, which extended to include merchants, foreign residents, volunteer soldiers and clergy and other revolutionary exiles who aroused suspicion.[240] But foreign bankers who had great economic and financial influence in France were particularly suspect.

The French populace had long held to conspiracy theories. The notion that the increasingly frequent and serious food shortages were the result of a plot – the famous famine plot persuasion – was the main *idée fixe*.[241] It was a common theme during the eighteenth century in both the countryside and the towns and became greatly accentuated during the revolution. The Great Fear that initiated the rural revolution was essentially conceived of as an aristocratic plot against the peasantry. The king's summoning of troops to Versailles, the court's suborning of politicians, as well as Louis's and his wife's flight to Varennes and suspected collusion with Austria in a war against France magnified the idea of counter-revolutionary conspiracies against the revolution.[242] By the time the Jacobins assumed power the notion of conspiracy focused on the idea of the foreign plot or the notion that those who opposed the government were in the service of foreign enemies. It was an idea which was commonplace among members of the government. As the Terror developed suspicions came to centre on the opponents of Robespierre and the Committee of Public Safety, i.e., the radical faction known as the Hébertists as well as the right-wing Jacobins clustered around Danton.

Suspicions of a foreign plot revolved around the directors and principal shareholders of the East India Company, many of whom were bankers. Accusations against the company combined suspicions of hoarding and speculation with counter-revolutionary conspiracy organised by France's enemies. Prior to the revolution the company had known great prosperity, paying extraordinary dividends to its shareholders. Its profitability was due to the fact that it enjoyed a monopoly of trade with Asia. But in conformity to the principles of laissez-faire, in early 1791 the National Assembly declared the company's monopoly over the Asian trade at an end. Despite this reversal, in May of the same year the stockholders, attracted by the ongoing profitability of the trade, decided to resume commercial operations and appointed commissioners to draw up new statutes for the company of which three of four – Delessert, Sabatier and Aimé-Gabriel Fulchiron – were Parisian bankers. In addition its leading shareholders included 20 other leading bankers including Perier, Grenus, Per-

240   Rapport 2000, pp. 191–2, 206–7, 189–258.
241   Kaplan 1982.
242   Hardman 2007, pp. 63–84.

regaux, Louis Greffulhe and Jean-Marc Montz, Jean Barthélemy and Laurent Lecouteulx, Balthasar-Elias Abbema and Boyd and Ker. Despite difficulties the company continued to return substantial profits, especially as the goods in the warehouses of the company appreciated as a result of inflation. The price of shares in the company actually rose as investors exchanged *assignats* for them in the wake of the depreciation of the latter.[243]

But on 26 July 1793, in the midst of growing popular paranoia about hoarding, Joseph Delaunay d'Angers, a Jacobin close to Hébert, accused the company of secretly stashing vast amounts of goods in its warehouses at Lorient for the purposes of speculation and in order to undermine the *assignat*.[244] As a follow-up, on the 6 August the revolutionary playwright Fabre d'Eglantine, an ally of Danton and himself suspected of corruption, denounced the speculation of the bankers in the following terms: 'Pitt has many agents in Paris, especially in banking. The majority of the bankers and the richest of them are foreigners – English, Dutch, German and Genevan. All of these bankers have no ties to France whatsoever ... Pitt has opened an unlimited line of credit for these ... bankers'.[245] The point of such credits, according to Fabre, was to speculate against the *assignat* in order to destroy it. In the meantime, he concluded, the shares of the Company of the Indies have sky-rocketed as a result of hoarding and speculation inspired by Pitt.[246] On 24 August, as we have noted, the activities of the company as well as all other joint stock companies, including the Caisse d'Escompte and the recently created Parisian Insurance, Water and Lighting Companies, were suspended.[247]

But the bankers who were especially signalled out by the Terror were not advocates of the Feuillant or Girondin cause. It was foreign bankers who professed to identify with the Jacobin Republic who were compromised. In the first place suspicion focused on two Moravian bankers of Jewish origin, Junius and Emmanuel Frey, who were attracted to France by the freedom promised by the revolution.[248] The family, the Dobruskas from Moravia, had made a fortune as wholesale merchants and military suppliers to the Hapsburg court and were strongly attracted to the syncretic ideas of the Sabbatarian and Frankist Jews. Influential among the Frankists, the family converted to Catholicism and were raised to the nobility by the Habsburgs, while the elder brother Junius became

243   Lefebvre 1954, p. 171.
244   Mathiez 1920, 1971, p. 35.
245   Mathiez 1920, 1971, p. 36.
246   Mathiez 1920, 1971, p. 37.
247   Mathiez, 1920, 1971, pp. 52–3; Bouchary 1940–2, vol. 3, pp. 42–3.
248   Scholem 1981; Wölfle-Fischer 1997.

a member of the Masonic Order. As a youth Junius had been educated in the Talmud and wrote Hebrew poetry while developing an enthusiasm for the German classics. The French Revolution drew Junius, his brother Emmanuel and sister Leopoldine to Strasbourg in 1792, from where Junius wrote to an Austrian friend: 'my beloved best brother Voss I have lived here in Strasbourg for three weeks, or to express myself better, I live in heaven, for to live in freedom no one can deny is to live a heavenly life, and the land of freedom is a heaven on earth'.[249]

From Strasbourg, Junius Frey moved along with his brother and sister to Paris, rented a mansion and began to associate with the Jacobins, lavishly entertaining some of their leaders. Based on his lengthy treatise *Philosophie sociale dédiée au peuple*, François Junius's commitment to the Jacobin democratic republic seems entirely genuine.[250] At the same time he seems to have retained an interest in Masonic ideas and Jewish philosophy.[251] Like many better-off Parisians, he undertook to support a widow whose sans-culotte husband had been killed in the attack on the Tuilleries, and also adopted a little boy whose father had likewise been killed.[252] On the other hand, like other Jacobins he appears to have carried over into the new epoch the corrupt practices of the former regime.

Fatefully, the Frey brothers entered into a close relationship with the politician and scoundrel François Chabot. A Capuchin monk prior to the revolution, Chabot studied theology at Rodez and Toulouse while developing anti-clerical opinions based on Enlightenment ideas.[253] In May 1790 he founded the Société des amis de la Constitution at Rodez. Elected to the Legislative Assembly from Loir-et-Cher, he adhered to the Jacobins in September 1791. Opposing the war policy of the Girondins, he helped rally the populace in the attack on the Tuilleries. After voting for the execution of the King he was sent as a representative on mission in the Tarn and Aveyron in March 1793. Over the next months he entered into increasingly close social and business contact with the Frey brothers and in September married their sister in return for a dowry of 200,000 livres.

As we have seen, growing hostility toward speculative profits had led to a decree of the National Convention calling for the liquidation of the Company

249   Wölfle-Fischer 1997, p. 88.
250   Frey 1793.
251   AN T 1524.
252   AN F7 4713.
253   Bonald 1908.

of the Indies (8 October 1793).[254] The Frey brothers were viewed as Chabot's principal financial backers, using his political influence to advance their financial interests. Chabot got himself named to the committee overseeing the liquidation of the assets of the company, while demanding an enormous payoff from the directors in order to protect the principal shareholders. At the same time Chabot and more than likely also the Frey brothers were profiting from shorting the shares of the company.

In the context of growing paranoia over foreign conspiracies, Chabot's role in the liquidation of the Company of the Indies inevitably drew attention to the Frey brothers, who after all were Austrian. By then Robespierre suspected Chabot of attempting to extort money from the company by offering to use his Jacobin connections to arrange for the liquidation of the company in a way which favoured the interests of its principal shareholders. Throughout the spring of 1793 Robespierre and other militant Jacobins urged more stringent measures against foreigners.[255] In July the moderate Cambon joined the attack. In a report to the Convention, Cambon asserted that foreigners were responsible for the growing economic crisis. According to him Pitt had deployed five million pounds sterling for secret purposes and as a result had been able to sow disorder throughout the country. Pitt had hold of millions in *assignats*, by means of which he was waging a fearsome monetary campaign which was ravaging France by spreading monetary chaos.[256] In the following weeks there were widespread reports of English agents undermining the French currency, promoting price rises, hoarding, speculation and even arson. It seems that the English, Austrian and émigré agents were in fact conducting counterfeiting operations in various places across the frontiers.[257]

By the end of summer the Convention was considering the suspension of the activities of all bankers and especially foreigners, who because of their ties abroad were more and more linked to subversion.[258] But contrariwise Chabot urged caution in cracking down on bankers and as a result he was increasingly viewed as acting on their behalf. In early October a motion by Robespierre ordering the arrest of all English residents and seizure of their property passed the Convention.[259] Two weeks later Robespierre called for the extension of these measures to all foreigners while bitterly attacking Chabot and what he

254   Claeys 2011, vol. 2, p. 979, n. 141.
255   Rapport 2000, pp. 121, 126, 131, 134.
256   Rapport 2000, pp. 136, 139.
257   Crouzet 1993, pp. 140, 220; Bouchary 1946, pp. 61–77.
258   Crouzet 1993, pp. 149–50.
259   Crouzet 1993, p. 157.

called the Austrian faction. According to Robespierre, since the beginning of the revolution there had been two factions hostile to the revolution, the Anglo-Prussian and the Austrian, each opposed to the other. The Convention has struck a powerful blow against the first, but the Austrian faction was still alive and had to be smashed.[260] The English faction was led by Brissot and other Girondins. The other group was the Austrian faction, including the Frey brothers, who were being protected by Chabot:

> I distrust all these strangers whose face is covered by the mask of patri- otism and who attempt to appear more republican and energetic than us. It is these ardent patriots who are the most treacherous artisans of our troubles. They are agents of foreign powers because I know that our enemies have resolved that agents ought to affect an ardent patriotism in order to insinuate themselves into our committees and assemblies. They are the ones who spread discord, who undermine our most estimable cit- izens. It is these agents that it is necessary to strike at. They come from every country. There are Spaniards, English, Austrians and they all need to be struck down.[261]

Denounced in the Convention on 15 November, Chabot vainly attempted to convince his audience that the bribery scheme had been launched by the aris- tocratic financier and royalist intriguer the Baron de Batz in order to discredit the republican regime and that he had entered the conspiracy not for his own gain but in order to expose it.[262] Chabot and his allies adhered to the Hébertists, but they began to be denounced by them in the pages of the Père Duchesne in November, 1793 especially following Chabot's incautious condemnation of the Law of the Maximum.[263] Arrested shortly afterwards the Frey brothers and Chabot were guillotined on 25 April 1794, executed ironically at the same time as the Dantonists, their erstwhile enemies.[264]

The Frey brothers and Chabot were part of the Hébertist faction. Although they espoused the radical economic programme of the *enragés*, many of the Hébertists were not craftsmen or workers but for the most part educated mem- bers of the lower middle class, who sought entry into the echelons of the

260   Crouzet 1993, p. 158.
261   Quoted in Crouzet 1993, p. 158.
262   Mathiez 1920, 1971, pp. 79–93.
263   Crouzet 1993, p. 156; Guérin 1968, vol. 2, p. 194.
264   Rapport 2000, p. 235.

expanding revolutionary state. They based their claims on their ardent patriotism and populism, designed to appeal to the sans-culottes.[265] But like the
brothers Frey some of the principal backers of the Hébertists were politically
well-connected foreign bankers like Pierre-Jean Berthold de Proli, Don Andrés
de Guzmán, Edward de Walckiers and Jean Conrad de Kock, who supported a
policy of war. These men who were exiled from their own countries favoured a
policy of no compromise with the enemy and a war of liberation vis-à-vis their
own states. Accordingly they called for an all-out mobilisation. In order to gain
political credibility among the sans-culottes they supported government control over the economy. This entailed control over prices, exchange rates and
foreign trade, forced use of the *assignat* and government requisition of private
property where necessary. At the same time, some like Walckiers benefitted
from the policy of war by becoming suppliers to the French army.[266] But their
affiliation with the extremism of Hébert, their direct involvement in internal
French politics and their foreign origins rendered them suspect in the eyes of
Robespierre.[267]

Proli was perhaps the most influential member of this faction. A most
unlikely revolutionary due to his foreign birth and aristocratic background,
as well as his profligate lifestyle, Proli was born in Brussels the son of Count
Balthazar Proli, head of an important bank in Antwerp and receiver-general of
the domains and finances of the Austrian Empress. It was widely believed that
Proli was the bastard son of the Prince of Kaunitz, the Austrian first minister.
Educated in Paris and Nantes, he sailed to India and created a company trading
in the Indian Ocean and the Red Sea. Settling in Paris in the 1780s, he became
involved in many of the spectacular financial ventures of that decade and
notably those of the East India Company.[268] By the time of the revolution he
was a ruined man and had turned to buying and selling paintings along with his
friend the banker Joseph Laborde de Mereville. In the wake of the revolution, he
took up residence in the Palais-Royal and frequented its salons and gambling
houses, later installing himself in the rue Vivienne and then the rue Saintes-
Filles de St. Thomas. While carrying on a dissolute life, he enlisted in the ranks
of the Hébertists and helped lead the attack on the National Convention at the
end of May and beginning of June 1793, which saw the ouster of the Girondins.
The Dantonists were unable to prevent him from organising the radical clubs
of the Parisian sections under the command of a central committee – a form

265   Guérin 1968, vol. 1, pp. 279–84.
266   Godechot 1958, p. 7.
267   Mathiez 1920c, pp. 139–40.
268   Lüthy 1959–61, vol. 2, pp. 654–5.

of dual power which threatened the authority of the Convention. In the wake of the fall of Chabot, Proli was denounced in the press and Convention as an Austrian. Robespierre took the lead in pointing the finger linking him with other foreign bankers:

> How does it transpire that Proli, a foreigner and son of the mistress of the Prince Kaunitz and for this reason suspect of being the bastard and pensioner of that Austrian prince, can pass himself off in Paris as a thirty-six carat patriot, and that, despite appearances, he has not been unmasked as the intriguer that he is? How does it come about that Proli, who is a nobody and who ought to concern himself with nothing, should involve himself in all aspects of political business? How can it be that Proli and his associate the wine merchant (François) Desfieux and their cabal know all the secrets of the government two weeks before they are known to the National Convention; that they know who will be promoted and at any given point know everything about public matters and conduct themselves so as to take advantage of their knowledge? How does it come to pass that Desfieux and Proli, great patriots that they are, are the constant companions of the most dangerous of the foreign bankers ...?[269]

Closely associated with Proli was the Spaniard Don Andrés de Guzmán y Ruiz de Castro t'Serclaes de Tilly, count de Guzmán, like Proli scion of an illustrious family. He studied at the military school of Sorèze and then did military service in Spain and France. He moved to Paris in 1778 and was naturalised three years later. In Paris he spent lavishly and gambled recklessly, accumulating enormous debts. In the course of pursuing these excesses he became fast friends with the bon-vivant Proli. Perregaux lent him large sums of money throughout the 1780s and continued to supply him with loans after the onset of the revolution. As a result Guzman acted as Perregaux's financial and political go-between with the Jacobins. Guzman's mansion on the rue Neuve-des-Mathurins was opened to the Jacobin leadership and it was there apparently that the radical Hébert met his wife, a friend of the celebrated Parisian beauty Mlle Louise Descoings. Guzman became an important investor in several gambling establishments in the Palais-Royal while continuing his relationship with Perregaux as well as the bankers Laborde and de Joseph Pestre de Séneffe. It is said that Perregaux provided Guzman with cash to help foment the Parisian revolutionary sections during the anti-Girondin movement of the spring of 1793. As part of the Jacobin

---

269   Robespierre 1828, pp. 75–8.

conspiracy on 31 May he sounded the tocsin which led to the final ouster of the Girondins.[270] Guzman was arrested, condemned and executed (15 prairial an. II) as part of the purge of the Hébertists instituted by Robespierre.[271]

Another Hébertist who went to the scaffold was the Dutch banker Jean Conrad de Kock. He likewise was born into a noble family but fled Holland in 1787 in the wake of invasion by the Prussian army. He and his wife ended up in Paris. His wife having died, De Kock quickly re-married into a banking family from Switzerland and became associated with the Sartorius-Chockard Bank. Ongoing hostility to the Prussians and their Austrian allies led him to travel to the camp of the French army of the North in Belgium. He journeyed there on behalf of the Batavian Committee of Paris which had sent a legion of volunteers to back up the French forces. After the defection of de Kock's friend, the general-in-command Charles François Dumouriez (5 April 1793) – an event which greatly increased Jacobin fears of conspiracy – de Kock returned to France, stopping at Lille and then returning to Paris. His primary goal was to rejoin the Section Bonne Nouvelle where he had first encountered Hébert and where they had become close friends. De Kock was rounded up along with other Hébertists and was condemned and executed (24 March 1794). His fellow Hébertist, the banker Edouard de Walckiers, named by Robespierre as an associate of Proli and as such denounced as one of the most dangerous of the foreign bankers, was also condemned but escaped.

Walckiers had been head of the most important bank in Holland, but faced with the triumph of a feudal and clerical reaction in 1790 fled to Paris and put himself at the head of the Belgian exiles, who espoused a democratic and liberal programme for their country. At the same time he became a contractor for the growing French Army of the North. While a French army marched into the Netherlands in March 1794, Walckiers was denounced as an Austrian agent and fled to Hamburg.[272]

The Controlled Economy

The revolutionary governments had step-by-step limited the ability of bankers to make money by manipulating government finance, engaging in speculation against the national currency, hoarding commodities and making profits

---

270   Senar 1978, p. 86.
271   Mathiez 1926, pp. 221, 226, 227.
272   Lüthy 1959–61, vol. 2, pp. 663–4.

off foreign exchange. But the most serious blow against them was the Jacobin seizure of control of foreign commerce. Despite the outbreak of war, foreign trade by the summer of 1793 was at a peak, as growing government interference in the market seemed to excite commercial activity in fear of the future. The decree of 26 July directed against hoarding, the imminence of the Law of the Maximum, the imposition of a forced loan and the growing interventions of the revolutionary armies led merchants to throw their goods onto the market in order to rid themselves of stocks. But faced with runaway prices and scarcity, the sans-culottes forced the government in August 1793 to prohibit export of goods and raw materials deemed indispensable.[273] Already from the beginning of the war in April 1792 until the formation of the Commission des subsistances in October 1793, exports and imports had been gradually choked off.[274] Through the *Commission* foreign commerce was essentially nationalised for the duration. This move, which radically centralised the export trade, drastically curtailed the operations of the private banks, whose principal function was the provision of credit to finance external commerce. In November the Committee of Public Safety attempted to restart foreign commerce but under its strict control. It demanded that the assets of bankers resident in France be used to finance necessary imports. On 6 nivoise II the Committee of Finances, Public Safety and General Security decreed the requisition of the industries and the assets of the bankers and capitalists of the Republic.[275] Five citizens including Cambon and another member of the Committee of Public Safety, Robert Lindet, were to see to the execution of this decree in concert with the Commission des subsistances.[276] Two days later the Commission decided to call the principal bankers of Paris before it. Cambon explained to them the intent of the government to institute an equal balance in trade and to repatriate all funds that had been expatriated out of fear or unscrupulous calculation of self-interest. A decree followed ordering all bankers, merchants, capitalists or others holding funds or merchandise abroad to declare these within four days. In order to block all manipulation of exchange rates no transfers of funds to or from France were allowed without permission. A committee of ten bankers and stock brokers was named to superintend the operation and among the bankers selected the foremost proved to be Perregaux.[277]

---

273   Lefebvre 1954, p. 172.
274   Poussou 1993, p. 103.
275   Bouchary 1939–43, Vol. 3, pp. 28–33, Caron 1913, pp. 182–3, 191–3.
276   Brugière 1986, pp. 84–6.
277   Mathiez 1920, pp. 242–52; Mathiez 1920a, pp. 237–43; Ducoudray 1989, pp. 836–7; Alain-Jacques Tornare and Claeys 1996, vol. 1, pp. 207–12.

Perregaux, who figures so largely in the revolution, was born in the canton
of Neuchâtel to a father who was a lieutenant-colonel in French service. He
apprenticed as a banker in Mulhouse, Amsterdam and London, establishing
himself in Paris in 1765, where he worked for Necker. With the help of his com-
patriot, the banker Isaac Panchaud, he founded his own bank in 1781. He quickly
accumulated a fortune and became a familiar figure in Parisian high society, as
well as a patron of the arts. When the revolution arrived he joined the national
guard, became a member of the Valois Club and appeared to favour the consolidation of a constitutional monarchy. He speculated particularly in grain,
while surreptitiously facilitating the movement of the gold and silver of aristocrats and émigrés outside the country, especially to London. As the revolution
radicalised it seems incontestable that he served as an English spy while being
closely associated with the banking house Boyd and Ker. But it also seems clear
that Perregaux backed members of the extreme radical faction the Hébertists
through agents like Proli and Guzman. Perregaux successfully assumed the role
of the *éminence grise* of both the revolution and counter-revolution, surviving
through all the vicissitudes of the revolution while prospering and carrying on
into the Napoleonic period. Arrested at the beginning of September 1793, he
was quickly released by the intercession of Barère, a conservative member of
the Committee of Public Safety. Arrested again 14 December 1793 by order of the
Committee of General Security, who accused him of aiding the fugitive Duke
du Chatelet, he was released on the intervention of Cambon. In the winter of
1794 he directed the commission of ten bankers and exchange agents charged
to survey and requisition the foreign debts that the banks held in neutral countries, by means of which the government sought to pay for foreign food and raw
materials.[278]

In response to the demands of the Commission des subsistances on the 14
nivoise, Perregaux proposed that bankers and stock brokers offer the government a credit of 50 million livres on their foreign holdings. Moreover a long
list of bankers, stock brokers and merchants was drawn up as more or less willing subscribers to the plan.[279] Four days later the Commission des subsistances
met to consider the offer. One of its members vehemently denounced the idea,
claiming that the Republic was abasing itself 'by putting itself in the hands of
these men without a country who despise and hate liberty'. He insisted that
'one could have little confidence in the operations of these egotists whose least
fault among others is to doubt the strength and power of the Republic'. But the

278   Bouchary, 1939–43, vol. 3, p. 33.
279   Bouchary, 1939–43, vol. 3, pp. 77–8.

offer was not at once rejected.[280] Lindet, a moderate among the members of the Committee of Public Safety, claimed that it was the spurning of the offer a few weeks later which set off the major wave of arrests of merchants and bankers in Paris.[281] Nonetheless France needed to import war supplies and grain, especially to meet the essential needs of the population of the Midi, Paris and the revolutionary army in the field, and it did so by tightening its control. On 28 Brumaire the Committee of Public Safety ordered that all authorisation to buy grain abroad, all export of numeraire, all voyages by French merchant ships were to be authorised by it. On 10 Frimaire it was decreed that all exports were to be under its control. By two decisions of 29 Pluvoise the disposition over all imported grain was placed in its hands.[282] In centralising foreign trade the role of private banks in financing overseas trade was more or less completely undermined. The scope for circulating capital whether commercial or financial had been reduced to virtually nil.

The ongoing war of course played an important role in interrupting commerce. During the conflict Basle remained the sole point of exchange between France and the rest of Europe, at which French provisioners would exchange *assignats* for foreign currency.[283] At Bordeaux the situation was complicated by the Girondin revolt. On the night of 29–30 November, more than two hundred merchants were arrested 'in order to purify commerce and exterminate speculators and hoarders'. In February 1793 an embargo was placed on enemy vessels while the coalition meanwhile instituted a blockade against French goods and shipping as well as French funds. The French government in turn sought especially to bar entry of English goods.[284] As time wore on the government's control of external trade was more and more relaxed. Nonetheless it was only after Thermidor that government restrictions on foreign commerce were definitively lifted. Chaffing over the remaining restraints, the disabused Jacobin regicide Charles Cochon de Lapparent, a member of the Commission des subsistences, could write in December 1794: 'the commission carries on the whole trade of the Republic. Seven or eight individuals undertake or wish to undertake what forty or fifty thousand merchants in other times could scarcely accomplish'.[285]

---

280   Bouchary, 1939–43, vol. 3, p. 33.
281   Pascal 1999, p. 221.
282   Lefebvre 1954, pp. 175–7.
283   Lüthy 1959–61, vol. 2, p. 739.
284   Lefebvre 1954, pp. 173–4.
285   Quoted in Crouzet 1993, p. 288.

Bankers and Productive Investment

At its height the revolutionary government had progressively suppressed the court loans, the foreign exchange operations and finally even the commercial activities of the bankers. At first glance the fate of the bankers during the revolution substantiates Taylor's perspective. Much of their activity seems external to the productive economy and was speculative and even parasitical, as the Jacobins and sans-culottes insisted. We can concede this with the important reservation that Taylor did not appreciate that the banks played a large role in the financing of external commerce, which was the most dynamic sector of the pre-revolutionary economy. Still, even this important export and import sector can likewise be seen as external to the internal economy. Taylor's point that banking operated mainly in the sphere of finance and circulation, divorced from production, appears tenable, and his conception of the French economy as non-capitalist at least discussable.

Yet we are brought up short by the case of Jacques Marc Montz, denounced by Robespierre as one of the most dangerous bankers in France. With Louis Greffuhle Montz he was head of one of the most important banks in Paris, operating through a vast network of international contacts.[286] As the Jacobins consolidated their power, Greffuhle moved to London, taking with him the bulk of the bank's assets. Meanwhile Montz tried to carry on but found himself under arrest in October 1793. According to testimony given against him in front of the Revolutionary Tribunal by one of the inhabitants of his section, Montz had contacts with many different kinds of people in his district, but since he never came to his section's assembly general, his political opinions were not really known. But the character and opinions of the class of men to which he belongs, concluded this testimony, leaves little doubt of his lack of revolutionary patriotism. Testifying in his own defence before the same tribunal, Montz claimed that he had done nothing wrong. Moreover setting him free was essential to more than 100 'brave sans-culottes' whom he was employing in his glass works in Sèvres. Without his presence the manufacture was in danger of shutting down.[287] This manufacture it turns out had long been under the control of Genevan and Parisian banks and had fallen under the control of the Greffulhe and Montz Bank.[288] In other words, Montz claimed that his revolutionary zeal was proven by the fact that he employed over a

---

286   Antonetti 1963, p. 8.
287   AN F7 4774.
288   Lüthy 1959–61, vol. 2, pp. 294–8.

hundred productive workers in Sevres and that their future employment was jeopardised by his detention.

But Montz's awakening interest in productive investment was not confined to his own factory. In 1791–2, Montz, along with his partner Greffulhe, loaned 300,000 livres to the so-called Chancellor of the Duke of Orleans, the liberal noble Levassor de la Touche, to establish a sugar refinery and cotton factory at Montargis.[289] This loan to Levassor de la Touche for the purpose of investing in industry points us initially away from the immediate pressure of the popular revolution in looking for the sources of the connection between financial and productive capital. It reminds us that the court financiers were at least until the middle of the eighteenth century deeply involved in textile manufacturing and armaments production, in close conjunction with the Bourbon state.[290] Although these financiers eventually became more and more preoccupied with state debt and for the most part removed themselves from involvement with productive activity, it was the nobility that replaced them. The latter played a large role in the growth of the cotton, mining, metallurgical and glass-making industries, making investment in manufacturing respectable in the decades leading up to the revolution.[291] Indeed, to the last of its days manufacture was closely associated with the system of privilege during the Old Regime.[292] The high nobility's interest in capitalist enterprises formed part of the noble reaction of the pre-revolutionary period. Among other aspects of this phenomenon was their drive to put their hands on capitalist mines, metallurgy, public works, financial companies and colonial plantations, often by gaining special privileges. Bankers among others were drawn into these ventures.[293]

An important example of the link between privilege and industrial develop- ment is the history of the De Dietrich family of Strasbourg. Mayor of Strasbourg at the time of the revolution, Philippe-Frédéric de Dietrich was a committed Girondin who was arrested and guillotined under the Terror. He was heir to a banking, mining and iron and steel company which was the third largest producer of iron in the Kingdom at the time of the revolution.[294] Philippe's grandfather was Jean de Dietrich, a banker at Strasbourg who in 1694 acquired the metallurgical factory at Jägerthal, in which he installed the first blast fur- nace. His son Jean extended the firm's activities to the nearby metallurgical

289   Lüthy 1959–61, vol. 2, p. 632.
290   Chaussinand-Nogaret 1970, pp. 102, 217–18, 225–30, 248, 251.
291   Chaussinand-Nogaret 1976, pp. 140–56.
292   Horn 2012, pp. 149–85.
293   Lüthy 1959–61, vol. 2, p. 697.
294   Hau 1993, pp. 77–92.

works at Niederbronn and Reichshoffen and to the forges of Reichshoffen. Among other products the firm manufactured arms for the French army as well as loaning the monarchy large amounts of money to fight wars – a service for which Jean de Dietrich was ennobled and showered with economic privileges. His son and heir Philippe was accordingly able to receive appointments to a series of high offices in the French state. A gifted geologist and friend to the *philosophes*, he was appointed head of all mining development in France on the eve of the revolution. Renouncing his noble status, Philippe became a staunch Girondin. He became the patron of Roger de l' Ile's *Marseillais*, which reputedly was played for the first time in his Strasbourg town house. Strasbourg, of which he was mayor, was key to the defence of France's eastern border. His Girondist sympathies aroused suspicion and cost him his head following the treason of Dumouriez. Nonetheless, Philippe's heirs survived the revolutionary period and made the iron and steel works they controlled one of the great industrial firms of the new century.

In its early stages cotton manufacturing – the point industry of the period – developed largely through self- or local financing. Industrialists at first were wary of the control of bankers and other outside investors.[295] Nonetheless we note an early commitment of the Cottin family to cotton manufacturing.[296] In this they were joined by their eventual partners the Jauge of Bordeaux. Delessert started out as a merchant banker in Lyons and there he provided loans to textile manufacturers interested in developing the production of gauze.[297] Lecouteulx and Co. developed a variety of industrial interests in the later half of the eighteenth century. Among their investments was a loan to help finance a cotton factory at Beauvais.[298] Perier likewise became involved in cloth making and sugar refining. Even the Boscary, for all their speculative activity, were invested in a hat factory. The Mallet Bank bought a large number of shares in the Amboise steel works, which was an ambitious establishment of the 1780s employing hundreds of workers.[299] As the revolution drew closer we note the growing involvement of bankers from Geneva, including Clavière and Bidermann in the textile sector.[300] Indeed, in the decades prior to the revolution a massive wave of Swiss capital was invested in French state debt and overseas commerce, but also the manufacture in France of Indian cottons,

---

295   Chassagne 1991, pp. 81, 118–9, 136–8, 282–3.
296   Lüthy 1959–61, vol. 2, pp. 81–4.
297   de Coninck 2000, pp. 17, 32.
298   Chassagne 1991, p. 119.
299   AN T 149. See Jagnaux 1891, vol. 2, pp. 249–53.
300   Lüthy 1959–61, vol. 2, pp. 104–6, 616, 665–7.

with capital flowing both from Geneva and other Swiss cities as well as through the Parisian branches of these banks.[301] By taking control of the Wesserling manufacture in Alsace, Bidermann put himself and his bank at the head of the largest cotton manufacturing and distributing complex on the European Continent.[302] We have noted furthermore that cotton manufacturers became more and more dependent on credit from Paris to finance their long-distance trade. We can conclude that a certain rapprochement between financial and productive capital is evident prior to the revolution.

If we look across the whole revolutionary period from 1789–1815 we note a highly uneven economic expansion, with considerable growth especially in the cotton and associated chemical industries. The Terror, during which the new regime was fighting for its life, saw no great economic expansion. On the other hand, the expropriation of the properties of the Church and the émigré nobles, which mainly fell into the hands of the bourgeois, can be described as an enormous process of primitive accumulation which reached its peak under the Jacobins. It is certainly comparable to the sixteenth-century primitive accumulation in England described by Marx in the first volume of *Capital*. Properties confiscated and transformed into private property included mainly agricultural land, the best of which was made up of capitalist farms. Most of these properties fell into the hands of the urban bourgeoisie, including bankers. As we have noted, the Parisian bankers bought land mainly in the île-de-France. But the Parisians were active much further afield. The Monneron family, for example, acquired a huge amount of national properties in the Ardèche, largely it seems for speculative purposes.[303] In the Haute Marne two bankers were among the largest purchasers of national properties. The Parisian banker Caroillon Vandeuil in particular bought 1,000 hectares owned by the Abbey of Auberville, which he transformed into a manufacture. He likewise bought the forge at Chateauville.[304] To the north the Lillois banker Placide-Joseph Panckouke, correspondent of the Parisian Bank Bontemps-Mallet, bought a vast number of national properties.[305] Closer to home following his release from prison at the end of the Terror, Delessert devoted himself to improving his newly acquired properties in the île-de-France, using fertilizers, crop rotation and machines, some of which were his own invention. He played a major part in the development of sugar beet production in place of West Indian cane sugar, from which

---

301   Veyrassat 1977, 145–59; Veyrassat 1982.
302   Lambert-Dansette 2001, vol. 1, p. 21.
303   Bodinier and Teyssier 2000, p. 424.
304   Bodinier, and Teyssier 2000, p. 259.
305   Brugière 1986, p. 83.

France was cut off. On the national level, he led an effort to import and dis-seminate thousands of merino sheep – dissemination designed to improve the quality of French wool and therefore to advance the development of wool cloth manufacturing.[306]

Indeed, it should be underscored that many ecclesiastical buildings which became national properties were transformed into factories, of which sixty became cotton factories, twenty-three metallurgical workshops, and nineteen chemical plants. Others became sugar refineries, breweries, oil-processing plants and saw and paper mills.[307] The transformation of many of the mon-asteries of the Cistercian Order into cotton factories was particularly notable. Of 148 cotton factories operating between 1785 and 1815, five percent were owned outright by bankers.[308] We should also recall that Le Creusot and Anzin, the largest industrial properties in France, fell into the hands of groups led by bankers. Analysis of the holdings of the initial directors of the Bank of France reveals that most combined financial holdings with an interest in indus-trial enterprises.[309] Although the tie between financial and productive capital would deepen in the course of the nineteenth century, such institutional and personal links had already been established by the Napoleonic period, with the bankers largely in control of these industries.[310]

Looking back we can conclude that Taylor was clearly incorrect in assert-ing that capitalism barely existed prior to the revolution and that banking was essentially speculative. Contrary to Taylor it seems that bankers were clearly involved in the development of both mining and metallurgy as well as large-scale commercial capitalism, the latter being the most dynamic sec-tor of the economy prior to the revolution. It was in this sector in particular that industrial enterprises developed prior to 1789. The revolutionary period further advanced the development of capitalism and the development of the capitalist class. While the establishment of a national currency during the Jac-obin period failed, the politically enforced development of a national market and rationalisation of the national debt were to prove important to the future development of both public and private finance. But the single most import-ant event of the revolution was the primitive accumulation of capital brought about by the expropriation of the property of the Church and émigré nobility.

---

306   de Coninck 2000, pp. 17, 32.
307   Perrot 1975; Chassagne 1991, p. 230.
308   Chassagne 1991, p. 274.
309   Szramkewicz 1974, pp. xlvi–vii.
310   Bergeron 1978, p. 319.

The transfer of ownership from clerical and noble hands into those of the bourgeoisie was of fundamental significance to strengthening the bourgeoisie. An important aspect of this process was the willing or coerced investment of the finance capital of bankers and other bourgeois in the process. Measures against speculation forced finance capital toward investment in production. The bias of the Jacobins and the sans-culottes toward production clearly helped pressure bankers and other investors toward productive investments when faced with a narrowing of their other financial and economic opportunities under the Terror. Indeed, part of the motive behind the purchase of national properties by bankers, the importance of which we have pointed out, was precisely to show where they stood with respect to the revolution. In other words, an essential thrust of the popular revolution seems to have been toward policies which would promote growth and the employment of productive labour. The popular revolution helped to force capital into investments in productive activity, buying labour power and furthering the advance of capitalism.

Bibliography

Manuscripts

Archives Nationales (AN)

F7 4667
F7 4713
F7 4774
T 149
T 508
T 1524
T 1671
W 182
W 300
W 324
W 348
W 357
W 389
W 429
W 431
W 437

Published Works

Ado, Anatoli 1996, *Paysans en Révolution: Terre, pouvoir et jacquerie 1789–1794*, translated by Serge Aberdam, Paris: Société des Études Robespierristes.

Alder, Ken 1997, *Engineering the Revolution: Arms and Enlightenment in France, 1763–1815*, Princeton: Princeton University Press.

Allen, Robert C. 1992, *Enclosure and the Yeoman*, Oxford: Oxford University Press.

Allen, Robert C. 1994 [1981], 'Agriculture during the Industrial Revolution', in *The Economic History of Britain since 1700*, Volume 1, 1700–1860, edited by Roderick Floud and Deirdre McCloskey, Cambridge: Cambridge University Press.

Allix, E. 1913, 'La rivalité entre la propriété foncière et la fortune mobilière sous la Révolution', *Revue, d'histoire économique et sociale*, 6: 297–348.

Althusser, Louis 1972, *Politics and History: Montesquieu, Rousseau, Hegel and Marx*, translated by Ben Brewster, London: New Left Books.

Anderson, Perry 1974, *Lineages of the Absolutist State*, London: Verso.

Andrews, Richard Mowery 1985, 'Social Structures, Political Elites and Ideology in

Revolutionary Paris, 1792–94: A Critical Evaluation of Albert Soboul's Les sans-culottes parisiens en l'an II', *Journal of Social History*, 19, 1: 71–112.

Antoine, Annie 1999, 'Systèmes agraires de la France de l'Ouest: Une rationalité méconnue?', *Histoire, économie et société*, 18, 1: 107–32.

Antonetti, Guy 1963, *Une maison de banque à Paris au 18e siècle: Greffulhe Montz et Cie (1789–1793)*, Paris: Editions Cujas.

Antonetti, Guy 2007, *Les ministeres de Finances de la Révolution française au Second Empire. Dictionnaire biographique 1790–1814*, Paris: Comité pour l'histoire économique et financières de la France.

Archives parlementaires de 1787 à 1860, Série 1. 1787 a 1799 (1879–), edited by M.M.I. Mavidal, Paris: Librairie Paul Dupont.

Aulard, F.A. (ed.) 1889–97, 1973, *La société des Jacobins: recueil de documents pour l'histoire du Club des Jacobins de Paris*, 6 Volumes, Paris: Librairie Jouaust, Librairie Nobelet, Maison Quantin, New York: AMS Press.

Autexier, M.-L. 1947, *Les droits féodaux et les droits seigneuriaux en Poitou de 1555 à 1799*, Fontenay le-Comte: P. & o. Lussaud frères imprimeurs.

Aymard, Maurice 1988, 'Autoconsommation et marchés: Chayanov, Labrousse ou Le Roy Ladurie?', in *La Terre et les Hommes: France et Grande-Bretagne, XVIe–XVIIIe siècle*, edited by Gérard Béaur, Paris: Hachette Littératures.

Aymard, Maurice 1975, *Condorcet: From Natural Philosophy to Social Mathematics*, Chicago: University of Chicago Press.

Aymard, Maurice 1990, *Inventing the French Revolution: Essays on French Political Culture in the Eighteenth Century*, Cambridge, New York: Cambridge University Press.

Aymard, Maurice and Joseph Zizek 1998, 'The American Historiography of the French Revolution', in *Imagined Histories: American Historians Interpret the Past*, edited by Anthony Molho and Gordon S. Wood, Princeton: Princeton University Press.

Ballot, Charles 1923, *L'introduction du machinisme*, Lille: O. Marquant.

Barnave, Antoine 1843, *Sur la révolution et sur l'état present de la France* in *Oeuvres*, edited by Alphonse Bérenger, Paris: J. Chappelle and Guiller.

Barnave, Antoine 1906, *Lettres inédites sur la prise de la Bastille et sur les journées des 5 et 6 octobre*, edited by J.de Beylié, Grenoble: Allier Frères.

Barnave, Antoine 1971, *Introduction à la Révolution française*, edited by Fernand Rude, Paris: A. Colin.

Barnave, Antoine 1971a, *Poverty, Property, and History: Bamave's Introduction to the French Revolution and Other Writings*, edited by Emanuel Chill, New York: Harper & Row.

Barral, Pierre 1964, *Les Perier dans l'Isère au 19e siècle, d'après leur correspondance familiale*, Paris: Presses universitaires de France.

Bates, David 2001, 'Political Pathologies: Barnave and the Question of National Identity in Revolutionary France', *Canadian Journal of History*, 36, 3: 427–52.

Baulant, Micheline 1979, 'Groupes mobiles dans une société sédentaire: La société rurale autour de Meaux au XVIIe et XVIIIe siècles', in *Les Marginaux et les exclus dans l'histoire*, Paris: Union générale d'éditions.

Béaur, Gérard 1984, *Le marché foncier à la veille de la Révolution: Les mouvements de propriété beaucerons dans les régions de Maintenon et de Janville de 1761 à 1790*, Paris: Éditions de l'École des hautes études en sciences sociales.

Béaur, Gérard 1991, 'Investissement foncier, épargne et cycle de vie dans le pays chartrain au XVIIIe siècle', *Histoire et Mesure*, 6, 3/4: 275–88.

Béaur, Gérard 1996, 'Les Chartier et le mystère de la révolution agricole', *Histoire et Mesure*, 11, 3/4: 367–88.

Béaur, Gérard 2000, *Histoire agraire de la France au XVIIIe siècle: Inerties et changements dans les campagnes françaises entre 1715 et 1815*, Paris: SEDES.

Becchia, Alain 2000, *La draperie d'Elbeuf des origines a 1870*, Rouen: Publication de l'Université de Rouen.

Beik, William 1985, *Absolutism and Society in Seventeenth-Century France: State Power and Provincial Aristocracy in Languedoc*, Cambridge, New York: Cambridge University Press.

Beik, William 1997, *Urban Protest in Seventeenth-Century France: The Culture of Retribution*, Cambridge, New York: Cambridge University Press.

Beik, William 2010, 'Response to Henry Heller's "The Longue Durée of the French Bourgeoisie"', *Historical Materialism*, 18, 2: 117–22.

Benedict, Philip 2002, *The Faith and Fortunes of France's Huguenots, 1600–85*, Aldershot: Ashgate.

Benoist, André 1985, 'Vie paysanne et protestantisme en "Moyen-Poitou" du XVIe siècle à la Révolution', *Annales de Bretagne et des pays de l'Ouest*, 92, 3: 161–82.

Benoist, André 2005, *Paysans du Sud-Deux-Sèvres, XVIIe–XVIIIe siècle: La terre, tes traditions, les hommes*, La Crèche: Geste.

Bercé, Yves-Marie 1990, *History of Peasant Revolts: The Social Origins of Rebellion in Early Modern France*, translated by Amanda Whitmore, Ithaca: Cornell University Press.

Berenson, Edward 1984, *Populist Religion and Left-Wing Politics in France, 1830–1852*, Princeton: Princeton University Press.

Berger, Denis n.d., 'Daniel Guérin et la Révolution française', available at: http://www.danielguerin.info.

Berger, Gérard 1985, *Le Pays de Saint-Bonnet-te-Château (Haut-Forez), de 1775 à 1975: Flux et reflux d'une société*, Saint-Etienne: Centre d'histoire régionale.

Bernet, Jacques 1999, 'Les grèves de moissoneurs ou "bacchanals" dans les campagnes d'Ile-de-France et de Picardie au XVIIIe siècle', *Histoire et sociétés rurales*, 11: 153–86.

Berryer, Pierre-Nicolas 1839, *Souvenirs de M. Berryer, doyen des avocats de Paris, de 1774 à 183*, Paris: A. Dupont.

Bianchi, Serge 1999, *La terre et les paysans en France et en Grande Bretagne: Du début du XVIIe à la fin du XVIIIe siècle*, Paris: Armand Colin.

Bianciarli, David-Paul 1995, 'Sophie Cottin, une romancière oubliée a l' oreé du Romantisme', Metz: PhD, Université de Metz.

Birnstiel, Eckart 1985, *Die Fronde in Bordeaux, 1648–1653*, Frankfurt-am-Main: Peter Lang.

Blackburn, Robin 1997, *The Making of New World Slavery: From the Baroque to the Modern 1492–1800*, London, New York: Verso.

Blackledge, Paul (ed.) 2011, 'Symposium on Chris Wickham's *Framing the Early Middle Ages*', *Historical Materialism*, 19, 1: 37–231.

Bloch, Camille 1910, *La verification des caisses patriotiques*, Paris: E. Leroux.

Bloch, Marc 1966, *French Rural History: An Essay on Its Basic Characteristics*, translated by Janet Sondheimer, Berkeley: University of California Press.

Bodinier Bernard and Eric Teyssier 2000, *L'événement le plus important de la Révolution: la vente des biens nationaux (1789–1867) en France et dans les territoires annexés*, Paris: Société des études robespierristes.

Bois, Guy 1976, *Crise du féodalisme: Économie rurale et démographie en Normandie orientale du début du 14e siècle au milieu du 16e siècle*, Paris: Presses de la Fondation nationale des sciences politiques.

Bois, Guy 1984, *The Crisis of Feudalism: Economy and Society in Eastern Normandy*, Cambridge: Cambridge University Press.

Bonald, Louis Gabriel Ambroise 1908, *François Chabot, membre de la Convention (1756–1794)*, Paris: Emile-Paul.

Bosher, J.F. 1970, *French Finances 1770–1795; From Business to Bureaucracy*, Cambridge: Cambridge University Press.

Bossis, Philippe 1972, 'Le milieu paysan aux confins de l'Anjou, du Poitou et de la Bretagne 1771–1789', *Études rurales*, 47:122–47.

Bossis, Philippe 1980, 'La foire aux bestiaux en Vendée au XVIIIe siècle: Une restructuration du monde rural', *Études rurales*, 78–80: 143–51.

Bottin, Jacques 1990, 'Marchands' in *Dictionnaire du Grand Siècle*, edited by François Bluche, Paris: Fayard.

Bouchary, Jean 1942, *Un famille d'agents de change sous l'ancien régime, la révolution, le consulat, l'empire et la restauration: les Boscary*, Paris: G. Thomas.

Bouchary, Jean 1937, *Le marché des changes de Paris à la fin du XVIIIe siècle (1778–1800)*, Paris: P. Hartmann.

Bouchary, Jean 1939–43, *Les manieurs d'argent à Paris à la fin du XVIIIe siècle*, 3 Volumes, Paris: Librairie des sciences politiques et sociales.

Bouchary, Jean 1940–2, *Les compagnies financièrs à Paris à la fin du XVIIIe siècle*, Paris: Librairie des sciences politiques et sociales.

Bouchary, Jean 1946, *Les faux-monnayeurs sous la révolution française*, Paris: Rivière et Cie.

Boudon, Jacques-Olivier, and Phillipe Bourdion 2006, 'Les heritages républicains sous le Consulat et l'Empire', *Annales historiques de la Révotution française*, 346, 4.

Bourdin, Isabelle 1937, *La Société de la Section de la Bibliothèque, 26 août 1790–25 floréal, an 11*, Paris: Sirey.

Bouton, Cynthia A. 1993, *The Flour War: Gender, Class, and Community in Late Ancien Régime French Society*, University Park, PA.: Pennsylvania State University Press.

Brass, Tom 2000, *Peasants, Populism, and Postmodernism: The Return of the Agrarian Myth*, London: Frank Cass.

Brass, Tom 2011, *Labour Regime Change in the Twenty-First Century: Unfreedom, Capitalism and Primitive Accumulation*, Leiden: Brill.

Brennan, Thomas 2006, 'Peasants and Debt in Eighteenth-Century Champagne', *Journal of Interdisciplinary History*, 37, 2: 175–200.

Brenner, Robert 1976 [1985], 'Agrarian Class Structure and Economic Development in Pre-Industrial Europe', *Past & Present*, 70, 170: 30–75, in *The Brenner Debate: Agrarian Class Structure and Economic Development in Pre-Industrial Europe*, edited by T.H. Aston and C.H.E. Philpin, Cambridge, London: Cambridge University Press.

Brenner, Robert 1986, 'The Social Basis of Economic Development', in *Analytical Marxism*, edited by John Roemer, Cambridge: Cambridge University Press.

Brenner, Robert 1989, 'Bourgeois Revolution and Transition to Capitalism', in *The First Modern Society: Essays in English History in Honour of Lawrence Stone*, edited by A.L. Beier, David Cannadine and James M. Rosenheim, Cambridge, New York: Cambridge University Press.

Brenner, Robert 1993, *Merchants and Revolution: Commercial Change, Political Conflict and London's Overseas Traders, 1550–1653*, Princeton: Princeton University Press.

Brenner, Robert 2001, 'The Low Countries in the Transition to Capitalism', in *Peasants into Farmers?: The Transformation of Rural Economy and Society in the Low Countries (Middle Ages–Nineteenth Century) in Light of the Brenner Debate*, edited by Peter Hoppenbrouwers and Jan Luiten van Zanden, Turnhout: Brepols.

Brenner, Robert 2003 [1993], *Merchants and Revolution: Commercial Change, Political Conflict, and London's Overseas Traders, 1550–1653*, London: Verso.

Brenner, Robert 2007, 'Property and Progress: Where Adam Smith Went Wrong', in *Marxist History – Writing for the Twenty-First Century*, edited by Chris Wickham, Oxford: Oxford University Press/British Academy.

Brenner, Robert and Christopher Isett 2002, 'England's Divergence from China's Yangzi Delta: Property Relations, Microeconomics, and Patterns of Development', *The Journal of Asian Studies*, 61, 2: 609–62.

Brenot, Edouard 1980, *Documents pour servir l'histoire de Grigny-en-Lyonnais des origines à 1789*, Lyon: L'imprimerie des Beaux-Arts, J. Tixier & Fils S.A..

Brissot de Warville, Jacques-Pierre 1877, *Mémoires*, edited by Adolphe de Lescure, Paris, Firmin-Didot.

Brockliss, Lawrence and Colin Jones 1997, *The Medical World of Early Modern France*, Oxford: Oxford University Press.

Brossard, E. and Joseph Delapoix de Fréminville 1904–7, *Histoire du département de la Loire pendant la Révolution française, 1789–1799*, Saint-Étienne: Chevalier.

Bruguière, Michel 1986, *Gestionnaires et profiteurs de la Révolution: l'administration des finances françaises de Louis XVI à Bonaparte*, Paris: O. Orban.

Brunelle, Gayle K. 1991, *The New World Merchants of Rouen 1559–1630*, Kirksville: Sixteenth Century Journal Publishers.

Brunet, Pierre 1960, *Structure agraire et économie rurale des plateau tertiaires entre la Seine et l'Oise*, Caen: Société d'impressions Caron.

Burke, Edmund 2001, *Reflections on the Revolution in France*, Stanford: Stanford University Press.

Burney, John M. 1995, 'Jerome Petion and the Practical Problems for the Mayor of Paris', *Proceedings of the Annual Meeting of the Western Society for French History*, 22:33–44.

Burney, John M. 1996, 'Conspiracy Rhetoric and the Jacobin Attack on Jerome Petion', *Consortium on Revolutionary Europe 1750–1850*: 100–7.

Burstin, Haim 2005, *Une révolution à l'oeuvre: le faubourg Saint-Marcel (1789–1794)*, Paris: Champ Vallon.

Butel, Paul 1974, *Les négociants bordelaises, l'Europe at les îles au XVIIIe siècle*, Paris: Aubier.

Byres Terence 1996, *Capitalism from Above and Capitalism from Below: An Essay in Comparative Political Economy*, London: MacMillan, New York: St. Martin's Press.

Byres Terence 2006, 'Differentiation of the Peasantry Under Feudalism and the Transition to Capitalism: In Defence of Rodney Hilton', *Journal of Agrarian Change*, 6, 1: 17–68.

Callinicos, Alex 1994, 'England's Transition to Capitalism', *New Left Review*, I, 207: 124–33.

Cambon, Joseph 1793, *Rapport sur la dette publique*, Paris: Imprimerie nationale.

Cambon, Joseph 1795, *Rapport sur les moyens à prendre pour retirer des assignats de la circulation*, Paris: Imprimerie nationale.

Camfield, David 2004, 'Re-Orienting Class Analysis: Working Classes as Historical Formations', *Science & Society*, 68, 4: 421–46.

Cathelineau, Léonce 1912, *Cahier de doléances des sénéchaussées de Niort et de Saint-Maixent, et des communautés et corporations de Niort et Saint-Maixent pour les États généraux de 1789*, Niort: G. Clouzot

Chagny, Robert 1990, '"Consommer la Révolution": L'évolution de la pense polititique de Barnave d'après ses interventions à l'Assemblée constituante', in *Terminer la*

Révolution: Mounier et Barnave dans la Révolution française: Colloque de Vizille 1988, edited by François Furet and Mona Ozouf, Grenoble: Presses Universitaires de Grenoble.

Chassagne, Serge 1991, *Le coton et ses patrons: France, 1760–1840*, Paris: EHESS.

Chaunu, Pierre and Richard Gascon 1977, *Histoire économique et sociale de la France: Vol. I – L'état et la ville*, Paris: Presses Universitaires de France.

Chaussinand-Nogaret Guy 1970, *Les financiers de Languedoc au XVIIIe siècle*, Paris: SEVPEN.

Chaussinand-Nogaret Guy 1976, *La noblesse au XVIIIe siècle: De la Feodalité aux Lumières*, Paris: Hachette.

Chenier, André 1872, *Oeuvres en prose*, Paris: Charpentier.

Chenier, André 1958, *Oeuvres Complètes*, Gérard Walter, ed., Paris: Gallimard.

Chevet, Jean-Michel 1994, 'Production et productivité: Un modèle de développement économique des campagnes de la région parisienne aux XVIIIe et XIXe siècles', *Histoire et Mesure*, 9, 1/2: 101–45.

Christofferson, Michael Scott 2001, 'François Furet: Between History and Journalism, 1958–65', *French History*, 5, 4: 420–47.

Christofferson, Michael Scott 2013, 'Les passeurs de depasseur: les historiens américains de la Revolution francaise et François Furet', in *Passeurs de révolution: actes de la journée d'étude organisée à Rouen, le 14 janvier 2013, par la Société des études robespierristes et le GRHis Université de Rouen*, edited by Jean-Numa Ducange and Michel Biard, Paris: Société des études robespierristes.

Claeys, Thierry 2011, *Dictionnaire biographique des financiers en France au XVIIIe siècle*, 2 Volumes, Paris: SPM.

Claeys, Thierry 2011a, *Les institutions financières en France au XVIIIe siècle*, 2 Volumes, Paris: SPM.

Clark, Gregory 1999 [1993], 'Too Much Revolution: Agriculture in the Industrial Revolution, 1700–1860', in *The British Industrial Revolution: An Economic Perspective*, edited by Joel Mokyr, Boulder, CO.: Westview Press.

Clifford, Dale Lothrop 1990, 'The National Guard and the Parisian Community, 1789–1790', *French Historical Studies*, 16, 4: 849–78.

Clouatre, Dallas L. 1984, 'The Concept of Class in French Culture Prior to the Revolution', *Journal of the History of Ideas*, 45: 2, 232–34.

Cobban, Alfred 1968, *The Social Interpretation of the French Revolution*, Cambridge: Cambridge University Press.

Cointet, J.-P. 1965, 'Le bataillon des filles Saint-Thomas et le 10 août', *Annales Historiques de la Révolution Française*, 37, 182: 450–68.

Collins, James 1994, *Classes, Estates and Orders in Early Modern Brittany*, Cambridge: Cambridge University Press.

Comité des travaux historiques et scientifiques, France, *Commission de recherche et de publication des documents relatifs à la vie économique de la Révolution: notes et documents sur ses travaux de 1903 à 1912*, edited by Pierre Caron, Paris: E. Leroux.

Comninel, George C. 1987, *Rethinking the French Revolution: Marxism and the Revisionist Challenge*, London, New York: Verso.

Condorcet, Jean-Antoine-Nicolas de Caritat 1793–4,1847, *Tableau général de la science, qui a pour objet l'application du calcul aux sciences politiques et morales*, edited by A. Condorcet O'Connor and M.F. Arago, Paris: Firmin.

Constant, Jean-Marie 1996, *La Ligue*, Paris: Presses Universitaires de France.

Cooper, J.P. 1985, 'In Search of Agrarian Capitalism', in *The Brenner Debate; Agrarian Class Structure and Economic Development in Pre-Industrial Europe*, edited by T.H. Aston and C.H.E. Philpin, Cambridge: Cambridge University Press.

Coudart, Laurence 1990, 'La contre-révolution parisienne: la section de la Bibliothèque (dite aussi section 92 et section Lepeletier), 1790–1792', *Annales historiques de la Révolution française*, 62, 2: 198–206.

Couturier, Henri 1909, *La préparation des États généraux de 1789 en Poitou, principalement d'après les cahiers des paroisses et des corporations: Étude d'histoire du droit*, Poitiers: Société française d'imprimerie et de librairie.

Crestin Jean-Francois 1792, *Discours et projet de décret, pronounceés à l'Assemblée nationale. a la séance du 29 mars 1792, sur les caisses d'escompte, patriotiques, de confiance & de secours, établies dans tout le royaume..., l'agiotage et les accaparements qui en sont la suite*, Paris: Imprimerie nationale.

Crouzet, François 1993, *La grande inflation: la monnaie en France de Louis XVI à Napoléon*, Paris: Fayard.

Daline, Victor 1960, 'Robespierre et Danton vus par Babeuf', *Annales historiques de la Revolution Française*, 23: 388–410.

Darnton, Robert 1984, *The Great Cat Massacre and Other Episodes in French Cultural History*, New York: Basic Books.

Davidson, Neil 2012, *How Revolutionary Were the Bourgeois Revolutions?*, Chicago: Haymarket Books.

Davis, Natalie Zemon 1975, *Society and Culture in Early Modern France: Eight Essays*, Stanford: Stanford University Press.

de Coninck, Severine 2000, *La Famille Delessert Banquiers et philanthropes (1735–1868): aux origines des Caisses d'épargne françaises*, Paris: Economica.

Dehergne, Joseph 1963, *Le Bas Poitou à la veille de la Révolution*, Paris: Centre national de la recherche scientifique.

Démier, François 1990, 'Les "economistes de la nation" contre "l'economie-monde" du XVIIIe siècle', in *La pensée économique pendant la Révolution française: actes du colloque international de Vizille, 6–8 septembre 1989*, edited by Gilbert Faccarello and Philippe Steiner, Grenoble: Presses universitaires de Grenoble.

Descimon, Robert, and Christian Jouhaud, *La France du premier XVIIe siècle: 1594–1661*, Paris: Belin.

Dessert, Daniel 1984, *Argent, pouvoir et société au Grand Siècle*, Paris: Fayard.

Devenne, Florence, 1991, 'La Garde Nationale, création et evolution', *Annales historiques de la Révolution françaises*, 283: 50–65.

Deyon, Pierre 1963, 'Variations de la production textile aux XVIe et XVIIe siècles: sources et premiers resultats', *Annales: ESC*, 18, 5: 939–55.

Dion, Roger 1959, *Histoire de la vigne et du vin en France des origines au XIX siècle*, Paris: Imprimerie Sévin et cie.

Dixon, Scott 2001, 'American Luther Research in the Twentieth Century', *Lutheran Quarterly*, 15,1; 1–21.

Dobb, Maurice 1946, *Studies in the Development of Capitalism*, New York: International Publishers, London: Routledge & Kegan Paul.

Dontenwill, Serge 2003, 'La mise en valeur des terres en Roannais Brionnais au dernier siècle de l'Ancien Régime (1670–1789)', in *Les contrats agraires de l'Antiquité à nos jours. Actes du colloque de Caen (10–13 septembre 1997)*, edited by Anne Varet-Vitu, Mathieu Amoux and Gérard Béaur, Rennes: Association d'histoire des societies rurales.

Dorigny Marcel 1983, 'Les Girondins et la droit à la propriété', in *Bulletin d'histoire économique et sociale de la Révolution francaise*, Paris: C.T.H.S.: 16–20.

Dorigny Marcel 1985, 'Etienne Clavière', in *Dictionnaire historique de la Révolution française*, edited by Albert Soboul, Paris: Presses universitaires de France.

Doyle, William 1996, *Venality: The Sale of Offices in Eighteenth-Century France*, Oxford: Clarendon Press.

Doyle, William 1999, *Origins of the French Revolution*, 3rd. ed., Oxford: Oxford University Press.

Ducange, Jean-Numa 2010, *Le socialisme et la Révolution française*, Paris: Demopolis.

Ducoudray Emile 1989, 'Jean-Frederic Perregaux', *Dictionnaire historique de la Révolution française*, edited by Albert Soboul, Paris: Presses universitaires de France.

Dupâquier, Jacques 1956, *La propriété et l'exploitation foncière à la fin de l'Ancien Régime dans la Gâtinais septentrional*, Paris: Presses Universitaires de France.

Dupâquier, Jacques 1995, 'Le peuplement', in *Histoire de la population française*, Volume 2, *De la Renaissance à 1789*, edited by Dupâquier, Paris: Presses Universitaires de France.

Dupâquier, Jacques, and Guy Cabourdin et al. 1988, *Histoire de la population française: Vol. II – de la Renaissance à 1789*, Paris: Presses Universitaires de France.

Durand, Georges 1979, *Vin, vigne et vignerons en Lyonnais et Beaujolais*, Lyon: École des hautes études en sciences sociales.

Elie, Jean 2003, 'Note sur l'économie agricole en Haut-Poitou au XVIIIe siècle. La

Chapelle Moulière: Un exemple ou un cas particulier?', *Revue historique du Centre-Ouest*, 2: 231–48.

Engelman Ralph 1973, 'The Problem of Jean Jaurès', *Science and Society*, 37, 2: 195–202.

Engels, Frederick 1972 [1884], *The Origin of the Family, Private Property, and the State*, New York: Pathfinder.

Fagniez, Gustave 1908, *La condition des commerçants étrangers en France au commencement du XVIIe siècle*, La Flèche: E. Beisner.

Fitzsimmons, Michael P. 2010, *From Artisan to Worker: Guilds, the French State, and the Organization of Labor, 1776–1821*, New York: Cambridge University Press.

Flamein, Richard 2010, 'Lecouteulx, identité bourgeoise, univers matériel, siège social, capitalisme familial, anoblissement', *Annales historiques de la Révolution Française*, 362,1: 3–30.

Foisil, Madeleine 1970, *La révolte des nu-pieds et les révoltes normandes de 1639*, Paris: Presses Universitaires de France.

Forestier, Albane 2011, 'A "considerable credit" in the Late Eighteenth-Century French West Indian Trade: the Chaurands of Nantes', *French History*, 25, 1:48–68.

Fossier, Robert 1968, *La Terre et les hommes en Picardie jusqu'à la fin du XIIIe siècle*, Volume 2, Paris: B. Nauwelaerts.

Forsyth, Murray 1987, *Reason and Revolution: The Political Thought of the Abbé Sieyes*, Leicester, UK: Leicester University Press/Holmes and Meier.

Fournial, Etienne and Jean Pierre Gutton 1974–5, 'Introduction', in *Cahiers de doléances de la province de Forez: Bailliage principal de Montbrison et bailliage secondaire de Bourg-Argental*, Saint-Etienne: Centre d' études foréziennes.

Fourquin, Guy 1970, *Seigneurie et féodalité au Moyen Âge*, Paris: Presses Universitaires de France.

Fourquin, Guy 1971, 'Le renouveau de la fin du moyen-age (du milieu du xve siècle aux années1520)', in *Histoire de l'Île-de-France et de Paris*, edited by Michel Mollat, Toulouse: Privat.

Frey Lucius Junius 1793, *Philosophie sociale dédiée au peuple François*, Paris: Froullé.

Fromont, Henry 1907, *Essai sur l'administration de l'assemblée provincial de la généralité d'Orléans (1787–1790)*, Paris: Imp. de la Fac. De Médecine.

Freudenthal, Gideon 2005, 'The Hessen-Grossman Thesis. An Attempt At Rehabilitation', *Perspectives on Science*, 13, 2: 166–93.

Friesen, Abraham 1974, *Reformation and Utopia, the Marxist Interpretation of the Reformation and Its Antecedents*, Weisbaden: F. Steiner.

Furet, François 1978, *Penser la Revolution française*, Paris: Gallimard.

Furet, François 1988, *Marx and the French Revolution*, Chicago: University of Chicago Press.

Furet, François and Denis Richet 1973, *La Révolution française*, Paris: Fayard.

Galley, J.-B. 1903, *L'élection de Saint-Étienne à la fin de l'ancien régime*, Saint-Étienne: Ménard.

Ganiage, Jean 1988, *Le Beauvaisis au XVIIIe siècle: La campagne*, Paris: Presses Universitaires de France.

Garnier, Josette 1982, *Bourgeoisie et propriété immobilière en Forez aux XVIIe et XVIIIe siècles*, Saint-Etienne: Centre d'études foréziennes.

Gascon, Richard 1971, *Grand commerce et vie urbaine au XVIe siècle: Lyon et ses marchands*, 2 Volumes, Paris: Presses Universitaires de France.

Gauthier, Florence 1992, *Triomphe et mort du droit naturel en Révolution: 1789–1795–1802*, Paris: Presses universitaires de France.

Gauthier, Florence 2006, '1793–94: La Révolution abolit l'esclavage. 1802: Bonaparte rétablit l'esclavage', *Révolution Française.net*, *Synthèses*, online 11 April 2006, http://revolution-francaise.net/2006/04/11/32-1793-94-la-revolution-abolit-l-esclavage-1802-bonaparte-retablit-l-esclavage.

Gay, François-P. 1955, 'L'agriculture en Berry au XVIIIe siècle: Les enquêtes agricoles de 1762 et 1786', *Mémoires de l'Union des Sociétés Savantes de Bourges*: 25–46.

Gay, François-P. 1967, *Essai sur la formation d'un paysage agraire et l'évolution d'une société rurale*, Bourges: Tardy.

Gendron, François 1993, *The Gilded Youth of Thermidor*, Montreal-Kingston: McGill-Queens University Press.

Genty, Maurice 1993, 'Controverses autour de la garde nationale parisienne,' *Annales Historiques de la Révolution Française*, 293: 61–88.

Gérard, Alain 1990, *Pourquoi la Vendée?*, Paris: Armand Colin.

Godechot Jacques 1958, 'The Business Classes and the Revolution outside France', *American Historical Review*, 64, 1: 1–13.

Goubert, Pierre 1990, *Mazarin*, Paris: Fayard.

Goubert, Pierre and Daniel Roche 1984, *Les français et l'Ancien Régime*, Volume 1, *La société et l'Etat*, Paris: Armand Colin.

Grantham, George 1975, 'Scale and Organization in French Farming, 1840 to 1880', in *European Peasants and their Markets*, edited by E.L. Jones and W.N. Parker, Princeton: Princeton University Press.

Grantham, George 1978, 'The Diffusion of the New Husbandry in Northern France, 1815–1840', *The Journal of Economic History*, 38, 2: 311–37.

Greer, Donald 1935, *The Incidence of the Terror During the French Revolution: A Statistical Interpretation*, Cambridge, Mass: Harvard University Press.

Greer, Donald 1966, *The Incidence of the Emigration During the French Revolution*, Gloucester, Mass.: P. Smith.

Gross, Jean-Pierre 1996, *Fair Shares for All: Jacobin Egalitarianism in Practice*, Cambridge, New York: Cambridge University Press.

Grüner, Shirley M. 1976. 'La concept de classe dans la Révolution française: une mise à jour', *Histoire Sociale*, 9,18: 406–23.

Gueniffey, Patrice 1990, 'Terminer la Révolution: Barnave et le révision de la Constitution (Août 1791)', in *Terminer la Révolution: Mounier et Barnave dans la Révolution
française: Colloque de Vizille 1988*, edited by Furet and Ozouf, eds., Grenoble: Presses
Universitaires de Grenoble.

Guérin, Daniel 1968, La lutte de class sous la première république 1793–97, 2 Volumes,
Paris: Gallimard.

Guilhaumou, Jacques 1989, 'Discourse and Revolution: The Foundation of Political Language', in *Cultural Ramifications of the French Revolution*, edited by George Levitine,
College Park, Maryland: University of Maryland Press.

Guilhaumou, Jacques 1989a, *La langue politique et la Révolution française: à l'événement
de la raison linguistique*, Paris: Méridiens-Klincksieck.

Guilhaumou, Jacques 1998, *L'avènement des porte-paroles de la république (1789–1792)*,
Villeneuve d'Ascq: Presses Universitaires de Septentrion.

Guilhaumou, Jacques, and Raymonde Mounier 200, *Des notions-concepts en révolution
autour de la liberté politique à la fin du 18e siècle: journée d'études du 23 novembre 2002
à la Sorbonne*, Paris: Société des études robespierristes.

Guillemet, Dominique, Nicole Pellegrin and Jacques Peret 1981, *Le Haut-Poitou au
XVIIIe siècle*, Volume 1, *La société d'une paroisse rurale, la Vitledieu-du-Clain*, Poitiers:
CNDP.

Guillet, Eric 2010, 'Les courbes et les droites. Patience en Allemagne et impatience
en France à l'époque révolutionnaire. L'interpretation de Jean Jaurès', *Annales historiques de la Révolution française*, 360: 173–96.

Guizot, Francois 1860, *Mémoires pour servir à l'histoire de mon temps*, Volume III, Paris:
Michel-Lévy.

Gutton, Jean Pierre 1971, *La société et les pauvres: L'exemple de la généralité de Lyon,
1534–1789*, Paris: Société d'édition 'Les Belles Lettres'.

Hafter, Daryl M. 2007, *Women at Work in Preindustrial France*, University Park: Pennsylvania State University.

Hamilton, Earl J. 1934, *American Treasure and the Price Revolution in Spain, 1501–1650*,
Cambridge, Mass., Harvard University Press.

Hardman, John 2007, 'The Real and Imagined Conspiracies of Louis XVI', in *Conspiracy
in the French Revolution*, edited by Peter R. Campbell, Thomas E. Kaiser and Marisa
Linton, Manchester, New York: Manchester University Press.

Hau, Michel 1993, 'Naufrage et redressement d'une grande entreprise métallurgique De
Dietrich', *Histoire, économie et société*, 12, 1: 77–92.

Harman, Chris 2008, 'An Age of Transition? Economy and Society in England in the
Later Middle Ages: The Field and the Forge: Population, Production and Power in
the Pre-Industrial West', *Historical Materialism*, 16, 1: 185–99.

Hayden, Michael J. 1996, 'Models, Mousnier and Qualité: The Social Structure of Early
Modern France', *French History*, 10, 3: 375–98.

Hébert, Jacques 1859, *Le Père Duchesne d'Hébert, ou Notice historique et bibliographique sur ce journal publié pendant les années 1790, 1791, 1792, 1793 et 1794*, edited by Charles Brunet, Paris: Librairie de France.

Heller, Henry 1969, 'Reform and Reformers at Meaux, 1518–1525', Ph.D Diss., Ithaca, New York: Cornell University.

Heller, Henry 1977, 'Famine, Revolt and Heresy at Meaux: 1521–1525', *Archiv für Reformationsgeschichte*, 5: 133–67.

Heller, Henry 1986, *The Calvinist Revolt in Sixteenth Century France*, Leiden: Brill.

Heller, Henry 1991, *Iron and Blood: Civil Wars in Sixteenth Century France*, Montreal, Kingston: McGill-Queens University Press.

Heller, Henry 1996, *Labour, Science and Technology in France 1500–1620*, Cambridge, New York: Cambridge University Press.

Heller, Henry 2000, 'Primitive Accumulation and Technical Innovation in the French Wars of Religion', *History and Technology*, 16, 3: 243–62.

Heller, Henry 2003, *Anti-Italianism in Sixteenth Century France*, Toronto: University of Toronto Press.

Heller, Henry 2006, *The Bourgeois Revolution in France 1789–1815*, New York: Berghahn Books.

Heller, Henry 2009, 'The Longue Durée of the French Bourgeoisie', *Historical Materialism*, 17, 1:31–59.

Heller, Henry 2010, 'Response to William Beik and David Parker', Historical Materialism, 18, 2: 132–42.

Heller, Henry 2010, 'Marx, the French Revolution, and the Spectre of the Bourgeoisie', *Science & Society*, 74, 2: 184–214.

Heller, Henry 2011, *The Birth of Capitalism: A Twenty-First Century Perspective*, London: Pluto Press.

Heller, Henry 2012, review article, Jeff Horn, *The Path Not Taken: French Industrialization in the Age of Revolution, 1750–1830*, Cambridge: MIT Press, 2006, *Historical Materialism*, 20, 1: 244–53.

Heller, Henry 2013a, review article, 'Guy Lemarchand, *Paysans et seigneurs en Europe: une histoire comparée, XVIe–XIXe siècle*', *Historical Materialism*, 21, 4: 304–13.

Heller, Henry 2013b, 'Stephen Miller on Capitalism in the Old Regime: A Response', *Historical Materialism*, 21, 3: 109–16.

Heller, Henry 2014, 'Bankers, Finance Capital and the French Revolutionary Terror (1791–94)', *Historical Materialism*, 22, 3–4, 172–216.

Heller, Henry 2015, Introduction to *A Socialist History of the French Revolution*, translated by Mitchell Abidor, London: Pluto Press.

Hermann-Mascard Nicole 1990, *L'emprunt forcé de l'An. II*, Paris: Aux Amateurs du Livre.

Heron, Louis 1791, *Complot d'une banquerote generale de la France, de l'Espagne, et par contre-coup de la Hollande et d'Angleterre ou les horreurs de l'ancien et nouveau regime*, Paris: Impr. de Marat.

Hessen, Boris, and Henryk Grossman 2009, *The Social and Economic Roots of the Scientific Revolution*, edited by Gideon Freudenthal, Dordrecht: Springer.

Higonnet, Patrice 2006, 'Terror, Trauma and the Young Marx's Explanation of Jacobin Politics', *Past & Present*, 191, 1: 121–64.

Hilton, Rodney (ed.) 1976, *The Transition from Feudalism to Capitalism*, London: New Left Books.

Hincker, François 1990, 'Y eut-il une penséee économique de la montagne?', in *La pensée économique pendant la Révolution Française: actes du colloque international de Vizille (6–8 septembre 1989)*, edited by Gilbert Faccarello and Philippe Steiner, Grenoble: Presses Universitaires de Grenoble.

Hirsch, Jean-Pierre 1979, 'Un fil rompu? À propos du credit à Lille sous la Révolution et l'Empire', *Revue du Nord*, 61, 240: 182–3.

Hirsch, Jean-Pierre 1989, 'Revolutionary France, Cradle of Free Enterprise', *American Historical Review*, 94, 5: 1281–89.

Hirsch, Jean-Pierre 1991, *Les deux rêves du commerce: Enterprise et institution dans la région lilloise 1780–1860*, Paris: Éditions de l'École des Hautes Études en Sciences Sociales.

Hobsbawm, Eric 1976, 'From Feudalism to Capitalism', in *The Transition from Feudalism to Capitalism*, edited by Rodney Hilton.

Hoffman, Philip T. 1996, *Growth in a Traditional Society: The French Countryside, 1450–1815*, Princeton: Princeton University Press.

Hoffman, Philip T. 2000, *Priceless Markets: The Political Economy of Credit in Paris, 1660–1870*, Chicago: University of Chicago Press.

Horn, Jeff 2006, *The Road Not Taken: French Industrialization in the Age of Revolution, 1750–1820*, Cambridge, Mass.: Harvard University Press.

Horn, Jeff 2012, '"A Beautiful Madness": Privilege, the Machine Question and Industrial Development in Normandy in 1789', *Past and Present*, 217, 1: 149–85.

Houssay, E. 1907, *Étude sur le papier-monnaie et les assignats émis en France de 1701 à 1796: Banque de Law, Caisse d'escompte, assignats de la Révolution, billets de confiance, assignats de la chouannerie, de Louis XVII, faux assignats*, Tours: Lebodo.

Hunt, Lynn Avery 1984, *Politics, Culture and Class in the French Revolution*, Berkeley: University of California Press.

Israel, Jonathan 1989, *Dutch Primacy in World Trade 1580–1740*, Oxford: Oxford University Press.

Jacoud, Gilles 1996, *Le billet de banque en France (1796–1803)*, Paris: Harmattan.

Jacquart, Jean 1974, *La Crise rurale en Ile de France, 1550–1670*, Paris: Publications de la Sorbonne.

Jacquart, Jean 1975, 'Le rente foncière, indice conjoncturel?', *Revue Historique*, 253, 2: 355–76.

Jacquart, Jean 1990, *Paris et Île-de-France aux temps des paysans*, Paris: Publications de la Sorbonne.

Jacquart, Jean 1992, 'Les problèmes de la paysannerie française au temps de Henri III', in *Henri III et son temps*, edited by Robert Sauzet, Paris: J. Vrin.

Jaurès, Jean 1901–4, Histoire socialiste *de la Révolution française*, 4 Volumes, Paris: Rouff.

Jagnaux Raoul 1891, *Histoire de la Chimie*, 2 Volumes, Paris: Baudry.

Jameson, Fredric 1981, *The Political Unconscious: Narrative As A Socially Symbolic Act*, Ithaca: Cornell University Press.

Jamoux, Philippe 1996, *Les bourgeois et la terre: Fortunes et strategies foncières à Rennes au XVIIIe siècle*, Rennes: Presses Universitaires de Rennes.

Jaurès, Jean 1901–4, Histoire socialiste *de la Révolution française*, 4 Volumes, Paris: Rouff.

Jaurès, Jean 1922–4, Histoire socialiste de la révolution française, edited by Albert Mathiez, 8 Volumes, Paris: Éditions de la Librairie de l'humanité.

Jaurès, Jean 1968–73, *Histoire socialiste de la Révolution française*, edited by Albert Soboul, 7 Volumes, Paris: Éditions sociales.

Jaurès, Jean 2014, *Histoire socialiste de la Révolution française*, 4 Volumes, Paris: Les Éditions sociales.

Jaurès, Jean 2015, *A Socialist History of the French Revolution*, introduction by Heller, translated by M. Abidour, London: Pluto Press.

Jean, Raymond 1989, *La dernière nuit d'André Chénier*, Paris: Albin Michel.

Jessenne, Jean Pierre 2007, *Vers un ordre bourgeois? Revolution française et changement social*, Rennes, France: Université de Rennes.

Johnson, Christopher H. 1993, 'Capitalism and the State: Capital Accumulation and Proletarianization in the Languedocian Woolens Industry, 1700–1789', in *The Workplace Before the Factory*, edited by Thomas Max Safley and Leonard N. Rosenband, Ithaca: Cornell University Press.

Jomand, Joseph 1966, *Chaponosten Lyonnais*, Lyon: E. Vitte.

Jones, Colin 1991, 'Bourgeois Revolution Revivified: 1789 and Social Change', in *Rewriting the French Revolution*, edited by Colin Lucas., Oxford: Oxford University Press.

Jones, Colin 2002, *The Great Nation: France from Louis XV to Napoleon: The New Penguin History of France*, Harmondsworth: Penguin Books.

Jones, Peter 2003, *Liberty and Locality in Revolutionary France: Six Villages Compared, 1760–1820*, Cambridge: Cambridge University Press.

Jouanna, Arlette 1989, *Le devoir de révolte: la noblesse française et la gestation de l'État moderne (1559–1661)*, Paris: Fayard.

Kaplan, Steven L. 1979, 'Reflections sur la police du monde du travail, 1700–1815', *Revue historique*, 256, 1: 17–77.

Kaplan, Steven L. 1982, *The Famine Plot Persuasion in Eighteenth-Century France*, Philadelphia: American Philosophical Society.

Kaplan, Steven L. 1995, *Farewell, Revolution: The Historian's Feud, France, 1789–1989*, Ithaca, New York/London: Cornell University Press.

Kaplan, Steven L. 2001, *La fin des corporations*, Paris: Fayard.

Kautsky, Karl 1988 [1899], *The Agrarian Question*, Volume 1, translated by Peter Burgess with an Introduction by Haniza Alavi and Teodor Shanin, London: Zwan Publications.

Kettering, Sharon 1986, *Patrons, Brokers and Clients in Seventeenth Century France*, Oxford: Oxford University Press.

Krumenacker, Yves 2002, *Des Protestatants au siècle des lumières: le modèle Lyonnais*, Paris: Champion.

Kuhn, Thomas S., *The Structure of Scientific Revolutions*, Chicago: University of Chicago Press.

Kurtz, Geoffrey 2006, 'A Socialist State of Grace: The Radical Reformism of Jean Jaure's', *New Political Science*, 28, 3: 401–18.

Labrousse, Ernest 1966, 'The Evolution of Peasant Society in France from the Eighteenth Century to the Present', in *French Society and Culture since the Old Regime*, edited by Evelyn M. Acomb and Marvin L. Brown, Jr., New York: Holt, Rinebart and Winston.

Labrousse, Ernest 1967, 'Preface', in Jaures, *Histoire socialiste de la Révolution française*, 1: 9–34.

Labrousse, Ernest 1990 [1943], *La crise de l'économie française à la fin de l'Ancien Régime et au début de la Révolution*, Paris: Presses Universitaires de France.

Lacombe, Paul 1908, 'Les historiens de la Révolution – Jean Jaurès', *Revue de synthèse historique*, 16, 1: 164–74, 2: 272–302.

Lacroix, Sigismond 1894–8, *Actes de la Commune de Paris*, série 2, 8 Volumes, Paris: Le Cerf.

Lafargue, Paul 1894, *Essai sur la langue français avant et après la Révolution*. The Paul Lafargue Internet Archive, http://www.marxist.org/archive/lafargue/index.htm.

Laffon de Ladébat, André-Daniel 1807, *Compte-rendu des opérations de la Caisse d'escompte, depuis son origine (24 mars 1776) jusqu'à sa suppression (24 août 1793) et de sa liquidation depuis l'époque de sa suppression*, Paris: A. Bailleul.

Lambert-Dansette, Jean 2001, *Le temps des pionniers: 1830–1880*, Paris: Harmattan.

Landes, David S. 1969, *The Unbound Prometheus: Technological Change and Industrial Development in Western Europe from 1750 to the Present*, Cambridge: Cambridge University Press.

Larkin, Paschal 1930, *Property in the Eighteenth Century with Special Reference to John Locke*, Cork: Cork University Press.

Lecouteulx, Jean-Barthélemy, and Laurent-Vincent 1792, *Le cri de la conscience, ou Réflexions d'un François, ami de la justice, adressées à la Convention nationale & à ses concitoyens, sur le procès de Louis XVI*, Paris: n.p.

Lefebvre, Georges 1924, *Les paysans du Nord pendant la revolution française*, Paris: F. Rieder et cie.

Lefebvre, Georges 1954, 'Le commerce extérieur en l'an ii', in *Études sur la Révolution française*, Paris: Presses universitaires de France, pp. 170–98.

Lefebvre, Georges 1954a, *Questions agraires au temps de la terreur*, La Roche-Sur-Yon: Potier.

Lefebvre, Georges 1976, 'Some Observations', in *The Transition from Feudalism to Capitalism*, edited by Rodney Hilton.

Legal, Pierre-Yannick 1995, 'Paysans Bas-Poitevins entre plaine, bocage, Gatine et marais (1730–1750)', *Recherches vendéennes*, 2: 317–53.

Legay, Marie-Laure, Joël Félix and Eugene White 2009, 'Retour sur les origines financières de la Révolution française', *Annales historiques de la Révolution française*, 356: 183–201.

Lehideaux-Vernimmen, Virginie 1992, *Du negoce à la banque: Les Andre, une famille nîmoise protestante, 1600–1800*, Nîmes: C. Lacour.

Lejosne, Raymonde 1989, 'Champarts autours d'Étampes', *89 en Essonne*, 2: 61–2.

Lemarchand, Guy 1989, *La fin du féodalisme dans le pays de Caux: conjuncture économique et démographique et structure sociale dans une région de grande culture de la crise du XVIIe siècle à la stabilisation de la révolution (1640–1795)*, Paris: Comité des Travaux historiques et scientifiques.

Lemarchand, Guy 2008, *L'économie en France de 1770 à 1830: De la crise de l'ancien régime à la révolution industrielle*, Paris: A. Colin.

Lemarchand, Guy 2011, *Paysans et seigneurs en Europe: une histoire comparée, XVIe–XIXe siècle*, Rennes: Université de Rennes.

Lenin, V.I. 1964, *The Development of Capitalism in Russia*, in *Collected Works*, 45 Volumes, Moscow: Progress Publishers, Volume 3.

Lenin, V.I. 1972, *The Agrarian Program of Social-Democracy in the First Russian Revolution, 1905–7*, in *Collected Works*, Moscow: Progress Publishers, Volume 13, pp. 217–429.

Léon, Pierre 1954, *La naissance de la grande industrie en Dauphiné*, 2 Volumes, Paris: Presses Universitaires de France.

Léon, Pierre 1963, *Marchands et spéculateurs dauphinois dans le monde antillais du XVIIIe siècle. Les Dolle, les Raby*, Paris: Les Belles Lettres.

Léon, Pierre 1970, 'Morcellement et emergence du monde ouvrier', in *Histoire économique et sociale de la France, Vol. II: Des derniers temps de l'âge seigneurial aux preludes de l'âge industriel (1660–1789)*, edited by Ernest Labrousse, Léon Goubert, et al., Paris: Presses Universitaires de France.

Leroux, Ernest 1922, 'Commission de recherche et de publication des documents relatifs à la vie économique de la Révolution', in *La Monnaie et le Papier-Monnaie*, Paris: Imprimerie Nationale.

Le Roy Ladurie, Emmanuel 1966, *Les paysans de Languedoc*, 2 Volumes, Paris: SEVPEN.

Le Roy Ladurie, Emmanuel 1969, *Les paysans de Languedoc*, Abridged Edition, Paris: Flammarion.

Le Roy Ladurie, Emmanuel 1975, 'De la crise ultime à la vraie croissance', in *Histoire de la France rurale*, edited by Georges Duby and Armand Wallon, Volume 2, *L'âge classique 1340–1740*, edited by Hughes Niveux, Jean Jacquart and Emmanuel Le Roy Ladurie, Paris: Seuil.

Le Roy Ladurie, Emmanuel 1977, 'Les masses profondes: La paysannerie', in *Histoire économique et sociale de la France*, Volume 2, *Des derniers temps de l'âge seigneurial aux préludes de l'âge industriel (1660–1789)*, edited by Fernand Braudel and Ernst Labrousse, Paris: PUF.

Le Roy Ladurie, Emmanuel 1978, 'En Haute-Normandie: Malthus ou Marx?', *Annales: Économies, Sociétés, Civilisations*, 33, 1: 115–24.

Le Roy Ladurie, Emmanuel 1979, *Le carnival de Romans: de la Chandeleur au mercredi des Cendres, 1579–1580*, Paris: Gallimard.

Le Roy Ladurie, Emmanuel 1994, *The Royal French State 1460–1610*, Oxford: Blackwell Publishers.

Le Roy Ladurie, Emmanuel 1996, *The Ancien Regime: A History of France 1610–1774*, Oxford: Blackwell Publishers.

Le Roy Ladurie, Emmanuel 2002, *Histoire des paysans français. De la Peste noire à la Révolution*, Paris: Seuil.

Le Roy Ladurie, Emmanuel 2008, 'Regards croisés: historiens et révolutions. Vers une "paix des braves"', *Annales historiques de la Révolution Française*, 351, 1: 177–96.

Lewis, Gwynne 1993, *The French Revolution: Rethinking the Debate*, New York: Routledge.

Lewis, Gwynne 1993, *The Advent of Modern Capitalism in France, 1770–1840: The Contribution of Pierre-François Tubeuf*, Oxford: Oxford University Press.

Lewis, Gwynne 1998, 'Book Review: David Parker, *Class and State in Ancien Régime France: The Road to Modernity?*', *History*, 270, 3: 343–45.

Lewis, Gwynne 2004, *France 1715–1804: Power and the People*, Harlow, London: Pearson Longman.

Liébart, Déborah 2008, 'Un groupe de pression contre-révolutionnaire: le club Massiac sous la constituante', *Annales historiques de la revolution francaise*, 354: 29–50.

Ligou, Daniel 1968, *Le Protestantisme en France de 1598 à 1715*, Paris: Société d'édition d'enseignement supérieur.

Livesey, James 2013, 'Capitalism and the French Revolution', available on *e-France*, Volume 4, edited by A. Fairfax-Cholmeley and C. Jones, *New Perspectives on the French Revolution*.

Lizin de Mily, Louis 1790, *Discours prononcé le 20 février 1790, par M. de Milly, américain, citoyen de Paris, avocat en Parlement, l'un des commissaires nommés par le district des*

Filles-Saint-Thomas; pour l'examen de la question relative à la liberté et à l'abolition de la traite des nègres, Paris: Didot.

Lods, Janine Driancourt-Girod 1992, *L'insolite histoire des luttheriens de Paris*, Paris: A. Michel.

Louis, Eugène (ed.) 1877–1880, *Le Bas-Poitou en 1788: Mémoires addresses à la Commission intermédiaire de l'Assemblée d'élection de Fontenay par les municipalités de Maillezais et de Chailté-les Marais*, La Roche-sur-Yon: L. Gasté, imprimeur de la Société d'émulation.

Loutchisky, I. 1933, 'Régime agraire et populations agricoles dans les environs de Paris à la veille de la Révolution', *Revue d'histoire moderne*, 7:97–142.

Lowy, Michael 1989, '"The Poetry of the Past": Marx and the French Revolution', *New Left Review*, 1, 177: 1–24.

Lublinskaya, A.D. 1968, *French Absolutism: the Crucial Phase 1620–29*, translated by Brian Pearce, Cambridge: Cambridge University Press.

Luckett, Thomas M. and Pierre Lachaier 1996, 'Crises financiers dans la France au XVIIIe siècle', *Revue d'histoire moderne et contemporaine*, 43, 2: 266–92.

Lüthy, Herbert 1998 [1959], *La banque protestante en France de la révocation de l'édit de Nantes à ta Révolution*, 2 Volumes, Paris: École des hautes études en sciences sociales.

Lyotard, Jean-François 1984, *The Post-Modern Condition: A Report on Knowledge*, Manchester: University of Manchester Press.

Marat, Jean-Paul 1789–92, *L'ami du peuple*, Paris.

Marat, Jean-Paul 1963, *Jean-Paul Marat, textes choisis*, edited by Michel Vovelle, Paris: Editions Sociales.

Markoff, John 1995, 'Violence, Emancipation and Democracy: The Countryside and the French Revolution', *American Historical Review*, 100, 2: 360–86.

Martin, Bernard 1988, *La vie en Poitou dans la seconde moitié du XVIIIe siècle: Mazeuil, paroisse du Mirebalais*, Maulévrier: Hérault.

Massé, Pierre 1956, *Varennes et ses maîtres: Un domaine rural, de l'Ancien Régime à la Monarchie de juillet (1778–1842)*, Paris: SEVPEN.

Marx, Karl 1963 [1862–3], *Theories of Surplus Value*, Volume 1, Moscow: Progress Publishers.

Marx, Karl 1977 [1867], *Capital*, Volume 1, translated by Ben Fowkes, New York: Vintage.

Marx, Karl 1978 [1851], *The Eighteenth Brumaire of Louis Bonaparte*, in Karl Marx and Frederick Engels, *Collected Works*, Volume 40, London: Lawrence and Wishart.

Marx, Karl and Friedrich Engels 1975 [1845/6], *The German Ideology*, in Collected Works, Volume 5, London: Lawrence and Wishart.

Mathiez, Albert 1913[1989], *Les grandes journées de la constituante*, Paris: Hachette, Monteuil: éd. de la Passion.

Mathiez, Albert 1918, *La révolution et les étrangers: cosmopolitisme et défense nationale*, Paris: La Renaissance du livre.

Mathiez, Albert 1920, 'Le banquier Perrégaux', *Annales révolutionnaires*, 11: 242–52.

Mathiez, Albert 1920a, 'Encore le banquier Perrégaux', *Annales révolutionnaires* 12: 237–43.

Mathiez, Albert 1920b [1971], *Un procès de corruption sous la Terreur: l'affaire de la Compagnie des Indes*, Paris: F. Alcan, New York: B. Franklin.

Mathiez, Albert 1920c 'Le programme hébertiste', *Annales revolutionnaires* 12: 139–4.

Mathiez, Albert 1926, *Autour de Danton*, Paris: Payot.

Mathiez, Albert 1927, *La vie chère et le mouvement social sous la Terreur*, Paris: Payot.

Mathiez, Albert 1929, 'Les banquiers et la politique à la fin de 1791', *Annales historiques de la Révolution française*, 6: 398–9.

Maury, Jean-Sifrein 1827, *Oeuvres choisis*, 5 Volumes, Paris: Aucher-Elay.

Mayer, Anna K. 2004, 'Setting up a Discipline II: British History of Science and the "End of Ideology", 1931–1948', *Studies in History and Philosophy of Science*, 35, 1: 41–72.

Mayerne, Louis Turquet de 1611, *La monarchie aristodémocratique ou le gouvernement composé et meslé des trois formes de légitimes republiques. Dédiée aux états-généraux des provinces conféderées des Pays-Bas*, Paris: J. Berjon.

Maza, Sarah 2003, *The Myth of the French Bourgeoisie: An Essay on the Social Imaginary, 1750–1850*, Cambridge, Massachusetts/London: Harvard University Press.

Mazauric, Claude 1985, 'A propos d'un mouvement populaire préprolétarien survenu à Rouen au cours de l'été 1789 et de sa valorisation dans le champ des affrontements politiques de la Révolution', in *Mouvements populaires et conscience sociale XVIe–XIXe siècles: actes du colloque de Paris 24–26 mai 1984*, edited by Jean Nicolas, Paris: Maloine.

Mazauric, Claude 2009, *L'histoire de la Révolution française et la pensée marxiste*, Paris: Presses universitaires de France.

Mazauric, Claude and Julien Louvrier 2008, 'Entretiens de Claude Mazauric avec Julien Louvrier', *Cahiers d'histoire: revue d'histoire critique*, 104:19–145.

McPhee, Peter 1989, 'The French Revolution, Peasants and Capitalism', *American Historical Review*, 94, 5:1265–80.

Menault, Ernest 1991, *Histoire de l'agriculture en Berry: La condition paysanne du ve au XVIIIe siècle*, Mayenne: Royer.

Mercier, Sebastien 1994, *Tableau de Paris*, 3 Volumes, edited by Jean-Claude Bonnet, Paris: Mercure de France.

Merle, Louis 1958, *La métairie et l'évolution agraire de la Gâtine poitevine de la fin du Moyen Age à la Révolution*, Paris: SEVPEN.

Meuvret, Jean 1987 [1977], *Le problème des subsistances à l'époque Louis XIV*, Volume 2, *La production des céréales et la société rurale*, Paris: Éditions de l'École des hautes études en sciences sociales.

Miller, Stephen 2002, *The French Revolution 1789–1799*, Oxford, Oxford University Press.

Miller, Stephen 2008, *State and Society in Eighteenth-Century France: A Study of Political Power and Social Revolution in Languedoc*, Washington, DC.: The Catholic University of America Press.

Miller, Stephen 2012, 'French Absolutism and Agricultural Capitalism: A Comment on Henry Heller's Essays', *Historical Materialism*, 20, 4: 141–61.

Minard, Philippe 1989, 'Identité corporative et dignité ouvrière: le cas des typograph-iques parisiens, 1789–1791', in *Paris et la Revolution: Actes du colloque de Paris I, 14–16 avril 198*, edited by Michel Vovelle, Paris: Publications de la Sorbonne.

Mireaux, Emile 1958, *Une province française au temps du Grand Roi: La Brie*, Paris: Hachette.

Miskimin, Harry A. 1994, 'Book Review: Robert Brenner, *Merchants and Revolution: Commercial Change, Political Conflict and London's Overseas Traders, 1550–1653*', *Journal of Interdisciplinary History*, 25, 2: 286–7.

Molà, Luca 2000, *The Silk Industry of Renaissance Venice*, Baltimore: Johns Hopkins University Press.

Monnier, Raymonde 1994, *L'espace public démocratique: essai sur l'opinion à Paris de la Révolution au Directoire*, Paris: Kimé.

Monnier, Raymonde 2003, 'Républicanisme, patriotisme et Révolution française', *French Historical Studies*, 26, 3: 87–118.

Monnier, Raymonde 2004, *Citoyens et citoyenneté sous la revolution française: actes du colloque international de Vizille, 24 et 25 septembre 2004*, Paris: l'Harmattan.

Monnier, Raymonde 2005, *Républicanisme, patriotisme et Révolution française*, Paris: l'Harmattan.

Moriceau, Jean-Marc 1985, 'Les 'Baccanals' ou grèves de moissoneurs en pays de France (second moitié du XVIIIe siècle)', in *Mouvements populaires et conscience sociale*, edited by Jean Nicolas, Paris: Maloine.

Moriceau, Jean-Marc 1989, 'Les gros fermiers en 1789: vice-rois de la plain de France', in *Les paysans et la révolution en pays de France: actes du Colloque de Tremblay-lès-Gonesse: 15–16 octobre 1988*, Paris: L'Association Tremblay-lès-Gonesse.

Moriceau, Jean-Marc 1989, 'Des Notables consolidés? Les "proprietaires-cultivateurs" au lendemain de la Révolution', in *Actes du Colloque de Tremblay-lès-Gonesse 15–16 octobre*, 1988, *Les Paysans et la Revolution en pays de France*, Tremblay-les-Gonesse: L'Association.

Moriceau, Jean-Marc 1990, 'Une nouvelle donne économique? Les adjudications de fermes autour de Paris (districts de Corbeil, Gonesse, Meaux et Versailles)', *Mémoires de Paris et Ile-de-France*, 41: 409–528.

Moriceau, Jean-Marc 1993, 'Le laboureur et ses enfants. Formation professionnelle et mobilité sociale en Île-de-France (seconde moitié du XVIe siècle)', *Revue d'histoire moderne et contemporaine*, 40, 3: 387–414.

Moriceau, Jean-Marc 1994, 'Au rendez-vous de la "revolution agricole" dans la France du XVIIIe siècle: à propos des régions de grande culture', *Annales: Economies, Sociétés*, 49, 1: 27–63.

Moriceau, Jean-Marc 1994, *Les fermiers de l'Ile-de-France: l'ascension d'un patronat agricole, XVe–XVIIIe siècle*, Paris: Fayard.

Moriceau, Jean-Marc 2002, *Terres mouvantes: les campagnes françaises du féodalisme à la mondialisation, 1150–1850: essai historique*, Paris: Fayard.

Moriceau, Jean-Marc and Gilles Postel-Vinay 1992, *Ferme, entreprise, famille: Grande exploitation et changements agricoles: Les Chartier, XVIIe–XIXe siècles*, Paris: Éditions de l'École des hautes études en sciences sociales.

Morilhat, Claude 1988, *La prise de conscience du capitalisme: économie et phiiosophie chez Turgot*, Paris: Méridiens Kliiicksieck.

Morrill, John 1994, 'Conflict Probable or Inevitable?', *New Left Review*, I, 207: 113–23.

Mottu-Weber, Liliane 1985, 'Marchands et artisans du Second Refuge à Genève', in *Genève au temps de la Révocation de l'Edit de Nantes*, Paris: Champion.

Mousnier, Roland 1955, 'L'opposition politique bourgeoise à la fin du XVIe siècle at au début du XVIIe siècle', *Revue historique*, 213, 1: 1–20.

Mousnier, Roland 1967, *Fureurs paysannes; les paysans dans lesrévoltes du XVIIe siècle (France, Russie, Chine)*, Paris: Calmann-Lévy.

Mousnier, Roland 1979, *The Institutions of France under the Absolute Monarchy, 1598–1789: Vol. 1*, translated by Brian Pearce, Chicago: University of Chicago Press.

Mousnier, Roland 1984, *The Institutions of France under the Absolute Monarchy, 1598–1789: Vol. 2*, translated by Brian Pearce, Chicago: University of Chicago Press.

Muir, Edward 1995, 'The Italian Renaissance in America', *American Historical Review*, 100, 4: 1095–118.

Nakane, Chie, and Shinzaburo Oishi (eds.) 1991, *Togukawa Japan: The Social and Economic Antecedents of Modern Japan*, Tokyo: University of Tokyo Press.

Najamy, John M. 2005, 'Politics and Political Thought', in *Palgrave Advances in Renaissance Historiography*, edited by Jonathan Woolfson, ed., Palgrave Macmillan: Basingstoke, Hampshire, New York.

Necker, Jacques 1820–1, 'Project d'une banque nationale 1789', *Oeuvres complètes*, edited by Auguste Louis de Staël-Holstein, 8 Volumes, Paris: Treuttel et Würtz, Volume 7, pp. 149–97.

Neveux, Hugues, Jean Jacquart and Emmanuel Le Roy Ladurie (eds.) 1975, *Histoire de la France rurale: Vol. II: L'Age Classique: 1340–1789*, Paris: Seuil.

Nicolas, Jean 2002, *La rébellion française: Mouvements populaires et conscience sociale, 1661–1789*, Paris: Éditions du Seuil.

North, Douglas C., and Barry R. Weingast 1989, 'Constitutions and Commitment: The Evolution of Institutions Governing Public Choice in Seventeenth-Century England', *Journal of Economic History*, 49, 4: 803–32.

Nygaard, Bertel 2007, 'The Meaning of "Bourgeois Revolution": Conceptualizing the French Revolution', *Science & Society*, 71, 2: 146–72.

Nygaard, Bertel 2009, 'Constructing Marxism: Karl Kautsky and the French Revolution', *History of European Ideas*, 35, 4:450–64.

O'Brien, Patrick, and Keyder Caglar 1978, *Economic Growth in Britain and France, 1780–1914: Two Paths to the Twentieth Century*, London: George Allen and Unwin.

Olsen, Mark 1992, 'A Failure of Enlightened Politics in the French Revolution: The Société de 1789', *French Historical Studies*, 6, 3: 303–34.

Ourliac, Paul, and Jean-Louis Gazzaniga 1985, *Histoire du droit privé de l'An mil au code civil*, Paris: Albin Michel.

Ozouf, Mona, and François Furet 1988, *Dictionnaire critique de la Révolution française*, Paris: Flammarion.

Parker, David 1971, 'The Social Foundation of French Absolutism 1610–30', *Past and Present*, 53: 67–89.

Parker, David 1978, 'The Huguenots in Seventeenth Century France', in *Minorities in History*, edited by A.C. Hepburn, London: Edward Arnold.

Parker, David 1980, *La Rochelle and the French Monarchy: Conflict and Order in Seventeenth Century France*, London: Royal Historical Society.

Parker, David 1996, *Class and State in Ancien Régime France: The Road to Modernity?*, London: Routledge.

Parker, David 2010, 'Henry Heller and the 'Longue Durée' of the French Bourgeoisie', *Historical Materialism*, 18, 2:123–31.

Pascal, François 1999, *L'economie dans la Terreur: Robert Lindet 1746–1825*, Paris: S.P.M.

Patnaik, Prabhat 2009, *The Value of Money*, New York: Columbia University Press.

Patnaik, Utsa 2011, 'The Agricultural Revolution in England: Its Cost for the English Working Class and the Colonies', in *Capitalism, Colonialism and Globalization: Studies in Economic Change*, edited by Shireen Moosvi, Delhi: Tulika Books.

Peace, William J. 2004, *Leslie A. White: Evolution and Revolution in Anthropology*, Lincoln: University of Nebraska Press.

Pellegrin, Nicole 1987, 'Ruralité et modernité du textile en Haut-Poitou au XVIIIe siècle: La leçon des inventaires après-décès', *Congrès national des Sociétés savantes, Lyon, Section d'histoire moderne et contemporaine*, Paris: Éditions du CTHS.

Peret, Jacques 1976, *Seigneurs et seigneuries en Gâtine poitevine: La duché de la Meilleraye XVIIe–XVIIIe siècles*, Poitiers: Au siège de la Société.

Peret, Jacques 1988, *Histoire de la Révolution française en Poitou-Charentes, 1789–1799*, Poitiers: Projets Éditions France.

Peret, Jacques 1998, *Les paysans de Gâtine poitevine au XVIIIe siècle*, La Crèche: Geste éditions.

Perrot, Jean-Claude 1975, 'Voies nouvelles pour l'histoire économique de la Revolution', *Annales historiques de la Révolution française*, 47, 1:30–94.

Peru, Jean-Jacques 2003, 'L'évolution de l'outillage aratoire dans trois communautés au nord-est de Paris (1600–1850)', in *Jardinages en région parisienne du XVIIe au XXe siècle*, edited by Jean-René Trochet and Jean-Jacques Peru, Paris: Créaphis.

Peyard, Charles and Michel Vovelle (eds.) 2002, *Héritages de la Révolution française à la lumière de Jaurès*, Aix-en-Provence, Publications de l'Université de Provence.

Pichón, Jack 2004, 'La taille tarifée dans quatre paroisses du Haut-Poitou: Approche statistique d'un essai de répartition équitable de l'impôt au XVIIIe siècle', *Revue historique du Centre-Ouest*, 3,1: 129–74.

Piuz, Anne-Marie and Liliane Mottu-Weber 1990, *L'économie genevoise de la Réforme à la fin de l'Ancien Régime XVI–XVIIIe siècles*, Geneva: Georg.

Plessis, Alain 1989, 'La Révolution et les banques en France: de la Caisse d'escompte à la Banque de France', *Revue économique* 40, 6: 1001–14.

Po-Chia Hsia, R. 1988, *The German People and the Reformation*, Ithaca, New York: Cornell University Press.

Porshnev, Boris 1963, *Les soulèvements populaires en France de 1623 à 1648*, Paris: SEVPEN.

Pocock, J.G.A. 1985, 'The Political Economy of Burke's Analysis of the French Revolution', in *Virtue, Commerce and History: Essays on Political Thought and History Chiefly in the Eighteenth Century*, Cambridge: Cambridge University Press, pp. 193–212.

Postel-Vinay, Gilles 1974, *La rente foncière dans le capitalisme agriculture: analyse de la voie 'classique' du développement du capitalisme dans l'agriculture à partir de l'exemple du Soissonais*, Paris: Maspero.

Potofsky, Allan 2009, *Constructing Paris in the Age of Revolution* London: Palgrave Macmillan.

Potofsky, Allan 2011, 'Paris on-the-Atlantic from the Old Regime to the Revolution', *French History*, 25, 1: 89–107.

Poussou, Jean-Pierre 1990, 'Commerce', in *Dictionnaire du Grand Siècle*, edited by François Bluche, Paris: Fayard.

Poussou, Jean-Pierre 1993, 'Les activités commerciales des villes françaises de 1789 à 1815', *Histoire, économie et société*, 12, 1: 101–18.

Pressnel, Leslie S. 1956, *Country Banking in the Industrial Revolution*, Oxford: Clarendon Press.

Price, Roger 1975, 'The Onset of Labour Shortage in Nineteenth-Century French Agriculture', *Economic History Review*, 28, 2: 260–79.

Prochasson, Christophe 2011, 'Sur une réception de l'Histoire socialiste de la Révolution française: François Furet lecteur de Jean Jaurès', *Cahiers Jaurès*, 200: 49–67.

Prunaux, Emmanuel 2006, 'La société des Mines d'Anzin', on the website 'Cambacérès', http://www.cambaceres.org/.

Rabourdin, Monique 1988, *Condamnés à mort par le Tribunal révolutionnaire, 1793–1795*, Paris: Les Editions de Saint Albin.

Ranum, Orest 1963, *Richelieu and the Councillors of Louis XII: A Study of the Secretaries of State and Superintendents of Finance in the Ministry of Richelieu, 1635–1642*, Oxford: Clarendon.

Ranum, Orest 1986, 'Book Review: William Beik, *Absolutism and Society in Seventeenth-Century France: State Power and Provincial Aristocracy in Languedoc*', *Renaissance Quarterly*, 39, 4: 775–9.

Rapport Michael 2000, *Nationality and Citizenship in Revolutionary France: The Treatment of Foreigners 1789–1799*, Oxford, New York: Oxford University Press.

Rebérioux, Madeleine 1967, 'Le livre et l'homme,' in Jaurès, *Histoire socialiste de la Révolution française*, edited by Albert Soboul, Volume 1.

Rebérioux, Madeleine 1974, 'Jaures et les historiens dreyfusards,' *Bulletin d'histoire économique et sociale de la Révolution française*: 19–31.

Rebérioux, Madeleine 1976, 'Histoire, historiens et dreyfusisme', Revue historique, 255: 2, 407–32.

Rebérioux, Madeleine 1994, *Jaurès, La parole et l'acte*, Paris: Decouvertes: Gallimard.

Redlich, Fritz 1948, 'Jacques Lafitte and the Beginnings of Investment Banking in France', *Business History Review*, 22, 4–6: 137–61.

Réimpression de l'ancien Moniteur ... 1789–99 (1843), edited by Léonard Gallois, Paris: Quai Malaquais, 13 au Bureau central.

Rémondière, Louis Alexandre 1894, *Les charges du paysan avant la révolution de 1789*, Paris: Guillaumin

Révolutions de Paris 1789–94, Paris: Prudhomme.

Reynard, Pierre Claude 1999, 'Early Modern State and Enterprise: Shaping the Dialogue Between the French Monarchy and Paper Manufacturers', *French History*, 13, 1: 1–25.

Riley, James C. 1973, 'Dutch Investement in France, 1781–1787', *Journal of Economic History*, 23, 4: 732–60.

Robbins, Kevin C. 1997, *City on the Ocean Sea, La Rochelle, 1530–1650: Urban Society, Religion, and Politics on the French Atlantic Frontier*, Leiden: Brill.

Robin, Régine 1970, *La société française en 1789: Semur-en-Auxois*, Paris: Pion.

Robespierre, Maximilien 1828, *Papiers inédits trouvés chez Robespierre, Saint-Just, Payan, etc., supprimés ou omis par Courtois*, Paris: Baudouin frères.

Roederer, Pierre-Louis 1831, *L'esprit de le Révolution*, Paris: Chez les principaux libraries.

Roederer, Pierre-Louis 1840, *Mémoires sur quelques points d'économie publique: lus au Lycée en 1800 et 1801*, Paris: Firmin Didiot.

Root, Hilton L. 1994, *The Fountain of Privilege: Political Foundations of Markets in Old Regime France and England*, Berkeley: University of California Press.

Rosenband, Leonard N. 1997. 'Jean-Baptiste Réveillon: A Man on the Make in Old Regime France', *French Historical Studies*, 20, 3: 481–510.

Roux, René 1951, 'La Révolution française et l'idée de lutte des classes', *Revue d'histoire économique et sociale*, 29, 3: 252–79.

Rowlands, Guy 1999, 'Book Review: David Parker, *Class and State in Ancien Régime France: The Road to Modernity?*', *English Historical Review*, 114, 457: 722–3.

Rude, George F.E. 1959, *The Crowd in the French Revolution*, Oxford: Clarendon Press.

Sarrazin, Hélène 1996, *La Fronde en Gironde: l'Ormée un mouvement révolutionnaire 1648–1654*, Bordeaux: Dossiers d'Aquitaine.

Schaeper, Thomas J. 1983, *The French Council of Commerce 1700–1715*, Columbus: Ohio State University Press.

Schiappa, Jean Marc 2003, *Les Babouvistes*, Saint-Quentin: Les amis de Gracchus Babeuf.

Schmidt, Wilhelm Adolf 1867, *Tableaux de la révolution française publiés sur les papiers inédits du département et de la police secrète de Paris*, 2 Volumes, Leipzig: Veit.

Scholem, Gershon 1981, *Du frankisme au jacobinisme. La vie de Moses Dobruska, alias Franz Thomas von Schönfeld, alias Junius Frey*, Paris, Gallimard/Seuil.

Scoville, Warren C. 1960, *The Persecution of Huguenots and French Economic Development: 1680–1720*, Berkeley: University of California Press.

Scurr, Ruth 2000, 'Social Equality in Pierre-Louis Roederer's Interpretation of the Modern Republic, 1793', *History of European Ideas*, 26, 1:105–126.

Seligman, Edmond 1904, *Madame de Kolly: une conspiration politique et financière*, Paris: F. Juven.

Senar Gabriel, Jérôme 1878, *Mémoires sur les Comités de Salut public de sureté générale et sur les prisons (1793–1794)*, edited by M. de Lescure, Paris: Firmin-Didot.

Sewell, William Hamilton 1980, *Work and Revolution in France: The Language of Labor from the Old Regime to 1848*, Cambridge, New York: Cambridge University Press.

Sewell, William Hamilton 1994, *A Rhetoric of Bourgeois Révolution: The Abbé Sieyès and What is the Third Estate?*, Durham, North Carolina: Duke University Press.

Shovlin, John 2006, *The Politicat Economy of Virtue: Luxury, Patriotism and the Origins of the French Revolution*, Ithaca, New York, London: Cornell University Press.

Sibalis, Michael David 1986, 'Parisian Labour During the French Revolution', *Historical Papers*, 21, 1: 11–32.

Sieyès, Joseph Emmanuel 1970, *Qu'est-ce que le Tiers-état?*, Geneva: Droz.

Skinner, Quentin 1969, 'Meaning and Understanding in the History of Ideas', *History and Ideas*, 8, 1: 3–53.

Skopcol, Theda 1979, *States and Revolutions*, Cambridge: Cambridge University Press.

Slavin, Morris 1995, *The Left and the French Revolution*, Atlantic Highlands, N.J., Humanities Press.

Smith, Adam 1999 [1776], *The Wealth of Nations*, Books I–III, edited with an Introduction and notes by Andrew Skinner, Harmondsworth: Penguin Books.

Smith, Michael Stephen 2005, *The Emergence of Modern Business Enterprise in France, 1800–1930*, Cambridge, MA.: Harvard University Press.

Soboul, Albert 1958, *Les sans-culottes parisiens en l'An II*, Paris: Librairie Clavreuil.

Soboul, Albert 1973, *Mouvement populaire et gouvernement révolutionnaire en l'an II, 1793–1794*, Paris: Flammarion.

Sonenscher, Michael 1997, 'The Nation's Debt and the Birth of the Modern Republic: the French Fiscal Debt and the Politics of the Revolution (Part II)', *History of Political Thought* 18, 2: 268–325.

Sonenscher, Michael 2007, *Before the Deluge: Public Debt, Inequality, and the Intellectual Origins of the French Revolution*, Princeton, New Jersey/Oxford, England: Princeton University Press.

Sonenscher, Michael 2008, *Sans-Culottes: An Eighteenth Century Emblem in the French Revolution*, Princeton, Oxford: Princeton University Press.

Stasavage, David 2003, *Public Debt and the Birth of the Democratic State: France and Great Britain, 1688–1789*, Cambridge, New York: Cambridge University Press.

Staum, Martin S., 1996, *Minerva's Message: Stabilizing the French Revolution*, Montreal/ Kingston, Canada: McGill-Queen's University Press.

Stein, Stanley, and Barbara H. Stein 2000, *Silver, Trade and War: Spain and America in the Making of Early Modern Europe*, Baltimore: Johns Hopkins University Press.

Stone, Lawrence 1965, *The Crisis of the Aristocracy: 1558–1641*, Oxford: Clarendon Press.

Stone, Lawrence 1979, 'The Revival of Narrative: Reflections on a New Old History', *Past & Present*, 85: 3–24.

Stuart, Robert 1992, *Marxism at Work: Ideology, Class and French Socialism during the Third Republic*, Cambridge: Cambridge University Press.

Surrateau, Jean-Reneé 1979, 'Georges Lefebvre, disciple de Jaurès', *Annales historiques de la Révolution française*, 237: 374–98.

Surrault, J.-P. 1990, *L'Indre: Le Bas-Berry de la préhistoire à nos Jours*, Saint-Jean-d'Angély: Bordessoules.

Swann, Julian 2003, *Provincial Power and Absolute Monarchy: The Estates of Burgundy, 1661–1790*, Cambridge: Cambridge University Press.

Sweezy, Paul M. et al. 1976, *The Transition from Feudalism to Capitalism*, London: NLB.

Szramkewicz Romuald 1974, *Les régents et censeurs de la Banque de France nommés sous le Consulat et l'Empire*, Geneva: Droz.

Tackett, Timothy 2003, *When the King Took Flight*, Cambridge, Mass.: Harvard University Press.

Taylor, George V. 1956, 'Prospectus for a Christian Consideration of the French Revolution', *Historical Magazine of the Protestant Episcopal Church*, 25, 3: 353–77.

Taylor, George V. 1962, 'The Paris Bourse on the Eve of the Revolution, 1781–1789', *American Historical Review*, 67, 4: 951–77.

Taylor, George V. 1963, 'Some Business Partnerships at Lyon, 1785–1793', *Journal of Economic History*, 23,1: 46–70.

Taylor, George V. 1964, 'Types of Capitalism in Eighteenth Century France', *English Historical Review*, 79, 312: 478–97.

Taylor, George V. 1967, 'Noncapitalist Wealth and the Origins of the French Revolution', *American Historical Review*, 72, 4: 469–96.

Ternaux, Mortimer 1866–81, *Histoire de la terreur, 1792–1794, d'après des documents authentiques et inédits*, 8 Volumes, Paris: M. Lévy.

Teschke, Benno 2003, *The Myth of 1648: Class, Geopolitics and the Making of Modern International Relations*, London: Verso.

Thirsk, Joan 1978, *Economic Policy and Projects: The Development of a Consumer Society in Early Modern England*, Oxford: Clarendon Press.

Thullier, Guy 1999, *Une ténébreuse affaire: la Caisse Lafarge, 1787–1892*, Paris: Comité d'histoire de la sécurité sociale.

Tilly, Charles 1964, *The Vendée*, Cambridge, Mass.: Harvard University Press.

Tomas, François 1965, 'Geographie sociale du Forez en 1788 d'après les tableaux des "propriétaires et habitants"', *Bulletin de la Diana*, 39: 80–117.

Tomas, François 1967, 'Alleux et parcellaire à Sury-le-Comtal (Forez): Un essai de recon-stitution du cadastre ancien', *Cahiers d'histoire*, 12, 4: 407–12.

Tomas, François 1968, 'Problèmes de démographie historique: Le Forez au XVIIIe siècle', *Cahiers d'histoire*, 13, 4: 381–99.

Tonnesson, Kare D. 1960, 'L' an II dans la formation du Babouvisme', *Annales historiques de la Revolution Française*, 23, 4: 411–25.

Tornare Alain-Jacques, and Thierry Claeys 1996, 'Jean-Frederic Perregaux, banquier (1744–1808)' in *Biographies neuchâteloises*, Volume 1, edited by Michel Schlup, Haut-erive, Neuchâtel, Switzerland: G. Attinger.

Tuetey, Alexandre (ed.) 1890–1914, *Répertoire général des sources manuscrites de l'his-toire de Paris pendant la révolution française*, 11 Volumes, Paris: Imprimerie Nationale.

Tulippe, Omer 1934, *L'habitat rural en Seine-et-Oise: Essai de géographie du peuplement*, Paris: Sirey.

Turgot, Anne-Robert-Jacques 1898, *Reflections on the Formation and the Distribution of Riches*, translated by William J. Ashley, New York: The Macmillan Co.

Venard, Marc 1957, *Bourgeois et paysans au XVIIe siècle: Recherché sur le role des bourgeois parisiens dans la vie agricole au Sud de Paris au XVIIe siècle*, Paris: SEVPEN.

Venturi, Franco 1966, *Historiens du XXe siècle: Jaurès, Salvemini, Namier, Maturi, Tarle, et discussion entre historiens italiens et soviétiques*, Geneva: Droz.

Veyrassat Beatrice 1977, 'Les investissements suisses en France a la fin du XVIIIe et au debut du XIX siècle', in *La position internationale de la France: Aspects économiques et financiers XIX–XX siècles*, edited by Maurice Lévy-Leboyer, Paris: EHESS.

Veyrassat Beatrice 1982, *Négociants et fabricants dans l'industrie cotonnière Suisse: 1760–1840*, Lausanne: Payot.

Vignon, Louis 1978, *Annales d'un village de France, Charly-Vemaison en Lyonnais 1715–1774*, Volume 3, Vernaison: Vignon.

Vovelle, Michel 1980, *Ville et campagne au 18'siècle: Chartres et la Beauce*, Paris: Éditions sociales.

Vovelle, Michel 1984, *The Fall of the French Monarchy 1787-1792*, Cambridge/ London, England: Cambridge University Press,

Vovelle, Michel 1988, *1793, La Révolution contre l'Église: de la Raison à l'Être Suprême*, Paris: Complexe.

Vovelle, Michel 1990, 'Reflections on the Revisionist Interpretation of the French Revolution', *French Historical Studies*, 16, 4: 749–55.

Vovelle, Michel 2004, *Les Mots de la Révolution*, Montpellier: Presses Universitaires de Mirail.

Wallerstein, Immanuel 1974, *The Modern World-System*, Volume 1, *Capitalist Agriculture and the Origins of the European World-Economy*, New York: Academic Press.

Walter, Gérard 1968, *Actes du Tribunal Révolutionnaire*, Paris: Mercure de France.

Weir, David R. 1991, 'Les crises économiques et les origines de la révolution française,' *Annales: ECS*, 46: 917–47.

Whatmore, Richard 2000, *Republicanism and the French Revolution: An Intellectual History of Jean-Baptiste Say's Political Economy*, Oxford, England: Oxford University Press.

Whatmore, Richard 2002, 'Adam Smith's Role in the French Revolution', *Past and Present* 175, 1: 65–89.

Whatmore, Richard 2012, *Against War and Empire: Geneva, Britain, and France in the Eighteenth Century*, New Haven: Yale University Press.

Whatmore, Richard and James Livesey 2000, 'Etienne Claviere, Jacques-Pierre Brissot et les fondations intellectuelles de la politique des girondins', *Annales Historiques de la Revolution Francaise*, 321, 3: 1–26.

White, Eugene N. 1990, 'Free Banking During the French Revolution', *Explorations in Entrepreneurial History*, 27, 3:251–76.

Wolf, John B. 1968, *Louis XIV*, New York: Norton.

Wölfle-Fischer, Susanne 1997, *Junius Frey, 1753-1794: Jude, Aristokrat und Revolutionär*, Frankfurt am Main, New York: P. Lang

Wood, Ellen Meiskins 2002, *The Origins of Capitalism: A Longer View*, London: Verso.

Wood, James B. 1986, 'Book Review: William Beik, *Absolutism and Society in Seventeenth-Century France: State Power and Provincial Aristocracy in Languedoc*', *American Historical Review*, 91, 5: 1212–13.

Woronoff, Denis 1984, *L'industrie sidérurgique en France pendant la Révolution et L'Empire*, Paris: EHESS.

Woronoff, Denis 1993, 'Un entrepreneur d'ancien type en révolution: le bourguignon Jean-Baptiste Bureau', *Histoire, économie et société*, 12, 1: 63–76.

Woronoff, Denis 1994, *Histoire de l'industrie en France: du XVIe siècle à nos jours*, Paris: Seuil.

Wrigley, E.A. 2006, 'The Transition to an Advanced Organic Economy: Half a Millennium of English Agriculture', *Economic History Review*, 59, 3: 435–80.

Young, Arthur 1969 [1794], *Travels in France during the Years 1787, 1788, and 1789*, Garden City, NY: Doubleday.

Zeller, Olivier 1990, 'Les mirages de la domination', in *Histoire de Lyon: Des origines à nos Jours*, Volume 2, *Du XVIe siècle à nos Jours*, edited by Françoise Bayard and Pierre Cayez, Le Coteau: Horvath.

Zylberberg, Michel 1993, *Une si douce domination. Les milieux d'affaires français et l'Espagne vers 1780–1808*, París: Comité pour l'Histoire Économique et Financière de la France, Ministère des Finances.

Zylberberg, Michel 2001, *Capitalisme et catholicisme dans la France moderne. La dynastie Lecouteulx*, Paris: Publications de la Sorbonne.

Index

CPSIA information can be obtained
at www.ICGtesting.com
Printed in the USA
LVHW04s1731220918
590997LV00002BA/2/P